Curriculum Today

Curriculum Today

David G. Armstrong

The University of North Carolina at Greensboro

Merrill
Prentice Hall

Upper Saddle River, New Jersey
Columbus, Ohio

Library of Congress Cataloging-in-Publication Data

Armstrong, David G.
   Curriculum today / David G. Armstrong.
     p. cm.
   Includes bibliographical references and indexes.
   ISBN 0-13-093885-8
   1. Curriculum planning—United States.   I. Title.

LB2806.15 .A75 2003
375′.001—dc21

2002190247

Vice President and Publisher: Jeffery W. Johnston
Executive Editor: Debra A. Stollenwerk
Editorial Assistant: Mary Morrill
Production Editor: Kimberly J. Lundy
Production Coordination: Lea Baranowski, Carlisle Publishers Services
Design Coordinator: Diane C. Lorenzo
Cover Designer: Jason Moore
Cover Image: Index Stock
Production Manager: Pamela D. Bennett
Director of Marketing: Ann Castel Davis
Marketing Manager: Krista Groshong
Marketing Coordinator: Tyra Cooper

This book was set in Guardi Roman by Carlisle Communications, Ltd.
The cover was printed by Phoenix Color Corp.

Pearson Education Ltd.
Pearson Education Australia Pty. Limited
Pearson Education Singapore Pte. Ltd.
Pearson Education North Asia Ltd.
Pearson Education Canada, Ltd.
Pearson Educación de Mexico, S.A. de C.V.
Pearson Education—Japan
Pearson Education Malaysia Pte. Ltd.
Pearson Education, *Upper Saddle River, New Jersey*

10 9 8 7
ISBN: 0-13-093885-8

Preface

Additions to knowledge occur today at a pace unknown to past generations. Sophisticated transportation systems and communications technologies allow for a quick global spread of new information. Curriculum decisions play important limiting and focusing roles that respond to the inability of any individual to know it all. As you engage in curriculum work, you will be involved in developing plans for designing, implementing, and evaluating educational programs that introduce learners to samples of the total universe of knowledge.

Curriculum development is a sophisticated enterprise. You and others with whom you work need a nuanced understanding of content knowledge, the developmental characteristics of students, learning theory, the perspectives of diverse cultural groups, the priorities of individuals from different economic and social strata, varying perspectives on the characteristics that students should have when they leave school, competing political forces, and economic realities (particularly as they pertain to education).

The good news is that, when you are involved in curriculum work, you rarely will work alone. The involvement of people who represent varied interests and who have different perspectives adds to the knowledge base of the entire group. The collaborative nature of much curriculum work encourages decisions that will win broad-based support without alienating and marginalizing individuals and groups with different views.

As you grow in your ability to engage curriculum responsibilities, you will work collaboratively with others on tasks that include

- Identifying the kinds of content to be emphasized
- Suggesting approaches to transmitting information
- Recommending ways to package decisions to make them accessible to broad audiences
- Devising approaches to implementing decisions
- Proposing approaches to assessing students' progress

Curriculum changes that you and those with whom you work propose and implement will not occur in a vacuum. New and revised curricula often displace certain aspects of programs with some history behind them. You will need to know something about the historical realities that provided support for the programs that you seek to either replace or modify. In addition, our diverse society includes people from many cultures and with many perspectives. Your effectiveness will increase as you become familiar with a cross section of personal views on the characteristics of "a good education."

You will also need to monitor political developments carefully. Public attention—and, hence, politicians' attention—rarely has focused so intensely on education as it does today. The nature of instructional experiences that legally may (or must) be provided to students is greatly affected by movements to establish official state standards and to impose other kinds of mandates. Requirements to explain programs to various audiences highlight the importance of developing good systems to package curriculum decisions. Since instructional programs are scrutinized carefully to determine their impact on students, you will need to know how to install appropriate new and revised curricula and to win teacher support for them. Finally, you and your colleagues will have to develop abilities to assess new and revised programs and to report results in ways that make sense to various kinds of audiences.

When you engage in curriculum work, you are involved in making decisions that influence students' views of the world. This book seeks to give you confidence as you and others weigh options and make decisions designed to provide learners with instructional experiences that facilitate their development into more caring, thoughtful, and satisfied human beings.

ORGANIZATION

Curriculum Today presupposes no background in the study of curriculum. However, the content is sufficiently rich to be of value also to people with some prior experience in curriculum work. The book is intended for use in courses such as "Introduction to Curriculum," "General Curriculum Development," "Curriculum Studies," "Developing and Managing Instructional Programs," "Elementary-School Curriculum," "Middle-School Curriculum," and "Secondary-School Curriculum."

Chapter 1 deals with issues associated with defining "curriculum" and points out how alternative curriculum decisions can give students remarkably varied perspectives, even when they focus on a common topic. You will also find a discussion of the constraints that prevent irresponsible curriculum decisions.

In Chapter 2, you will find information related to how various traditions affect instructional programs and students' attitudes toward them. In addition to details on the legacies of Europe, the Mediterranean, and the United States, you will also find examples of the legacies of non-Western sources. These non-Western influences assume more importance each year as the diversity of students in U.S. classrooms increases.

Chapter 3 introduces you to three key influencers on the curriculum: (1) society, (2) learners, and (3) knowledge. The information provided in this chapter includes details that you can use as you consider alternative curriculum decisions. You will find useful information sources in this chapter, including kinds of help available from specialty-content organizations.

If you have long worked in education, you will be aware that state governments' involvement in public education is increasing. One reflection of their influence is the spread of state-level curriculum standards for public schools.

Chapter 4 introduces you to the standards movement and suggests approaches for embedding state standards into your curriculum decisions in responsible ways.

Information from philosophy, learning theory, and sociology influences curriculum decisions. Chapter 5 introduces information related to each of these three areas and suggests ways you can accommodate various perspectives when involved in curriculum work.

Individuals working alone almost never accomplish curriculum work. It is quintessentially a group activity. Chapter 6 introduces you to the various settings in which curriculum-development work takes place and to the types of people who often are involved. You will learn that the composition of curriculum groups varies with the nature of the setting and the nature of the task.

Several key design principles underpin much curriculum-development work. Chapter 7 introduces several of these. In addition, you will learn some basic types of curriculum designs. Needs-assessment procedures often are implemented as part of the curriculum-development process. This chapter provides you with guidelines for conducting an activity of this kind.

When you and others work on a project to develop a new or revised instructional program, one of your challenges has to do with selecting, sequencing, organizing, and prioritizing the content that is to be included. Chapter 8 introduces you to guidelines for accomplishing the tasks in each of these important areas.

Once curriculum decisions are made, they need to be disseminated to individuals and groups who were not part of the curriculum-development group. Often, these decisions are packaged in the form of curriculum documents. Chapter 9 introduces you to some criteria that you should strive to meet when preparing curriculum documents, some individual document types, and a scheme for developing an interrelated set of documents.

Chapter 10 points out procedures you can follow to encourage the smooth adoption of a curriculum change and strong user commitment to the new or modified program. You will learn about the value of a guiding coalition, the key role teachers play in the process, and guidelines from the Concerns-Based Adoption Model (CBAM) that may help you during the implementation process.

Chapter 11 focuses on the issue of program evaluation. You will be introduced to some historical approaches to assessment, to standardized tests and their limitations, and to a number of formal approaches to curriculum evaluation. The content in this chapter will be particularly useful to you, given the public's interest in evaluating the effectiveness of school programs.

 ## SPECIAL FEATURES OF THIS TEXT

- Each chapter opener features a **graphic organizer,** which facilitates learning by providing you with a visual depiction of the chapter's organizational scheme.
- The **Introduction** section of each chapter provides you with a useful overview of the content that is covered.

- **Figures** appear at selected places throughout the book to reinforce and elaborate on the content introduced in the body of the text.
- Each chapter includes numerous **Learning Extension** features, which seek to augment the text information and to provide you with opportunities to use what you have learned.
- Chapter components titled **Curriculum Realities** expand your understanding by providing real-world examples of circumstances faced by curriculum specialists today.
- **Exercises** encourage you to extend your understanding by engaging in application activities that build on the content introduced in the text.
- Many enrichment activities direct you to **the accompanying website** at http://www.prenhall.com/armstrong. The website's section titled "Curriculum" identifies numerous links to websites that feature information of interest to curriculum developers.
- An end-of-the-chapter feature titled **Review and Reflection** reinforces learning by helping you recapitulate the key elements of the chapter content and think about their implications for you as you engage in curriculum work.
- **References** at the end of each chapter direct you to sources of information that were consulted during the processes of researching and writing the text.
- A **glossary** at the end of the book provides you with a convenient way to review your understanding of the meaning of specialized terms associated with the field of curriculum.

 ## TO THE INSTRUCTOR

This text provides an overview of the curriculum field that can serve the needs of both curriculum beginners and curriculum specialists. You will find content that relates to issues surrounding the foundational base of the field and to the application of curriculum decisions in the day-to-day world of practicing educators. With respect to the latter orientation, you will find considerable attention to a topic that often is not treated explicitly in curriculum texts—namely, preparing documents to package curriculum decisions. Without careful attention to document preparation, curriculum decisions reflecting even the finest thinking may not get the attention they deserve.

You may be familiar with the frustration experienced by many newcomers to the study of curriculum when they encounter different writers and speakers using the same terminology to refer to different things. A lack of a common professional vocabulary featuring widely recognized and accepted definitions continues to plague the curriculum field. In an effort to assist the users of this text, a *glossary* has been provided. It features definitions that large numbers of curriculum specialists would support. At a minimum, the glossary will provide your students with a clear understanding of how terms are used throughout *Curriculum Today*.

The content at the end of Chapter 1 provides an overview of the important tasks that curriculum specialists discharge. Each task receives attention in one of the subsequent chapters. Because of differences in the backgrounds and interests of the students enrolled in the courses in which this text is used and because of your own priorities as an instructor, there is no presumption that these chapters will be introduced to your students in the same order as they appear in the book. Neither is it assumed that each class will be asked to read every chapter. Instead, the intent is for you to use the book as a resource, making accommodations you deem appropriate to your special teaching circumstances. In this light, please feel free to challenge assumptions you find implicit in the content you will encounter and to otherwise engage students in active thought about the curriculum field. To the extent that the book functions as a catalyst for thinking, my purposes will be served.

ACKNOWLEDGMENTS

Many outstanding professionals had a hand in the development of *Curriculum Today*. I am pleased to acknowledge the assistance of the following instructors who provided comments on early drafts of the chapters: William Brown, Purdue University; India Broyles, University of Southern Maine; Jane McGraw, Cal Poly University; Robert C. Morris, State University of West Georgia; William A. Ricck, University of Louisiana, Lafayette; and Mark Ryan, Loyola Marymount University. I wish particularly to thank my friend and colleague, Ada Vallecorsa of The University of North Carolina at Greensboro, for helping me think through some issues associated with certain content areas. I also want to express my appreciation to Debbie Stollenwerk, my editor at Merrill/Prentice Hall, for her support of this project and for the encouragement she has provided for many years for other writing projects I have been associated with. Finally, I want to thank my wife, Nancy, for her tolerance and unwavering support while I was in my study, "working on the book."

Discover the Companion Website Accompanying This Book

THE PRENTICE HALL COMPANION WEBSITE: A VIRTUAL LEARNING ENVIRONMENT

Technology is a constantly growing and changing aspect of our field that is creating a need for content and resources. To address this emerging need, Prentice Hall has developed an online learning environment for students and professors alike—Companion Websites—to support our textbooks.

In creating a Companion Website, our goal is to build on and enhance what the textbook already offers. For this reason, the content for each user-friendly website is organized by topic and provides the professor and student with a variety of meaningful resources. Common features of a Companion Website include:

FOR THE PROFESSOR—

Every Companion Website integrates **Syllabus Manager™**, an online syllabus creation and management utility.

- **Syllabus Manager™** provides you, the instructor, with an easy, step-by-step process to create and revise syllabi, with direct links into the Companion Website and other online content without having to learn HTML.

- Students may log on to your syllabus during any study session. All they need to know is the web address for the Companion Website and the password you've assigned to your syllabus.

- After you have created a syllabus using **Syllabus Manager™**, students may enter the syllabus for their course section from any point in the Companion Website.

- Clicking on a date, the student is shown the list of activities for the assignment. The activities for each assignment are linked directly to actual content, saving time for students.

- Adding assignments consists of clicking on the desired due date, then filling in the details of the assignment—name of the assignment, instructions, and whether it is a one-time or repeating assignment.
- In addition, links to other activities can be created easily. If the activity is on-line, a URL can be entered in the space provided, and it will be linked automatically in the final syllabus.
- Your completed syllabus is hosted on our servers, allowing convenient updates from any computer on the Internet. Changes you make to your syllabus are immediately available to your students at their next logon.

 FOR THE STUDENT—

- **Topic Overviews**—outline key concepts in topic areas
- **Web Links**—a wide range of websites that provide useful and current information related to each topic area
- **Lesson Plans**—links to lesson plans for appropriate topic areas
- **Projects on the Web**—links to projects and activities on the web for appropriate topic areas
- **Education Resources**—links to schools, online journals, government sites, departments of education, professional organizations, regional information, and more
- **Electronic Bluebook**—send homework or essays directly to your instructor's email with this paperless form
- **Message Board**—serves as a virtual bulletin board to post—or respond to—questions or comments to/from a national audience
- **Chat**—real-time chat with anyone who is using the text anywhere in the country—ideal for discussion and study groups, class projects, etc.

To take advantage of these and other resources, please visit the *Curriculum Today* Companion Website at

www.prenhall.com/armstrong

Brief Contents

Contents

Curriculum Today

Defining "Curriculum" and Recognizing Its Influence on Perception

Graphic Organizer

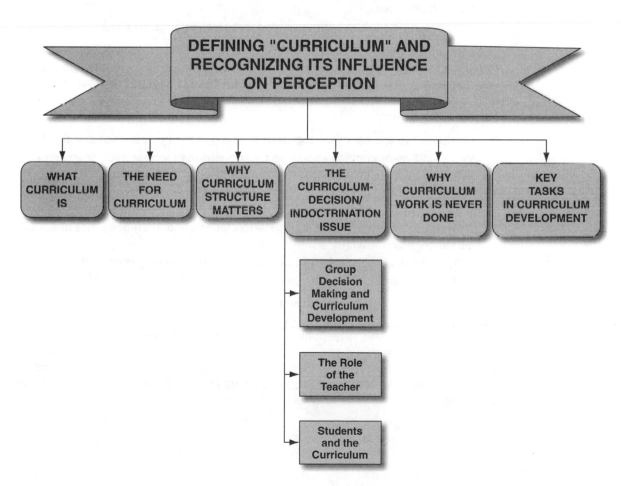

INTRODUCTION

Nineteenth-century American poet John Godfrey Saxe (1816–1887) reworked an old tale from India in his poem "The Blind Men and the Elephant" (Fabun, 1968). These verses describe the conclusions of six people who lacked sight and who were asked to describe an elephant based only on the part of the animal they touched. They arrived at widely differing conclusions, none of which adequately described an elephant's true characteristics. Here are their thoughts:

- The person who touched the broad side of the animal declared that elephants are creatures that looked like walls.
- The person who felt the tusk suggested that elephants are animals shaped like spears.
- The person who grasped the tail proclaimed the elephant to be a creature that grows rope.
- The person who put arms around one of the animal's legs asserted that elephants are built like trees.
- The person who felt an ear proclaimed that elephants resemble fans.

The point of the poem is that generalizations based on accurate, but highly limited, information can lead to faulty conclusions. Recognizing that this may be a problem is the easy part. For you, as a prospective curriculum specialist, the more important issue you face is identifying an appropriate remedy. In doing so, you'll need to answer questions such as the following:

- Of alternative approaches, which is best suited to the particulars of this situation?
- What kind of "authority" should lie behind information selected for inclusion in school programs? What should the sources of this information be?
- Who are the "experts," how do you identify them, and how heavily do you weigh their views?
- How should information based on interpretations and inferences, not direct observation, be dealt with?
- What actions should be taken to respond to concerns of groups with vested interest in conclusions that may be at odds with newly found knowledge?

These are just a few of the many questions that you and others involved in curriculum work will seek to answer as you work to make appropriate content-selection decisions. In addition, you will have to respond to other categories of questions having to do with (1) identifying suggested methods for transmitting information to students, (2) packaging your curriculum decisions, (3) devising approaches to implementing new and revised programs, and (4) preparing approaches for assessing the quality of new and revised programs.

CURRICULUM REALITIES 1–1

Limited Data and Faulty Conclusions

Inexperienced students, even bright ones, may develop false generalizations when they lack an adequate knowledge base. As was the case of the people in "The Blind Men and the Elephant," often a certain logic underlies their mistaken impressions. Although their thinking processes may be sound, the conclusions miss the mark because students lack the information they need to arrive at defensible conclusions.

Some years ago, the author of this textbook helped judge finalists in a geography-skills contest for bright sixth graders. This group consisted of about 10 talented young people who had won several lower-level competitions. For the most part, these students had a remarkable grasp of content associated with the field of geography. However, answers that a few of them provided revealed some surprising misunderstandings. For example, several students claimed that the following statements were true:

1. No river can run from south to north.
2. In the Northern Hemisphere, if place "A" is located south of place "B," then place "A" will definitely have warmer winters than place "B."

These answers do not reflect an absence of logic. They represent, instead, an inadequate information base.

At the end of the contest, the students were asked about these answers. Their responses quickly identified possible places their mistaken impressions had come from. With regard to statement 1, the culprit seemed to be classrooms in which geographic information sources were limited to flat wall maps of the United States. Such maps have "north" at the top and "south" at the bottom. These students looked at the maps, falsely assumed that, in the real world, gravity acts much as it might if these rivers were flowing on a flat map attached to a classroom wall. Since water will not run from the bottom of a wall to the top of a wall, the students concluded that no river could run in this direction (i.e., from south to north).

Student responses about statement 2 suggested that they had internalized information about a climate pattern that features colder winter temperatures as distance north of the Equator increases. However, these students lacked information about other influences on climate such as elevation, proximity to water, and prevailing wind patterns. These variables sometimes give places in northerly locations fairly mild winter temperatures. For example, Juneau, Alaska, has winters that typically are less severe than those in Philadelphia, a city that lies far to the south of Juneau.

The key point is that students' thinking does not stop when they have inadequate information to work with. They *will* arrive at conclusions. The drive students have to make sense of their world puts great pressure on curriculum developers to create and revise programs in ways that will provide learners the information base they need to arrive at intellectually defensible conclusions.

Curriculum decisions are important. The conclusions you and others make will greatly affect how students see the world. This text seeks to give you professional competence as you develop new and revised programs that describe "elephants" as the best evidence suggests they *truly are,* rather than as fantasy creatures that look like "living walls," "walking spears," "producers of rope," "surrogate trees," or "ambulatory fans."

WHAT CURRICULUM IS

At one level, **curriculum** acts as a filtering mechanism, which allows some content to survive to be included in instructional programs and other content to be eliminated. At another level, it functions as an ordering mechanism. That is, it not only helps you identify instructional content but also assists you and other educators as you seek to assign higher priorities to some topics than to others. Finally, curriculum decisions provide some guidance about the order in which material should be introduced. The very term "curriculum" acknowledges the importance of this important sequencing function. The expression derives from an ancient Latin word meaning a "running course." Through time, the meaning evolved to imply a sequence of learning experiences or courses. Although there is some agreement about these historic origins of the term, you will find that various authorities have defined "curriculum" in somewhat different ways (Armstrong, 1989; Doll, 1986; Tanner & Tanner, 1995).

In this text, the term will be used in a consistent way. Here we will view curriculum as referring to *decision-making processes and products that focus on preparation and assessment of plans designed to influence students' development of insights related to specific knowledge and skills.* This definition highlights three key curricular emphases (Smith, 2001):

1. Transmission of *knowledge*
2. *Processes* that seek to facilitate student learning
3. *Products* of learning used to ascertain whether students have acquired new information

Do not confuse curriculum with a simple listing of content. Instead, think of it as a collection of decisions that relates to the selection, ordering, emphases, and breadth of the treatment of the content elements chosen for presentation to students and to the assessment of students' proficiency levels.

You will often find the term "curriculum" used in tandem with the related term "**instruction.**" *Instruction focuses on the specific means of achieving the purposes of the overall plan reflected in the curriculum.* Think of curriculum as the grand strategy. Think of instruction as the tactics you use to achieve the ends implied by the strategy.

THE NEED FOR CURRICULUM

At this point, you may be prompted to say, "The information about curriculum is all well and good, but isn't it a bit theoretical? Why is curriculum work necessary? Why not just present people with information and let them make sense of it on their own?" At first blush, this idea has appeal. It respects the individuality of learners, and it helps you avoid a concern that your decisions might be denying students access to some kinds of content that you might decide not to include. There are two major problems with this position. First of all, if you are a teacher, you and others with whom you work have only limited time to spend with students. You simply cannot teach it all. Second, content that students encounter that comes to them in an unorganized way often is not comprehensible. To help you better appreciate this point, take a few moments to read the following:

> The process is not complex. In fact, large numbers of people do it at least once a day. Some authorities wish they would do it at least three times as frequently, and some people do.
>
> To begin, you need to use both hands, but just one ordinarily will do most of the work. Which you use most will depend on special circumstances. Ordinarily, you set aside a particular place in your apartment or house to accomplish this task. To begin, you may have to open some drawers or receptacles and prepare the necessary equipment.
>
> Some people begin the process by applying a strand of special textile material in a particular way. Others skip this phase. They work with a special tool fitted with a set of short appendages, which typically are set perpendicular to the handle. You prepare these appendages for the activity by covering them with a special chemical mixture.
>
> You typically will not find the action phase of the process to be exhausting. However, frequent movements are required. At the conclusion, you may initiate action to eliminate any of the chemical additives that you earlier placed on the special appendages of the tool. You may also desire to briefly ingest some liquid.
>
> When you have completed the process, you usually will return the tool, the supply of chemical additives you have used, and the special textile material (if you have used it) to appropriate storage locations. It will not be too long until you will need them again, and you want to be sure they remain easily accessible. You (as is the case with many others) may find this whole set of procedures to be tedious. Nevertheless, you probably will remain committed to do them all again. These actions have become a well-established routine of life that promises to be with us for some time.

What subject is being discussed? Did you consider any of the following possibilities?

- It is a description of some kind of at-home weaving process that involves use of special chemicals and equipment.
- It is a tedious aerobic activity that doctors recommend but that many people find troublesome to maintain over time.
- It is a description of a disreputable, nonmainstream practice that might be detailed in a cheap novel but that would not be printed in publications designed to support traditional family values.

These, of course, are just examples of some conclusions you might reasonably have drawn from your reading. You may have come up with a number of other interesting possibilities.

Suppose that, instead of reading this material as it was presented, you had first been given its title: "Brushing Teeth." If you thought it was something else, your mistake is understandable. Even as mundane a curriculum decision as giving new material a good, descriptive title makes it more comprehensible. Had you seen the "Brushing Teeth" label, you would have immediately been cued to the kind of information that would follow, and you probably would have had little difficulty in understanding exactly what was being described in the article. Good curriculum decisions provide students with contextual information that makes learning easier and more efficient.

LEARNING EXTENSION 1–1

Preparing Good Titles

Think about a topic or process you know well. Prepare a short written description that you might use to introduce this information to others. (Four or five paragraphs will do.) When you have completed your work, think about choosing a title. Identify three alternatives. Prepare three printed versions, each including just one of the three possible titles you have selected.

Invite several people to read the three versions. When they have completed this task, ask them to tell you which title gave them the best information about your material. What did they especially like about this title? In what specific ways was it better than the alternatives?

 ## WHY CURRICULUM STRUCTURE MATTERS

If you accept that curriculum decisions that involve selecting, prioritizing, and sequencing content influence what students learn, does the particular structure you select make a difference? Indeed, it does. General topics can be organized in many ways. The particular pattern chosen affects what a teacher does to enact the curriculum. That is, the adopted arrangement encourages strong emphases on some elements of content, moderate emphases on others, and no emphases at all on still others. To see how this is so, read through the two examples that follow. Both deal with the same general topic: *settlement of the United States from 1840 to 1920.* However, as you will see, there are great differences in the perspectives embedded within each arrangement.

EXAMPLE 1: Settlement of the United States from 1840 to 1920

South-to-North Patterns

The treaty of Guadalupe Hidalgo, which ended the Mexican-American War in 1848, and the Gadsden Purchase of 1853 added enormous new territories to the United

States. These agreements halved the extent of Mexico's total land area. The United States gained lands having a large Mexican population.

In these newly acquired territories, the numbers of people of Mexican descent varied greatly from place to place. In California, the gold rush of 1849 led large numbers of English-speaking Americans to the northern part of this region. For many years, traditional Mexican culture continued to dominate in southern parts of California. This began to change in the 1880s, when railroads improved overland access to California from states in the East.

In Texas, a large migration of English-speaking Americans occurred after Texas declared its independence from Mexico in 1836. This influx was so large that, in just a few years, people of Mexican heritage became a small minority within the borders of Texas. For example, in 1840, Mexicans represented only about 10 percent of the Texas population. By 1860, this figure had dropped to 6 percent.

In the 1870s, people from Mexico began to cross back into Texas in large numbers. Expansion of Texas's sheep industry provided jobs for these newcomers from south of the border. During the 1880s and 1890s, many more people arrived from Mexico as the spread of cotton farming in Texas increased the demand for farm labor.

During the 1840s, more Mexicans lived within the boundaries of today's New Mexico than in either California or Texas. In the 1870s, even more people from Mexico moved into New Mexico and Arizona to work in the mines. Some English-speaking Americans began moving to New Mexico and Arizona in the 1880s and 1890s, after railroads made travel to these areas from the East less difficult. However, even as late as 1910, life in New Mexico and Arizona retained much of the flavor of Mexico.

In general, the movement of people from Mexico in and out of the United States resulted from what geographers call push-pull migration. The "pull" was the prospect of better jobs in the United States. The "push" was the presence of poor conditions in Mexico, which prompted many people to leave.

There were extremely difficult times for Mexicans during the presidency of Portfirio Diaz from 1877 to 1910. During these years, much of Mexico's land passed into the hands of a small number of owners. At the same time, there was an enormous jump in population, from about 9.4 million in 1877 to about 15.2 million in 1910. Competition for jobs was fierce, and wages were low.

These conditions led many people in Mexico to think about moving to the United States. The completion of rail lines from Mexico's heavily populated interior to the United States border made it easier for Mexicans to make the move north. At the same time that physical movement was becoming easier, there was a huge increase in the demand for Mexican workers in the United States between 1900 and 1910. The construction of railroads generated a need for large numbers of workers. Demand for workers from Mexico accelerated when new U.S. laws made it illegal to bring in workers from China and other countries in Asia.

In the last years of the presidency of Portfirio Diaz, there was growing political unrest in Mexico. Some of his opponents fled north to the United States. An election scandal in 1910 forced Diaz to resign. This event was followed by a 10-year period of bloody revolutionary activity. During this terrible time, more than 1 million Mexicans were killed. Others, as many as 1 million, fled north to the United States.

During World War I, the supply of immigrants from Europe was cut off. War industries in the United States enjoyed boom times. Their demand for labor generated a ready employment market for workers from Mexico. In agriculture, farmers in the United States expanded their operations. One result was a great increase in their need for field workers. Sugar beet growers were especially eager to have workers from Mexico. Large numbers went to work for farmers in Colorado. A large, permanent settlement of Mexican-Americans took root in Denver and had its beginnings in the movement of workers from Mexico who originally were attracted north to work in the sugar beet fields.

As you think about the material in Example 1, reflect on what you recall from your own high school U.S. history course. You may not remember reading much (or even anything) about the content included in this passage. Aside from any forgetting that might have occurred over the years, chances are that your text didn't include this information. What you read in your own text and what you read here reflect the writers' curriculum decisions.

First of all, note that the subtitle of the material in this selection is *South-to-North Patterns*. If you think back on U.S. history courses you took and their accompanying textbooks, you probably never encountered material organized from a south-to-north perspective. Almost always, U.S. history content is presented within the framework of an east-to-west design. Do you remember those lessons about colonial settlement of the East Coast, followed by treatments of crossing over the Appalachian Mountains into Tennessee, Ohio, and the middle sections of the country? Then you went on to learn about the Mississippi, about pioneers following the trails to the Rockies, and finally about the Oregon Country, the California gold rush, and other topics associated with settlement of the Pacific Coast.

This traditional framework has some advantages. For example, it allows for an understandable presentation of content that many writers of history consider to be important. On the other hand, it presents a barrier to the inclusion of other kinds of content. The growing influence of Latino cultures in our national life cannot easily be embedded within narratives organized according to a traditional east-to-west perspective. This is true because, over time, Latino peoples have worked north from entry points in the southern part of the United States. It is for this reason that the writer of Example 1 chose a curriculum design featuring a south-to-north organizational framework.

Let's take a look at some other decisions the writer made in preparing and organizing this material. If you examine this passage carefully, you will see that a small number of generalizations influenced the selection of the included historical examples. A **generalization** is a statement of relationship among ideas that summarizes the best available information about a topic or an issue. The following are the generalizations this writer selected and some content from the passage that illustrates them:

Generalization 1: Revolutionary conditions in a country that pose an extreme danger to its citizens, perhaps even threatening their lives, provide a heavy incentive for people to leave.

- *Information from the passage.*   The bloody revolution in Mexico during the second decade of the twentieth century resulted in the deaths of more than 1 million people and led many to go to the United States for personal safety reasons.

Generalization 2: Immigration flows between two countries vary in their intensity and direction over time as conditions within the two countries change.

- *Information from the passage.* For much of the period between 1848 and 1920, most immigration flowed north from Mexico into the United States. However, for some years following the Mexican-American War, there were few attractions for Mexicans in the United States, and many Mexicans moved back to Mexico.

Generalization 3: If economic conditions, particularly the opportunity to find work at an acceptably high wage, are poorer in one country than in one of its neighbors, then there is a tendency for people to leave the poorer country to seek work in the neighboring country where economic conditions are better.

- *Information from the passage.* Opportunities for Mexican workers to be employed in the United States as railroad workers, ranchers, and farmers led many to move to the United States.

Generalization 4: Political decisions and conflicts can affect the overall demand for workers who are not residents of a country, as well as the countries where employers are authorized to seek needed employees.

- *Information from the passage.* U.S. laws adopted in the early decades of the twentieth century greatly limited the number of Asian workers who could enter the country. As a result, U.S. employers in need of workers looked increasingly to Mexico as a source of employees, and many Mexicans began moving north.

- *Information from the passage.* World War I made sea travel dangerous, and it had the effect of shutting off the supply of new workers from Europe. This situation generated a greater demand for workers from Mexico.

To recapitulate, the content included in this selection reflects a point of view, resulting from the writer's conscious curriculum decisions. Remember that other content arrangements that deal with the same general topic (settlement of the United States from 1848 to 1920) may present quite different information. To better appreciate how this can happen, go on to Example 2.

EXERCISE 1–1

Embedding a Perspective

There are many points of view expressed in material written about controversial issues in education. Basic information almost never speaks for itself. It is organized and introduced by people whose thinking processes are filtered through personal values and perspectives.

Action

Write three separate, free-standing paragraphs on a topic related to education (voucher plans, standardized testing, requirements for students in public schools to wear uniforms, single-sex schools, the adequacy or inadequacy of services for special categories of students, the fairness of school funding formulas, tests of academic competence of teachers, business advertisements in schools, alternative approaches to teaching reading, and so forth). Each paragraph will reflect a different perspective on the topic.

In paragraph 1: Assume you have yet to take a personal position on the issue; strive to present a balanced view of the facts.

In paragraph 2: Assume you have a generally positive view of the actions that are proposed related to your topic.

In paragraph 3: Assume you have a generally negative view of the actions that are proposed related to your topic.

Analysis

Conclude by comparing and contrasting what you wrote.

1. What are some similarities and differences among these accounts?
2. Which one did you find easiest to write? most difficult? How do you explain these differences?
3. What might each account communicate to a reader about your personal values?

Key Points

Curriculum decisions made even for brief treatments of topics require choices. These choices reflect priorities and values.

EXAMPLE 2: Settlement of the United States from 1840 to 1920

The Nineteenth-Century "Case" for Settling the West

By the middle years of the nineteenth century, millions of Americans had moved west of the eastern mountain ranges. Especially large numbers had settled in the rich agricultural lands of the Mississippi, Ohio, and Tennessee river valleys. Rail lines had begun to penetrate these regions. The new rail connections and existing water routes made it possible for the abundant agricultural bounty of these interior lands to reach the cities and ports of the East. The high demand for these agricultural goods and the availability of highly productive and inexpensive agricultural lands proved to be irresistible attractions to East Coast farmers. They were faced with increasing prices for lands with productive capacities much below those lying west of the mountains.

In addition to the lure of inexpensive and rich agricultural land, there were historical and psychological supports that encouraged movement into the western territories of the United States. For several centuries, leading European thinkers had noted a gradual movement of so-called progressive civilizations from east to west. In Europe, this had been reflected in a shift over the centuries in continental leadership from the heartland of ancient civilization in Greece to France, England, and other countries on the western margins of the continent. In time, these civilizations had reached farther west to the "New World" of the Americas. Indeed, many in Europe who had observed this historic east-to-west trend simply assumed that the pattern would continue as "civilization" crossed the Atlantic and spread into the new continent. For example, in 1726, Irish philosopher and bishop George Berkeley included these lines in his widely read work *On the Prospect of Planting Arts and Learning in America:*

> Westward the course of empire takes its way;
> The first four acts already past,
> A fifth shall close the drama of the day;
> Time's noblest offspring is the last.*

Implicit in these lines is the idea not only that westward movement is natural but also that it is good. The feelings of many nineteenth-century Americans on this matter traced to perspectives of the Puritan settlers of early New England. Though individuals among them probably had different motives for undertaking the harrowing sea journey to the New World, a common thread was a desire to escape religious "error" in England. They wanted to establish a "New Jerusalem," where religious and political practices would be better than those prevailing in the Old World. These early settlers went west across the Atlantic, convinced that they could improve on what they had left, could selectively impose the most desirable features of the lives they had left behind, and could greatly enhance the quality of any people and conditions they encountered in the new American lands.

These assumptions continued to greatly influence American settlers as they continued the move westward during the latter half of the nineteenth century. Their inclination to accept these attitudes was reinforced by a doctrine that became hugely popular at midcentury. This was the idea of manifest destiny.

John O'Sullivan, editor of a paper called *The Democratic Review,* coined the term in the 1840s as he argued strongly for the annexation of Texas to the United States. The basic manifest destiny argument was that God had placed a unique obligation on the United States to accommodate its growing population by expanding its territorial boundaries. Vacant lands to the west had been put there to be filled. Indeed, the United States had a moral obligation to bring them under civilizing influences that could come about only by filling them with migrants from the East and, in time, by making them part of the American union.

But what if other people were occupying these lands? The racial superiority premise of manifest destiny easily handled this dilemma. Such people as Senator Thomas Hart Benton of Missouri argued that Native Americans would be the beneficiaries of the "higher civilization" that would be taken to them by white settlers of European descent (Horsman, 1981). In time, the original settlers of the continent would appreciate how the imposition of an unfamiliar culture had made them "better" people.

---

*From Bartlett, John, comp. *Familiar Quotations,* 10th ed, rev. and enl. by Nathan Haskell Dole. Boston: Little, Brown, 1919; Bartleby.com, 2000. *www.bartleby.com/100.* [May 1, 2001]. © 2000 Copyright Bartleby.com, Inc. Reprinted with permission.

LEARNING EXTENSION 1–2

Observing How Different Textbooks Treat the Same Basic Subject

As text Examples 1 and 2 above illustrated, varying perspectives on similar topics are common in student learning material. To illustrate this point, do the following.

Suppose you have been asked to choose a textbook for a subject you teach regularly. Look at two or more available texts. Make a comparative analysis that includes responses to the following questions:

- What identical topics are treated by each text?
- What is the relative emphasis given to the common topics in each text? (One way to determine this is to compute the percentage of the total number of pages devoted to the topic in each text.)
- Are there some topics treated in one or more of the texts but not in the others? If so, what are they? What differences are there in how topics are sequenced?
- How would you describe the differences among the priorities of the writers of each of the texts?
- If you were to improve the available texts, which existing topics would you eliminate and which new ones would you add? How much emphasis would you give to missing topics that you might add? Why would you make these changes?

In terms of the basic subject treated, the selection in Example 2, like the earlier one in Example 1 focusing on immigration from south-to-north, deals with settlement patterns in the United States from about 1840 to 1920. However, the writer of Example 2 has different priorities. For example, there is no challenge to the idea that teaching the settlement of the United States within a traditional east-to-west framework might in any way limit the inclusion of certain kinds of information. It is assumed that the only pattern of any consequence flowed from east to west. The purpose of this material is to help readers understand the *reasons* that prompted people to move inexorably westward.

If you read Example 2 carefully, you will uncover several generalizations that guided this writer's choice of examples. Note these generalizations and some of the information that was provided in this material to illustrate them:

Generalization 1: When one region has good transportation connections to a bordering region with better economic opportunities, there is a tendency for people to move to the region with better economic opportunities.

- *Information from the passage.* As transportation via rivers and railroads from the eastern seaboard to the lands west of the Appalachian Mountains became easier, more and more people moved from the East to new lands in the western interior.

Generalization 2: Studies of historical patterns sometimes lead people to conclude that these patterns are likely to be repeated in other times and at other places.

- *Information from the passage.* Many people in the United States in the middle of the nineteenth century noted that so-called progressive civilizations had tended to move gradually westward from their points of origin in Eastern Europe.

Generalization 3: Motives that are claimed to be larger than self-interest often are used to justify acts that otherwise might appear to be selfish.

- *Information from the passage.* The manifest destiny doctrine, among other things, presumed that the displacement of Native Americans that would occur as settlers of European descent moved westward would benefit the Native Americans, who, for the first time, would come into contact with a "more advanced" and "progressive" civilization.

- *Information from the passage.* In part, the movement of the first settlers to New England was taken out of a view that they would establish a new, better society, which would be a model for older civilizations in Europe.

As was the case in the first example, the content in Example 2 reflects the author's decisions regarding what information related to the settlement of the United States is important and, therefore, should be included in a discussion of this subject. As noted earlier, this writer accepts the idea that the settlement of the United States is something that occurred primarily in an east-to-west pattern. The author's key point is that, today, many might question the logic and even the morality used to support and encourage this east-to-west filling in of the country.

What these two examples should help you appreciate is that curriculum decisions matter. They establish guidelines that make the inclusion of some content more convenient than other content. They lay out a pattern that governs how the content will be sequenced. These processes impose order on complex and often messy realities. On the one hand, curricular decisions make new knowledge more accessible to learners. On the other hand, they inevitably reflect the perspectives of those who make the choices. Hence, different materials that focus on identical topics often include quite different information.

LEARNING EXTENSION 1–3

Curriculum Decisions Reflect Choices That Are Based on Values

Curricula embed values. To illustrate this point, you may be interested in looking at the results of some curriculum decision making. Curriculum documents are available at numerous locations on the World Wide Web. To see an example of how certain values and priorities are embedded within school curricula, follow these directions:

1. Clicking on http://cw.prenhall.com/bookbind/pubbooks/methods-cluster/ will take you to the home page of Merrill Education's Link to General Methods Resources. At the bottom of this page, select "Topic 1—Curriculum" and click on "Begin."

2. This action will take you to a page titled "Topic 1—Curriculum Overview." On the left side, you will see a list of several topics. Click on "Web Links."

3. You will find yourself at a page labeled "Topic 1—Curriculum: Web Links." Click on "Outlines and Guides."

4. You will now be looking at a page titled "Topic 1—Curriculum: Outlines and Guides." On this page, click on "Arts Education Curriculum."

5. You should be looking at a page titled "Arts Education Curriculum Guide." At the bottom of the page under the heading "Secondary Level," click on "Arts Education: An Information Bulletin for Administrators."

6. On the table of contents, click on "General Information: Kindergarten to Grade 12." This will take you to a document that contains highly detailed information about the kindergarten-to-12 arts program.

Look at the information included on the first three or four pages of this document. Then respond to the following questions:

- What do the three components tell you about the priorities of the developers?
- What do you learn about previous versions of the arts curriculum? How does the program introduced here differ from what was done in the past? What does this tell you about the values of the developers?
- What specific features of the new program are highlighted in this overview for administrators? Why do you think the curriculum developers took pains to draw attention to these components?
- What social or political changes may have influenced the decisions reflected in this document?

The arts education document cited here is just an example of one you might use as a focus for this exercise. Feel free to use others that interest you. If you do so, you may want to make some adaptations in the list of questions.

All of this means that, when you engage in curriculum work, you function as one of education's power players. The results of your decisions will influence what new information students receive and how they acquire it. Students simply cannot learn everything. There is just too much. You must select information you teach from a huge range of possibilities. When you engage in curriculum work, your objective is to make certain that the processes associated with content selection and organization go forward in a responsible way. This text will help you do that.

 ## THE CURRICULUM-DECISION/INDOCTRINATION ISSUE

What can you do to ensure that your involvement in curriculum work will not result in the development of material that presents a biased view of reality? This question concerns most curriculum professionals. Though there is always the potential for distorted perspectives to get into completed curriculum materials, professional curriculum development typically is organized in ways that tend to make this less of a concern than you might suppose.

Group Decision Making and Curriculum Development

When you engage in curriculum development, you rarely work alone. Curriculum work almost always involves groups of people, and the likelihood is high that many points of view will be represented. The negotiations and discussions in which the members of your group engage as you discharge your responsibilities lessen the probability that your decisions will reflect an excessively narrow point of view.

In addition, professional curriculum tasks require you and others in your group to look for help from sources lying well beyond membership of the curriculum-development team. For example, you will find that the views of subject-matter experts nearly always come into play. Groups working on mathematics curricula will seek some guidance from leaders in mathematics. Groups working on reading curricula will seek help from recognized authorities in the reading field. Other groups will look for assistance from experts in areas relevant to the subject or subjects for which they are responsible.

When you find yourself engaged in curriculum tasks, you and your associates will be forced to consider important context variables. For example, you will want to know something about the social setting within which the materials you are preparing will be taught. The need for this kind of information may lead you to consult the work of leading educational sociologists. You certainly will want to develop materials that are appropriate to the age and sophistication levels of the learners who will use them. To assure an appropriate fit with the intended learners, members of your group will want to consider findings related to learners' cognitive and psychological development. The curriculum decisions your group makes will guide instruction in a particular setting. Political conditions and philosophical assumptions related to such questions as "What kinds of programs are associated with 'good' education?" vary enormously from place to place. Given this reality, you and your colleagues may spend time gathering information related to the political constraints and philosophical perspectives that characterize the locations where the materials will be taught. In summary, the complexity of the curriculum-development process and the need to involve many people establish conditions favorable to the production of programs and materials that (1) consider multiple points of view, (2) reflect up-to-date scholarship, and (3) respond to important characteristics of the settings where they will be taught.

The Role of the Teacher

The content of curriculum materials never flows directly and uninfluenced into the minds of learners. There is no hard-wire connection that allows a teacher to turn on a switch and perfectly implant new information in students' brains. As enactors of the curriculum, teachers interpret, modify, augment, and choose selectively from any materials that are made available to them (Ben-Peretz, 1990). For example, if you have spent time as a teacher, you probably often have drawn on your own professional background as an important content-accuracy screen.

When you had doubts about whether information in new material was correct, at a minimum you probably checked other reliable sources to either confirm your suspicions or modify your own original understandings of what is accurate and what is not. It is unlikely that you incorporated into your instructional program any content that was clearly inaccurate. For example, you probably would have quickly rejected a program featuring wonderfully designed graphic illustrations, numerous student-engaging activities, and state-of-the-art computer-support software if the content asserted such nonsense as "all tomatoes contain deadly poisons" or "Mars is made of cream cheese, whereas Venus is a giant, spinning ball of cotton candy."

Students and the Curriculum

The term "curriculum" as used in this text refers to a development of general plans to guide instruction. The curriculum that students receive as a result of their exposure to instruction will be affected somewhat by the overall plan *and*—this is the key point—will be highly influenced by their individual characteristics. Curriculum specialists R. Murray Thomas and Dale L. Brubaker (2000) use the term **"inner curriculum"** to refer to the kind of sense each of us makes when we find ourselves confronted with new information and new situations. Students you teach in your classes bring widely divergent life experiences with them. They vary in terms of their prior knowledge about what you are teaching. They differ in how they value what you teach. They reflect wide-ranging opinions about all sorts of things as a result of their family background, their religious orientation, their ethnicity, and other variables that give special tint and tone to individuals who come to maturity in our highly diverse society.

What all this means is that students interpret the "realities" embedded within the curriculum in highly individualistic ways. Given that the instructional experiences flowing out of any adopted curriculum are filtered through the unique perspectives of individual students, any delivered instruction is unlikely to affect all students in the same way. On the one hand, this makes teachers' work challenging and difficult. On the other hand, it all but assures that even instruction associated with the best-designed curriculum has little likelihood of producing narrow-thinking students who passively take on the perspectives of those who prepared it.

Good curriculum functions as a stimulus. It should lead to instruction that provides excellent raw material for students to consider as they engage and interpret content in light of their own experiences. It is illusory to suppose that the curriculum itself has the power to produce students who will unthinkingly embrace the views of the curriculum developers. Students, even young ones, always bring something of their own worldview to bear on any school program. Curriculum decisions exert some control over what students are taught, but such decisions have a much more tenuous affect on what students learn.

WHY CURRICULUM WORK IS NEVER DONE

You may have observed that thousands, perhaps millions, of products of curriculum thinking already exist. Textbooks often are organized into chapters, and the chapters within those texts frequently follow predictable patterns. School districts and universities have long had printed courses of study. Curriculum guides for every grade level and subject are available in libraries, school administrative offices, and on the web. Why not just do some occasional "scissors and paste" work and take advantage of curriculum decisions that have already been made?

Although it often is useful to look at existing curricula for ideas related to such issues as formatting, suggestions for presentations to students, and approaches to assessment, knowledge refuses to stand still. Building school programs by simply borrowing from existing curricula is a recipe for teaching students information that has less and less connection to the best knowledge available. To avoid the calamitous results of school programs built on out-dated information, it is essential for curriculum work to be an ongoing activity. There is no other way to keep what is taught reasonably aligned with the best available knowledge.

Despite the logic supporting continuous curriculum development and improvement, from time to time shortsighted people do take a public stand in support of the proposition that "we can stop now, because we've gone about as far as we can go, and the world tomorrow will be pretty much as it is today." Through the years, even some bright people have committed to this faulty assumption. The following are some examples of comments made by sincere, educated adults who went public with statements that, in later years, proved to be laughably off the mark:

- "There are defects about the electric light which, unless some essential change takes place, must entirely prevent its application to ordinary lighting purposes" (Keates, 1879).

- "Jupiter's moons are invisible to the naked eye, and therefore can have no influence on the earth, and therefore would be useless, and therefore do not exist" (Williams-Ellis, 1930). (Comments made by Aristotelian professors who were Galileo's contemporaries).

- "The advancement of the arts from year to year taxes our credulity and seems to presage the arrival of that period when further improvements must end"[1] (comments by Henry L. Ellsworth, U.S. Commissioner of Patents, 1844).

- "It was argued that inoculation of the kind employed by Jenner would produce a cow-like face; that those who had been vaccinated ... would grow hairy and cough like cows ..."[2] (reaction of some members of the English medical

---

[1]Woods, R. L. (1966, October). Prophets can be right and prophets can be wrong. *American Legion Magazine,* p. 29.
[2]Butler, R. R. (1947). *Scientific discovery* (p. 100). London: English Universities Press.

establishment in 1796 to Dr. Edward Jenner's efforts to develop a vaccine for smallpox).

- " 'Knife' and 'pain' are two words in surgery that must forever be associated in the consciousness of the patient. To this compulsory combination we shall have to adjust ourselves"[3] (comments of Alfred Velpeau, a famous surgeon, in 1839).

As these amusing examples illustrate, it is dangerous to let respect for past thinking grow into an assumption that yesterday's knowledge will serve the needs of today's students. It won't. This means that curriculum development must be a continuous process that seeks to assure that instructional programs incorporate the best available contemporary information.

KEY TASKS IN CURRICULUM DEVELOPMENT

The complexities associated with the curriculum thinking that is needed to produce guidelines for high-quality instruction often seem overwhelming to newcomers. To help you grapple confidently with critical issues, each subsequent chapter in this text deals with a single basic curriculum-development topic. This approach will help you focus on important areas of concern one at a time. The intent is to help you develop a high level of comfort and expertise with each of these important topics. (For a graphic identifying chapters where each topic is treated, see Figure 1.1.)

The following are the 10 topics you will learn about in Chapters 2 through 11:

- History and Its Influence on the Curriculum (Chapter 2). Some topics treated include
  - Dealing with the power of tradition
  - How technology affects school practices
  - Non-Western curricular legacies
  - Legacies from Europe, the Mediterranean, and America's past
  - Positive influences of history
- Society, Learner Characteristics, and Academic Content as Curriculum Influencers (Chapter 3). Some topics treated include
  - Society as a source
  - Learners as a source
  - Knowledge as a source
- Working with Curriculum Standards (Chapter 4). Some topics treated include
  - The nature of standards and the history of the standards movement
  - Rationale for standards

---

[3]Gumpert, M. (1936). *Trail-blazers of science* (p. 232). New York: Funk and Wagnalls.

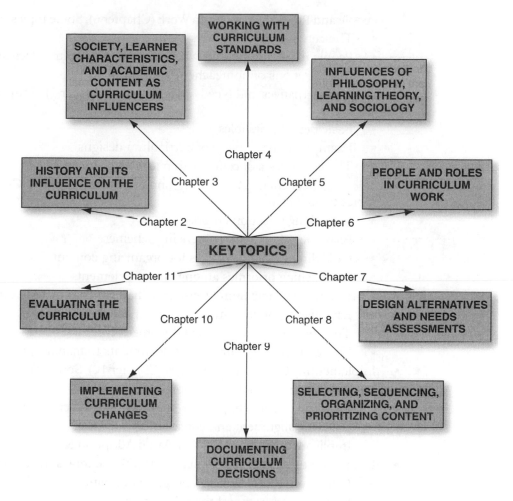

FIGURE 1.1   Categories of Information Used by Curriculum Specialists

- State-level responses to standards
- The implications of standards for curriculum workers
- Work to be done that goes beyond existing standards
- Influences of Philosophy, Learning Theory, and Sociology (Chapter 5). Some topics treated include
  - Philosophies of education and their impact on curriculum decisions
  - Learning theories and how they influence curricula
  - Sociological perspectives and their effects on program development

- People and Roles in Curriculum Work (Chapter 6). Some topics treated include
  - The central role of teachers
  - People in varying settings who influence curriculum decisions
  - Contributions of nonteacher participants
- Design Alternatives and Needs Assessments (Chapter 7). Some topics treated include
  - Basic design principles
  - Examples of basic types of curriculum designs
  - The processes associated with needs assessment
- Selecting, Sequencing, Organizing, and Prioritizing Content (Chapter 8). Some topics treated include
  - Identifying selection criteria
  - Examples of content-sequencing schemes
  - Guidelines and frameworks for organizing content
  - Establishing priorities among content elements
- Documenting Curriculum Decisions (Chapter 9). Some topics treated include
  - Establishing document-quality criteria
  - The components of selected document types
  - Using interrelated curriculum documents to manage programs
- Implementing Curriculum Changes (Chapter 10). Some topics treated include
  - Assembling a guiding coalition
  - Winning teacher support for new and changed curricula
  - Assuring alignment and consistency
  - Implications of the Concerns-Based Adoption Model (CBAM)
- Evaluating the Curriculum (Chapter 11). Some topics treated include
  - Objectives-based tests and program evaluation
  - Standardized tests and their limitations
  - Examples of formal curriculum-evaluation models

Review and Reflection

1. How can curriculum workers help in the effort to prevent students from generalizing from either sparse or inaccurate information?
2. Many texts that purport to cover the same basic subject matter do so in vastly different ways. What accounts for these differences?
3. Curriculum often is thought of as a master plan to guide instruction. Some critics of this view argue that, once programs are in the hands of individual teachers, they adapt the programs so profoundly to meet the needs of their own settings and students that the provided curriculum simply doesn't matter. How do you feel about this issue, and why?

4. In what ways can curriculum decisions affect what students take away from instruction related to a particular topic?

5. Suppose a group of people in your state examined demographic patterns and found that relatively small numbers of students who were enrolled in the grade 7 state history course would be living in the state as adults. Suppose, too, that this group decided to recommend eliminating the state history course. What do you think might happen, and why?

6. Students of Latino heritage represent one of the fastest growing groups in the schools today. Over time, what curricular changes might you anticipate as Latinos come to represent an ever larger percentage of the total school population?

7. What factors militate against adopted curricula "indoctrinating" students?

8. How do students' personal backgrounds affect what they take away as a result of their exposure to adopted school programs?

References

Armstrong, D. G. (1989). *Developing and documenting the curriculum.* Boston: Allyn and Bacon.

Ben-Peretz, M. (1990). *The teacher-curriculum encounter: Freeing teachers from the tyranny of texts.* Albany: State University of New York Press.

Doll, R. C. (1986). *Curriculum improvement: Decision making and process* (6th ed.). Boston: Allyn and Bacon.

Fabun, D. (1968). *Communications: The transfer of meaning.* New York: Macmillan.

Horsman, R. (1981). *Race and manifest destiny.* Cambridge, MA: Harvard University Press.

Keates. (1879). *Report from the Select Committee on Lighting by Electricity* (p. 43). London: House of Commons.

Smith, M. K. (2001). *Curriculum.* [http://www.infed.org/biblio/b-curric.htm]

Tanner, D., & Tanner, L. (1995). *Curriculum development: Theory into practice* (3rd ed.). Upper Saddle River, NJ: Merrill/Prentice Hall.

Thomas, R. M., & Brubaker, D. L. (2000). *Theses and dissertations: A guide to planning, research, and writing.* Westport, CT: Bergin & Garvey.

Williams-Ellis, A. (1930). *Men who found out* (p. 43). New York: Coward-McCann.

History and Its Influence
on the Curriculum

Graphic Organizer

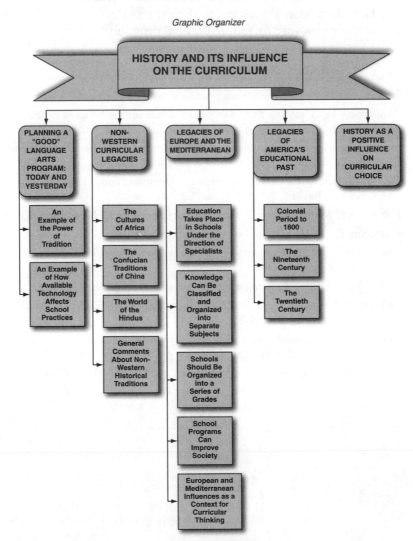

HISTORY AND ITS INFLUENCE ON THE CURRICULUM

- **PLANNING A "GOOD" LANGUAGE ARTS PROGRAM: TODAY AND YESTERDAY**
  - An Example of the Power of Tradition
  - An Example of How Available Technology Affects School Practices

- **NON-WESTERN CURRICULAR LEGACIES**
  - The Cultures of Africa
  - The Confucian Traditions of China
  - The World of the Hindus
  - General Comments About Non-Western Historical Traditions

- **LEGACIES OF EUROPE AND THE MEDITERRANEAN**
  - Education Takes Place in Schools Under the Direction of Specialists
  - Knowledge Can Be Classified and Organized into Separate Subjects
  - Schools Should Be Organized into a Series of Grades
  - School Programs Can Improve Society
  - European and Mediterranean Influences as a Context for Curricular Thinking

- **LEGACIES OF AMERICA'S EDUCATIONAL PAST**
  - Colonial Period to 1800
  - The Nineteenth Century
  - The Twentieth Century

- **HISTORY AS A POSITIVE INFLUENCE ON CURRICULAR CHOICE**

INTRODUCTION

Historical realities influence curriculum decisions. As you engage in curriculum-development work, you will come face to face with several challenges that relate to the issue of curriculum history:

* You will find that some people will argue that long-standing tradition makes a case for retaining the status quo, even when proposed changes are conceptually sound, well grounded in the research literature, and widely supported by respected professionals.

* You will find that existing technologies will limit your thinking about what should go into program designs that provide appropriate learning experiences for students.

* Though curricular practices in today's schools for the most part derive from earlier European and American practices, in an increasingly multicultural society, many students have ties to non-European and non-American traditions. As you consider curriculum changes, you will need to be sensitive to the varied cultural traditions from which today's students come.

 ## PLANNING A "GOOD" LANGUAGE ARTS PROGRAM: TODAY AND YESTERDAY

Suppose you are part of a curriculum-development team working on a language arts program for sixth graders. Among other things, you have been assigned to prepare units and lessons that require students to write short essays. You are expected to provide specific recommendations for teachers about how students should approach these tasks. Given this set of circumstances, it would hardly be surprising if your group were to suggest that teachers encourage members of their classes to begin by preparing rough drafts. Their students would be expected to submit completed papers only after revising their work to smooth over rough spots and correcting errors. These teachers might have their students use computers to generate the rough drafts, the intermediate versions, and the final copies they will turn in.

Now let's change the scenario by moving back the date. Suppose you and your group were doing your curriculum work in the middle 1880s. Obviously, during these years, you wouldn't expect students to do their work on a computer. But what about having them do extensive handwritten revisions? Although that might seem to be a logical choice, it is one that fails to recognize what tools were available for teachers and students at the end of the nineteenth century. The most readily available writing tool for students was the steel pen. They dipped the tips of their straight pens into inkwells, which were built into their desks. The teacher filled them when writing tasks were assigned. Paper was expensive. This meant that students did not do drafts. They were expected to do any revising in their heads. When students committed pen to paper, the resultant product was assumed to be the final one. As a result of the conditions in place in schools in the 1880s and the prevailing views about what "good" students should do when writing, in all likelihood your group would not have recommended that teachers allow students to prepare rough drafts of their essays.

This discussion of differences in assumptions about how students should approach the task of preparing essays underscores a key point: Conditions that exist at a given time exert a strong influence over instructional practices. If you look at circumstances affecting what teachers did at different periods in history, you will find two key influences at work. First, you will observe that typically educators rarely have done everything they *could* have been doing. Instead, they have been engaged in what prevailing opinion allowed or wanted them to do. Second, you will find that available and affordable technologies have exerted considerable influence on the nature of teachers' work.

LEARNING EXTENSION 2–1

Changes in Tests

You may be interested in some examples of test questions for school students that were developed at different times. A short article titled "Testing Across Time" appeared in the June 16, 1999, edition of *Education Week*. You may be able to access this information at the *Education Week* website (http://www.edweek.org). At this site, click on the button at the top, labeled "Archives," and follow directions.

How do you explain differences in the kinds of questions asked at different times? What accounts for some of the differences you observe? Which of these examples would you and your colleagues be most likely to endorse today?

An Example of the Power of Tradition

Practices that seem novel when they are first introduced gain legitimacy over time. Long-legitimized practices become traditions that resist—often with astonishing tenacity—attempts to displace them. For example, think about the traditional school year. This arrangement (1) initially developed in response to a particular condition, (2) continues to exist even though the condition no longer exists, and (3) maintains itself simply because large numbers of people wish it to continue.

The familiar nine-month or nine-and-one-half-month school year traces its origins back to a time when most Americans lived in rural areas. Young people were needed to help out on the farms during the prime summer growing months. A school calendar developed that built in a long summer break, so that children could help their families tend and bring in the crops. Today, the conditions that gave rise to a school year of this length no longer exist. Less than 3 percent of our total population lives on farms. Tradition maintains the length of the typical school calendar, not the need to release children so they can help grow and harvest crops.

To understand the power of tradition, you have to do more than consider the conditions that initially gave rise to a given way of doing things. It is also important to think through all the supports that have grown up around the practice in the years since it was first introduced. These supports give staying power to a school tradition. Think again about the traditional school year. Over time, the assumption that the school year should be nine or nine-and-one-half months in length gave rise to a vast instructional materials development industry that produces mostly items designed for use within a nine- or nine-and-one-half-month time period. Large numbers of family vacation and travel plans assume children will be out of school during the summer months. Many professional development courses and workshops for teachers provided by universities and colleges are offered during the weeks of summer when public schools are not in session.

It is true that some schools around the country do operate on calendars that differ from the traditional nine- or nine-and-one-half-month model. However, such calendars remain in a distinct minority. Resistance to changing the school calendar—particularly, attempts to keep schools in session during the summer months—often face stiff resistance. Such proposals require parallel changes that many people simply do not want to make. When you engage in curriculum work, all of this underscores the importance of staying alert both to how your proposals will affect what teachers and students study and do and to how these changes may affect other patterns that have grown up in support of existing arrangements.

An Example of How Available Technology Affects School Practices

Individuals who have planned school experiences for young people throughout history have been interested not just in describing the kinds of content to be taught, and in suggesting ways to introduce it, but also in determining that students have learned the material to which they have been exposed. How students have been expected to demonstrate what they have learned has varied tremendously over time. Today, for example, if you and some colleagues wanted to deal with this issue, you might expect students to prepare for a written test. You could have them do a traditional pencil-and-paper test, or you could consider a test that would require them to type in responses to questions using a personal computer. Either alternative basically involves students in providing written responses. Today's available technologies make this kind of student assessment an easy choice for educators.

CURRICULUM REALITIES 2–1

Teachers' Resistance to Pencils in Schools

As technologies of production improve, expensive and scarce items become cheap and abundant. Let's consider the case of pencils. Though their large-scale manufacture began in the late 1860s, it wasn't until after 1900 that inexpensive pencils—and ones with an important refinement, a *built-in eraser*—became widely available. For the first time, these wonderful writing tools, now in 1900 available at a price of one cent each, came within the budgetary reach of many schools.

Teachers were not thrilled (Coles, 1999). Many of them had taught for years under conditions in which students could not easily correct writing errors. In response to these conditions, they had taught their students to think very carefully about what they wished to say before committing pen to paper. Many teachers of this era feared the arrival of a writing tool that would allow errors to be quickly and easily erased. Such a device, they felt, would encourage bad writing habits. The pencil with an eraser made it possible for students to make corrections "on the fly" instead of making them in their heads as they carefully preplanned what they intended to write. Despite these concerns, pencils with erasers soon became common in schools, and teachers came to appreciate that there were benefits as well as potential dangers of a device that allowed written mistakes to be corrected quickly.

Think about how more recent technologies have changed what students logically can be expected to do. Can you cite examples of how teachers, at least initially, have reacted to them? You might begin by considering how teachers' expectations of appropriate student behavior might have been influenced as the following technological innovations became widely available in schools.

- The ballpoint pen
- Educational films
- Handheld calculators
- The personal computer
- School-based access to the World Wide Web

If you are interested in more information about the history of the pencil, you might like to read Henry Petroski's *The Pencil: A History of Design and Circumstance* (New York: Knopf, 1989).

Suppose you had been teaching in the 1860s. Think about the kinds of technological supports available to teachers and students in those days, as compared with our own time. Though pencils were invented in the 1500s, not until the late 1860s were processes invented that allowed them to be manufactured in huge numbers. Few pencils were in the hands of school children before the waning years of the nineteenth century. Steel pens did not come into common use until the 1880s. Student writing in schools was largely confined to small slates. These were not easy surfaces to write on, and they were small. The space constraints of slates made them unsuitable for recording anything but brief notes. Because the technologies of the day failed to provide inexpensive, easy-to-use ways for students to provide written responses to questions, it was unusual for teachers to ask students to write out responses to questions.

If you had been teaching in the 1860s, you probably would have given your students oral rather than written examinations (Coles, 1999). Logically, too, you probably would have spent a good deal of instructional time helping students learn how to develop good oral presentation skills (clear movement from point to point, logical organization of expressed ideas, and so forth). Given the importance of careful and clear oral expression for evaluating student learning, curriculum work you might have done at this time probably would also feature a great deal of emphasis on developing students' oral presentation skills.

Today, teachers spend much less time working to develop their students' oral expression abilities. This change has much to do with the arrival of technologies that make it easy to give pencil-and-paper tests. Present-day students with inadequate oral expression skills are less likely to do poorly on examinations than their counterparts of 150 years ago. Only rarely do twenty-first-century students take oral examinations.

Changes in assessment practices influence how teachers work with students, in terms of both helping them master new content and preparing them for opportunities to demonstrate what they have learned. As you engage in curriculum work, you need to think carefully about technologies that lead teachers to prefer certain kinds of evaluation processes. If technologies are not readily available to support the kinds of evaluation approaches you and your group recommend, you may find it difficult to generate wide support for your proposals.

LEARNING EXTENSION 2–2

Do New Technologies Really Improve Schools?

Today, we frequently hear claims that the personal computer has the power to transform the school. Hopes that technological innovations will be the salvation of education were a recurring feature of twentieth-century discussions centering on improving education. For the most part, the impact of technological innovations on school programs and practices has fallen short of their supporters' expectations.

Suppose your school board, as part of its member education program, wanted to learn more about the probable impact of new technologies on teaching practices and on student learning. If you were asked to address this issue, what would you say? In preparation for your remarks, one of the sources you might wish to consult is Larry Cuban's fine book *Teachers and Machines: The Classroom Use of Technology Since 1920* (New York: Teachers College Press, 1986). Though the book was written some years ago, you will find examples and arguments that continue to be relevant to today's schools.

NON-WESTERN CURRICULAR LEGACIES

For many years, educators in this country gave little thought to educational traditions and practices originating outside of Europe and the United States. When they were mentioned at all, they often were treated dismissively as "primitive," "backward," or even "barbarian." Such descriptions marginalized the influence of alternative educational traditions (Reagan, 2000). The children of parents with roots in non-Western culture were expected to shed their cultural identities and embrace the traditions and values that came as a birthright to sons and daughters of the European-tied majority. In some cases, the non-European cultural roots were so devalued that substantial numbers of educators presumed that members of such groups either had highly limited learning capacities or should not be taught at all. In many places, the children of African-American parents were especially vulnerable to educational maltreatment.

The attitude that "different means inferior" undermined the self-images of young people from minority cultures. This perspective led not only to school programs that sometimes were not responsive to students' backgrounds but also to public statements that denigrated entire classes of people. For example, in the 1870s, leaders of residential schools for Native Americans often regretted that these youngsters occasionally had to be allowed to go home to visit their families. One Federal employee, working with Nez Percé children, in Idaho commented: "The only way Indian children can be taught successfully, in my opinion, is to take them away from their parents. . . . If they are allowed to run home every day or two they keep up their Indian customs in part and consequently make very little progress (Monteith, 1872, pp. 953–954). School programs designed for these children almost certainly did little or nothing to give them pride in their heritage and confidence in their standing as worthy human beings.

Today, these attitudes are much changed. There is broader acceptance of the idea that the varied cultural backgrounds students take to school add strength to the learning experiences of all. However, even now, not much systematic thought is given to how the curriculum can embrace certain historical realities that have helped shaped the worldviews of members of non-Western groups (Reagan, 2000). As you engage in curriculum work, you may wish to think seriously about ways in which program designs might respond to some of these historical patterns. Let us look briefly at some patterns associated with (1) the cultures of Africa, (2) the Confucian traditions of China, (3) the world of the Hindus, and (4) general patterns reflected in many non-Western cultures.

The Cultures of Africa

Timothy Reagan (2000), a well-known non-Western cultures expert, takes care to point out that Africa covers a huge extent of territory and that it is a continent featuring tremendous cultural diversity. Nevertheless, he asserts, there are some commonalities that tie together the perspectives of peoples who live in widely separated parts of the continent. This situation is much akin to what exists in Europe. Though southern Greeks and northern Swedes have lives that differ in many respects, still there are enough commonplaces among most areas on the continent for people to make legitimate references to a general "European" culture.

Historically, many African cultures have viewed education as a communal function. It is not something that resides exclusively in the hands of a professional class of teachers. There are blurry lines between the education that occurs in interactions between the child and his or her parents, relatives, and community members and the education that may occur between the child and a teacher in a formal school setting. A highly important objective is for the child to develop a sense that he or she is rooted in and belongs to the larger society. There is a strong oral learning tradition. Important precepts are passed down to the young through stories, riddles, anecdotes, and word games.

As you think about needs of young people of African-American heritage, you may wish to reflect on some of these historical traditions. Some curricular implications include the following:

- Providing abundant opportunities for group work
- Embedding messages within lessons that involve word play
- Tying content to the perceived needs of the larger community, not just to those of the individual students
- Developing lessons that help students see how what they learn will enable them to play a meaningful role in the larger community

The Confucian Traditions of China

An examination system, supported by schools, was in place in China more than 3,000 years ago (Cleverly, 1985). This system was designed to produce well-educated employees to work in governmental services. It survived until 1905 (Reagan, 2000). Only male children participated in this system. Though technically open to a larger population, for the most part, the focus was on preparing sons of the upper class for the civil service examinations.

Examinations were held at several levels. Those who received high scores on local-level tests were allowed to sit for further examinations given at the provincial level. Those who passed these tests were eligible for lower-level government positions. A small percentage of this group went on to take national-level tests. All who passed received higher-level positions. From this elite group, a few were selected to take palace-level exams. Those who passed were appointed to particularly important posts in the imperial Chinese government.

Preparation for these tests involved memorizing a specific set of classic texts. Many of these texts featured the thoughts of Confucius, who emphasized the importance of the relationships people enjoyed with one another because of their individual stations in life. Although each party in one of these relationships bore certain obligations to the other, they were not relationships of equals. According to Confucius, these were hierarchical arrangements, in which one party always stood in a position superior to the other. Much of his thought focused on how mutual obligations in this unequal arrangement should be discharged. Confucius also had a negative view of certain occupations. For example, he did not hold manual labor in high esteem, and he was especially critical of those engaged in farming.

A key point in thinking about the Chinese examination system is that each candidate studied exactly the same material. Further, grading of the examinations did not involve creative interpretations of the material. Rather, grading focused on the examinees' abilities to conform to a prescribed style of written argumentation.

Today, the Chinese examination system is an artifact of history. However, as a tradition that lasted centuries, some of the patterns of thinking associated with Confucius's thought may continue to influence the worldviews of those tied to traditional Chinese culture. As you think about developing curricula that will respond well to the needs of young people from a Confucian tradition, you may wish to reflect on issues such as these:

- How will these students react to a program premised on the idea that human relationships should be based on equality rather than inequality?

- Will students see attempts to promote creative thinking as a poor substitute for tasks that require them to master a prescribed set of content?

- Will students want particularly explicit information related to the form in which their work is to be presented, and will they be disappointed if some grading recognition is not accorded to their ability to follow the prescribed format?

Of course, as you think about these questions, you have to recognize that today's young people with historic ties to a Confucian tradition have worldviews that have been conditioned by many other forces. However, only infrequently have curriculum developers paused to consider the residual effects of historic traditions from other cultures. Time spent thinking about this issue may help you make some programmatic adjustments that will encourage some students to embrace your new program who, absent this kind of attention, might fail to do so.

The World of the Hindus

Most followers of the Hindu religion live in India. Huge numbers of native-born or second-generation Hindus live in the United States. Accordingly, large numbers of students from this tradition are in the public schools. Hinduism is a highly decentralized religion. Although there is no rigidly defined creed, many Hindus believe that (1) there is a supreme being; (2) there is a system of reincarnation, which involves people in a continuous cycle of death and rebirth; (3) through a series of birth and death events, the souls of all people evolve in the direction of a liberating end, which will free them from this cycle; and (4) every variety of life is sacred and deserves protection.

For Hindus, the key life problem is ignorance. This ignorance stands in the way of the kind of knowledge that, in time, has the potential to free the soul from the death and rebirth cycle. Because of the importance of overcoming ignorance, Hindu thinkers have placed great importance on many different approaches to acquiring knowledge. Traditional Hindu education, for males only, featured several key steps (Reagan, 2000). Instruction, following an oral tradition, began with the student's listening to a teacher and learning basic information. This was followed by a step requiring the student to reflect on this new knowledge. Finally, the student was expected to engage in personal meditation based on this reflection, in an attempt to establish a fuller consciousness of the supreme being.

This brief description scarcely does justice to the complexities of Hinduism and the processes used to bring the young into full participation in the spiritual community. However, even this limited discussion underscores two important points. First of all, the Hindu tradition placed great store on multiple approaches to acquiring knowledge. Second, it tended to focus its attention on students' individual development—their personal growth toward a relationship with the supreme being. These features suggest that you might want to think about these issues in developing programs for students with ties to a Hindu tradition:

- Are learning experiences that feature extensive use of group work a good fit for these students?
- Is the logic promoted by the proposed program limited to scientific rationalism, or are other approaches to truth incorporated and valued?

EXERCISE 2–1

Identifying Historical Traditions of a Non-Western Culture

Today's schools enroll students from a variety of cultural backgrounds. The historical traditions of a culture continue to influence how its members see the world. You may wish to explore the traditions of some non-Western cultures not treated in this chapter.

Action

Identify a specific non-Western group as your focus. For example, you might choose to look at the world of Buddhism, the world of Native Americans, or the world of Islam. Feel free to select a group that interests you. Begin by preparing a short description that references a number of the core beliefs and values of each group. (You probably will want to acknowledge the existence of differences *within* some of these groups. The idea is to identify some commonalities that, in a general sense, tend to characterize the focus group.)

Analysis

Suppose you are invited to make a presentation to the members of a local community group whose members are not well informed about the diversity of the student population in today's schools. To illustrate the point that educators need to vary approaches to accommodate the characteristics of one of the non-Western cultural groups represented within the local school district population, describe some points you will make about the group you select as your focus. Include responses to the following questions:

1. Are there patterns of expected behavior within this group that differ from what we typically expect of students in our schools?

2. What kinds of accommodations might we make as educators to better serve the needs of students from this group?

3. How might educational experiences for all be improved by incorporating some perspectives of this group as we make decisions about operating the schools and teaching students?

Key Points

Traditions exert an influence on a culture's members, including the young. Students from non-Western traditions may take to school the thought and behavioral patterns that are at odds with those of majority-group students from European and Mediterranean traditions. In thinking about developing programs that respond to the needs of all students, curriculum developers must take into account the broad range of cultural differences represented among students in the schools today.

General Comments About Non-Western Historical Traditions

The African, Chinese, and Hindu traditions represent merely samples of the non-Western traditions represented in an American classroom. Large numbers of students are members of other groups. For example, the numbers of Americans who are Muslims increase each year. Today, followers of Islam represent the third largest religious group in the country. By 2010, only Christians will be a larger group (Esposito, 1994). Native Americans are present in significant numbers in some of the nation's school systems. Buddhist-heritage Asian students represent a fast growing non-Western minority in the schools.

There are important differences within and among these groups. As you think about curriculum work, you need to look carefully at the backgrounds of the students who will be served. Your decisions will be better if, as your efforts go forward, they are grounded in a consideration of historical antecedents from both Western and non-Western sources. If you would like to acquire more information about non-Western perspectives, you might want to read Timothy Reagan's book *Non-Western Educational Traditions: Alternative Approaches to Educational Thought and Practice,* 2nd ed. (Mahwah, NJ: Lawrence Erlbaum, 2000).

LEARNING EXTENSION 2–3

Approaches That Have Succeeded with Cultural Minority Students

Special histories of cultural and ethnic minorities increasingly interest educators. What curricular approaches have teachers found to be effective in working with these young people? For answers, go to Merrill Education's Link to General Methods Resources website at http://cw.prenhall.com/bookbind/pubbooks/methods-cluster/.

Once there, go to the bottom of the page and select the topic "Curriculum". Click on the "Begin" button. This will take you to a page with topics listed on the left side of your screen. Click on "Web Links." This will take you to a page that includes the topic "Reform and Improvement Movements and Issues." Click on this topic. This will bring up a page with another set of topics. Click on the one titled "School Reform and Diversity Papers." You will find a list of topics, including some material by Beverly McLeod titled "School Reform and Student Diversity: Lessons Learned: Educating Students from Diverse Linguistic and Cultural Backgrounds (1995)." There will be a link printed immediately below this title named "Curriculum and Instruction." Follow this link. You will find an excellent article detailing some successful approaches to working with culturally and linguistically different students. What would you do differently in light of information you have learned from this review?

LEGACIES OF EUROPE AND THE MEDITERRANEAN

Throughout much of American educational history, school authorities little valued cultural perspectives that originated outside of Europe and the lands of the Mediterranean. School practices consistent with the traditions rooted in this part of the world posed few adjustment problems for students from the White majority culture. The values they encountered at school, by and large, tracked closely those they brought with them from home. On the other hand, students from ethnic and cultural minorities often found some practices and expectations of teachers to be jarringly at odds with the traditions of their parents. The lack of congruence between the values and practices of the school and the patterns of living prized in these students' homes often contributed to their academic difficulties. However, because large numbers of majority-group Americans long believed that cultural traditions of minority populations were inferior, for many years school leaders did little to modify programs and practices in response to the needs of students with ties to non-European and non-Mediterranean cultures. It was not that cultural practices originating outside of Europe were unknown; rather, they were considered irrelevant in an environment where legacies from Europe and the Mediterranean were broadly viewed as superior (Armstrong, Henson & Savage, 2001).

For the most part, curriculum leaders today have a much more enlightened view. In part, this has been driven by the increasing diversity of the school population. In part, it has been a result of better international communication and broader public understanding of people from cultural traditions throughout the world. However, even with a sensitivity to the need to develop school programs that take into account the perspectives of students from many cultural traditions, prevailing school practices in this country continue to reflect many patterns that originated in Europe or in Mediterranean areas close to Europe.

You will be better able to think about ways of serving *all* students if your thinking about this issue is informed by an understanding of how patterns originating in Europe continue to influence many school practices. Some of these features are so common that you may find it difficult to imagine an educational system that does not have them. Let's look at some examples in the following sections.

Education Takes Place in Schools Under the Direction of Specialists

Few in the United States would challenge the idea that education occurs in special institutions called schools. Though parents, families, and friends clearly play a nurturing role, there is broad agreement that the depth and range of learning that young people need require the attention of specialists. Though a growing number of people are interested in homeschooling their children, the percentage of students who are taught at home continues to be small. It might also be argued that, when a child is homeschooled, the home takes on many of the characteristics of a school. There is a parent functioning as a teacher, and educational publishing houses professionally prepare many of the learning materials. Relatively few secondary-school students are homeschooled. The sophistication of the content that must be taught at this level is beyond the capacity of many parents. At this level, many homeschooled students take at least a few classes in traditional schools, or they take them at home from teachers at distant locations who communicate with them via educational television or via the World Wide Web.

Ancient Sumer was the place of origin of some of the first schools. They were established in small cities between the Tigris and Euphrates rivers nearly 5,000 years ago. The Sumerians had a particularly challenging writing system. They were a trading people, and their economic survival depended on writing skills that were sufficiently well developed for them to keep good commercial records. Young people were gathered together and taught by teachers who had developed an effective, simple-to-complex approach for teaching writing. The Sumerian beginnings spawned the development of what has become a widely held assumption of American education: Young people need knowledge that is best transmitted to them by an individual who is a specialist.

It was many centuries later that leading thinkers began speculating about the need for special training in teaching methodologies for those who would be instructing children. Johann Pestalozzi, an eighteenth-century Swiss educator (1746–1827), believed that many students were not treated humanely in school by their teachers. He advocated interactions with students that would give the classroom some of the warm and supportive characteristics young people associated with their homes. He believed teachers needed to be taught these patterns of behavior, and many aspiring teachers from Europe visited Pestalozzi and his schools to learn his methods.

The view that it is educationally sound for students to be taught by well-prepared instructors is a thread that has antecedents in practices originating in Europe and the Mediterranean. It is an idea that continues to underpin thought about the nature of American education in our own day.

Knowledge Can Be Classified and Organized into Separate Subjects

When you first started teaching, you may have come face to face with a problem that has challenged educators for centuries: how to help students make sense of the huge amount of information that is out there. If you prepared as an English teacher, the breadth and depth of content you encountered at the university far exceed what 14-, 15-, or 16-year-olds can absorb. In responding to this dilemma, you had to make choices, and you had to impose an organizational scheme on the material you decided to teach. This process of selection and classification has its origins in Europe.

In particular, the work of Greek philosopher Aristotle (384–322 B.C.E.) made important contributions that continue to benefit educators today. If you use major concepts to organize your instruction, you are following a pattern Aristotle established. He recognized that students' learning was facilitated when they understood that objects sharing certain characteristics could be placed into common categories.

In the Middle Ages, cathedral schools in Europe extended Aristotle's classification ideas and began organizing content into huge subject-area categories. The **seven liberal arts** were among the earliest subjects to be identified. These included the *Trivium* (1. grammar, 2. rhetoric, 3. dialectic) and the *Quadrivium* (4. arithmetic, 5. geometry, 6. astronomy, and 7. music) (Meyer, 1965). Over time, more subjects were added.

Present-day schools continue to feature the organization of content into traditional academic subjects. On the one hand, this arrangement is consistent with the pattern many teachers experienced as university students. Also, it is one with which many parents are familiar and support. On the other hand, traditional subjects are human constructions. Some critics argue that they artificially divide content into categories that are inconsistent with what students encounter in the real world. They argue for more cross-subject organization of content. You may have encountered people taking positions on both sides of this issue. (See Chapter 7, "Design Alternatives and Needs Assessment," for more information related to this topic.)

Schools Should Be Organized into a Series of Grades

That schools should be divided into grades and that students should progress through them in a sequential fashion are notions so embedded in our thinking that we find it difficult to imagine another arrangement. If we consider the long extent of education's history, these ideas are relative newcomers. They trace to the work of a seventeenth-century Moravian thinker, John Amos Comenius.

Comenius recommended that children stay at home with their mothers until they were 6 years old. Then, all children were to go to the *vernacular school*. This school was divided into six class levels, according to students' ages. Students would graduate at about age 12. At this point, some students would go on to the *grammar school*, a school divided into grades that would serve young people from the ages of 13 to 18. A few graduates of the grammar school would go on for further education at a university (*Education in 17th Century Europe*, 1999).

Comenius's scheme, developed in the 1600s, bears a striking resemblance to our familiar way of thinking about schooling as being divided between elementary and secondary levels. (Of course, in recent years, we have tended to think about a three-level scheme: elementary, middle, and high school.) In addition to his ideas about establishing grade levels, present-day American schools owe a debt to Comenius for his advocacy of education for all children regardless of social class, his assertion that females as well as males should be educated, and his appreciation that books for young people needed to be designed differently than those for adults.

LEARNING EXTENSION 2–4

Challenges to the Idea That Schools Should Be Divided into a Series of Grades

Not all educators endorse the idea that schools should be divided into grades and that students should progress through them one year at a time. Some argue in favor of "nongraded" schools, in which students are moved along according to measures of their ability and achievement whenever their teachers believe they are ready to do more advanced work. Do some reading on the topic of nongraded schools.

Suppose that a parents' group in a local school that was considering a switch to a nongraded arrangement invited you to speak to them about the pros and cons of such a change. In your remarks, how would you address the following questions?

- What are some problems proponents have had in attempting to institute nongraded schools?
- Where such schools have proved successful, how have these problems been overcome?
- What characteristics of this school seem particularly congenial to the establishment of a nongraded program, and what characteristics may pose challenges if such an approach were adopted?

School Programs Can Improve Society

You can probably think of dozens of occasions when you have picked up a newspaper and read about a particularly intractable problem. As often as not, you will find buried somewhere in these articles a recommendation that the cure for the cited difficulty is "better education." For all the positions represented in debates about public education, one common article of faith is that schools and schooling have the capacity to "make things better." This conviction applies to challenges as diverse as (1) reducing the incidence of teenage pregnancy, (2) diminishing the use of tobacco products, (3) lowering the amount of greasy food people consume, (4) producing students with a stronger work ethic, (5) making the air cleaner, and (6) improving dental hygiene practices.

The high expectations our citizens have of the schools are reflections of a widely held view that "the best times lie ahead." Certainly, not everyone feels this way, but this positive view of the future is widespread and influential. Not all societies have viewed the future so positively, however. For example, for much of their history, the ancient Egyptians looked back on a highly superior prior "golden age." They saw present and potential future deviations from this past as negative movements away from perfection. This perspective stands in stark contrast to many Americans' optimistic view of the future.

How we see the future and our tendency to view the school as an agency for social improvement stem from European educational thought. In particular, we owe a great debt to the thinking of Johann Pestalozzi, who thought that good schooling could improve not just the character of each child but, ultimately, society itself. Well-educated people of good character would, inevitably, work to eliminate social evils. The connection Pestalozzi saw among schooling, students brought to maturity with good understandings and good character, and the solution of social problems continues to influence much present-day discussion about American education.

European and Mediterranean Influences as a Context for Curricular Thinking

The preceding discussion focused on only a few examples of how European and Mediterranean thought continues to affect American educational practices. European and Mediterranean thinking has helped to build broad American support for many additional ideas about schools and schooling, including the following:

- The idea that governments have an obligation to pay for schools and schooling
- The idea that one important aim of education is the development of attitudes associated with good citizenship
- The idea that schools should provide students with some understandings and skills needed in the adult workplace
- The idea that as many people as possible should be educated
- The idea that social class and personal wealth should not determine how much education a person can receive

To most Americans, there is nothing strange about any of these ideas. They are so familiar that they form a nearly invisible backdrop to our daily experiences. They fall into categories of accepted realities that are akin to our unthinking acceptance of an obligation to drive on the right-hand side of the road or to stop when the light turns red and go when it turns green. The very familiarity of these ideas may lead some people to conclude that these perceptions of reality are universals, representing the beliefs of people everywhere. They are not.

Many of our common assumptions about schools and students are not absolute truths but, rather, human constructions. Because not all Americans (and, hence, not all young people in the schools) come from traditions in which these are the assumed ways of looking at the world, it makes sense for curriculum workers to bring these majority-group assumptions to a conscious level. If you do this as you engage in curriculum tasks, you will be better able to ask critical questions about the appropriateness of your decisions. These questions will assist you and your group as you strive to develop programs that will receive a positive response from *all* the students to be served, not just from those who have been conditioned to see the world through majority-group lenses.

 ## LEGACIES OF AMERICA'S EDUCATIONAL PAST

The introduction of particular organizational patterns and content emphases into our schools often has been triggered by events or circumstances. Once new patterns have been introduced, they prove remarkably resistant to elimination. Instead, they are incrementally modified to adjust to new conditions. In addition, they tend to be sustained by traditions and to support activities that have developed as supportive side effects. You will recall the earlier discussion of the nine- or nine-and-one-half-month school year. This pattern, begun in days when students were expected to be out of school and helping on the farm during the summer months, to this day remains the overwhelming calendar of choice in American schools. The original need for this arrangement is long past, but the system continues to be maintained in large measure because a wholesale move to another pattern would necessitate more changes than the general public has been willing to accept.

You might also be familiar with the beginnings of vocational education. The famous Kalamazoo case of 1874 established a legal precedent in support of the idea that state legislatures can legally impose taxes to support secondary schools. Previously, there were solid legal grounds to support taxation only for the purposes of paying for elementary-level education. When school leaders considered the implications of the **Kalamazoo case,** they quickly concluded that secondary schools shortly would increase greatly in numbers and that the total secondary-school enrollment would skyrocket. They feared that many of the young people who would attend would have neither the intellectual talent nor the inclination to go on to colleges and universities when they graduated. Because so many high-school graduates were expected to go directly into the workforce, educational leaders in the last quarter of the nineteenth century pushed hard for the introduction of practical, vocationally related subjects.

High schools today continue to accept education for work as one of their functions. However, what constituted vocational education in the late nineteenth century bears only a tenuous resemblance to what goes on in today's work-readiness programs. Most early programs focused on preparing students for work in an era in which there was an enormous demand for semiskilled labor. There was an emphasis on activities that required students to work at least as much with their hands as with their heads. Many of today's school-to-work programs feature a heavy dose of mathematics and technical subjects that are essential tools of employees working in today's technologically sophisticated workplaces. The continued presence of programs designed to prepare students for the world of work, in large measure, has come about because these programs have been able to adapt to changing needs.

In the sections that follow, you will find examples of historical circumstances that helped shape today's educational practices.

LEARNING EXTENSION 2–5

What Should High Schools Strive to Do?

For well over 100 years, debates about the primary purpose of high schools have raged. Should they strive to give young people the background they need for successful college and university work? Should they devote their attention to preparing students for various vocational roles? Should they seek to produce "good" citizens? Take time to review more recent proposals (since 1980) to make high schools better. What issues are in dispute? Did you find any ideas that tend to appear over and over again?

Colonial Period to 1800

In the Colonial Period, quite different educational practices developed in the New England Colonies, the Middle Colonies, and the Southern Colonies. Settlers in New England had come from England in part to escape what they perceived to be religious error. They were concerned that their children learn to read the Bible and other appropriate religious texts. The **Massachusetts School Law of 1642** represented the first attempt in America to make schooling compulsory. Some teeth were put into this legislation in 1647, when the so-called **Old Deluder Satan Act** was passed. This law required every town of 50 or more families to hire a teacher to be paid out of local funds.

The population of the Middle Colonies was more diverse than that of New England. In New York, merchants were concerned about a future supply of trained employees, and they started a number of private schools to train young people for future careers in business and trade. Groups of Quakers in Pennsylvania started schools that, highly unusual for the time, welcomed all children, including African-Americans and Native Americans. These schools were very early examples of a tendency of American education over time to broaden the range of young people to be served. However, many more boys than girls attended school.

There were few large towns and cities in the Southern Colonies. Rather, the population tended to be located on widely dispersed individual farms sited along the region's many large rivers. The lack of a concentrated population made it difficult to establish schools. Upper-class children were tutored on individual plantations and, in many cases, male children were sent back to England to complete their educations. Relatively few young people from less affluent families were educated.

Few secondary schools existed in the years prior to 1800. One of the famous early ones was the **Boston Latin Grammar School,** established in 1635 to prepare boys for Harvard. In the middle of the eighteenth century, Benjamin Franklin proposed a new kind of secondary school—one that would focus on practical subjects, such as mathematics, bookkeeping, and navigation, and that would be free of religious ties. To put these ideas into practice, he established the **Franklin Academy** in 1751. The **academy,** a private school to which students paid tuition, proved to be a popular approach to secondary education. Academies became popular, and they were the most common form of secondary school until the second half of the nineteenth century. Some present-day patterns that trace back to the Colonial-to-1800 period include

- The principle that schools should be locally controlled
- The debate over the relative emphasis that should be placed on academic as opposed to practical school subjects
- The idea that schools have some responsibility for moral education
- The idea that school attendance should be compulsory (in Colonial times, these regulations applied only to young children)

The Nineteenth Century

Interest in establishing new secondary-level academies increased greatly during the first half of the nineteenth century. By 1850, when they reached their highest number, there were over 6,000 of them (Barry, 1961). Though these institutions were popular, their growth potential was limited. Because they were private, tuition-charging institutions, young people from poor families could not attend. Over time, pressures mounted in support of a public-funded alternative that would open up secondary-level education to many more students. In response to this need, the nation's first public high school, the **Boston English Classical School,** was established in 1821.

Though the first high school was established in the 1820s, the new school type was slow to catch on. Funding was a major problem. For many years, there were questions about the legality of using public money to pay for secondary schools. This was not resolved until the 1870s. It was only then that high schools began to increase greatly in number. During all of the nineteenth century, the private academy remained the dominant secondary-school type. It was as late as 1900 before the number of high schools exceeded the number of academies (Barry, 1961).

Though some legal bases for supporting elementary schools traced back to Colonial times, there were vast place-to-place differences in the numbers of schools that were built and supported. This pattern changed, thanks greatly to the work of Horace Mann, who, in the late 1820s, took up the cause of the **common school.** As a result of Mann's efforts, there was a tremendous school-building boom from the 1830s to the 1860s. In 1860, for the first time, over half of the nation's young people were enrolled in public schools (*Historical Statistics of the United States,* 1975).

Mann also promoted the need to train instructors in special teacher-training institutions called **normal schools.** The first of these was established in 1839. By 1900, they existed in every state. However, for many years, large numbers of states did not require people hired as teachers to be graduates of formal training programs. As late as 1921, 31 states had not a single official academic requirement on the books for awarding a teaching certificate (Bowen, 1981).

In the second half of the nineteenth century, the forerunners of today's National Education Association and American Federation of Teachers were organized. Committees affiliated with these groups began to exercise an influence on school curricula. In concert with university officials, some of them brought pressure to bear on high schools to develop curricula that would help graduates cope better with university-level work. Other committees offered countersuggestions in support of the view that high schools should not abandon the needs of students who would enter the workforce after graduation.

EXERCISE 2–2

Recommendations of the Committee of Ten

In 1893, the National Education Association's Committee of Ten recommended the following program of study for *all* high school sophomores (National Education Association, 1893, p. 4):

- Latin
- Greek
- German (continued from the freshman year)
- Algebra (could be replaced by bookkeeping or commercial arithmetic)
- Botany
- English history to 1688

Action

Review the list against a program for a typical high-school sophomore today. If you teach high school, consider what students take at your school. If you do not, and have no access to either a high-school student or a high-school program of study, think about what you studied as a high-school sophomore. Suppose you were asked to comment on how a proposal to put this set of course requirements in place today might be received. What would you say?

Analysis

Look at one or more present-day school reform proposals. (As a beginning, put the term "school reform" in a standard web search engine, such as Google. You might also check the *Education Index* in the library. Your instructor may also provide you with some suggestions.) Do these 1893 ideas continue to live in some present-day school improvement proposals? If so, what are some examples?

Key Point

For over 200 years, people interested in American education have argued about whether schools should place heavier emphases on academic subjects that tie closely to programs of study in colleges and universities or on more practical subjects designed to help students prepare for the world of work.

The last decades of the nineteenth century witnessed a huge influx of immigrants to the United States. Many came from Eastern and Southern Europe. Many politically influential groups saw these new arrivals as a threat and put pressures on schools to "Americanize" them as quickly as possible. School programs tended to treat the cultures of many of these newcomers as "undesirable baggage," and little that went on in schools was designed to enhance the cultural pride and self-worth of the sons and daughters of immigrants.

Some present-day patterns that trace to the 1800s include

- The idea that secondary as well as elementary education should be publicly funded
- The idea that public schools should be available in every part of the country
- The idea that teachers should have special training for their roles
- The idea that teachers can emphasize educational policy through organized professional groups
- The idea that schools have an obligation to produce citizens committed to American values

The Twentieth Century

The numbers of high schools grew rapidly in the early years of the twentieth century. High-school teachers complained that many of the additional students they were getting were not capable of doing the required work. These concerns led to a focus on the special needs of students as they prepared to transition from elementary schools to high schools. In time, a new school type, the junior high school, was created to serve the needs of preadolescents. The first junior high school opened in Berkeley, California, in 1909 (Popper, 1967).

Many supporters of the new institution hoped that it would provide programming responsive to the needs of the young people in this age group and would give them the tools needed for success in high school. However, as the century progressed, critics of the junior high school emerged, who charged that the institutions were not adequately responding to the needs of preadolescent and early adolescent children. These concerns spread rapidly after World War II. As an alternative, a new school type, the *middle school,* began to catch on in the 1960s. The middle school, designed with a strong concern for the developmental needs of children in their pre-high-school years, by the last decades of the twentieth century had displaced the junior high school as the most common school type between elementary and high school.

LEARNING EXTENSION 2–6

How Well Are Middle Schools Serving Their Students' Needs?

The middle school, as originally conceived, was supposed to provide programming for preadolescents and early adolescents that was uniquely suited to their needs. Have these schools actually delivered on this expectation? Do some research, and think about how you would answer these questions: (1) What features do experts in middle-school education want to see in the curricula for these schools? (2) How widely have such curricula been adopted? (3) What barriers have there been to establishing middle-school curricula that are uniquely suited to the needs of their students?

Debates between those seeing secondary schools as college-preparatory institutions and those seeing them as places to prepare students for the world of work heated up in the first two decades of the twentieth century. In 1918, the National Education Association's Commission on the Reorganization of Secondary Education came up with a grand compromise. The commission identified seven *Cardinal Principles* (health, command of fundamental processes, worthy home membership, vocational preparation, citizenship, worthy use of leisure time, and ethical character), which collectively describe the ends toward which secondary education should be directed. By suggesting that the secondary school, among other things, should embrace a focus on both academics and preparation for work, the commission sought to put to rest the concerns of people on both sides of the issue. This hope was illusory. Though the report acknowledged the legitimacy of both the academic and the work-related ends of secondary schooling, it said nothing about questions such as the following: How much money should be placed behind academic as opposed to work-related programs? How many students should be enrolled in each? How should they be selected? In short, the Cardinal Principles proposal proved to be a 1918 response to a debate that continues into the twenty-first century.

The work of educational philosopher John Dewey (1859–1952) had a tremendous influence on twentieth-century education. For curriculum specialists, among his notable contributions was his inquiry-teaching model. Dewey's (1910) classic book, *How We Think,* laid out a simple, five-step plan for an inquiry lesson: (1) describe the problem, (2) suggest possible solutions, (3) gather evidence to test their accuracy, (4) evaluate the solutions in light of the evidence, and (5) arrive at a conclusion.

Dewey believed that schools should focus on the needs of individual students. He was suspicious of schools' efforts to promote society's goals at the expense of the needs and aspirations of learners. He contended that students are best served when they are taught the processes of learning, rather than specific elements of content. Once mastered, these processes allow individuals to engage in a program of continuing self-education.

While John Dewey was doing work focusing on the needs of particular learners, others in the first decades of the twentieth century were directing their attention to the problem of gaining information about large groups of individuals. As early as 1905, Alfred Binet and his co-workers developed the *intelligence quotient (IQ)* test. It was designed to predict how well learners would do in regular school classrooms. Initially, the available technology limited the numbers of people who could take group tests.

In the nineteenth century, most assessment took the form of oral exams or, sometimes, essays. Neither format lent itself well to situations in which hundreds of people might be tested. Even short-answer tests required a great deal of time to correct. What was needed was a forced-choice test type that could be used to assess many topics and varying levels of difficulty. The technological breakthrough that allowed this to happen did not come until 1914, when the multiple-choice test was invented (Clarke, Madaus, Horn, & Ramos, 1999). Technological developments later in the century, such as the optical scanner, invented in the 1950s, and computer-based scoring systems—made possible the quick scoring of exams from thousands of test takers. These innovations gave states the technological tools needed to support implementing and monitoring mandated standardized curricula and associated testing programs.

In the second half of the twentieth century, a series of events focused public attention on education and led to an enormous number of proposals to make schools better. In 1957, the former Soviet Union's launch of the earth satellite *Sputnik* challenged Americans' views of themselves as the world's technological leaders. Almost immediately, schools faced demands to adopt more rigorous curricula, particularly in the areas of mathematics and the hard sciences. Federal funding to produce new, rigorous curricula and to train teachers to use them came with the passage of the National Defense Education Act in 1958.

The reform initiatives of the late 1950s were scarcely underway when concerns about the nation's involvement in the Vietnam War led to widespread public suspicion of governmental authority of all kinds. School leadership was not immune. Many articles in the educational press began depicting schools as repressive sorts of places, where graduation requirements and other school regulations unnecessarily interfered with students' individual development (Armstrong, 1986).

A strong push for more rigor in schools, spawned with the appearance of *Sputnik* and undermined by concerns about the Vietnam War, reappeared in the 1980s. This time, economic worries, especially those related to Japan's rapid rise, played a key role in shaping public attitudes. The publication of *A Nation at Risk: The Imperative for Educational Reform* (1983) prompted a wave of subsequent reports and recommendations. Though specific suggestions varied, most called for more academic rigor, better preparation of teachers, and more testing of students to assure that they were progressing satisfactorily.

Since the 1980s, there has been a tremendous increase in the number of tests students take. Increasingly, scores are used to make school-to-school comparisons, and often there are important negative consequences for principals and teachers when scores fail to improve over time. The desire to make meaningful school-to-school comparisons has also prompted many states to develop standardized programs of study and related sets of assessment items. Some educational leaders worry that this trend forces teachers to spend too much time teaching good test-taking skills and too little time teaching content.

This section has focused on just a few of the twentieth-century developments that continue to influence the efforts of curriculum workers. Space considerations prevent a more comprehensive review of such issues as homeschooling, educational television, school voucher proposals, tech-prep programs, web-based course delivery, charter schools, full-service schools, and magnet schools.

As you think about doing curriculum work today, you might want to recall such twentieth-century developments as the following:

- The evolution of technologies that are now available to support plans for administering and scoring huge numbers of student responses to standardized tests
- The recognition that schools have some responsibility to respond to the individual needs of students
- The ongoing debate between those seeing education as preparation for college and university work and those seeing education as preparation for the world of work
- An appreciation for the point that "negative surprises" that affect the entire nation often result in negative looks at the public schools and accompanying proposals for their improvement
- A recognition that, over time, there have been different responses to the question "What is wrong with today's schools?"
- The recognition that a growing public demand for meaningful school-to-school comparisons has been a force supporting the development of state-level curriculum guidelines that all schools are expected to follow

EXERCISE 2–3

Educational "Excellence" Is Not Always Defined the Same Way

Had you been in a position to survey public opinion about education in the 1960s, you might have found support for ideas including the following: (1) There is no problem with the quality of school graduates—the nation has responded to *Sputnik* and has sophisticated engineers with the talent for planning moon landings; (2) as evidenced by the "Vietnam mess," it is evident that government authority at all levels (including educational bureaucracies) has become too heavy-handed; (3) something should be done to make schools less repressive places; and (4) secondary schools, in particular, should give students opportunities to take many more elective courses.

Were you to survey public opinion today, you would probably find broad support for quite different ideas, including the following: (1) There should be rigorous academic programs that are common enough that school-to-school comparison is easy, (2) students should have no way of escaping the need to take challenging courses, (3) there should be widely used standardized tests to provide evidence that students are learning, and (4) teachers and administrators should suffer consequences when students' performance levels are low.

Action

Do some reading focusing on possible causes for changes in the kinds of issues that have drawn the attention of critics of the schools over the past 40 years. Consult professional as well as general-circulation periodicals, sites on the World Wide Web, and other information sources your instructor might recommend.

Analysis

Suppose you are asked to address a group of people who are new to curriculum-development work. In your comments to them, what responses would you provide to the following questions?

- What historical events contributed to changes in how the general public views problems facing the schools today, as compared with four decades ago?
- How have these events altered the criteria people have used to decide which schools are doing a good job?
- In your opinion, how should curriculum professionals cope with the issue of shifting public opinion?

Key Points

At no time in our history has there been absolute consensus regarding what good schools do. However, at different times in our history, strong majorities have lined up behind particular points of view. Curriculum workers need to think about how shifting public priorities can affect what they do.

 ## HISTORY AS A POSITIVE INFLUENCE ON CURRICULAR CHOICE

The nub of the history/curriculum issue is simple. People most readily accept ideas for curricular change when these proposals do not challenge deeply held values. The values that go together to form individuals' worldviews derive, in large measure, from the history and traditions of their cultural groups. Even when professional educators align solidly behind a proposed change and needed technologies are available to support it, if large numbers of people, particularly parents and relatives of students, find that it challenges deeply held values, the change will face stiff opposition.

As you engage in curriculum work, you need to be sensitive to the varied perspectives of today's students, parents, relatives, and other school patrons. History, in one sense, limits what you can do. However, you might consider this to be a positive restriction. Reflection on diverse cultural histories encourages you to look beyond the assumptions of the members of your own cultural group as you bring to a conscious level the often quite different perspectives of other groups. Seen in this light, the restraint of history can be a liberating force, which leads to curriculum decisions that benefit all members of today's culturally diverse community of students.

Review and Reflection

1. Why do some curricular patterns persist even though the conditions that originally gave rise to them no longer exist?

2. At various times throughout American educational history, new technologies have appeared that, to some, seemed to threaten traditional and "appropriate" ways of doing things. For example, debates continue today about the wisdom of allowing younger elementary children to use calculators. Opponents suggest that these devices stand in the way of their mastery of the multiplication tables. Proponents suggest that they open up the possibilities of engaging younger children in more demanding work at a younger age than was possible in the pre-calculator age. What are your thoughts on the issue of technological innovation and students? Are your positions shaped by any special experiences you have had? If so, what are they?

3. Describe some ways today's curriculum developers might take into consideration the historical legacies of students from families with non-European, non-Mediterranean cultural traditions.

4. What are some present-day school practices that reflect the perspectives of education that originally developed in Europe or the lands around the Mediterranean?

5. American educational history has witnessed many occasions when contradictory forces were at work. For example, today the pressure for accountability is a force supporting the adoption of statewide curricula and accompanying standardized testing. This force tends to lead to more centralization of authority at the state level. At the other end of the spectrum, there is a strong movement in support of charter schools. For many, the attraction of the charter school is its standing as an institution that does not have to abide by a large number of state-level mandates. What other present-day policy issues involve well-organized support groups favoring a stronger role for state-level authorities and other, well-organized support groups favoring much more local-level autonomy?

6. What explains the relatively slow growth of high schools in the nineteenth century, and what nineteenth-century debates about their purposes continue today?

7. Some critics of high schools accuse them of dealing with groups that favor a particular course or set of experiences by simply adding more courses to the curriculum. Over time, these critics allege, high-school programs no longer require students to learn anything at much depth. You might wish to look at the work of people such as Theodore Sizer, who argue that less

is more and that high schools should provide a much more limited range of course options for students than many do today. What are your reactions to this position?

8. What developments in the past 125 years have provided the kind of techno-logical support needed for today's broad use of standardized tests?

References

Armstrong, D. G., Henson, K. T., & Savage, T. V. (2001). *Teaching today: An introduction to education* (6th ed.). Upper Saddle River, NJ: Merrill/Prentice Hall.

Barry, T. N. (1961). *Origin and development of the American public high school in the 19th century.* Ph.D. Diss. Palo Alto, CA: Stanford University.

Bowen, J. A. (1981). *A history of western education. Vol. III, The modern west, Europe, and the new world.* New York: St. Martin's Press.

Clarke, M. M., Madaus, G. F., Horn, C. L., & Ramos, M. A. (1999). Retrospective on educational testing and assessment in the 20th century. *Journal of Curriculum Studies, 32*(2), 159–181.

Cleverly, J. (1985). *The schooling of China: Tradition and modernity in Chinese education.* Sydney, Australia: Allen & Unwin.

Coles, A. D. (1999, July 16). Mass-produced pencil leaves its mark. *Education Week on the Web.* [http://www.edweek.com/ew/vol-18/40pencil.h18]

Dewey, J. (1910). *How we think.* Boston: D. C. Heath.

Education in 17th century Europe. (1999). [http://www.britannica.com/bcom/eb/article/4/0,5716,108334+4+105951,00.html]

Esposito, J. (1994). Islam in the world and in America. In J. Neusner (ed.), *World religions in America: An introduction* (pp. 243–258). Louisville, KY: Westminster/John Knox.

Historical statistics of the United States. (1975). Washington, DC: U.S. Department of Commerce, Bureau of the Census.

Meyer, A. E. (1965). *An educational history of the western world.* New York: McGraw-Hill.

Monteith, J. B. (1872). Annual Report No. 98. *Report of the Commissioner of Indian Affairs, 1872.* Washington, DC: U.S. Department of the Interior.

A nation at risk: The imperative for educational reform. (1983). Washington, DC: U.S. Department of Education, National Commission on Excellence in Education.

National Education Association. (1893). *Report of the Committee of Ten on secondary school social studies.* Washington, DC: Author.

Popper, S. H. (1967). *The American middle school: An organizational analysis.* Waltham, MA: Blaisdell.

Reagan, T. (2000). *Non-Western educational traditions: Alternative approaches to educational thought and practice* (2nd ed.). Mahwah, NJ: Lawrence Erlbaum Associates.

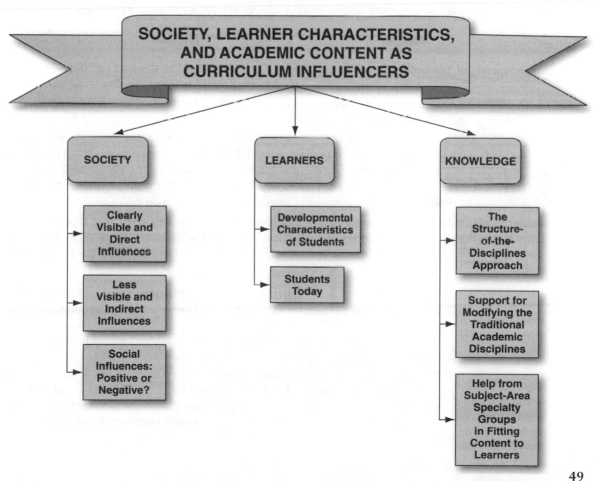

Society, Learner Characteristics, and Academic Content as Curriculum Influencers

Graphic Organizer

49

INTRODUCTION

If you have spent much time in the field of education, you probably have encountered the following question and the accompanying answer:

Question: What should school programs attempt to do?
Answer: They should seek to meet each student's unique needs.

The wording may have varied just a bit from the two sentences in this example, but the sense probably did not deviate significantly.

This question-and-answer pair exemplifies a difficult problem curriculum workers face. It boils down to this: *Often, proposed solutions to complex educational problems are expressed in ways that appear to provide meaningful remedies but that, on further inspection, raise at least as many questions as they answer.* To see how this is so, think about what the stock answer to the "What should school programs attempt to do?" question tells you. That is, what kind of practical guidance do you get about what you are to do as you "seek to meet each student's unique needs"? The answer, of course, is that the phrase provides little specific direction. At best, it prompts you to consider answers to a number of challenging additional questions, such as the following:

- What is meant by "needs"? Are these simply intellectual or academic needs, or do they embrace physiological and emotional needs as well?
- What happens if your assessment of students' needs is at odds with how parents and guardians see those needs?
- If these individual needs can be identified, what is the best programmatic response to each?
- Is it possible to "atomize" school programs so completely that every need of every student can be accommodated, or will it be necessary to develop a more restricted set of programmatic responses? If a restricted set must be developed, what will it consist of, and how will you know that it is the set that will respond to the largest number of needs represented among the students to be served?
- How can you judge whether the needs that are the targets of the program are being met? What criteria will you use, what standards of performance will you set, and what assessment tools will you employ to gather data for making necessary judgments?

For many years, curriculum specialists have identified three major sources of or major influences on the curriculum: (1) society, (2) learners, and (3) knowledge (Doll, 1996; Taba, 1962; Tanner & Tanner, 1995; Tyler, 1949). Knowing that there are three major sources of the curriculum, in and of itself, provides you and others with little specific direction as you ponder actions you might take as members of a curriculum development or revision group. They simply identify three dimensions of concern that can help frame your deliberations. These major categories suggest the kinds of information that will be helpful to you as you engage in curriculum decision making. As you participate in this process, you may find it useful to seek answers to questions such as these:

Society

- What are some core values that our society expects to be prized by *all* citizens, and how might these be embedded in school programs?
- Is our society better thought of as a group of individuals who share certain perspectives, or is it better thought of as consisting of groups that openly compete on behalf of narrowly defined interests?
- Will programs that reflect present social values only replicate what we now have and, hence, stand in the way of improved ways of doing things?
- Who speaks for society? That is, where can credible information be obtained that adequately reflects society's needs?

Learners

- Are learners adequate judges of their own needs and interests? If not, who should make this determination, and what procedures should be used?
- What is the appropriate balance between responding to learners' needs as individuals and responding to their needs as members of a multiperson society?
- Are learners better served when their school programs emphasize the fundamentals?
- How are learners' performances to be judged and on what authority?
- Should school programs emphasize preparation for the world of work, or should they be oriented toward the mastery of traditional academic subjects?

Knowledge

- Should the curriculum feature emphases on facts, concepts, and generalizations taken from traditional academic disciplines?
- Should the knowledge selected be interdisciplinary?
- To what extent should issues associated with assessment drive the selection of knowledge?
- How will knowledge that a "typical citizen" needs be identified, and how will it differ from what academic specialists (or people preparing to be academic specialists) need to know?
- How will the accuracy of knowledge be verified, and how will changes in "what is known" be accommodated?

Much interest in sources of the curriculum traces to the work of John Dewey. Toward the end of the nineteenth century, Dewey's thinking led educators to focus increased attention on the connections among students, their social world, and applications of academic knowledge (Tanner & Tanner, 1995). His efforts encouraged curriculum developers to orient school programs around the idea that lines of separation between the school and the larger society should be blurred. He argued that learning experiences that are selected should fit well with students' individual characteristics and should require them to make active use of academic content as source material as they hone their problem-solving skills.

Despite Dewey's influence, over the years, many curriculum specialists have observed that many school programs are built more around the perspectives of academic knowledge than around knowledge about society and about learners (Broudy, 1982; Caswell, 1978; Sowell, 1996). In his influential 1949 text *Basic Principles of Curriculum and Instruction,* Ralph Tyler made a strong case in support of the idea that each of these three curriculum sources—society, learners, and knowledge—merits serious consideration. These three categories continue to frame much curriculum-development work.

How should curriculum developers interpret and incorporate into their decisions societal influences, knowledge influences, and information-about-learners' influences? Although there is no agreement on an answer to this question, experts do agree that major tensions adhere to each of these categories of concern. These tensions give rise to further questions you might wish to consider, such as the following:

- In making curriculum decisions, to what extent can the needs of society be differentiated from the interests of narrow groups that merely claim that their agenda represents the needs of society?

- What is the appropriate balance point between (1) providing students with the kinds of educational background they will need to be a contributing participant of a multiperson world and (2) providing them with educational experiences that are uniquely fitted to their individual needs?

- Since it is impossible to teach everything, what aspects of knowledge should be emphasized, how should they be organized, and what should be done to assure that the selection process does not result in school programs that unacceptably distort reality?

SOCIETY

Civilizations encompass clusters of groups that share certain perspectives. Activities, including education, take place within a set of assumptions. This means that curriculum decisions are made within a social context. When you engage in thinking related to curriculum, in some cases the influences you confront will take the form of rules and regulations promulgated by constituted legal authority. In other cases, pressures you face will be indirect and subtle. Indeed, it is quite probable that some of them will almost never be raised to a conscious level. This is especially true in the case of decisions you make that seem to be so "natural" that you might have a difficult time imagining how anyone would oppose them.

Are there assumptions about how the world should be that are universally accepted? This question prompts heated debates. Those on one side of the issue tend to see social influences on curricular decision making as generally benign. Those on the other see them as influences that support decisions that advantage some people at the expense of others.

Clearly Visible and Direct Influences

Decisions of various governing bodies are among the social influences that most directly impinge on curriculum workers' thinking. For example, you and others involved in curriculum development cannot disregard the federal regulations related to providing certain kinds of services for students with disabilities. Similarly, if your state has set content standards for specific school courses, you cannot ignore them. Some places have state or local regulations mandating the use of specific textbooks. When such regulations are in place, you and members of your curriculum-development group are not free to propose a program that would require the use of other texts. (Of course, you certainly can lobby for a change in a local textbook regulation; however, as long as one is on the books, it constrains your ability to choose other titles.)

LEARNING EXTENSION 3–1

Federal Regulations Regarding Gifted and Talented Students

In addition to federal legislation related to learners with disabilities, legislation also exists that pertains to school services for gifted and talented students. Go to your library or seek information on the World Wide Web about the provisions of The Jacob K. Javits Gifted and Talented Students Act of 1994 (P.L. 100-297).

*   What are the provisions of this legislation?
*   What constraints, if any, does it potentially impose on curriculum developers who are charged with preparing or revising programs for gifted and talented students?
*   To what extent do the provisions of this legislation influence the curricula in local school districts?

Clearly visible social influences sometimes exert their power over curriculum decisions less directly than do decisions that tie clearly to such issues as adequately serving special needs students, offering certain required courses, and using a selected set of textbooks. For example, in some places, local school budgets depend heavily on annual school tax elections. If a district has had a poor history of providing funds for local schools, one result may be an increase in average class size. If you are involved in curriculum development and your group knows that teachers who use the new program will be teaching classes of 30 or more, rather than classes of 20 to 25, this information places limitations on the kinds of recommendations you are likely to make.

In recent years, school districts have faced tremendous numbers of lawsuits. In response to this situation, many districts have sought ways to limit their exposure to future court actions. As a result, suggestions for curricular change that may be perceived to involve students in situations in which an injury might result (and, hence, a potential lawsuit) tend to be looked at very carefully. In some places, for example, out-of-school field trips are discouraged because they put students in relatively uncontrolled environments, where the possibility of an accident's occurring is higher than when they are in school classrooms.

In summary, you will have to consider a wide spectrum of local rules and regulations that affect the kinds of decisions you make. These restrictions are a basic feature of the context within which curriculum work occurs.

Less Visible and Indirect Influences

Colleges and universities periodically change their entrance requirements and lists of courses they strongly recommend that students take in high school. When such changes are announced, local school districts feel great pressure to modify their curricula to bring them into line with the new guidelines. Many of the parents who expect their children to enter the world of higher education after graduating from high school are leaders in their communities. They constitute strong lobbies, which work to influence curriculum workers to align local programs quickly with the recommendations of college and university officials.

Pressure groups of all kinds work to influence curriculum decisions. At the local level, for example, there may be well-organized groups supporting the expansion of services for gifted and talented learners. The ultimate goal of such groups often is to obtain a school district mandate in support of more funding for the programs they espouse. When they are successful in doing so, the influence on curriculum workers shifts from less visible and indirect to clearly visible and direct. In reality, what often happens is that curriculum groups, in an effort to ward off a possible official mandate from a local school district, provide some expansion of services in an area of interest to the lobbying group within new programs it is planning. For example, if you were working on a new mathematics program for the middle grades, your group might decide to prepare some materials for a gifted and talented track within the new program. Even though you would not be under any official pressure to do so, the action you and members of your group take would be influenced by the threat of a more prescriptive guideline that could come down in the form of a school-district mandate.

Other pressure groups include national and state affiliates of professional organizations that are dedicated to improving instruction in various academic subjects. (For additional information about the efforts of these groups to establish national subject-area standards, see Chapter 6, "People and Roles in Curriculum Work.") Some examples of these groups are

- American Alliance for Health, Physical Education, Recreation and Dance (AAHPERD)
- Association for Career and Technical Education (ACTE)
- Council on Exceptional Children (CEC)
- International Reading Association (IRA)

- International Society for Technology in Education (ISTE)
- Music Teachers National Association (MTNA)
- National Art Education Association (NAEA)
- National Association for Gifted Children (NAGC)
- National Business Education Association (NBEA)
- National Council for the Social Studies (NCSS)
- National Council of Teachers of English (NCTE)
- National Council of Teachers of Mathematics (NCTM)
- National Science Teachers Association (NSTA)

There are other professional groups that focus on more general program design and management issues. One is the Association for Supervision and Curriculum Development (ASCD). This is a group concerned with curricular issues affecting public schools. Another organization is the American Society for Training and Development (ASTD). This group serves the interests of curriculum specialists and trainers in business and private industry.

As you engage in curriculum work, you will probably encounter discussions of the guidelines produced by professional groups. Positions taken by these organizations have no legal standing, but their views enjoy wide respect, and it is common for curriculum workers to reference the groups' positions as they work to build a rationale in support of their own decisions.

The kinds of content assessed on standardized tests greatly concern today's curriculum developers. Two forces drive this interest. First, in recent years, there has been a tremendous increase in the numbers of standardized tests students take (Stake, 1999). Second, the test results increasingly are used to make school to school, school district to school district, and even state to state comparisons. This practice is opposed by many assessment experts, but it is a part of today's educational reality. As a result, school leaders, who must face questions from a skeptical public when test scores are not good, often push for academic programs that tie clearly to the content of the standardized tests students must take.

LEARNING EXTENSION 3–2

Standardized Testing and Content Selection

The increase in standardized testing has placed new pressures on educators to align curricula with topics and issues students are likely to encounter on these assessments. Attention to the tests has been especially pronounced in places where results are being used to make school to school and, sometimes, teacher to teacher performance comparisons.

Choose a school level (elementary, middle, high school) and survey some administrators or teachers in your local area. Ask the respondents the following questions:

- Are your students taking more standardized tests today than they were 10 years ago?
- If so, where is the pressure to increase testing coming from?

- How are the test results being used?
- What revisions to your curricula have been influenced by standardized tests?
- Are there other revisions you are contemplating because of concerns related to standardized tests?
- Do you regard the influences of standardized testing on the curriculum as positive or negative, and why do you take this position?

Testing technology, at least as applied when thousands of students must take tests that have to be scored within a reasonable period of time, restricts the kinds of content that can be assessed. Nicholas Burbules (1997) has written and spoken about this issue. He cites an example of an attempt to introduce a new civics course in Australia. The stated purpose was to produce students who would become active, engaged citizens as adults. The available testing technology restricted the test items to the recall of the names of former prime ministers and the dates of key events in Australian political history. The need for students to pass this test skewed instruction away from the intent of the course and in the direction of the more narrow outcomes to be tested.

CURRICULUM REALITIES 3–1

Technology as a Constraint on Intended Learning Outcomes

A number of social forces today encourage educators to incorporate more and more technology into school programs. Part of the agenda is to make students more aware of technologies they will encounter in the workplace. Another purpose is to make education more accessible to students who live far from places where certain kinds of instruction can be provided. Still another claimed benefit is that using technology to disseminate information can reduce school costs.

Dr. Ada Vallecorsa, a professor and administrator at The University of North Carolina at Greensboro, has long worked with special education teachers and administrators. In recent years, she has developed programs for delivery via the World Wide Web. She points out that this approach makes it possible for students to engage materials according to their own time schedules. On the other hand, this technology imposes constraints on the kinds of learning experiences that can be provided (Vallecorsa, 2001).

Vallecorsa finds that courses transmitted exclusively on the web function well to deliver basic information. She sees problems occurring when there is an intent to provide activities requiring the teacher to monitor students as they engage in higher-level thinking and decision-making processes.

In special education, decision making often occurs in a group setting. Hence, these skills are best nurtured under conditions in which people directly engage one another in a discussion, listen to what others say, react to their perspectives, and in general take advantage of a collective dialogue focusing on a common issue. To facilitate the development of these skills, Vallecorsa believes that teachers need to be in a position that allows them to listen to discussions as they unfold, to interject comments as appropriate, and to read and respond to students whose physical demeanor or comments convey they are having difficulties.

Vallecorsa suggests that programs that depend exclusively on the World Wide Web as a vehicle for disseminating information and interacting with students limit the range of what teachers can expect of their students. As you think about technology and its implications for curriculum workers, consider these questions:

- Has technology been oversold as a way to make instructional programs better? Why or why not?
- Vallecorsa's comments reference programs that are exclusively web-based. If some instruction were delivered on the web and some in more traditional classroom settings, could these difficulties be overcome? If so, what would be the emphases of the components of the course on the web and of those provided in the classroom?
- The discussion in this feature centers on some potential limitations certain technologies impose on the kinds of learning outcomes teachers might logically expect of their students. Are there other examples of technology expanding the range of potential learning outcomes? If so, what are they?

Social Influences: Positive or Negative?

Are social forces that impinge on curriculum decision making good or bad? How you and others answer this question varies with how you view our society as a whole. Do you see it as an agency that, for the most part, has acted in ways that have benefited most people and have treated them in sensitive, humane, and respectful ways? Or do you see our society as controlled by narrow interest groups that provide benefits to a selected few while denying benefits to others (Sirotnik, 1988)?

Whether you regard influences of society on curriculum as positive or negative can lead you to have quite different reactions to particular decisions. For example, suppose a school district decided to offer a new advanced calculus course as an elective for talented high-school seniors. If you have a generally positive view of our society, you might see this as an excellent response to a social need to provide better high-school-level mathematics preparation for high-school seniors who aspire to go on to colleges and universities. On the other hand, if you have a negative view of social influences on curriculum decisions, you might see the authorization of this new course as an irresponsible approval to spend scarce funds to support the sons and daughters of elite local citizens who want to provide their own children with special advantages. You might argue that money would be better spent on programs designed to serve a broader cross section of the community.

Another way to look at the society as a positive influence vs. society as a negative influence debate is to think about an answer to this question: Do individual human beings have more characteristics that make them similar to one another than characteristics that make them different from one another? If you believe that people are more alike than different, then you subscribe to the idea that there are general curricular approaches that will make sense for school learners, regardless of who they are. If you take the contrary position, you will seek highly individualized programs, which place more emphasis on person-to-person differences than on their similarities.

A group of thinkers associated with **postmodernism** often question the alleged benefits of new technologies, including those proposed for use in school programs. They argue that human misery is an often overlooked side effect of scientific advances. Postmodernists hold the uniqueness of the individual human being as their highest value (Chagani, 1998). They challenge the assumption that human commonalities exist that support the appropriateness of developing school curricula that seek to serve the needs of groups of learners as well as individuals. They contend that attempts to impose common educational experiences marginalize the views of some individuals while giving too much honor to those of others.

The label **critical theorist** has been given to a group of scholars who, in general, take the position that groups that have been in a position of power in our society have served narrow interests and have, in general, not worked hard enough to abolish social injustice (Bronner, 1993). They point out that the overrepresentation of minority students in special education classes, the underrepresentation of females in top school-district leadership posts, and advisement practices that have tracked students from less affluent families into less rigorous academic programs stand as evidence that our society sends messages to educational leaders that undermine the goal of promoting social mobility and that devalue the worth of people from certain groups.

Critics of postmodernism and critical theory acknowledge that injustices continue to exist. They accept, too, that there are sometimes unintended consequences when well-intentioned curriculum decisions are made. However, they assert that most people have been well served by a school system that features programs that assume that some student to student commonalities exist. They point out further that there is strong evidence that schools do act to promote social mobility. Many members of today's middle class, as a result of the education they received in the nation's schools, escaped the impoverished conditions of their youth. Though racism and sexism continue to be problems, because of the success of the American education system, support for maintaining their demeaning and dehumanizing effects has disappeared from mainstream thinking. In summary, the messages society has sent to schools and, more particularly, to curriculum developers have been good ones. What is needed is more thought about how we can leverage those things we share as we continue to attack some problems associated with those things that continue to make us different.

What will be the final outcome of the society is a good influence vs. society is a bad influence debate? No one knows. What you can be sure of is that curriculum discussions will continue to feature debates about how to seek an appropriate balance between programs that aim to meet the needs of society and those that seek to respond to the needs of each student.

LEARNERS

In thinking about how the characteristics of learners influence curriculum decisions, you need to weigh information that will help you strike a reasoned balance between providing some common experiences to all learners and providing other, student-specific experiences that speak to the more narrowly defined needs of individuals. Researchers have found that some categories of classroom practice seem to facilitate the learning of large numbers of students. The findings included in *How Teaching Matters*, produced under the auspices of the Educational Testing Service and The Milken Family Foundation, support this view (Wenglinsky, 2000). This report points out that students who are taught by teachers who use techniques designed to elicit higher-level thinking skills and who engage members of their classes in active, hands-on learning experiences do better on achievement tests than students in classes where these approaches are not used (Wenglinsky, 2000).

LEARNING EXTENSION 3–3

Building an Entire Program Around Students' Interests

In the 1920s, an English educator, A. S. Neill, started a school designed to respond to the basic goodness of young people. Students, freed from the threat of discipline, exercised enormous influence in decisions related to all aspects of the school and its program. In 1960, Neill published a book, *Summerhill* (NY: Hart Publishing), in which he described his philosophy and his school. The highly student-centered philosophy found in Neill's school underpins programs and practices in some schools today. A notable example is found in the free, democratic practices associated with *Sudbury Model* schools. Sudbury model school practices respect the key ideas of freedom, democracy, trust, and responsibility. These values underpin an arrangement that encourages learners to shape the nature of their own educational experiences.

Go to the web and use a standard search engine, such as Google (http://www. google.com), and type in "Sudbury Schools." You will find links to sites with information about basic features of the Sudbury Model and particular information about practices followed by individual schools with programs that subscribe to it. Using the information you locate, respond to these questions:

- How feasible do you think it would be to organize all schools along lines consistent with the Sudbury Model?
- Which particular features of the Sudbury Model do you find most attractive? most problematic?
- If you decide that it would not be desirable (or feasible) to organize an entire school program around the Sudbury Model, are there aspects of the Sudbury approach that you might like to implement in your own school or in schools you know about? If so, how would changes you would recommend make these schools better? What barriers and challenges might supporters of changes you would endorse encounter in winning approval for these recommendations?

- In general, do you think it would be easier to implement the Sudbury Model in private schools than in public schools? On what do you base your conclusion?
- Are there general insights you have gained from learning about the Sudbury Model as you engage in curriculum-development work? If so, what are they?

On the other hand, substantial evidence also exists that there are teaching approaches that work better with some kinds of students than with others. You may be interested in reading some research findings that support this view, reported in an excellent book titled *Looking in Classrooms* (Good & Brophy, 2000).

As you think about the issue of providing sets of common learning experiences to large groups of individuals, you may find it useful to review some information related to the developmental characteristics of young people. As you think about how programs can be fitted to the special needs of individuals, you need to think about the incredible diversity among students in our schools today.

Developmental Characteristics of Students

Curriculum decisions based on the developmental levels of students emphasize important physiological and psychological changes young people experience as they mature. The operating assumption is that all young people pass through similar periods, or stages. Further, there are patterns associated with each stage that suggest the kinds of learning experiences that represent a best fit with students at a particular developmental level.

Students pass through a given developmental stage when they are approximately the same age. However, individuals differ, and it is never possible to make definitive statements about a student's developmental stage based only on his or her chronological age. The general sequence is consistent from person to person, but the actual times individuals enter and leave a particular stage vary. There is some evidence that the rate of a student's progress from one stage to another can be influenced by the quality of the experiences he or she had at the earlier stage (Armstrong, Henson, & Savage, 1989). This suggests that the work you do in designing appropriate instructional programs can help students prepare for a smooth transition to the next stage.

The statements in the following list represent the core beliefs of individuals who state that developmental levels of learners should be an important influence on curriculum decision making:

- Young people pass through a predictable series of stages as they grow to maturity.
- Students do best when educational experiences are designed in light of their developmental levels.
- Challenging students with schoolwork for which they are developmentally unprepared is a prescription for failure.
- Diagnoses of the developmental levels of intended users of new programs must precede program planning.

Many developmental models exist. The work of Jean Piaget, who identified stages of intellectual development, is particularly well known (Elkind, 1981). The following four are Piaget's stages and some general characteristics associated with each:

1. *Sensorimotor stage (birth to age two)*. Development largely is of a nonverbal nature at this stage. What intellectual activity exists is based on immediate experiences that the child takes in through the basic senses. As language begins to develop, children at this stage begin manipulating objects and understanding the connections between words and the concrete objects for which they stand.

2. *Preoperational thought stage (ages two to seven)*. At this stage, children's behavior is very self-centered. They find it difficult to adopt the viewpoints of others. Their language abilities improve dramatically. Increasingly, they are able to recognize and use symbols that stand for objects. However, their perspective is limited. They have a difficult time dealing with multiple variables at the same time. For example, they may insist that a tall, thin glass of water holds more volume than a much more capacious short and stubby one. These children cannot deal with abstract thinking.

3. *Concrete operations stage (ages 7 to 11)*. There is a great increase in the ability to think logically about concrete objects and situations. Children at this stage tend to be very literal-minded. They have great difficulty in detecting parody, irony, or any other approaches in written material that expect the reader to go beyond the language of the literal text. Young people at this age are not comfortable with ambiguity. They prefer to work on problems that have answers of a kind that can be unarguably declared right or wrong.

4. *Formal operations stage (ages 11 to 16)*. As students move toward the kind of mature thinking reflected in this stage, they become much more comfortable dealing with abstractions. They are able to go beyond the givens and consider alternative implications of situations and events. Some young people at this stage become so enamored of logic that they become frustrated when some of the realities they see in the world seem at odds with what their logic tells them should be the case. This disjunction explains some of the alienation students in this age group feel as they observe their parents, guardians, and others behaving in ways that appear to them to be illogical.

Psychoanalyst Erik Erikson (1982) identified a somewhat different set of developmental stages. Erikson argued that there are tasks that, ideally, young people master at each stage. If these tasks are completed successfully, problems they experience at subsequent stages will be minimized. If they are not, self-doubt and other problems may emerge as young people pass through later stages. Erikson's stages extend from infancy through older adulthood. Those that cover early childhood and the school years are:

1. *Infancy stage (birth to age two)*. During this stage, the child's psychological challenge is dealing with "trust vs. mistrust." The child seeks an emotional,

trusting connection to an adult—typically, the parent. If such a connection is not established, the child may develop feelings of mistrust, which can interfere with subsequent development.

2. *Early stage (ages two to three).* During this stage, the child struggles to deal with the issue of "autonomy vs. shame." Tasks associated with autonomy involve climbing, walking, and learning to do things unaided. Shame and self-doubt can result when parents or guardians come down too hard when the child fails to behave as desired.

3. *Play stage (ages three to five).* During this stage, the child is challenged to cope with a potential "initiative vs. guilt" conflict. The individual at this stage of development may sense that mixed messages come from adults. On the one hand, parents and guardians praise the child's initiatives when they involve carrying out certain simple tasks. On the other hand, parents and guardians criticize the child's initiatives when they result in behaviors adults do not deem appropriate. For the child, the distinction between desirable and undesirable behaviors often appears confusing.

4. *School age (ages 6 to 12).* During this stage, young people face "industry vs. inferiority" challenges. They ask questions such as "Am I capable, or am I incapable?" A sense of industry (e.g., personal efficacy) comes when these young people receive praise for what they do. On the other hand, feelings of inferiority result when their sense of self is diminished as a result of too many signals from adults telling them their performances are inadequate. The major tasks of young people in this age group is to develop skills that will be highly regarded and, hence, will give them a stronger sense of self-worth.

5. *Adolescence (ages 12 to 18).* Students in this age group are challenged to deal with the "identity vs. role confusion" conflict. Young people in this age group have varied interests, diverse groups of friends, and potentially many different "faces" they show to the world. For example, among other characteristics, an individual may be described as an athlete, a churchgoer, a coin collector, an avid reader of mystery novels, and a good mathematics student. One of the challenges students in this age group face is sorting through their many interests, establishing priorities, and deciding who they really want to be.

When you are involved in curriculum work, you and others in your group may be asked to develop programs that will include recommendations for lessons designed to enhance students' decision-making abilities. Decision making is a value-laden process. Developmental psychologist Lawrence Kohlberg (1975, 1980) argues that the logic people use in making value judgments depends on the kind of moral reasoning they use. Further, he suggests that there are moral reasoning stages that people pass through:

1. *Stage 1: punishment and obedience orientation.* At this stage, people make decisions based on their fear of raw power. Decisions are based on whether a wrong response will result in punishment. There is no internal conflict or guilt about

doing something wrong if the person engaged in the activity senses no possibility that punishment inevitably will follow the action.

2. *Stage 2: instrumental relativism.* Students who are at this stage make decisions based on their views of the special advantages that will come to them as a result of choosing "A" as opposed to "B." The operating principle is "What's in it for me?"

3. *Stage 3: interpersonal concordance.* Decisions made by students at this stage are taken in light of how they think others in their peer group will react. The operating question is "Will people I like and respect approve or disapprove of me if I choose 'A' instead of 'B'?"

4. *Stage 4: law and order orientation.* Students who are at this stage make their decisions based on a recognition of and a respect for established rules, regulations, and traditions. Decisions are not made out of any thought that they are right or moral in any abstract sense. The operating question is "Is the decision I am about to make consistent with the rules?"

5. *Stage 5: social contract–legalistic orientation.* Individuals at this stage do not make their judgments based just on a consideration of formally adopted rules, regulations, or laws. Rather, they consider broader guidelines—for example, the common law court system and the possibility it affords people wanting to challenge established laws and regulations. The operating question in making decisions at this stage is "Is the decision I am making broadly consistent with our general legal, cultural, and social traditions?"

6. *Stage 6: universal ethical principles orientation.* The very few people who arrive at this stage make decisions based on their own consciences. In making their decisions, they take into account such universal principals as respect for human life and the imperative of not diminishing the self-worth of individual human beings. The operating question in making decisions at this level is "Will the decision I am making enhance or diminish the human condition?"

Kohlberg recognizes that very few people will ever arrive at stage 6. Indeed, large numbers will never arrive at stage 5. His general argument is that decisions made using logic based at higher stages generally is to be preferred over logic associated with lower stages. Hence, it makes sense to provide school instruction that will facilitate students' transitions from lower to higher stages of moral development.

Kohlberg points out that, generally, people are incapable of understanding the logic used by people operating at more than two stages higher than their own level of moral development. They can, however, understand logic based on a stage one level higher than their own. In fact, exposure to logic that is one stage higher can help shift them to this level. Hence, Kohlberg suggests that teachers take time to diagnose the moral levels of individual students and that they provide opportunities for them to hear logical arguments based on one stage higher than the students' own moral stages. Such lessons can help them move to higher stages—an occurrence that will promote thinking based on more preferable moral standards.

LEARNING EXTENSION 3–4

Moral Reasoning Discussions

The professional literature in education includes much discussion of various classroom adaptations of Kohlberg's work. Various approaches to classroom discussions designed to enhance students' levels of moral reasoning have been proposed. A number of these suggest that students be presented with and asked to comment on a situation representing a moral dilemma. The teacher is supposed to listen to each student's comment, quickly assess the level of moral reasoning the student is using, and make a response that includes logic at one level higher than the one the student is using. The idea is to familiarize the student with logic of a more advanced kind than the one he or she presently is using. Over time, it is hoped that exposure to higher levels of moral reasoning will encourage students to adopt logical patterns associated with more advanced Kohlberg levels.

Classroom programs that emphasize moral reasoning have drawn both supporters and critics. Do some reading focusing on classroom discussion related to such issues as moral reasoning, moral discussions, or moral dilemmas. You might enter these terms into a web search engine, such as Google (http://www.google.com); look for periodical articles in the *Education Index* in your library; or seek out information elsewhere as your instructor directs. Seek answers to questions such as the following:

- Is it possible for students using a high level of Kohlberg's moral reasoning to make highly irresponsible decisions?

- Are the kinds of moral dilemmas focused on in classroom discussions the kinds of situations that students will probably encounter in their own lives, or are they highly artificial episodes contrived only to stimulate active participation in classroom lessons?

- In a rapid-fire discussion, how practical is it for a teacher to listen to a student's response, immediately identify the stage of moral reasoning it reflects, and reply with a comment that features moral reasoning at a stage precisely one stage higher?

- What can you conclude about moral reasoning discussions in classrooms, and why?

Carol Gilligan, a well-known professor of human development and psychology at Harvard University, found that many developmental theorists have based their findings on studies that included only males. She and her colleagues established that girls and boys often follow somewhat different developmental paths, particularly in terms of the patterns of thinking they use to resolve dilemmas. Gilligan (1982) found that many girls make decisions based on an *ethic of caring*, whereas many boys make decisions based on an *ethic of justice*. The top priorities of the ethic of caring are the maintenance of relationships and a concern for how decisions will directly affect individuals. The ethic of justice holds as its highest value a consistency with established rules, regulations, and procedures.

Gilligan (1982) found that girls go through three general developmental phases:

1. *Preconventionial stage.* At this stage, the focus is on a selfish concern for personal survival.
2. *Conventional stage.* At this stage, a responsibility for maintaining relationships with others, even at the cost of sacrificing personal interests and priorities, is the defining characteristic.
3. *Postconventional stage.* At this stage, there is a recognition of the importance of sustaining an interplay between (1) an obligation to maintain relationships with others and (2) a need to take actions consistent with personal priorities.

Gilligan's work has implications for curriculum developers. For example, consider her finding that male and female students may assign quite different values priorities when making decisions about sophisticated issues. An understanding of these potential differences may lead you to think more broadly about the kinds of student responses that should be considered appropriate when students are asked to engage in learning activities that require them to engage in complex analyses.

If you are intrigued by school programs that are organized around an ethic of caring, you may wish to read an excellent book by Nell Noddings. In her *The Challenge to Care in Schools: An Alternative Approach to Education* (New York: Teachers College Press, 1992), Noddings describes school curricula organized around centers of care.

Students Today

If you want to fit programs to meet students' individual differences, you will need to look closely at the characteristics of students in schools where new and revised programs will be installed. Nationally, the student population has never been as diverse at it is today. Some of the characteristics cited in this section may not match those typifying student bodies in schools with which you are familiar. However, regardless of your location, you and your colleagues probably work with a highly diverse group of young people. You may find some of the categories used in this section to describe characteristics of the national pool of students useful as you think about student characteristics in your own area.

Race and ethnicity.   Recent data released by the U.S. Census Bureau reveal that the Latino population of the United States now exceeds the African-American population (*Census 2000 Brief,* 2001). Further, the Latino population continues to grow at a rapid rate. This finding suggests that many more Latino students will be in the schools in the years ahead. Today, close to 40 percent of the school population consists of students from minority groups. This percentage has more than doubled in the past 30 years (U.S. Department of Education, National Center for Education Statistics, 2000). For curriculum developers, these statistics suggest the importance of giving careful consideration to issues associated with ethnic, cultural, and language differences when planning new programs and revising old ones.

Language spoken at home.   Students who are proficient users of English do better in school than students who are not. More than 40 percent of Latino students do not routinely speak English at home. The use of Spanish at home is particularly prevalent in cases where students' mothers were born outside of the United States (U.S. Department of Education, National Center for Education Statistics, 2000). This information should alert curriculum developers to the possibility that difficulties experienced in school by some Latino students may tie as much to a lack of proficiency in English as to problems with handling academic concepts. Experts in bilingual education have developed approaches for helping these students, and these experts need to be involved as consulting specialists when programs for these students are developed.

Parental education levels.   Students whose parents have had more formal education typically do better in school than students whose parents have had less formal education. Curriculum workers welcome the news that, over the past quarter century, there have been increases in the percentage of school-aged children with parents or guardians who have had at least a high-school education. These increases cross all ethnic groups. However, these improvements still have not closed the gap between the educational levels of White parents and those of parents who are either African-American or Latino. A look at the percentages of mothers with less than a high-school education (1999 data) illustrates this point (U.S. Department of Education, National Center for Education Statistics, 2000):

White mothers with less than a high-school education = 6.9 percent
African-American mothers with less than a high-school education = 19.6 percent
Latino mothers with less than a high-school education = 49.2 percent

These data might lead you to reflect on issues such as communicating the school's expectations to parents who have not graduated from high school, considering the kinds of academic help available in homes where parents are not high-school graduates, and assuring parents who are not high-school graduates that their children can profit from taking rigorous, precollege courses.

Students with disabilities.   Recent data reveal that about 13 percent of all American students have disabilities qualifying them for services under the Individuals with Disabilities Education Act. Nearly half of these students spend all day in regular classrooms, as opposed to resource rooms, special classes, or facilities separate from schools other learners attend. Especially large numbers of students with speech or language impairments (about 88 percent of the total group) spend all day in regular classrooms (U.S. Department of Education, National Center for Education Statistics, 2000). These figures highlight the need for you to consider that large numbers of students with disabilities will be among the students served by any new or revised curriculum.

Percentages of young people enrolled.   Today, well over 95 percent of young people ages 5 to 17 are enrolled in schools. These figures are particularly significant when we look at what has happened to the enrollment patterns of individuals in the 14- to 17-year-old age group. When World War II began, more than 20 percent of all young people in that age range had already dropped out of school. Today, less than 5 percent are no longer in school (U.S. Department of Education, National Center for Education Statistics, 2000). These figures suggest that, as you engage in curriculum work, you need to recognize that students who will be consumers of new and revised programs represent virtually the nation's entire population of 5- to 17-year-olds. They represent incredible diversity, and programs that will accommodate their needs have to be designed in ways that will respond to a wide spectrum of student characteristics.

Summary.   The statistical profiles described in this section are just examples of data categories that might be used in an effort to paint a more comprehensive picture of the diversity represented among today's students. Data are readily available from such sources as the National Center for Education Statistics, ranging across such topics as economic status of students' families, students' perceptions of various aspects of schools and schooling, programs for gifted and talented learners, students' concerns about and involvement with illegal drugs, and students' fears and concern for their personal safety while at school.

As noted earlier, national data on student characteristics, although interesting, shed little light on the nature of student bodies in individual school districts. However, some categories used to gather national-level information may prove interesting to you and your colleagues as you think about the nature of student diversity in schools where programs you are preparing or revising will be implemented. To help inform your work, you might consider seeking answers to questions such as these:

- From what range of economic backgrounds do students to be served by this program come?

- What do you know about the educational attainment levels of students' parents and guardians?

- How many students with various disabilities are there in classrooms where new and revised programs will be implemented, and how can these programs be designed to make it possible for students to succeed who have different kinds of disabilities?

- How have students' academic histories prepared them to cope with the kinds of learning challenges that the new or revised programs will require?

- What other data do you need that would help you better fit new and revised programs to the special characteristics of your students, and how can you obtain this information?

 ## KNOWLEDGE

By definition, a teacher is a person who is charged with imparting knowledge or skills to learners. As curriculum specialist Ronald Doll (1996) points out, though professional discussions sometimes center around such priorities as meeting children's needs, the assumption is that teachers will draw on certain kinds of knowledge as they discharge this responsibility. There is little debate about the importance of teachers' knowledge-dissemination function. Disputes, instead, center on the following questions:

- How can knowledge be organized?
- What organized knowledge deserves to be taught?

You will recall from Chapter 2 that efforts to simplify reality by organizing knowledge into categories or disciplines trace back to Ancient Greece. Individual academic disciplines provide a means of drawing together related elements of content. They provide organizational frameworks, which give coherence to the information they contain and make this knowledge more easily accessible to learners. In addition, over time, the academic disciplines have developed their own approaches to generating and validating new knowledge. Specialists are challenged to meet high standards and, over time, a tremendous body of scholarship has developed within each discipline.

Although the academic disciplines represent extremely deep repositories of information about their respective subjects, when you are involved in curriculum work, knowledge from the academic disciplines represents an important but insufficient source of content information. This is the dilemma you must consider: Academic disciplines simplify reality by extracting a certain category of information and studying it in isolation from others; however, students encounter reality "all of a piece," not cut up into compartmentalized parts, with labels such as "history," "mathematics," and "English."

Your challenge is to identify what aspects of scholarship from the academic disciplines should be included in school programs and how this scholarship should be organized and delivered. Some suggestions have come from people who have wanted to increase the influence of the traditional academic disciplines in school programs. Others have come from individuals who want school curriculum developers to modify content significantly from the academic disciplines before it is presented to school learners.

The Structure-of-the-Disciplines Approach

Curriculum specialist Joseph Schwab, a strong supporter of school programs centered on the academic disciplines, recognized the danger of simply embedding existing findings from subject-matter specialists in programs for elementary-, middle-, and secondary-school students. He understood that new knowledge is developed so rapidly that attempts to put today's "best information" into school curricula would subject students to too much information, which would quickly become outdated. As an alternative, he proposed teaching students the **structure of the disciplines** (Schwab, 1962). This approach would result in K–12 programs that focused not on the findings of historians, scientists, and other subject-matter specialists but, rather, on the processes they use to identify problems, weigh evidence, and arrive at conclusions. Schwab argued that each discipline has its unique approaches to knowledge and that school curriculum developers should focus their attention on teaching those approaches to young people in the schools. One benefit would be high-school graduates who are able to tackle more advanced work in the academic disciplines when they entered college or university programs.

Schwab's ideas influenced a number of curriculum-development projects in the middle to late 1960s. The idea that high-school graduates could move quickly to do advanced work in higher-education institutions held particular appeal at a time when the Soviet launch of the first earth satellite had convinced many Americans that our universities were not producing enough top-level research scientists. Enthusiasm for programs built around Schwab's ideas waned when some initial new curricula developed around the structure-of-the-disciplines approach proved too difficult for many students. Beginning in the 1970s, worries about governmental decisions related to the Vietnam War, about the treatment of minorities, and about other issues eroded support for structure-of-the-disciplines approaches. Many education specialists came to believe that curricula designed to assure a fast track for the development of future research specialists in the academic disciplines were too narrow in scope to serve the needs of the entire population of young people in the schools.

Support for Modifying the Traditional Academic Disciplines

Because of the need for school programs to serve an ever more diverse group of school learners, you may have an interest in using content from academic disciplines selectively and in assuring that your choices will connect with students who have wide-ranging backgrounds, interests, and aptitudes. Curriculum specialist Ralph Tyler (1949) recommended a useful approach to working with subject-matter experts. He suggested that curriculum workers too often ask specialists from the academic disciplines only to provide lists of topics and other worthwhile information from their fields. This kind of request encourages them to outline content appropriate for someone who, in future years, might become an academic specialist in physics, mathematics, economics, English, or another academic specialty. To avoid this kind of recommendation, Tyler (1949) proposed that curriculum developers ask experts from the academic disciplines to answer this question: "What can your subject contribute to the education of young people who are not going to be specialists in your field . . . ?" (p. 26). This question prompts thought about the relevance of discipline-based content for audiences much broader than that represented by students who might become future academic specialists. As Ronald Doll (1996) points out, answers to this question tie closely to individuals' views about the purposes of general education. For example, you will probably arrive at different conclusions if you see education's primary purpose as (1) providing students with the tools needed to improve society, (2) providing every student with a solid grounding in the liberal arts, or (3) teaching every student skills that he or she will need to enter the workplace.

Some curriculum experts argue that the rigid lines of the traditional academic disciplines are breaking down as specialists come to recognize that many problems that need to be solved require information that draws on the expertise of people with diverse kinds of academic training. For example, Evelyn Sowell (1996) points out that "new" subjects, such as biophysics and biochemistry, are amalgams of two, formerly independent disciplines ((1) biology and physics; (2) biology and chemistry). She suggests that more combinations may be expected in the future and that, as a result, the influence of the individual, traditional academic disciplines may diminish.

Other curriculum specialists take a contrary view. While acknowledging that there have been successful combinations of new, composite disciplines, such as biophysics and biochemistry, they are few in number (Armstrong & Savage, 2002). Efforts to achieve new, integrated disciplines face important challenges. For example, it is difficult to identify exactly which elements of the source, or parent, disciplines will be included and to determine a distinctive focus for the new combination. There are also difficulties associated with accountability. What constitutes high-quality work in a newly created academic discipline is harder to discern than in one with years of history behind it.

Help from Subject-Area Specialty Groups in Fitting Content to Learners

To identify which aspects of academic knowledge to include into programs being developed for school learners, you need to consider two key categories of expertise. You should consider information from academic subject-matter specialists, and you should incorporate ideas from people who are familiar with the issues associated with classroom teaching and learning and sound program design. Curriculum and instruction specialists and academic subject-matter experts come together in national specialty organizations such as the National Council for the Social Studies, the National Council of Teachers of English, the National Council of Teachers of Mathematics, and the National Science Teachers Association. These organizations publish content guidelines that represent the combined thinking of subject-matter experts and of professionals who are familiar with K–12 school settings and students. For a listing of a large number of these organizations and the titles of some recent **curriculum standards** published by each, see Chapter 6, "People and Roles in Curriculum Work." See Figures 3.1, 3.2, 3.3, and 3.4 for some examples of academic content guidelines from four large, national specialty organizations.

Though the specialty organizations bring together academic subject specialists and professionals with expertise in curriculum and instruction, the work they do to identify what students in school programs should know by no means excuses local-level curriculum developers from making decisions of their own. To understand why this is true, you need to consider that individuals who are active in subject-area professional groups have an especially keen interest in the focus areas of their organizations. Members invariably favor more, not less, emphasis in schools on their subject areas. Because of time constraints and a need to maintain

1. Students read a wide range of print and nonprint texts to build an understanding of texts, themselves, and of the cultures of the United States and the world; to acquire new information; to respond to the needs and demands of society and the workplace; and for personal fulfillment. Among these texts are fiction and nonfiction, classic and contemporary works.
2. Students read a wide range of literature from many periods in many genres to build an understanding of many dimensions (e.g., philosophical, ethical, aesthetic) of human experience.
3. Students apply a wide range of strategies to comprehend, interpret, evaluate, and appreciate texts. They draw on their prior experience, their interactions with other readers and writers, their knowledge of word meaning and of other texts, their word identification strategies, and their understanding of textual features (e.g., sound-letter correspondence, sentence structure, context, graphics).
4. Students adjust their use of spoken, written, and visual language (e.g., conventions, style, vocabulary) to communicate effectively with a variety of audiences and for different purposes.
5. Students employ a wide range of strategies as they write and use different writing process elements appropriately to communicate with different audiences for a variety of purposes.
6. Students apply knowledge of language structure, language conventions (e.g., spelling and punctuation), media techniques, figurative language, and genre to create, critique, and discuss print and nonprint texts.
7. Students conduct research on issues and interests by generating ideas and questions, and by posing problems. They gather, evaluate, and synthesize data from a variety of sources (e.g., print and nonprint texts, artifacts, people) to communicate their discoveries in ways that suit their purpose and audience.
8. Students use a variety of technological and informational resources (e.g., libraries, databases, computer networks, video) to gather and synthesize information and to create and communicate knowledge.
9. Students develop an understanding of and respect for diversity in language use, patterns, and dialects across cultures, ethnic groups, geographic regions, and social roles.
10. Students whose first language is not English make use of their first language to develop competency in the English language arts and to develop understanding of content across the curriculum.
11. Students participate as knowledgeable, reflective, creative, and critical members of a variety of literacy communities.
12. Students use spoken, written, and visual language to accomplish their own purposes (e.g., for learning, enjoyment, persuasion, and the exchange of information).

FIGURE 3.1   Standards for the English Language Arts

Source: *Standards for the English Language Arts* (1996). Urbana, IL: National Council of Teachers of English and Newark, DE: International Reading Association (p. 3). Copyright © by the International Reading Association and the National Council of Teachers of English. Reprinted with permission.

Note: *Standards for the English Language Arts* provides many additional details related to English and language arts instruction. Professional organizations regularly update information about content standards. For the most current information, go to the website of the National Council of Teachers of English (http://www.ncte.org/).

some balance across subject areas, when you engage in curriculum work, you simply cannot make all your decisions based on the recommendations of specialty groups. Information they provide will be just part of the total mix you consider. Your decisions will also be influenced by context variables, including state and local regulations, the expectations of the local community, and the specific characteristics of the students to be served.

Numbers and Operations

Instructional programs from prekindergarten through grade 12 should enable all students to:

- understand numbers, ways of representing numbers, relationships among numbers, and number systems;
- understand meanings of operations and how they relate to one another;
- compute fluently and make reasonable estimates.

Algebra

Instructional programs from prekindergarten through grade 12 should enable all students to:

- understand patterns, relations, and functions;
- represent and analyze mathematical situations and structures using algebraic symbols;
- use mathematical models to represent and understand quantitative relationships;
- analyze change in various contexts.

Geometry

Instructional programs from prekindergarten through grade 12 should enable all students to:

- analyze characteristics and properties of two- and three-dimensional geometric shapes and develop mathematical arguments about geometric relationships;
- specify locations and describe spatial relationships using coordinate geometry and other representational systems;
- apply transformations and use symmetry to analyze mathematical situations;
- use visualization, spatial reasoning, and geometric modeling to solve problems.

Measurement

Instructional programs from prekindergarten through grade 12 should enable all students to:

- understand measurable attributes of objects and the units, systems, and processes of measurement;
- apply appropriate techniques, tools, and formulas to determine measurements.

FIGURE 3.2 Selections from *Principles and Standards for School Mathematics*

Source: Reprinted by permission from *Principles and Standards for School Mathematics:* pp. 392–402, copyright © 2000 by the National Council of Teachers of Mathematics. All rights reserved.

Note: *Principles and Standards for School Mathematics* provides much additional information that is of interest to planners of school mathematics programs. Professional organizations regularly update information about content standards. For the most current information, go to the website of the National Council of Teachers of Mathematics (http://www.nctm.org/).

EXERCISE 3–1

The Debate over National History Standards

In 1992, the National Center for History in the Schools (NCHS) received a grant to develop a set of voluntary national history standards for the schools. The intent was to provide local curriculum specialists with a framework they could use in making decisions about the structure and content of history programs in their schools. The NCHS completed its work in fall 1994. Almost immediately, critics began to attack the proposed standards.

Science as Inquiry

As a result of activities in grades 5–8, all students should develop

- Abilities necessary to do scientific inquiry
- Understandings about scientific inquiry

Physical Science

As a result of activities in grades 5–8, all students should develop an understanding of

- Properties and changes of properties in matter
- Motions and forces
- Transfer of energy

Life Science

As a result of activities in grades 5–8, all students should develop an understanding of

- Structure and function in reproduction and heredity
- Reproduction and heredity
- Regulation and behavior
- Populations and ecosystems
- Diversity and adaptations of organisms

Earth and Space Science

As a result of activities in grades 5–8, all students should develop an understanding of

- Structure of the earth system
- Earth's history
- Earth in the solar system

Science and Technology

As a result of activities in grades 5–8, all students should develop

- Abilities of technological design
- Understandings about science and technology

Science in Personal and Social Perspectives

As a result of activities in grades 5–8, all students should develop an understanding of

- Personal health
- Populations, resources, and environments
- Natural hazards
- Risks and benefits
- Science and technology in society

History and Nature of Science

As a result of activities in grades 5–8, all students should develop an understanding of

- Science as a human endeavor
- Nature of science
- History of science

FIGURE 3.3 Examples of Content Standards for Grades 5–8 from *National Science Education Standards*

Source: *National Science Education Standards.* Washington, DC: National Academy Press, 1996, pp. 143, 149, 155, 158, 161, 166, 170. Copyright © 1996 by the National Academy of Sciences. Reprinted with permission.

Note: *National Science Education Standards* provides detailed information related to many aspects of school science programs. Professional organizations regularly update information about content standards. For the most current information, go to the website of the National Science Teachers Association (http://www.nsta.org/).

Culture

Social studies programs should include experiences that provide for the study of *culture* and *cultural diversity* so that the learner can:

Early Grades	Middle Grades	High School
explore and describe similarities and differences in the ways groups, societies, and cultures address similar human needs and concerns	compare similarities and differences in the ways groups, societies, and cultures meet human needs and concerns	analyze and explain the ways groups, societies, and cultures address human needs and concerns
give examples of how experiences may be interpreted differently by people from diverse cultural perspectives and frames of reference	explain how information and experiences may be interpreted by people from diverse cultural perspectives and frames of reference	predict how data and experiences may be interpreted by people from diverse cultural perspectives and frames of reference
describe ways in which language, stories, folktales, music, and artistic creations serve as expressions of culture and influence behavior of people living in a particular culture	explain and give examples of how language, literature, the arts, architecture, other artifacts, traditions, beliefs, values, and behaviors contribute to the development and transmission of culture	apply an understanding of culture as an integrated whole that explains the functions and interactions of language, literature, the arts, traditions, beliefs and values, and behavior patterns
compare ways in which people from different cultures think about and deal with their physical environment and social conditions	explain why individuals and groups respond differently to their physical and social environments and/or changes to them on the basis of shared assumptions, values, and beliefs	compare and analyze societal patterns for preserving and transmitting culture while adapting to environmental or social change
give examples and describe the importance of cultural unity and diversity within and across groups	articulate the implications of cultural diversity, as well as cohesion, within and across groups	demonstrate the value of cultural diversity, as well as cohesion, within and across groups
		interpret patterns of behavior reflecting values and attitudes that contribute to or pose obstacles to cross-cultural understanding
		construct reasoned judgments about specific cultural responses to persistent human issues
		explain and apply ideas, theories, and modes of inquiry drawn from anthropology and sociology in the examination of persistent issues and social problems

FIGURE 3.4 The "Thematic Strand," Culture, and Related Performance Expectations from *Expectations of Excellence: Curriculum Standards for Social Studies*

Source: *Expectations of Excellence: Curriculum Standards for Social Studies.* Washington, DC: National Council for the Social Studies, 1994, p. 33. Copyright © 1994, National Council for the Social Studies. Reprinted with permission.

Note: *Expectations of Excellence* provides many additional details. Professional organizations regularly update information about content standards. For the most current information, go to the website of the National Council for the Social Studies (http://www.ncss.org/).

As a result, NCHS personnel went back to work and prepared a revised edition of the standards. This new material appeared in 1996. The revisions satisfied some, but not all, critics of the original version.

Action

Seek out information on this controversy. Go to the web. Put the phrase "history standards" in a search engine, such as Google (http://www.google.com). What points did critics of the original 1994 standards make? How did supporters respond? Prepare a list of arguments that were made both in opposition to and in support of these standards. Conclude by looking at the revised set. What specific changes were made?

Analysis

Reflect on what you have learned, and think about how you would answer the following questions:

- What kinds of groups or constituencies were among those who complained about the original standards?
- What specific aspects bothered the critics?
- How did the people involved in developing the original standards respond to the reactions of the people who challenged their work?
- How have the modifications to the standards, reflected in the revised 1996 version, been accepted?
- Was there information that the developers of the original 1992 version lacked that contributed to their going forward with recommendations that many critics found unacceptable?

Key Points

Specialty groups that develop proposed subject-area standards typically include representatives of professionals from the relevant academic disciplines, as well as professional K–12 educators. However, these two groups by no means represent all elements of the public with interests in the contents of school programs. Hence, proposed national standards have the potential to generate heated debate.

Review and Reflection

1. Cite some examples that illustrate how proposed solutions to complex educational problems sometimes raise as many questions as they answer.
2. When curriculum decisions are made in the name of serving the needs of society, what assurances are there that these decisions are not serving the needs of a narrow group, rather than the needs of society in general?
3. In your view, in general, are society's influences on school curricula positive or negative? Why?

4. What are examples of (1) direct and visible and (2) indirect and less visible influences on curriculum decisions?

5. Some critics say the increase in testing in schools is undesirable because it encourages instructors to teach to the test. Others argue that, if tests are good enough, teachers should be encouraged to teach to the test. What is your view on this issue, and how do you support it?

6. To what extent should people who are involved in local-level curriculum work heed content recommendations made by national subject-matter specialty organizations?

7. What is the relevance for curriculum workers of the findings of experts who have identified developmental stages that young people pass through en route to adulthood?

8. As you build programs that are well suited to the needs of the students in your own school district, what kind of information about the students would you like to have, where would you get it, and how would you use it?

References

Armstrong, D. G., Henson, K. T., & Savage, T. V. (1989). *Education: An introduction* (3rd ed.). Upper Saddle River, NJ: Merrill/Prentice Hall.

Armstrong, D. G., & Savage, T. V. (2002). *Teaching in the secondary school: An introduction* (5th ed.). Upper Saddle River, NJ: Merrill/Prentice Hall.

Bronner, S. (1993). Of critical theory and its theorists: Introduction. [http://www.uta.edu/english/dab/illustrations/bron1.html]

Broudy, H. (1982). What knowledge is of most worth? *Educational Leadership, 8*(5), 574–578.

Burbules, N. C. (1997). Why practice doesn't make perfect: The pragmatics of teaching knowledge. [http://faculty.ed.uiuc.edu/burbules/ncb/papers/perfect.html]

Caswell, H. L. (1978). Persistent curriculum problems. *Educational Forum, 43*(1), 99–110.

Census 2000 brief. (2001). Washington, DC: U.S. Department of Commerce, U.S. Census Bureau.

Chagani, F. (1998). Postmodernism. Rearranging the furniture of the universe. [http://www.geocities.com/Athens/Agora/9095/postmodernism.html]

Doll, R. C. (1996). *Curriculum improvement: Decision making and process* (9th ed.). Boston: Allyn and Bacon.

Elkind, D. (1981). *Children and adolescents: Interpretive essays on Jean Piaget* (3rd ed.). New York: Oxford University Press.

Erikson, E. H. (1982). *The life cycle completed: A review.* New York: W. W. Norton.

Gilligan, C. (1982). *In a different voice: Psychological theory and women's development.* Cambridge, MA: Harvard University Press.

Good, T. L., & Brophy, J. E. (2000). *Looking in classrooms* (8th ed.). New York: Longman.

Kohlberg, L. (1975). The cognitive-developmental approach to moral education. *Phi Delta Kappan, 56*(10), 670–675.

Kohlberg, L. (1980). Education for a just society: An updated and revised statement. In B. Munsey (Ed.), *Moral development, moral education, and Kohlberg* (pp. 455–470). Birmingham, AL: Religious Education Press.

Noddings, N. (1992). *The challenge to care in schools: An alternative approach to education.* New York: Teachers College Press.

Schwab, J. (1962). The concept of the structure of a discipline. *The Educational Record, 40,* 197–205.

Sirotnik, K. A. (1988). What goes on in classrooms? Is this the way we want it? In L. E. Beyer & M. W. Apple (Eds.), *The curriculum: Problems, politics, and possibilities* (pp. 56–70). Albany: State University of New York Press.

Sowell, E. J. (1996). *Curriculum: An integrative introduction.* Upper Saddle River, NJ: Merrill/Prentice Hall.

Stake, R. (1999). The goods on American education. *Phi Delta Kappan, 80*(9), 668–672.

Taba, H. (1962). *Curriculum development: Theory and practice.* New York: Harcourt, Brace, and World.

Tanner, D., & Tanner, L. (1995). *Curriculum development: Theory into practice* (3rd ed.). Upper Saddle River, NJ: Merrill/Prentice Hall.

Tyler, R. W. (1949). *Basic principles of curriculum and instruction.* Chicago: University of Chicago Press.

U.S. Department of Education, National Center for Education Statistics. (2000). *The condition of education 2000,* NCES 2000-602. Washington, DC: U.S. Government Printing Office.

Vallecorsa, A. (2001, March 21). Personal interview. Greensboro, NC: The University of North Carolina at Greensboro.

Wenglinsky, H. (2000). *How teaching matters.* Princeton, NJ: The Milken Family Foundation and the Educational Testing Service.

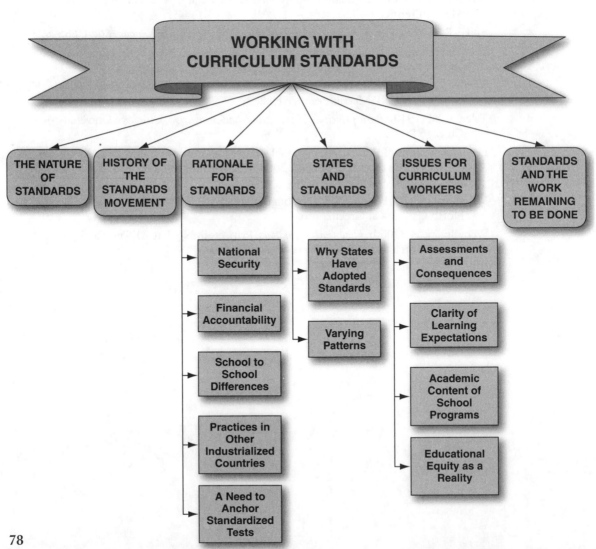

4

Working with Curriculum Standards

Graphic Organizer

WORKING WITH CURRICULUM STANDARDS

- THE NATURE OF STANDARDS
- HISTORY OF THE STANDARDS MOVEMENT
- RATIONALE FOR STANDARDS
  - National Security
  - Financial Accountability
  - School to School Differences
  - Practices in Other Industrialized Countries
  - A Need to Anchor Standardized Tests
- STATES AND STANDARDS
  - Why States Have Adopted Standards
  - Varying Patterns
- ISSUES FOR CURRICULUM WORKERS
  - Assessments and Consequences
  - Clarity of Learning Expectations
  - Academic Content of School Programs
  - Educational Equity as a Reality
- STANDARDS AND THE WORK REMAINING TO BE DONE

INTRODUCTION

Suppose someone poses the following questions about young people who have just completed a year's work in any school grade from kindergarten through 12:

● What do these students know now, and what can they do that they could not do at the beginning of the last school year?

● Is what they learned of any value, and how do you know?

● Can their progress be compared easily with the work of similar students who have attended other schools?

● Is what they learned adequate, and what evidence is there to support your position?

Do not be surprised if you have difficulty answering these questions. Many variables affect what individual students learn. Young people differ in their interests and aptitudes. Parents and guardians establish varying expectations for their school-aged children. Curricular content, teacher expertise, levels of administrative support, and resources to fund programs are not the same from school to school. Collectively, the number and complexity of the influences that affect what students learn make it difficult to identify common performance expectations for students in different places. You will find this to be true even when you are asked about probable characteristics of students who have gone through the same grades and have studied the same subjects.

Today, frustrations associated with making meaningful student to student and school to school comparisons prompt great interest in **standards-based education.** The movement toward this concept gained much momentum in the middle and late 1990s, after former Assistant Secretary of Education Diane Ravitch (1995) made the case that "standards are created because they improve the activity of life" (p. 89). In brief, standards-based education seeks to do the following (Robson & Latiolais, 2000):

● Establish clear statements regarding what students should learn

● Develop reliable and valid assessment systems that can be used to ascertain whether, in fact, the desired learning has occurred

Though opinions vary, recent data indicate that large numbers of parents and teachers support the establishment of clear standards (Morin, 2001). Supporters point out that the establishment of standards motivates students by helping them better understand what teachers expect of them. The testing programs established alongside of standardized curricula make student to student and school to school comparisons easier. One result has been an increase in the percentage of people who now believe that public schools have high academic standards (Morin, 2001).

LEARNING EXTENSION 4–1

Standards and Testing in the Local Area

Nationally, there has been an increasing trend for educational practices to be guided by officially adopted standards and for tests to be developed that are consistent with these standards. Has this happened in your area? Gather information from administrators or teachers that can provide answers to questions such as these:

- Are standards now in place that establish clear learning expectations for students?
- Were these standards developed nationally, at the state level, at the local level, or at a combination of the three levels?
- To what extent are tests that students take tied to these standards?
- If there has been a move toward establishing learning standards and testing student levels of proficiency against them, have there been any implementation problems? If so, what are they?
- If actions have been taken to establish standards, has there been a generally positive, negative, or neutral impact on levels of student performance?

Not everyone supports standards-based education, however. Much of the concern has to do with testing programs that have been developed to determine whether students have met standards (Sanchez, 2001). Some argue that tests reflect flawed designs, focus on trivial aspects of content, and fail to provide meaningful measures of what students know and can do. Others argue that there is no real measurement of students' abilities to perform tasks associated with the standards because tests assess content unrelated to the standards. Still others worry that the standards and accompanying assessments take control of school content away from parents and teachers in local schools. Members of some religious communities have been especially concerned that content embedded in standards may be contrary to the values these groups espouse and want transmitted to younger people in their communities.

In this chapter, you will learn more about the nature of standards, the history of the standards movement, and the rationale for establishing standards. When you engage in curriculum work, you will probably have to make some adjustments in light of state-level standards. You will want to know something about how states have approached the business of establishing standards and about the various patterns that states have followed in describing them. This information will help you better appreciate that standards pose both opportunities and challenges for curriculum workers.

 ## THE NATURE OF STANDARDS

Personnel at Mid-continent Research for Education and Learning (McREL), a private, nonprofit organization located in Colorado, have been national leaders in helping states develop and implement standards-based education programs. As state officials have worked to develop standards, they have worried about the issue of quality control. Specialists at McREL have worked to define the nature of standards and to describe approaches to developing assessment procedures that are consistent with adopted standards.

Robert Marzano and John Kendall (1997) point out that standards sort into two broad categories. Curriculum standards focus on the kinds of activities that should take place in the classroom as teachers work to convey specific types of information to students. **Content standards** focus on what students should know or be able to do as a consequence of instruction. If you find yourself involved in work that will establish or modify standards, Marzano and Kendall (1997) argue that you should pay less attention to establishing curriculum standards than to establishing content standards. An emphasis on curriculum standards inappropriately places the focus on instructional processes, rather than on the kinds of student learning that should be the "ends" of teaching. Further, standards have the potential to constrain teachers' instructional choices by prescribing an authorized way of introducing students to new content. Content standards, on the other hand, focus on the specific knowledge, understandings, and skills students will be expected to demonstrate. How individual teachers get their students up to the expected performance levels remains largely a matter of personal choice—a circumstance that allows them to develop approaches well fitted to their individual teaching contexts.

Educational researchers at McREL have identified three types of content standards (Marzano & Kendall, 1997). **Procedural standards** identify the processes students need to master. **Declarative standards** identify the basic information students need to know about specific topics. **Contextual standards** identify the knowledge and skills that take on a particular meaning because of the special conditions within which they occur. See Figure 4.1 for examples of each basic type of content standard.

If you spend much time working with content standards, you will find that they are written at many levels of specificity. For example, you might encounter a standard as broad as "Students will appreciate influences on nineteenth-century American novelists." Obviously, such a standard provides little specific information. It raises a huge number of additional questions, such as the following:

- What kinds of influences are important?
- Who are the novelists with whom students should be familiar?

Procedural	Declarative	Contextual
Performing long division	Understanding the concept of a numerator	Modeling numbers using a number line
Setting up an experiment	Knowing what an amoeba is	Classifying organisms
Editing an essay	Knowing the conventions of punctuation	Using appropriate tone and style for a selected audience

FIGURE 4.1   Examples of Procedural, Declarative, and Contextual Content Standards

Source: From Robert J. Marzano and John S. Kendall. "The Fall and Rise of Standards-Based Education." *Issues Brief* (September 1997), p. 13. Copyright © National Association of State Boards of Education. Reprinted with permission.

- What will be the measure of "appreciation"?
- How will expectations differ for students of different ages?

Not all standards are constructed using this kind of broad language. For example, you might find one that reads something like this: "Students will identify the economic causes of the Civil War." This standard focuses on a narrower spectrum of content, yet it, too, raises questions:

- To which specific economic causes should students pay attention?
- How will a student know when an economic stress becomes serious enough to be regarded as a "cause" of the war?
- How will expectations differ for students at different points in their school careers?

Ambiguities associated with content standards prompt additional thought about what students are really being asked to demonstrate. More precise descriptions of intended learning outcomes are an essential prerequisite of any attempt to develop a reliable assessment program to accompany established sets of content standards. To respond to this need, specialists in standards-based education have worked to develop **performance indicators** to accompany each content standard. Performance indicators describe specific behaviors that, if mastered, collectively suggest mastery of the content standard. Researchers at McREL have identified clusters of performance indicators for four school levels (K–2, 3–5, 6–8, and 9–12). These indicators are called **benchmarks**. Their purpose is to provide clear descriptions of learning expectations for students that are consistent with their ages and developmental levels (Marzano & Kendall, 1997). The benchmarks describe expected behaviors in specific terms, and they provide useful beginning points for assessment specialists developing tests that tie clearly to the related content standards.

A comprehensive discussion of technical issues associated with the development of standards goes beyond the scope of this text. If you are interested in this subject, you may find it useful to visit McREL's website (http://www.mcrel.org/).

LEARNING EXTENSION 4–2

Performance Indicators in State Curriculum Standards Documents

State curriculum standards are available on the web at sites maintained by state departments of education. To locate a state department of education, use a standard search engine, such as Google (http://www.google.com), and type in the name of the state, followed by "state department of education"—for example, "Illinois State Department of Education." By following this procedure, you should be able to identify the appropriate URL.

Choose three states to look at. Make an effort to include a set of standards from your state when you select and study these materials. Focus on a subject area that interests you. Look for the presence of performance indicators. (Remember, these are descriptions of explicit behaviors that, if present, collectively suggest that a standard has been met. You may not find them called "performance indicators" in the documents themselves.) Respond to the following questions:

- Do all three of the state standards have performance indicators?
- How adequate are these indicators?
- How consistently are these indicators used throughout the documents? That is, are some standards accompanied by a reasonable number of indicators, whereas others have only a few?
- Do the stated indicators lend themselves easily to assessment? If so, what kinds of tests/assessments could be designed to identify students' proficiency levels?
- Do you get any feeling that the developers of the standards experienced more difficulty in identifying performance indicators for some topics than for others? If so, do you think the topics for which the development of performance indicators poses a challenge are less likely to be included in standards than are the topics for which it is relatively easy to develop performance indicators?

 ## HISTORY OF THE STANDARDS MOVEMENT

Today's standards-based education movement represents a recent example of a recurring curriculum theme: the desire to specify learning outcomes, organize school programs in support of them, and use test results tied to learning expectations to ascertain both performance levels of students and quality levels of instructional programs. For the first 30 years of the twentieth century, many curriculum specialists were influenced by the scientific management work of Frederick Taylor. Taylor developed time-and-motion studies designed to help factory owners organize work to promote higher levels of efficiency. As applied to schools, Taylor's ideas spawned efforts to identify clear learning outcomes, instructional strategies that would facilitate student learning, and measurement approaches that could be used to assess instructional adequacy. High student scores were taken as an indication of "curricular efficiency"; lower scores were taken as evidence of a need for change. This view of curriculum assumed teachers to be technicians who applied their talents to the student raw material as they worked to transform them in directions suggested by the specified learning outcomes. It assumed that teaching and learning could be mechanized (Eisner, 1995).

Influential curriculum expert John Franklin Bobbitt, in his 1918 text *The Curriculum,* embraced the idea that school programs should be directed at helping students master "specific activities" that adults need for success in the world. He proposed that studies be made to identify these knowledge needs. Once this was done, learning objectives could be designed to guide instruction in schools. As you might imagine, followers of Bobbitt's thinking experienced some difficulties in trying to implement this approach. For one thing, lists of essential knowledge and skills tended to get longer and longer. For another, the approach viewed students as malleable creatures, who went to school ready to be molded into whatever form adult society deemed appropriate. Individual student differences did not come in for much serious attention. Finally, Bobbitt's approach seemed to assume an unchanging society; the knowledge and skills needed in the future would differ little from those needed today (Smith, 2001). In fairness, we need to acknowledge that, by the 1940s, Bobbitt's commitment to efficiency had cooled, and he had come to recognize the importance of social change as an influence on the curriculum (Null, 1999).

Ralph Tyler's influential 1949 book, *Basic Principles of Curriculum and Instruction,* stands as another precursor of today's movement to establish educational standards. Tyler (1949) suggested that curriculum specialists have four basic tasks to accomplish:

- To identify educational purposes for the school
- To identify learning experiences likely to help students attain these purposes
- To organize instructional experiences in ways well suited to promoting learning
- To develop ways to determine whether educational purposes are being attained (p. 1)

If you are a curriculum developer, Tyler admonishes you to decide exactly what students are to learn, identify and sequence some instructional approaches, and test to see whether students' achievement levels are up to your expectations.

Robert Mager (1962) refined Tyler's work by suggesting that measurable behavioral objectives should be identified for each important learning outcome. Mager's book, *Preparing Instructional Objectives,* enjoyed an enormous audience throughout the 1960s and into the 1970s. In time, teachers and others in school districts generated thousands of objectives. Enthusiasm for the approach waned as questions arose about the wisdom of cutting complex content into pieces small enough to accommodate individual objectives. Educators also raised concerns about the volume of paperwork required to keep track of student performance levels on dozens of individual objectives (Marzano & Kendall, 1997).

Although the work of such figures as Taylor, Bobbitt, Tyler, and Mager provide an important historical backdrop, today's standards movement traces more immediately to the 1983 publication of the National Commission on Excellence in Education's *A Nation at Risk*. The inflammatory language in this report ("We have, in effect, been committing an act of unthinking, unilateral educational disarmament" [p. 5]) raised the specter of future national economic impoverishment unless school programs were dramatically improved. *A Nation at Risk* generated tremendous interest in schools and school programming. These debates and discussions prompted many states to pass legislation designed to raise school standards.

LEARNING EXTENSION 4–3

Examining Selected Reform Proposals

The publication of A *Nation at Risk* occurred at a time when dozens of groups around the country were beginning to look carefully at schools and school programs. Interest in making recommendations aimed at "improving education" has continued unabated since the early 1980s.

To extend your understanding of the issues that have attracted the attention of people who wish to make schools better, look at three or four of these improvement proposals. (A few examples include: *Action for Excellence* (Task Force on Education for Economic Growth, 1983), *A Nation Prepared: Teachers for the 21st Century* (Carnegie Forum on Education and the Economy, 1986), *Time for Results* (National Governors' Association, 1986), *The State of America's Children* (Children's Defense Fund, 1994), *Breaking Ranks: Changing an American Institution* (National Association of Secondary School Principals and the Carnegie Foundation, 1996), *Interstate New Teacher Assessment and Support Consortium* (INTASC, 1999), *The Academic Achievement of Minority Students: Perspectives, Practices, and Prescriptions* (Gregory, 2000), (Your instructor may be able to suggest titles of others you may wish to examine.) Think about the following questions as you review these materials:

- What did the materials you reviewed point out as "causes" of any perceived problems involving schools and schooling?
- What solutions were proposed?
- What similarities and differences did you find in recommendations you found in the materials you reviewed?
- Did you find information in any of these materials that may have supported the move toward standards-based education?

In 1989, President George Bush joined with the nation's governors to host a national Education Summit. People who attended this event, held in Charlottesville, Virginia, identified a number of academic achievement goals for American schools. Following this meeting, two groups were formed: (1) the National Educational Goals Panel and (2) the National Council on Education Standards and Testing. They were charged with seeking answers to questions related to the subject matter schools should teach, the kinds of testing that should be used, and the standards of performance that should be expected of students (Marzano & Kendall, 1997). In 1994, Congress passed the Goals 2000 legislation. Among other things, this legislation established the National Education Standards and Improvement Council, charged with overseeing the development of national content standards. As noted earlier in this chapter, the standards-based education movement received an additional boost in 1994, when former Assistant Secretary of Education Diane Ravitch published *National Standards in American Education: A Citizen's Guide.*

The middle 1990s represented a high-water mark for direct federal involvement in standards setting. By 1995, a strong contingent of conservative members of the U.S. Senate and House of Representatives had begun arguing persuasively against developing and imposing education standards at the national level. They saw such an effort as inconsistent with the tradition of state and local control of schools. These legislators did not oppose the idea of standards, but they wanted the work to be shifted to authorities closer to people who would be affected by adopted standards. This change was reflected in the federal *No Child Left Behind Act* of 2002, an important law that requires the states, not the federal government, to develop rigorous curriculum standards. To comply with this legislation, in time all 50 states will have to have state curriculum standards.

 ## RATIONALE FOR STANDARDS

Supporters of standards-based education favor the approach for differing reasons. Among their arguments are those that relate to

- National security
- Financial accountability
- School to school differences
- Patterns in other industrialized countries
- A need to anchor standardized tests

National Security

The national security argument runs along the following lines. A strong economy stands as a bulwark against international troubles of all kinds. The economy can grow only as long as the talents of new American workers are as good as (if not better than) those of new workers in other countries. If school programs are weak, new generations of workers will lack the intellectual strength needed to keep the nation economically competitive. Over time, our standard of living will fall. Among other negatives associated with this development will be a reduced capacity to defend ourselves against the hostile interests of other nations. The best way to avert this problem is for schools to set high standards, hold students to them, and demand high levels of performance.

Financial Accountability

Public education is expensive. In a recent year, about $8,000 was spent for every enrolled student in the nation (Snyder, 2000). Educational costs total in the billions. Costs for other public services, such as highways, police protection, and welfare programs, continue to escalate. As legislators face pressures for increased allocations of money from various groups, they increasingly demand data that verify that benefits received are commensurate with costs incurred. Test scores have become a convenient source of information for legislators and other concerned citizens to use as they attempt to judge the quality of school programs. When there are great program differences, school to school comparisons are difficult. Standards-based school programming promotes commonalities among school instructional programs. These, in turn, make it easier for those who wish to hold schools accountable for appropriate expenditures of funds to gather meaningful comparative data.

School to School Differences

As previously noted, in many places there are significant differences in programming from one school to another. These differences make it difficult to make comparative judgments about relative quality of education. In addition, these school to school differences place a great burden on students who transfer from one school to another. Because curricula vary, they may find themselves in a situation where their levels of learning lag behind their classmates, a situation sure to lead to high levels of frustration. On the other hand, they may find they are being retaught information they have already learned, which can promote boredom and lead to discipline problems. Finally, there are enormous variations in grading policies from school to school and teacher to teacher. Hence, it is practical to make judgments neither about individual students in different schools nor about individual schools based only on comparisons of awarded grades.

Practices in Other Industrialized Countries

The decentralization of authority over academic content that typifies American education differs from the pattern in many other industrialized countries. These nations have recognized the importance of identifying specific content outcomes for all students, regardless of where they live and go to school. Supporters of standards argue that the American model permits each state to have islands of excellence, where students receive exemplary educations, and islands of despair, where programming is far from anyone's conception of high quality. The absence of common curriculum patterns can also undermine our sense of membership in a broader national community.

   An 11-year-old in France, for example, goes to school knowing that he or she is following a program of study that is pretty much identical to that being experienced by all 11-year-olds in the country. One positive result of this kind of standardized programming is that it develops a citizenry who share many experiences with their age counterparts throughout the entire country. These common experiences are part of the social glue that bonds individuals and contributes importantly to their sense of nationhood. Supporters of standards-based education believe that the United States would benefit from school programming that broadens the common experiential base of the nation's students.

A Need to Anchor Standardized Tests

Standardized tests are here to stay. These tests do not operate in an academic-content vacuum. Questions focus on various aspects of school subjects. But, you might ask, which ones and under whose authority? In an absence of adopted content standards, the tests themselves tend to establish the curriculum (Finn & Petrilli, 2000). Today, standardized test scores are important not just for students who take them but also for their teachers and principals. Supporters of standards-based education argue that these tests have great influence on what teachers emphasize in the classroom. In the absence of standards, the people who designed the tests and their priorities are invisible. It would be preferable to have a standard curriculum and to require the developers of standardized tests to tie their test items to it. For example, the development of state-level curriculum standards is a public process; there are opportunities for many constituencies to have their views represented. In the long run, these curriculum standards will establish a broad base of support for what is taught and emphasized and will help assure that assessments are focusing on high-priority content.

 ## STATES AND STANDARDS

Increased state-level interest in curriculum standards has been driven by several key concerns. This trend breaks with long-standing tradition: "Historically, states and districts haven't organized curriculum around a clearly-defined set of expectations, nor have they developed assessment systems that measure whether students are meeting rigorous, publicly available standards" (American Federation of Teachers, 1999, p. 1). While states have adopted state-level curriculum standards, the contents of these standards and implementation policies vary.

Why States Have Adopted Standards

States' actions to adopt curriculum standards have been taken in reaction to worries about issues related to such topics as

- Allocating scarce resources strategically
- Assessing the impact of programs on students
- Deploying statewide expertise to attack common educational problems
- Improving levels of student performance
- Promoting educational equity principle

Allocating resources   States and individual communities face multiple demands on their resources. Education needs compete for funds with the needs of many other government-supported activities and programs. Increasingly, school leaders who seek funds are asked, "What will we get for the money?" The kinds of well-defined learning expectations that characterize sets of curriculum standards help provide answers. Descriptions of what students are to learn represent well-defined targets, which allow state and local school budget makers to explain what allocated money will be used for. They provide assurances that allocated money will be used in support of significant, widely supported educational "ends."

Assessing program impact.   Clear statements of student learning expectations encourage the development of related tests. The results of these tests can be used to generate information that can be used when additional support for educational programs is sought in subsequent years. At a time when policy makers and the public want schools to be accountable, standards-related assessments generate evidence that can be used to defend present practices or to suggest areas in need of modification. The demand for assessment has prompted a huge increase in standardized testing. The adoption of state curriculum standards encourages the development of tests tied to the standards, a highly desirable development. As noted previously, without state standards, the tests may become *de facto* standards themselves, and the results may or may not relate well to the kinds of instruction students have received.

EXERCISE 4–1

Unintended Side Effects of Standardized Assessment

Recently, educators in California have been surprised to learn that attorneys specializing in divorce law and child custody have taken an interest in standardized test score averages of individual schools (Garrison, 2001). Newspapers now routinely publish the information. Attorneys use the information in custody cases, arguing that children should be awarded to the parent the attorneys represent because this parent lives in an area where the local school's test scores are higher than those in the school that serves the area where the other parent resides.

Action

The use of standardized test score averages by attorneys who specialize in custody cases was not a purpose the framers of legislation requiring the public posting of these scores had in mind. Are there other examples of unintended side effects of school accountability legislation? For example, are teachers harder to find for grade levels in which tests are given? Do newcomers to the profession avoid accepting positions in schools where standardized test scores are low? Interview some local school leaders about this issue.

Analysis

If you find evidence of some unintended side effects of standardized testing, what caused them? Why were these difficulties not foreseen? Do the unintended side effects create negatives, which outweigh any positives associated with the policy? If so, how might this situation be rectified?

Key Points

It is difficult for even the best-intentioned framers of new educational policy to antici-pate everything that will occur once the policy is in place. Frequently, there are impor-tant unintended consequences. In some cases, these may be serious enough to pose major questions about the merits of the policy that allowed them to occur.

Deploying statewide expertise.   The probability is high that there is more ex-pertise related to educational problems represented in the population of an entire state than in the populations of most of its individual school districts. When states develop curriculum standards, a common educational agenda is established for students, teachers, administrators, parents, guardians, and other interested citi-zens. This condition encourages the expertise of the entire population to be de-ployed in support of a common education agenda. It builds a statewide commu-nity of interest in support of improved student learning.

Improving student learning.   Students perform better when they have clear ideas about what they are to know and do (Good & Brophy, 2000). Ideally, state curriculum standards attack ambiguity and frame statements about what students should learn in explicit terms. These clear statements about learning expectations help teachers communicate their intentions to learners, develop instructional plans in support of them, and prepare test items that tie back to the standard. When all elements of the instructional system are mutually supportive, student levels of achievement tend to rise.

Promoting educational equity.   Many state constitutions either state directly or imply that education for all of the state's children is a high priority, yet, if you look around your own state, you probably can cite numerous examples of instances in which some students are receiving higher-quality educational services than oth-ers. In all states, there are schools where programs encourage students to engage in high-level academic tasks, and there are schools where programs allow many students to do work at a much less rigorous standard of excellence. Proponents argue that state curriculum standards have the potential to establish high and rig-orous learning expectations for *all* students. The standards establish intended learning outcomes for college-bound students as well as workforce-bound stu-dents, for gifted and talented students and for students with disabilities of various kinds, for students who are nonnative speakers of English and for students who are native speakers of English, and for students from economically impoverished families and for students from relatively affluent families.

In addition, the equity principle is served when students can move from one school in a state to another and find that they are held to the same set of learning expectations. This is critical, given that nearly 20 percent of all students change schools each year (American Federation of Teachers, 1999). Supporters of state standards point out that many transfer students experience great difficulty when the program in their new school fails to mesh well with the one in the school they just left.

Varying Patterns

Individual states adopted somewhat varied approaches as they set about identifying and adopting curriculum standards. Many states included steps similar to the following:

1. A steering committee identified some writing teams, whose members were selected because of their familiarity with national standards (often developed by specialty groups from individual academic subject areas) and with state standards from across the country.

2. Writing teams for individual grade levels and subject areas developed drafts and presented them to the steering committee.

3. Arrangements were made to solicit comments on the draft standards from constituencies, which often included state board of education members; representatives from local school boards; selected superintendents, principals, and teachers; state leaders from relevant specialty organizations (state affiliates of such groups as the National Council of Teachers of English, National Science Teachers Association, National Council for the Social Studies, National Council of Teachers of Mathematics, and so forth); university faculty members; parent-teacher organizations; additional groups with interests in particular parts of the academic program; and other citizens.

4. The steering committee working with various writing groups, and perhaps some *ad hoc* task forces, reviewed comments, arranged for revisions to the drafts, and ultimately presented the standards to the state board of education for approval.

Though there were commonalities among many of the processes the states followed in establishing curriculum standards, you will see important state-to-state differences when you look at the substance of the adopted standards. To illustrate some examples, consider some differences in state curriculum standards in the area of English/language arts. As the twenty-first century began, North Carolina, Texas, California, and Nebraska had separate standards for students in every grade from K to 12. Other states—for example, New York, Massachusetts, Kansas, Pennsylvania, Florida, Missouri, and Montana—had standards to be met by students by the time they were at the end of a cluster of grade levels (e.g., at end of grade 8 for a cluster including grades 5, 6, 7, and 8). For specific examples of state curriculum standards, go to the state department of education website for states you are interested in. You can locate these easily using a standard search engine, such as Google (http://www.google.com).

LEARNING EXTENSION 4–4

Establishing and Modifying State Standards

Since 49 of the 50 states now have state curriculum standards, you probably live in a state that has such a document. If this is the case, gather some information in response to the following questions. (Your instructor may be able to suggest some in-formation sources.)

- What processes were followed in adopting the standards?
- In particular, what kinds of groups were formally represented when adoption of the standards was considered?
- What procedures and mechanisms are in place to review and revise the standards?

If you are living in a state without state standards, what kinds of answers can you find to the following questions? (Your instructor may be able to suggest some infor-mation sources.)

- What arguments have been used to oppose the establishment of a set of state cur-riculum standards in your state?
- Given the nature of the discussion of this issue in your state, is it likely or unlikely that your state will adopt a set of standards in the near future?

In addition to the number of standards and their grade-level placement, standards also vary in terms of the content they describe, their specificity, the presence or ab-sence of performance indicators that will be considered to determine whether they have been met, and references to associated assessment procedures. As noted earlier in this chapter, Mid-continent Research for Education and Learning (McREL) has been engaged in work designed to improve the technical quality of standards. For ex-ample, McREL has done the following (*McREL's Contributions to K–12 Standards, 2001*):

- Published a database of grades K–12 content standards built on information gathered from existing state and national sources
- Posted an extensive list of standards-based resources on the McREL website
- Assisted dozens of school districts as they have worked to align their own standards and programs with state-level standards
- Developed a comprehensive list of terms related to standards-based education
- Prepared numerous books and monographs focusing on standards-based education

For more about McREL's efforts to assist states in preparing and implementing standards-based education programs, go to the group's website (http://www.mcrel.org).

Several groups have undertaken to critique the adequacy of present standards and to suggest criteria that the standards should be expected to meet. The Amer-ican Federation of Teachers (AFT) (1999) has proposed that good state curricu-lum standards and accompanying policies should

- Be fully developed for the four core academic areas of English, mathematics, science, and social studies
- Be explicit enough to provide the basis for a required core curriculum to be pursued by all students

- Be accompanied by an assessment system that aligns clearly with the standards
- Be backed up by state policies that tie promotion decisions, in part, to student performance on standards-related tests

In the early 2000s, the AFT found that the states had made progress in implementing the standards but that much work remains to be done (American Federation of Teachers, 1999).

The Thomas B. Fordham Foundation is another group that has issued periodic reviews of state curriculum standards. This group favors standards that place a heavy emphasis on academic content and is less enamored of standards that focus on either processes of learning or processes of teaching. In a recent report, the foundation reported that increasing numbers of states are focusing standards on academic content and are stating them in ways that allow for the reliable measurement of student performance (Finn & Petrilli, 2000).

The work of McREL and the concerns of such groups as the American Federation of Teachers and the Thomas B. Fordham Foundation attest to the widespread interest in using state curriculum standards as an approach to improving the overall quality of instruction in the schools. Though opinions vary regarding the adequacy of the existing standards, present trends suggest that state curriculum standards will continue to be a strong influence on individual school districts and schools as they plan programs for their own students. As you engage in curriculum activities of various kinds, the likelihood is high that you and your colleagues will consider state standards as you engage in curriculum decision making.

ISSUES FOR CURRICULUM WORKERS

As you engage in curriculum revision and development, you will find both positives and negatives associated with the standards-based education movement. These pluses and minuses center around concerns related to the following topics:

- Assessments and consequences
- Clarity of learning expectations
- Academic content of school programs
- Educational equity as a reality

Assessments and Consequences

Proponents of educational standards believe that school programs can be improved when students know what they are expected to do, when testing programs tie clearly to these assessments, and when the results of testing have consequences for students, teachers, and school leaders. The results of assessment are key features of a signal system that provides information about whether an instructional program is doing an excellent, a mediocre, or a poor job of serving students. Many supporters of curriculum standards believe that the impact of assessment information must go beyond simply publishing student scores. Both good and bad assessments must have associated consequences.

Examples of arguments supporting assessments and consequences.   It is true that the publication of poor student scores on tests tied to curriculum standards provides the incentive of public embarrassment to teachers and their school leaders. Similarly, good publicity that comes when student scores are high provides validating, emotional support for teachers and school leaders. However, if scores result in nothing beyond publicity, it is too easy for school staffs to continue doing business as usual. To avoid this possibility, it is important for both extremely good and extremely bad testing results to be accompanied by consequences that students, teachers, and school leaders see as important.

When students' failure to do well on tests associated with state curriculum standards is accompanied by a consequence, such as denial of graduation or graduation with a class of diploma that reflects mediocre academic performance, there is incentive for students (and their parents and guardians) to take schoolwork seriously. In addition, if teachers and school leaders understand that extremely low student scores may have consequences ranging from dismissal to the transfer to other, perhaps less desirable, buildings, there is an incentive for them to develop instructional programs that will lead to high levels of student mastery. Similarly, if the same educators understand that benefits in the form of higher salaries or special bonuses will come their way when students do well on these tests, there is an incentive for them to work hard to improve instructional programs that already may be satisfactory or even somewhat better than satisfactory. This set of conditions encourages educators to study test results carefully and to use them as part of a data-based approach to strengthening instructional programs.

Today, states vary in terms of their policies on imposing consequences related to levels of student performance on assessments. Some states (such as California and North Carolina) have established elaborate systems for rewarding teachers and leaders in schools where scores are high and for imposing negative sanctions of various kinds when student scores are extremely low. At present, only about one-tenth of the states with state curriculum standards impose strong negative or positive consequences on teachers and school leaders based on student test performance. This is a matter of concern, and groups interested in supporting state curriculum standards hope more states will adopt such policies in the future (Finn & Petrilli, 2000).

Examples of arguments questioning assessments and consequences.   Individuals who are skeptical of tying assessments to a set of predictable consequences often accept the importance of having tests that relate clearly to state standards. However, they take issue with the idea of imposing either positive or negative consequences on students, teachers, and school leaders that tie to test scores. One argument is that consequences tend to be limited to students, teachers, and building-level administrators. This arrangement presumes that all the variables associated with what students have learned and how they perform on a test are under the control of individuals in these three categories. This assumption is untenable.

If you are presently in education, you will recognize that what students learn, though directly affected by teachers and building-level administrators, also is influenced by the actions of parents and guardians, school boards, local superintendents, state boards of education, legislators, governors, colleges and universities, the business community, and the media. John Goff (1999), a former Ohio state superintendent of schools, argues that a more comprehensive accountability system is needed that systematically gathers data about the actions of *all* these groups. Unless there is documented support for responsible actions on the part of these many external groups, even the hardest working teachers, building-level principals, and students may not perform at high levels on standardized achievement tests. (See Figure 4.2 for an illustration of John Goff's "comprehensive accountability model.")

If there are variables over which professionals at individual schools have little control, what kinds of teacher and administrator behaviors are probable when the incentives associated with score levels of students on tests are tied to curriculum standards?

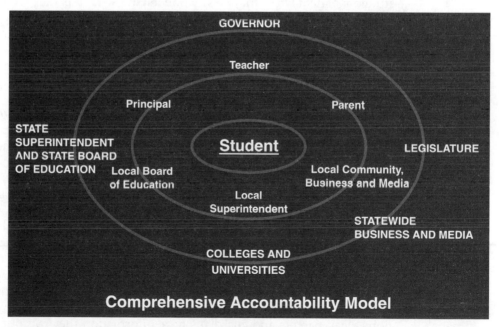

FIGURE 4.2   A Comprehensive Accountability Model

Source: Model is from John M. Goff. "A More Comprehensive Accountability Model." *Basic Education Online Edition.* October, 1999, *44*(2). Copyright © by the Council for Basic Education. Reprinted with permission. (John M. Goff is former Ohio Superintendent of Public Instruction, retired, and Senior Advisor with the Council for Basic Education.)

For one thing, these educators are likely to seek employment in schools in affluent districts with highly supportive, highly educated parents and with relatively homogeneous learner populations. Students in these schools generally do better on tests of all kinds than their counterparts in schools in less affluent areas that enroll more diverse student populations. Tying teacher and administrator incentives to student test performance may be an incentive that keeps good teachers and principals away from the schools and students most in need of their talents.

Critics of using test results to reward or sanction teachers and administrators for student performance allege that, in some places, assessments have not been tied closely enough to adopted state curriculum standards. For example, this issue has been raised in California, where teachers and others point out that what is being tested is at variance with what they are now required to teach (Garrison, 2001). This puts professional educators in an impossible situation; on the one hand, they are accountable to teach content included in an adopted set of state curriculum standards while, on the other hand, they are pressed to raise student scores on tests that sample different kinds of content.

Clarity of Learning Expectations

Discourse about standards-based education uniformly features mention of how students benefit when they clearly understand what it is they are to do and learn. Many parents and guardians who want to know what their children are supposed to be learning and how they can help them do so are also eager to have this information. Other individuals and groups support explicit, concise descriptions of intended learning outcomes as ways to identify what public schools are supposed to accomplish and to hold them accountable for doing so.

Examples of arguments supporting clarity of learning expectations.   Students dislike ambiguity; they do not want to guess what their teachers want them to study and learn. They benefit from structure, and there is evidence that they do better when they have a clear understanding of what they are expected to learn and do (American Federation of Teachers, 1999; Good & Brophy, 2000). American students are capable of doing very sophisticated work. In the past, part of the problem has been that schools have failed to establish high expectations for students and to communicate exactly what those expectations are. When this is done, student levels of psychological serenity improve, their performance levels go up, and their confidence in their abilities to succeed at difficult academic tasks increases.

Parents and guardians want their children to do well; however, unless they have a clear grasp of what the school expects, they have no focus for their academic support activities. When curriculum standards make these learning intentions clear, parents and guardians have information they can put to good use as they help their sons and daughters with their schoolwork.

Many individuals and groups outside of public education understand that schooling is an expensive enterprise. Billions of dollars are spent each year to support the nation's public schools. Increasingly, the public wants evidence that there is a reasonable return on the money that is invested. Knowledge and skill are the products of schooling, and assessments are the tools used to define their quality. To develop good assessments, there must be explicit descriptions of the kinds of learning to be tested. For this reason, clear and explicit descriptions of intended learning outcomes are essential.

Examples of arguments questioning clarity of learning expectations.   Opposition to identifying clarity of student expectations usually does not stake out a position in opposition to the *idea* of clarity. Rather, what some critics allege is that the press for clarity too often leads developers of curriculum standards to identify learning outcomes because it is easy to state them clearly rather than because they are truly important. The possibility for easy to define but relatively unimportant student-learning expectations is especially serious at a time when there are demands for assessment schemes that tie directly to curriculum standards. Some kinds of learning are simply easier to test than others. This means that some clear statements of student expectations reflect a desire to make testing easy rather than a sincere effort to identify really important kinds of academic content (Garrison, 2001).

CURRICULUM REALITIES 4–1

Trivializing Content and Teaching to the Test

Many people believe that state curriculum standards and their associated tests place great pressures on educators to focus students on low-level content that can be assessed easily on forced-choice tests (Garrison, 2001). The intent of legislation establishing these requirements was to make school programs more rigorous. Critics argue that it has had quite the opposite effect. Increasingly, teachers avoid dealing with academic content and, instead, spend time honing students' test-taking abilities. Further, since the tests, for the most part, feature easy to mechanically score forced-choice items, they focus on atomized bits of academic content and avoid complex issues that stretch students' mental capacities.

Ask a number of local teachers about how tests associated with state standards affect what they do in the classroom. You might wish to ask for responses to questions such as the following as you think about this issue:

- Has legislation establishing state curriculum standards lessened the rigor of academic content treated in the classroom?

- Is more and more instructional time devoted to developing students' test-taking skills, rather than encouraging them to engage new content?

- Overall, has the adoption of state curriculum standards improved the overall quality of education in the schools? What evidence supports your view?

Assessment programs tied to curriculum standards feature the testing of thousands of students. When large-scale testing of this kind occurs, correction is a huge task. It is much easier to design and correct tests requiring students to provide responses to true-false and multiple-choice items, which can be scored electronically, than essay items, which cannot. There are limitations on the kinds of thinking that can be addressed by forced-response test items. It is especially difficult to assess students' abilities to interpret, synthesize, and evaluate information using items of this type. (Essays are better suited to this task.) Cost considerations and the need to correct vast numbers of tests quickly provide an incentive for the adopters of state curriculum standards to develop low-level, unchallenging kinds of student learning outcomes. These may be defined with eminent clarity, but they signal to students that trivial kinds of learning are important. In the long run, the effect can be to dumb down the educational experiences students receive in our schools.

Academic Content of School Programs

State curriculum standards have the potential to do something about the proliferation of separate subjects and courses in American schools. From the 1940s until about the mid 1970s, the common response to a desire to meet individual student needs was to add new academic offerings to the curriculum (Marzano & Kendall, 1997). As a result, there was a huge increase in the number of subjects taught, and this expansion led to significant school to school differences. A key part of the agenda of the supporters of standards-based education is to reduce the total number of subjects taught and to focus students' attention on a more limited body of content, which all learners should master.

Examples of arguments supporting the identification of academic content. If someone were to ask you what subjects should a product of American schools be able to discuss knowledgeably, you probably would have to respond, "Well, it depends on what he or she studied in school." Many high schools provide varied course paths high-school students may follow en route to receiving a diploma. Even middle and elementary schools provide different learning experiences to some of their students—for example, to those enrolled in gifted and talented or special education programs. Though there are considerable differences in what individual students study within a school, they pale in comparison to school to school differences. The lack of a common set of academic experiences makes it difficult to compare the adequacy of instruction provided to students who have not been exposed to the same academic content.

What we need is a standard curriculum that requires all students to take some of the same basic courses in the traditional areas of English, science, mathematics, and social studies (American Federation of Teachers, 1999). A huge body of scholarship is available for academics and school curriculum specialists to draw on in selecting experiences appropriate for school learners. Subject-area specialty organizations are eager to assist in this effort. (For more information about the work of subject-area specialty organizations, see Chapter 6, "People and Roles in Curriculum Work.") A limited number of required school subjects, which all students should be required to study, would make it possible to do meaningful teacher to teacher and school to school comparisons. A common academic curriculum also would present fewer academic challenges to students who must transfer from one school to another.

Examples of arguments questioning the identification of academic content. Although it makes sense to provide a more common academic core for students in all schools, the real issue has to do with the actual content taught within each of the selected courses. Although there is much scholarship associated with each traditional academic discipline, there continue to be debates about what kinds of content should receive emphasis. As the states attempt to identify the content of curriculum standards, state leaders often involve people representing many constituencies. What is unclear is how much influence people with narrow interests or perspectives have had in the selection process. Identifying a narrow range of subjects all students must take will not result in educational improvement unless the content is sound.

Though one of the avowed purposes of standards-based education is to direct students' attention to a limited amount of required academic content, this purpose has been difficult to achieve. Heated debates about what content elements to include have, in many cases, resulted in enormously bloated sets of state standards (Marzano & Kendall, 1997). The effort to simplify, in many cases, has added unnecessary complexity to the lives of teachers and administrators who must work with state curriculum standards.

In some places, groups of parents and teachers have actively opposed content components of state standards (Garrison, 2001). Some of their concerns link to the assessment issue. They worry that the need to develop easy-to-correct standardized tests may have influenced the identification of relatively unimportant content. For example, a social studies learning expectation requiring students to identify the names of leading generals and to cite dates is easier to test than is one requiring them to analyze social and economic causes of a war.

Educational Equity as a Reality

Supporters of standards-based education argue that, over time, too many separate programs have been developed for too many separate categories of learners. To provide equal educational opportunity for all, state standards should outline a core set of academic requirements that is expected of all students (American Federation of Teachers, 1999). To do otherwise is to disadvantage some categories of students.

Examples of arguments supporting educational equity. Developing school programs that seek to respond to the special characteristics of certain groups of students may either fail to serve them well or, when they do work as designed, divert resources away from programs to support other students. For example, money for gifted and talented students often supports excellent, innovative instructional practices. Students who are enrolled in them may experience significant educational benefits. On the other hand, support for these programs, by definition, takes money away from programs directed at other students. This practice violates the educational equity principle.

Similarly, some programs for students with disabilities place learning demands on these young people that are less rigorous than those expected of other students. There is the potential, at least, for these students to emerge from their school years with achievement levels that lag well behind those of other students. It is not proper to establish a set of instructional programs that establishes varying learning expectations for different students. Rather, the emphasis should be on requiring *all* students to meet a common set of academic standards. The proper way, the *equitable* way, to respond to individual differences is to provide particular students with the kinds of learning experiences they need to achieve the common objectives. In other words, maintain the same set of learning objectives for all but vary instructional approaches to respond to the characteristics of particular students.

Examples of arguments questioning educational equity.   No one opposes the idea of educational equity. But what does the concept mean? Years of experience suggest to teachers and principals that students vary in terms of what they can learn and do. The standards-based education movement has been driven, in part, by a desire to establish high and rigorous student learning standards. It makes no sense to expect that students who cannot cope with aspects of programs that have been in the schools for years will somehow manage to master content associated with more rigorous and sophisticated standards.

At a theoretical level, there may be merit in the argument that students who fail to learn information embedded within state curriculum standards could do so if there were appropriate modifications to the instructional program. However, in the practical world in which teachers and administrators go about their business, instructional money is limited. It is illusory to expect state legislatures to pour large sums of additional dollars into teaching budgets for the purpose of providing special support for small groups of students. These resources are nice to dream about, but the needed dollars are unlikely to be allocated anytime soon.

 ## STANDARDS AND THE WORK REMAINING TO BE DONE

Has the proliferation of state curriculum standards taken all important decisions out of the hands of curriculum workers at the local level? Not to worry—much remains to be done. For one thing, standards seek to define a required core program of study. A statement issued by the Illinois State Board of Education (1999) speaks to this point: "The Illinois Learning Standards cannot possibly incorporate all the learning students will accomplish. If schools and their communities believe that important content has been omitted, it will be their responsibility to develop local standards. . . ." There is much local work to be done, even in states that have highly detailed, highly prescriptive sets of standards (Carr & Harris, 2001).

LEARNING EXTENSION 4–5

Areas in Need of Local Standards

If you are in one of the 49 states with an adopted set of state curriculum standards, locate a copy of this material. A good way to do so is to go to the website of your state department of education. You can find this location with a search engine, such as Google (http://www.google.com). Type in the name of your state, followed by the words "state department of education."

If you live in a state lacking state standards, choose one from any other state.

Look over the standards for a grade level and subject area that interests you. Think about the issue of developing additional standards that might make sense for your local district or for an individual school. Think about the following questions:

- Are there already so many standards in the state document that adding new local ones would place too much of a burden on teachers?

- If there is a need for additional local standards, how many should be developed?

Conclude this exercise by preparing one or two local standards in an area that interests you. For each, write two or three related performance indicators.

Personnel at Mid-continent Research for Education and Learning (McREL) have discovered that state standards tend to be huge, unevenly developed, and inconsistent in the presentation of information across grade levels and subject areas, and they are often lacking in terms of important implementation specifics (Marzano & Kendall, 1997). Further, standards tend to focus on academic content standards. You will find that much of your curriculum work will involve developing recommendations related to instructional processes. Relatively little of this kind of information is included in state standards documents.

One hope of the supporters of standards-based education is that the tests associated with content standards will generate data that teachers and administrators will use to improve programs. Relatively few educators have a great deal of background in this kind of data-based decision making (Council for Basic Education and the Johnson Foundation, 2000). Organizing staff development projects designed to teach people how to incorporate test data into discussions related to curriculum development and revision are likely to become an increasingly important responsibility of curriculum specialists.

Finally, curriculum standards continue to evolve. As you have learned in this chapter, critics have called attention to many alleged deficiencies in existing documents. As you work in curriculum, you will want to make your voice heard when changes are considered. As you do so, you may wish to reflect on questions such as the following:

- Who made decisions about the contents of existing standards, and how do you know they represent the best choices?
- What processes were followed as decisions were made about establishing the present standards, and should these processes be changed?
- Have local school districts abdicated too much authority to state and national authorities as state-level curriculum standards have been developed?
- Are existing standards driving good teachers away from the schools most in need of their expertise and, if so, what might be done to change this situation?
- To what extent do required tests reflect the learning expectations embedded within your state curriculum standards?
- Is there evidence that the need for easy-to-correct standardized tests has led to the selection of low-level, trivial content?
- Are groups other than teachers and local school administrators being held accountable for the student learning of content embedded in the state curriculum standards?
- If the promotion of equity is a guiding principle of state standards, what evidence is there that additional money has been deployed to make such a hope a reality?

These, of course, are just examples of questions you might begin thinking about. Perhaps this list will suggest others you might wish to consider. Your answers (and the answers of others) will vary. However, what seems clear is that the standards-based education movement and the accompanying proliferation of state curriculum standards will give you and others interested in curriculum work much to consider and do in the years ahead.

Review and Reflection

1. Why is it difficult to respond with confidence when someone asks you a question such as "What should a fourth grader be able to know at the end of the school year?"
2. What is standards-based education, and why has there been so much interest in this topic over the past 10 years?
3. What are benchmarks, and what difficulties do you suppose curriculum specialists encounter when they develop benchmarks for the first time?
4. What are some historical underpinnings of today's efforts to establish curriculum standards in each state?
5. How reasonable is it to judge the quality of individual schools based on how well their students do on standardized tests? What are some arguments used to support and oppose this practice?

6. Will establishing state curriculum standards serve the principle of educational equity? Why or why not?

7. Do you think curriculum standards strengthen or weaken the quality and rigor of the academic content that teachers treat in the classroom? Why do you take this position?

8. Has the adoption of content standards eliminated the need for local level curriculum work? Why, or why not?

References

American Federation of Teachers. (1999). *Making standards matter 1999: An update on state activity. Educational Issues Policy Brief, 11*. Washington, DC: Author.

Bobbitt, F. (1918). *The Curriculum*. Boston: Houghton.

Carnegie Forum on Education and the Economy. (1986). *A nation prepared: Teachers for the 21st century*. Washington, DC: Carnegie Task Force on Teaching as a Profession.

Carr, J. F., & Harris, D. E. (2001). *Succeeding with standards: Linking curriculum, assessment, and action planning*. Alexandria, VA: Association for Supervision and Curriculum Development.

Children's Defense Fund. (1994). *The state of America's children*. Boston: Beacon Press.

Council for Basic Education and The Johnson Foundation. (2000). *Closing the gap*. A report on the Wingspread conference. Washington, DC: Author.

Eisner, E. W. (1995). Standards for American schools: Help or hindrance? *Phi Delta Kappan, 76*(10), 758–764.

Finn, C. E., Jr., & Petrilli, M. J. (Eds.). (2000). *The state of state standards 2000*. Washington, DC: Thomas B. Fordham Foundation.

Garrison, J. (2001, January 14). School testing has unintended side effects. *Los Angeles Times*. [http://www.latimes.com/cgi-bin/print.cgi]

Goff, J. M. (1999). A more comprehensive accountability model. *Basic Education Online Edition, 44*(2). [http://www.c-b-e.org/articles/goff.htm]

Good, T. L., & Brophy, J. E. (2000). *Looking in classrooms* (8th ed.). New York: Longman.

Gregory, S. T. (Ed.). (2000). *The academic achievement of minority students: Perspectives, practices, and prescriptions*. Lanham, MD: University Press of America.

Illinois State Board of Education. (1999). *Introduction to the standards*. Springfield: Illinois State Board of Education. [http://www.isbe.state.il.us/ils/intro.history.html]

INTASC. (1999). *Interstate new teacher assessment and support consortium*, Washington, DC: Council of Chief State School Officers.

Mager, R. F. (1962). *Preparing instructional objectives*. Palo Alto, CA: Fearon.

Marzano, R. J., & Kendall, J. S. (1997). *The fall and rise of standards-based education*. Alexandria, VA: National Association of State Boards of Education.

McREL's contributions to k–12 standards. (2001). Aurora, CO: Mid-continent Research for Education and Learning. [http://www.mcrel.org/standards/factsheet.asp]

Morin, R. (2001). A lesson in public education: Parents, teachers and students are showing improved attitudes toward schools and testing. *Washington Post National Weekly Edition, 18*(20), 34.

National Association of Secondary School Principals and the Carnegie Foundation. (1996). *Breaking ranks: Changing an American institution.* Reston, VA: Author.

National Commission on Excellence in Education. (1983). *A nation at risk: The imperative for educational reform.* Washington, DC: U.S. Department of Education.

National Governor's Association. (1986). *Time for results.* Washington, DC: Author.

Null, J. W. (1999). Efficiency jettisoned: Unacknowledged changes in the curriculum thought of John Franklin Bobbitt. *Journal of Curriculum and Supervision, 15*(1), 35–42.

Ravitch, D. (1995). *National standards in American education: A citizen's guide.* Washington, DC: Brookings Institution.

Robson, R., & Latiolais, M. P. (2000). Standards-based education. *MAA Focus, 20*(5), 12–13.

Sanchez, C. (2001, March 30). Testing backlash. *All things considered.* Washington, DC: National Public Radio broadcast.

Smith, M. K. (2001). *Curriculum.* [http://www.infed.org/biblio/b-curric.htm]

Snyder, T. D. (Ed.). (2000). *Digest of education statistics, 1999.* Washington, DC: National Center for Education Statistics.

Task Force on Education for Economic Growth. (1983). *Action for excellence.* Denver, CO: Education Commission of the States.

Tyler, R. W. (1949). *Basic principles of curriculum and instruction.* Chicago: The University of Chicago Press.

Influences of Philosophy, Learning Theory, and Sociology

Graphic Organizer

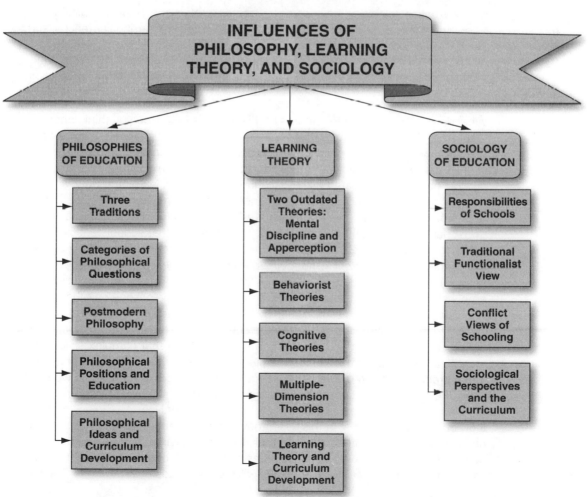

INTRODUCTION

Suppose business leaders in your community complained that the high-school gradu-ates they were hiring lacked the kinds of writing skills they expected in new employ-ees. In response to their concerns, your school board might direct the superintendent to make some changes in the grade 12 English program. If this happened, the director of curriculum, acting on a directive from the superintendent, probably would assemble a curriculum development group. The members might generate recommendations for a revised grade 12 English program that included the following:

- A change in the present English program from one in which about 20 percent of class time is devoted to developing students' written composition skills and about 80 percent of class time is devoted to developing their appreciation of outstanding literary works to a program in which about 40 percent of class time is devoted to developing students' written composition skills and about 60 percent of class time is devoted to developing their appreciation of outstanding literary works
- Instruction related to developing students' written composition abilities empha-sizing the traditional parts of speech, the components of strong sentences, and the basic skills of effective writing
- Because society in general expects all high school graduates to have good written communication skills, a requirement that all students enroll in the new grade 12 English program

What do you think about the features of this proposal? How do you think others might react to it? As you think about the answers to these questions, you need to consider that identifying these ideas as good, bad, or in between depends on how you and oth-ers are affected by several important perceptual filters or mediators. These include in-dividual positions associated with educational philosophy, learning theory, and educa-tional sociology. Let's look at these influences one at a time and think about how they might affect reactions to the proposal to revise the grade 12 English program.

A person who is philosophically attuned to the idea that schools should train stu-dents to meet the practical needs of the real world might find much to applaud in this proposal. On the other hand, people who think education should focus primarily on passing on the "wisdom of the ages" to students might balk at the decision to de-emphasize the study of literature. Others might oppose the change on other grounds.

The decision to teach composition by focusing on specific skills is an approach con-sistent with the views of people who are committed to learning theories that fall un-der the general heading of "behaviorism." They believe that complex skills are best taught when they are broken into small pieces, which are learned one-at-a-time as stu-dents progress toward mastering the larger whole. A decision to do this would likely draw fire from people committed to cognitive learning theories. Cognitive theorists generally suggest that learning best occurs when students learn "wholes," rather than individual parts of wholes. In this case, they might argue that the emphasis should be on writing paragraphs and papers, rather than on studying the basic components of sentences. Advocates of "multiple-dimension theories" might attack the proposal be-cause it presumes that a single approach will suit the needs of all students. They might argue that varied modes of presentation should be developed and fitted to particular characteristics of each student.

How individuals see our society also plays a role in how they evaluate this proposal. People who are "functionalists" basically see our society as organized in ways that are beneficial to nearly everyone and believe that the school has an obligation to provide students with an education that will help them fit in. If students who leave schools with better writing skills are more attractive to employers, then functionalists will see merit in the proposed program.

On the other hand, people who have a "conflict" view of society argue that we are not organized in ways that promote the general good. Rather, society features conflict among groups, which produces clear winners and losers. The present proposal, conflict theorists may argue, will divert resources to support a school program that will benefit the employers of those students who enter the workforce immediately after leaving high school. Funds to support it may be drawn away from programs designed to support the needs of other kinds of students.

This brief discussion highlights the point that many perspectives come into play when people make judgments about the quality of curriculum decisions. For this reason, it makes sense for you to have some understanding of the views associated with various educational philosophies, learning theories, and sociological positions.

PHILOSOPHIES OF EDUCATION

Philosophy is highly attuned to the real world. Your own philosophical positions help you answer such questions as the following:

- In general, do people have more good than bad characteristics?
- How do I determine what is right and wrong?
- How can I tell whether something is really true?
- What kind of information is really worth knowing?
- How should I treat others, and how should I expect them to treat me?

These questions have been asked for centuries. Over time, discussions related to them have occurred within the context of three traditions: idealism, realism, and pragmatism.

Three Traditions

Idealism traces back to the thought of Ancient Greek philosopher Plato. Idealists believe that reality is not found in what we take in through our senses. What is real is a mental world of "ideas" or "ideals." What we encounter every day is only a representation of the ultimate reality that is out there somewhere in the form of an intangible concept or idea.

For idealists, important universal truths and values exist. As an educator, your charge is to bring these abstract ideas to a conscious level. To do this, it is important that your students learn about the cultural heritage of human beings and, particularly, about people's attempts through the ages to develop more complete understandings of the ultimate verities. Curricula that strongly emphasize philosophy, theology, the liberal arts, and the fine arts often are consistent with the worldviews of people who associate themselves with idealism.

Realism asserts that there are important, unchanging truths to be learned. These truths are to be found in the real world of things that exist apart from any intangible ideas about them. It is a position that is historically associated with Ancient Greek philosopher Aristotle. For a realist, the test of truth is whether a given idea can be verified by examining its consistency with what is found in the real world. To make this judgment, the idealist relies on rational thinking powers.

Realists place a high priority on teaching young people to develop their thinking abilities. They want curriculum specialists to identify school subjects that help students organize information and make judgments based on the careful consideration of evidence. School subjects such as science and mathematics are among those realists often cite as having these characteristics. Sometimes realists challenge interdisciplinary programs out of a fear that blending content from separate subjects will dilute students' abilities to appreciate the special organizational features of individual academic disciplines.

Pragmatism focuses on the changing nature of the universe and rejects the idea that there is a huge body of unchanging knowledge that young people should learn. Truth is a concept that evolves over time. What people must do as they live is consider the circumstances of their own time and make judgments about what makes sense within the framework of their own time and culture. American educational philosopher John Dewey was highly influential in disseminating this perspective. Dewey particularly emphasized the need for young people to develop outstanding problem-solving skills. Individuals with these kinds of skills would have the tools needed to think about and adapt to changing social conditions.

Pragmatists see your job as an educator as that of providing learning experiences for students that will engage and develop their problem-solving powers. It is important that you provide them with learning examples that are relevant to their own experiences, and that you help them to understand that the thinking abilities developed in one context have relevance for many others. School curricula that emphasize the scientific method and other systematic approaches to problem solving are among those that pragmatists often favor. In supporting a given course, they are more interested in its capacity for teaching good thinking skills than in its standing as a repository for a particular body of information. Problem-solving abilities endure; academic content changes over time.

Categories of Philosophical Questions

Questions related to traditional philosophies sort into several major categories: metaphysics (or ontology), epistemology, axiology, and logic.

Issues associated with **metaphysics** (or **ontology**) focus on the nature of reality. Questions associated with this category are speculative and cannot be answered by reference to traditional problem-solving techniques, such as the scientific method. The following are some examples:

- Is there a more perfect and ideal state of things that exists beyond the physical manifestations we encounter in our daily lives?
- Is there a universal purpose to life that can be discerned, or is life essentially meaningless?
- Is it fruitless to search for truth because the changing nature of reality makes everything relative to its own place and time?
- Do what we perceive to be cause-and-effect relationships truly exist, or are they simply mental creations we use to impose order on a world that lacks it?
- Are there unchanging principles that can be found that will explain the operation of things?
- Are people fundamentally good or bad?

Individuals' answers to metaphysical questions affect their views of curricular programs. For example, consider a person who denies the existence of overarching truths that explain what we experience in our daily lives. This individual is unlikely to be receptive to arguments that students should study works of classical literature because they are repositories of such truths. Think also about someone who thinks cause-and-effect relationships are mental illusions. This person may hold in low esteem programs featuring a strong emphasis on teaching students to use the scientific method.

Questions associated with **epistemology** seek answers about the nature of knowledge. Some examples include

- Is it ever possible to know for certain that something is absolutely true?
- Does knowledge exist that is true in some situations but not true in others?
- What constitutes knowledge?

Individuals' epistemological positions affect their attitudes toward school programs. For example, if you ever find yourself working on a revision of a biology program, you may find that people who believe that truth is revealed through a literal reading of the *Bible* have quite different views of evolution than many professional biologists, who ground their position in the scientific method. People from some non-European cultural groups are much enamored of myths and information from unwritten oral traditions as sources of truth.

LEARNING EXTENSION 5–1

The Evolution Issue

A recurring issue having to do with epistemology concerns the theory of evolution. Supporters, who base their conclusions on evidence derived from application of the scientific method, from time to time find the theory challenged by people who argue that the account of creation in the *Bible* should be the definitive authority on this matter. Several years ago, a group of state-level education policy makers in Kansas adopted guidelines that banned the teaching of evolution in Kansas schools. This decision, subsequently, was reversed.

Using information from the World Wide Web or from other sources recommended by your instructor, gather information about the debate concerning the appropriateness of teaching the theory of evolution to public-school students. Respond to questions such as these:

- Where the theory of evolution has been attacked, what have supporters done to build support for including the theory in school programs?
- What kinds of coalitions have been built by opponents of the theory of evolution, and what strategies have they used as they have sought the adoption of policies to ban or limit the teaching of evolution in schools?
- What kinds of policies have school boards and other governing authorities adopted in response to this debate? Have they typically adopted compromise positions, or have they come down firmly on one side of this issue?

Questions associated with **axiology** focus on the nature of values and ethics. Examples of axiological questions include

- Is it better to seek gratification now or to defer it for potentially greater gratification at a later date?
- What is moral and immoral?
- What is the highest good?

People have different views on axiological questions. For example, should schools have common behavioral expectations of all students? Individuals who support this view take the position that there are agreed-on principles of good and appropriate living, which should apply to all. Others argue that differences associated with culture and other circumstances make it inappropriate for schools to have common expectations for all students.

Many issues associated with morality and good professional practice concern axiology. For example, if you are a teacher, is it better for you to work hard to make sure that all of your students achieve a certain minimum level of expertise, or is it better for you to concentrate your efforts on fewer, academically talented young people? Do you have a responsibility to assist young people in areas that go beyond what you teach, or does your responsibility end once your instructional duties are discharged?

Questions of **logic** focus on the issue of exact thought. They concern relationships among ideas and procedures for distinguishing between accurate and inaccurate information. Logic divides into two basic categories, **inductive logic** and **deductive logic.** Deductive logic begins with a general conclusion and attempts to make it clear through the presentation of illustrative examples to students. Inductive logic begins by presenting students with examples and asks them to develop an explanatory conclusion. Some examples of questions associated with logic include

- What steps should be followed as students pursue a problem from beginning to end?
- How should these steps be sequenced?
- For what kinds of content are inductive approaches preferred?
- For what kinds of content are deductive approaches preferred?

Many school programs claim to aim at developing students' thinking abilities. If you are involved in developing curricula with this focus, you need to consider what guidelines are provided that give students a model they can follow (either inductive or deductive) as they confront problems and work through them to a solution.

Postmodern Philosophy

Proponents of **postmodern philosophy** reject many positions associated with the perspectives of traditional idealism, realism, and pragmatism. They often also reject the question categories discussed in the previous section (Jacobsen, 1999). Among other things, they suggest that these positions have been built almost exclusively around European patterns of thought. This kind of cultural baggage distorts reality and imposes a highly limited set of perspectives on individuals. To counter this problem, postmodernists propose that efforts to identify reality should focus on individuals and communities and the unique approaches they take to construct a worldview. This involves a wide-ranging study of cultural artifacts of various kinds, including legends and myths.

Postmodernists see reality as individual-centered. Because every one of us has a private set of purposes and understandings, we have a unique view of reality (Beck, 1993). You may have encountered an application of this position, called *constructivism*. Constructivism holds that each student builds a personal set of knowledge, which evolves as he or she relates new information and puts it together with previously held understandings. Because individuals construct their own meanings, educators have an obligation to provide curricula that provide them with opportunities to engage rich and diverse perspectives. This is true because today's students will come to adulthood in a culturally and racially mixed world. As an educator, your task is to assure that students have opportunities to encounter the perspectives of many cultures and to consider diverse value sets as they strive to work out their own personal priorities. Instructional approaches should emphasize democratic decision making, open-ended conclusions, and the importance of ongoing dialogue about important issues.

Philosophical Positions and Education

Over the years, a number of philosophical positions have developed that relate directly to education:

- Essentialism
- Progressivism
- Perennialism

- Reconstructionism
- Existentialism

Essentialism derives its name from its intent to provide students with the "essentials" of academic knowledge and good citizenship characteristics. It owes much to the thinking of William Bagley in the 1930s and early 1940s (Bagley, 1941). This position assumes that the present social, political, and economic structures of American society are good and that they tend to benefit most citizens.

The essentialist defines reality as what we experience physically through the senses. Hence, science and technology have important roles to play in the curriculum because they help students better understand the world in which they live. All students should be taught basic academic subjects that include content that will equip them well for their roles as contributing citizens. These basics include mathematics, the sciences, history, foreign languages, and literature. On the other hand, schools should place less emphasis on music, the arts, and humanities. Although such subjects are interesting, they should not be high priorities because they fail to give students the basic understandings they will need as citizens. In addition, vocational programs are suspect because they have the potential to divert students' attention away from mastery of the essentials.

Progressivism owes much to the work of American educational philosopher John Dewey (1902, 1910, 1916, 1938). Progressives view change as the major constant of life. Change, when properly channeled, can improve society. Progressives see educators' task as giving students the kinds of problem-solving skills they will need to study difficult situations as they arise, to apply rational thinking powers as they make decisions about difficult issues, and to apply solutions that will help shape change in a positive direction.

When you engage in curriculum work, you will know you are encountering a view coming out of the progressive tradition when you hear someone argue that "we should teach these students how to think, not just the facts." Progressives reject the view that there are many lasting truths, which each student must learn. Truth changes constantly. However, sound rational thinking processes have lasting worth because they can be applied over time to diverse settings. Hence, school programs that emphasize rational thinking—for example, those from the physical and social sciences—have promise as vehicles for helping students master the problem-solving skills that will serve them well throughout their lives.

EXERCISE 5–1

Attacking Progressivism

To build support for a change or series of changes they favor, proponents of some school reform initiatives follow a two-pronged strategy. On the one hand, they carefully describe benefits that will result when the proposed change is adopted. On the other, they depict opposing ideas as unworthy and, sometimes, downright evil.

Action

In recent years, some enthusiastic supporters of a back-to-the-basics curriculum featuring common requirements for all students, frequent testing, and high academic standards have promoted these views on the grounds that their proposals would undo pernicious features of progressivism. This raises an interesting question: How do the features of progressivism as described by present-day critics square with the thinking of John Dewey and others whose thinking forms the intellectual support for this perspective? To get some answers, do the following:

- Read some accounts in journals, newspapers, or web articles in which supporters of any present-day school reform initiative defend the proposed change, in part, on the grounds that it will respond effectively to some bad influences associated with progressivism. From how progressivism is described in these accounts, what are its chief features?

- Read some material by John Dewey and his followers or about them and their work. From your reading, what do you conclude about the chief features of progressivism?

Analysis

Specifically, how did the critics define "progressivism"? How did their descriptions vary from how John Dewey and other intellectual founders of the tradition defined the term?

Key Point

Zealous proponents of certain kinds of changes sometimes distort the characteristics of approaches favored by others.

Perennialism owes much to the work of Robert Hutchins (1936), Arthur Bestor (1955), and Mortimer Adler (1982). Perennialists believe that some kinds of knowledge have been authenticated over and over again through the centuries. This information is as valid today as it ever was. Today's students benefit when school programs immerse them in the study of these enduring verities. When they are exposed to this kind of school program, not only do students get a store of wisdom that will serve them well but they also learn how to exercise the kinds of reasoning powers that led good thinkers throughout history to arrive at these conclusions.

You will recognize a perennialist perspective when you hear a recommendation for organizing school programs around the study of the great literary works of civilization. You will also find perennialists to be highly vocal critics of vocational education. They see such programs as sellouts of the school's purpose to develop the intellect. Perennialists also have little use for programs espoused by essentialists, claiming that so-called essential knowledge does not last and that programs with this orientation end up teaching students outdated information.

Essentialists place heavy emphases on knowledge derived from the sciences and technology. Perennialists worry that many such findings have limited value and that school programs that place too much emphasis on these subjects may end up teaching students knowledge that quickly becomes outdated. It is much better, they assert, to teach truths that have lasted through time and that have been presented to the world by great thinkers over the centuries. This implies an emphasis on many sources of knowledge and on broad, explanatory concepts, as opposed to isolated "findings" with the potential to lose their validity over time.

George Counts (1932) popularized **reconstructionism** in the 1930s in his book *Dare the Schools Build a New Social Order?* Reconstructionists have views of society that contrast sharply with those of essentialists. You will recall that essentialists believe that present-day social, political, and economic arrangements are good and should be preserved. Reconstructionists, on the other hand, contend that they are not good at all, that they give unconscionable advantages to some groups as opposed to others, and that they should be replaced. Reconstructionists argue that schools and school curricula should be in the vanguard of fundamental social change. The objective is to create a more democratic, fair, and just society.

As you engage in curriculum work, you will recognize the perspectives of reconstructionists in proposals for programs that focus students' attention on pressing social problems, such as racism and poverty. The intent is to give students the ability to analyze these problems and to consider potential solutions. The long-term purpose is to produce citizens who will press for social change. The academic proposals of reconstructionists often draw heavily on content from the behavioral sciences.

Existentialism owes much to the thinking of French philosopher Jean-Paul Sartre. Existentialists hold that there are no principles or truths that apply to all people. The only objective reality is that all of us come into this world facing one key task: making sense out of our own life with the understanding that ultimately it will end in our death. Existentialists are wary of programs that seek to impose the perspectives of others on individual students. Freedom of personal choice ranks as a very high value. The function of education is to provide students with opportunities to create their own personal meanings (Morris, 1996).

When doing curriculum work, it sometimes is difficult to know whether a given proposal reflects an existential orientation. For example, you cannot assume that every idea that comes forward about individualizing instruction reflects the position of someone who identifies with existentialism. It is quite possible to individualize instruction in programs where others identify the ends of learning. The key for existentialists is not individualization but, rather, freedom of choice regarding what is studied. Given present public demands for accountability and the increased interest in testing, you probably will encounter only limited support for curriculum revisions in directions that existentialists favor.

For a graphic representation of the curricular emphases of various educational philosophies, see Figure 5.1.

Philosophy	Curricular Emphases
Progressivism	Content and experiences involve students in problem solving and reflection. There should be opportunities for students to learn in situations that do not isolate them from the world beyond the school. Content drawn from the social sciences often has relevance for programs associated with progressivism.
Essentialism	All students should be taught a common core of knowledge that they will need to function as productive, contributing adult members of society. Serious knowledge is particularly likely to be found in the sciences and technical fields. Content from the arts and humanities generally fails to prepare young people for adulthood and should be deemphasized. New instructional technologies that help make instruction more efficient should be incorporated into school programs.
Perennialism	School programs have put far too much emphasis on scientific experimentation and technology. As a result, there have been diminished emphases on the insights into quality living that are generations old and that are found in the humanities and the world's great literature. Content from these areas should be emphasized. Programs that focus on vocational and other subjects that are not clearly directed at developing the intellect should be abandoned.
Reconstructionism	Society has lost its way because narrow groups with selfish interests have imposed their values through the application of strong-armed power. As a result, the values of fairness, equity, and humanity have been compromised. School programs should prepare students to study these social inequities with a view to turning them into social reformers who will work for a more just society. Some content from the behavioral sciences is a useful resource for educators committed to this philosophical perspective.
Existentialism	Since the only important commonality that all people face is the inevitability of their own deaths, they should be as free as possible to make personal choices regarding what they should think and how they should live their lives. There should be no imposition of a common curriculum on all students. Ideally, students should be free to choose what they study, and they should have a strong voice in school governance.
Postmodernism	Postmodernists hold that knowledge is individually created and that people determine reality as they interact with others and with the perspectives of their culture. Because of the variety of people and conditions individual learners encounter in their lives, school programs should provide students with opportunities to learn about different peoples and cultures. To accomplish this purpose, there should not be too much reliance on science as a source of truth. Instead, students should have opportunities to encounter myths, legends, narratives, and other forms of information that bring them into contact with the perspectives of peoples and communities. Teachers should act democratically and should strive to engage students in open dialogue and inquiry.

FIGURE 5.1 Curricular Emphases Associated with Selected Philosophical Positions

Philosophical Ideas and Curriculum Development

An understanding of some positions associated with various philosophies can assist you when you engage in curriculum work in two distinct ways. First of all, a familiarity with these perspectives will help you appreciate the values of the individuals making proposals. An understanding of the priorities that underpin recommendations coming from individuals who hold varying philosophical positions will help you better grasp their concerns and will enable you to take them into account as your work goes forward.

Second, once new programs are proposed or adopted, often there are public reactions from individuals and groups. These reactions frequently reflect identifiable philosophical positions. When you understand the positions that lie behind individual comments, you are in a better position to respond to them in ways that will make sense to the people who have gone public with their reactions. For example, if a parent wonders whether an emphasis on "problem solving" may divert teachers' attention away from "basic information" that students might need to know on standardized tests, you should know that you are dealing with an essentialist perspective. You might want to respond by pointing out the features of the program that encourage teachers to emphasize basic content knowledge as well as those that develop students' thinking powers.

 ## LEARNING THEORY

An important category of curriculum decisions relates to organizing, sequencing, and introducing content to students in ways that facilitate their ability to learn it. You may find yourself asking questions such as the following as you consider how new or revised programs might best meet students' needs:

- Should complex content elements be broken down into their constituent parts, so that they can be taught one at a time?
- Should somewhat smaller "wholes" be carved out of the entire body of content and taught as complete entities?
- Should there be extensive personal diagnoses of each student to determine the particular kinds of learning approaches that are suitable, and should there be an accompanying preparation of multiple instructional approaches, which can be selected according to the identified needs of each class member?

Your answers to these questions can be better if a sound understanding of learning theory supports them. In the sections that follow, you will learn about two outdated learning theories that occasionally continue to influence curriculum decisions and about three categories of present-day theories.

Two Outdated Theories: Mental Discipline and Apperception

The theory of **mental discipline** traces back to the thought of German philosopher Christian Wolff, who did most of his work in the first half of the eighteenth century.

Wolff argued that the mind has distinct "faculties," which include feeling, perception, imagination, and will (Bigge, 1963). Wolff and his followers believed that teachers should strive to provide school experiences that strengthen each faculty.

Suppose you were committed to this perspective and that you wished to focus some attention on the faculty of "will." This characteristic is defined as a person's ability to see a decision through, even at the risk of unpleasant consequences. One instructional implication of a commitment to strengthen this faculty is a need to confront students with work that they find difficult, and perhaps even distasteful. This means that you need to put aside any present-day commitment you might have to the idea of motivating students by convincing them that what they are to learn is interesting and exciting. Instead, you want to impose requirements that you know they may not like. You do this not because you are a harsh, uncaring person but, rather, because you know, in the long run, they will become better people for having gone through the kinds of frustrating experiences you intend to provide.

Today, we hear relatively little support for this "frustration will make you strong" approach to providing learning experiences. However, as you engage in curriculum work, you may occasionally hear arguments in support of a particular subject on the grounds that "dealing with this difficult content" is good for students—an argument that puts more weight on the importance of the frustration than on the substance of the material to be learned.

Another learning theory that has greatly waned in influence is **apperception.** The theory originated with Johann Friedrich Herbart, a German philosopher who did his work in the first half of the nineteenth century (Bigge, 1963). Herbart saw the mind as a collection of ideas or mental states. Initially, the child's mind holds nothing. This void is filled as new ideas are introduced. Once these ideas have been taken in, they join to form an *apperceptive mass.* Subsequently, any new ideas that are taken in must be consistent with those already present in the apperceptive mass.

Herbartian apperception put great pressure on teachers to present young students with the "right" ideas. This step was critical for their subsequent learning. If incorrect information somehow got into the apperceptive mass, then students would reject teachers' attempts to teach them correct information at a later date because such content would appear to be inconsistent with what they already knew.

Two key logical flaws undermined the theory of apperception. First, its proponents never adequately explained how children acquire their initial understandings. If the acquisition of knowledge depends on its congruence with what they already understand, there must be a store of information that was in the mind before any kind of instruction began.

Second, the supporters of apperception placed great emphasis on students' being taught what is "right." They presumed a social condition in which there was broad agreement regarding what constitutes appropriate knowledge. As populations of students became more diverse and the values orientations of parents more varied, this assumption failed to mirror the reality. Teachers found that others did not necessarily share their individual visions of "right" and "proper."

Despite some of its logical inconsistencies, there are some abiding legacies of apperception. Perhaps most important of these relates to apperception's emphasis on diagnosing students' present levels of understanding. (This is a key task if the intent is to provide instruction that is consistent with what students already know.) This concern for "beginning instruction where students are" continues to be a high priority for educators.

In addition, supporters of apperception developed a lesson plan format with categories that are startlingly similar to those in use today. The plan included five steps (Meyer, 1975):

1. *Preparation:*   the teachers helps students recall previously learned information
2. *Presentation:*   the teacher introduces new material
3. *Comparison:*   the teacher relates new material to what the student has already learned
4. *Generalization:*   the teacher asks students to describe new content in their own words
5. *Application:*   the students apply new information

LEARNING EXTENSION 5–2

Comparing Lesson Plan Formats

Locate two or three lesson plan formats from your own school district, a curriculum or instruction text, a professional journal, a web article, or another source suggested by your instructor. Compare categories on your present-day formats with those developed by followers of Herbart. Then, respond to the following questions:

- Do you find many categories similar to those developed by the followers of Herbart?
- Which categories on today's lesson plans are different?
- How do you account for any differences? In particular, do you note any that may be based on learning theories that are more widely held today than apperception?

Behaviorist Theories

Behaviorism assumes that the world we perceive through our senses is real. Any whole is equal to the sum of its parts. The study of individual parts of wholes leads to the identification of patterns that are consistent from person to person. Individuals who subscribe to this position believe that relevant information about learning manifests itself in behavior that can be observed. Therefore, they define "learning" as a change in observable behavior.

Ivan Petrovich Pavlov was one of the most influential early-twentieth-century behaviorists. In his famous experiment, Pavlov began by providing food (an "unconditioned stimulus") to a dog. The dog, in turn, salivated (a natural, or "unconditioned, response"). Pavlov began ringing a bell at the same time the food was presented (a "conditioned stimulus"). In time, the dog began salivating when the bell was rung (a "conditioned response"), even in the absence of the food. Pavlov's work suggested ways to elicit existing behaviors through conditioning (the dog already possessed an ability to salivate) but said little about how brand new behaviors might be prompted. In the twentieth century, theorists including John B. Watson, Edward Thorndike, E. R. Guthrie, Clark Hull, K. W. Spence, and B. F. Skinner addressed this problem. In recent years, applications of the work of B. F. Skinner have been particularly influential among curriculum specialists with a behaviorist orientation.

LEARNING EXTENSION 5–3

Comparing Views of Selected Theorists

Select two of the following theorists:

- John B. Watson
- Edward Thorndike
- E. R. Guthrie
- Clark Hull
- K. W. Spence

Do some research to identify how each of the two theorists you selected views learning. Then, describe how each might recommend that a lesson should be organized and sequenced to maximize student learning.

Skinner and his followers argued that the kinds of responses Pavlov studied account for only a tiny fraction of human behavior. The initial cause of Pavlov's dog's salivation was known: the presence of food. Unlike this situation, most human behaviors have causes that cannot be so easily identified. If we don't know what causes a given behavior, we cannot ring a bell or do something else to condition the desired behavior when we observe an instance of the "cause." What we need to do is to stop worrying about causes and to think about ways of increasing the frequency of behaviors we like. Skinner said the way to do this was to manipulate **reinforcers.** This scheme requires the focus behavior to be observable. When we see it, we are in a position to determine whether it is appropriate and, if it is, to provide reinforcement that will increase its tendency to recur in the future. A full discussion of kinds of reinforcements, reinforcement schedules, and other characteristics of Skinner's scheme is beyond the scope of this discussion. Suffice to say that some of the following implications for instructional planning flow logically from Skinner's work:

- Because reinforcement focuses on observable behavior, it is desirable for students to be active rather than passive.

- Skills are hierarchical and need to be taught from simplest to most complex.
- Desired levels of performance should be identified in advance and communicated to students.
- Reinforcement of appropriate responses is important.
- Complex content should be divided, and its parts should be presented to students as they strive for mastery.
- Practice in a variety of situations enables students to apply their learning to new situations.

Cognitive Theories

Theories associated with *cognition* share a conviction that reality is not restricted to what comes to us unaltered through the senses. Instead, reality consists of what we make of what we encounter in the world. There is an internal mental transformation of sensory inputs that takes place as we strive to ascribe meaning to new experiences. In other words, reality does not exist in some abstract form independent of our own thought processes. Learning, given this perspective, is not viewed as a change in behavior. Rather, it is defined as a change in insight.

Cognitive theory suggests that we use sets of internal thought structures, called **schema,** as we compare new knowledge with what we already understand. These schema may be extended or changed over time to accommodate novel information. Information is easier understood if it is meaningful. This kind of information comes in the form of wholes—that is, in the forms we actually encounter in the world—rather than in the form of individual parts that have been artificially separated from something larger and more complete. There are numerous theorists associated with this general orientation. Among the prominent thinkers associated with this perspective are Max Wertheimer, Wolfgang Kohler, Kurt Koffka, Kurt Lewin, Jean Piaget, Lev Vygotsky, David Ausubel, and Jerome Bruner.

LEARNING EXTENSION 5–4

Vygotsky and Piaget

The developmental stages espoused by Jean Piaget generally are more widely known than those of Lev Vygotsky. Do some reading to learn about Vygotsky's developmental perspectives. Many articles related to his work are available on the web. Your instructor may suggest other sources for you to consult. When you have completed your reading, answer the following questions:

- What are the similarities and differences in the work of Piaget and Vygotsky?
- Suppose you were charged with planning curricula for (1) children in the early elementary grades and (2) students in one or more of the middle-school grades. What differences would there be between your two proposals if you were to base your work on Vygotsky's ideas?

Max Wertheimer suggested that educators keep some basic principles in mind when they organize materials for students to learn. His "law of similarity" holds that it is easier for students to learn the defining features of groups when group members share many, rather than few, common characteristics. His "law of closure" points out that students dislike something that is incomplete or ambiguous and will use mental processes to arrive at some kind of conclusion to avoid mental discomfort (Wertheimer, 1959).

Jean Piaget is an example of a developmental cognitive theorist. He argued that individuals pass through a series of stages en route to adulthood. The kinds of thought processes they use to make sense of what they encounter vary, depending on their developmental stage. For more details about Piaget's stages, you may wish to review the material in Chapter 3, "Society, Learner Characteristics, and Academic Content as Curriculum Influencers." Lev Vygotsky is another developmental theorist. He suggested that what students can learn faces limits associated with their stages of development and that the ability to expand their cognitive capacities depends on social interaction with others.

David Ausubel (1963) suggests that learning take place as students identify large categories, which become repositories for new information. Initially, a category might be quite broad. For example, with very young students, it might be "dog." As they learn more about dogs, through a process Ausubel labeled **progressive differentiation,** they develop a series of subordinate categories, which hold more detailed information (perhaps categories such as "spaniel" and "terrier"). Ausubel suggested that a complementary process works when people begin to forget certain details. Over time, through a process he called **obliterative subsumption,** narrow categories of information are reorganized into larger, more general ones. From Ausubel's work comes the recommendation that teachers provide students with **advance organizers** (labels that help students organize new content and, thus, facilitate its easy retrieval).

The following are some general principles that flow from the work of cognitive theorists:

- Problems should be presented as wholes, so that students can have simultaneous access to all information that is relevant to their solution.

- Organization should proceed from simple wholes to more complex wholes, not from simple parts to complex parts.

- Opportunities to engage each student's thinking—for example, in classroom discussions—should be encouraged in the effort to help students make reasoned interpretations of reality.

- Students bring unique personal perspectives to their learning tasks.

- Students always impose their own meanings as they confront new content and new situations.

Multiple-Dimension Theories

Multiple-dimension theories proceed from the assumption that individual intelligence is not a unitary factor. Rather, our ability to learn and our interests result from numerous mental abilities. Each of these abilities varies somewhat in its importance from person to person. Hence, it is unlikely that a single instructional approach will be equally effective with all students in a given classroom.

In the middle of the twentieth century, J. P. Guilford developed a three-dimensional **structure-of-the-intellect model** (Guilford, 1967). Guilford developed three major divisions of the intellect (contents, products, and operations) and identified a number of categories under each. His model predicted the existence of 150 components of intelligence. Guilford spent much of his career developing tests to identify proficiency levels associated with these major components.

Robert Sternberg and Howard Gardner are scholars who have done more recent multiple-dimension work. Sternberg (1977, 1990) formulated a **triarchic theory of intelligence.** He identified three major categories of intelligence: componential, experiential, and contextual. **Componential intelligence** includes our abilities to distinguish between relevant and irrelevant information, to engage in abstract thought, and to make decisions leading to action. **Experiential intelligence** describes our capacity for responding to new experiences by generating new ideas and combining separate pieces of information to solve problems. It also refers to our ability to convert a new approach to solving a problem into a pattern that, subsequently, we follow automatically. **Contextual intelligence** is our general ability to make adaptations in light of new experiences and to consider carefully the contexts within which our decisions are made.

Howard Gardner (1999) suggests the existence of at least nine kinds of mental abilities:

- Logical-mathematical
- Linguistic
- Musical
- Spatial
- Bodily-kinesthetic
- Interpersonal
- Intrapersonal
- Existential
- Naturalist

LEARNING EXTENSION 5–5

Programs Keyed to Varying Mental Abilities

Suppose you had a reliable way to identify students with (1) high levels of logical-mathematical intelligence and (2) high levels of spatial intelligence. What would be some characteristics of the two instructional programs you might develop to take advantage of the particular kinds of high intelligence reflected in each group? To get a better understanding of each of these intelligence types, you may wish to read some of Howard Gardner's writings on multiple intelligences.

Respond to these questions:

- What would be some specific characteristics of the program you would devise for the group high in logical/mathematical intelligence?
- What would be some specific characteristics of the program you would devise for the group high in spatial intelligence?
- Which of these programs would be more difficult for you to design, and why?

Individuals are thought to have varying proportions of each of these intelligences. It is quite possible for a person to have an extremely high intelligence in one of these categories while having a moderate or even a low intelligence in one of the others.

Multiple-dimension theories challenge curriculum developers to use fine-grained analyses of students before planning instructional programs. For example, proponents of this view would challenge the wisdom of your planning a single music curriculum for all gifted and talented middle-school students. They would argue that there is no such thing as general gifted-and-talentedness. Some middle-school students are capable of doing gifted and talented work in music, but not in mathematics. Others are capable of doing gifted and talented work in mathematics, but not in music. Few, if any, are gifted and talented across all curricular areas. Hence, careful diagnoses of individual student characteristics—particularly in terms of their intelligence in different categories—must precede any attempt to develop instructional programs that are well fitted to their needs.

Learning Theory and Curriculum Development

Individual learning theories provide hints about how curricula can be designed to suit students' learning needs. However, you will be disappointed if you delve into the learning theory literature expecting to find definitive answers that will free you from making important judgments. Recommendations for instructional practice that derive from learning theory raise as many questions as they answer. For example, look at the following two principles, one found in many behaviorist theories and one found in many cognitive theories:

- Complex subject matter should be divided into simple parts; these parts should be taught to students in a simple-to-complex fashion. (behaviorist position)
- The best way to teach a complex whole is to begin by teaching somewhat smaller wholes; however, there should be no atomization of content down to small, meaningless parts. (cognitivist position)

Let's look first at the behaviorist position. Into exactly how many parts should a complex whole be divided? Where does the process end? Can too much simplification make it more difficult for students to learn? Consider, for example, what might happen were you to list every step involved in tying a shoelace. You could end up with a long, long list, one that might convince a learner that the task was simply not "learnable."

A similar set of concerns can be generated for the cognitivist position. Exactly what are the dimensions of the lesser wholes that are to be taught to students as they seek to understand the larger one? How many of these should there be? Is there a danger that the selected lesser wholes will be too complex?

To be fair, neither behaviorist nor cognitive theorists expect their recommendations to be anything other than general guidelines. It is clear that the quality of decisions about the breakdown of content, the sequencing of content, and content delivery depends on information from people who know the students to be served, the nature of the community, the culture of the schools, the background of the teachers, and other key pieces of contextual information. For this reason, you do not want to see learning theory as a substitute for curriculum workers' decision-making responsibilities. Rather, think of it as a body of knowledge that may prove useful as you and others who are knowledgeable about your local context think and decide about how best to serve your students' needs.

SOCIOLOGY OF EDUCATION

Sociologists study groups, their values, and their priorities. What is the importance of their work for you and others who are involved in curriculum work? As a starting point, consider all the things you have come to understand in your life. How much of your knowledge came to you as a result of first-hand experience? If you are like most of us, your answer will be "very little." What we "know" in large measure comes to us as a result of interactions with other people—our parents, our friends, our professional organizations, our social groups, our associates in the workplace, and our religious affiliations. The perspectives we adopt as a result of these relationships lead to conceptions of reality that reflect many of the values of the members of these groups. Although our conceptions of right and wrong and appropriate and inappropriate seem perfectly natural and logical to us, they are, in fact, largely human creations shaped by the values of the groups we belong to and respect.

Students come from highly diverse cultural and linguistic backgrounds. Their group associations may have given them assumptions about how the world operates and what acceptable behavior is that are at odds with what you and many other professional educators believe. As a result, some of these young people have a difficult time adjusting to schools, and many of them may be labeled "problem" students. Many years ago, professional educators gave scant heed to disjunctions between the values of students from certain minority groups and those espoused by the school. When these differences were acknowledged at all, it was assumed that these young people had "character faults," which the school should strive to overcome. For example, in the late nineteenth century, schools were thought to be a last hope for the children of Native American parents, who, in the view of mainstream educators, were all too willing to let their children "run wild" (Coleman, 1993).

Even today, sometimes proposals to "make schools better" presume that differences among student groups are relatively unimportant. Consider the common suggestion that more parent involvement in classrooms is desirable. This proposal, motivated by excellent intentions, overlooks differences in such things as the ages of students in different grades, the interests of individual teachers in having parents in the classroom, and the abilities of truly representative groups of parents to defer other responsibilities (employment and so forth) to spend time working in school classrooms. One study (Crozier, 1999) of the parent involvement issue revealed, for example, that secondary students are less than eager to have their parents present in their classrooms and that teachers at this level are hard-pressed to know what kind of substantive contributions parents might make. Elementary students, on the other hand, welcome parental presence, and teachers at this level have little difficulty putting parents to work, helping youngsters with academic tasks.

Differences within schools and, at a more general level, differences in how groups see the world comprise the area of study for educational sociologists. They study ways in which individuals from different groups perceive the various roles schools play. They seek answers to such questions as

- What interests do schools serve?
- What groups are advantaged and disadvantaged by existing school practices and proposals for change?

Responsibilities of Schools

Educational sociologists point out that our society expects schools to discharge several important responsibilities. Because of place to place differences, the relative emphases given to each responsibility varies from school to school. These responsibilities include the following:

- Disseminating knowledge
- Passing on the common culture
- Promoting social mobility
- Preparing students for the world of work
- Teaching students appropriate social and group skills
- Encouraging social change

Disseminating knowledge is a classic responsibility of schools. Indeed, the need for schools as institutions developed when the complexity of knowledge needed by young people exceeded what their parents could pass on to them. What debate there is surrounding this function does not focus on the appropriateness of passing on knowledge to the young. Rather, it centers on the question "What knowledge should schools teach?"

LEARNING EXTENSION 5–6

Roles and Public Concerns About the Schools

For a period of about one month, look at letters to the editor that focus on issues related to public schools. Look either in a local newspaper or in another source that your instructor might recommend. Indicate the specific school roles that are referenced in each letter. (Use the six school roles listed in the text.) A single letter may address topics related to several of these. Using information you have gathered as evidence to support your conclusions, respond to the following questions:

• Which school roles seem to involve schools in practices that generate the highest amounts of public comment and concerns?

• Which roles seem to have been seldom, if ever, mentioned in the letters you read?

• How do you account for apparent differences in attention to the six roles as reflected in these letters?

You will recall from Chapter 1 that the curriculum acts as a filter that makes it easy to incorporate some kinds of information into school programs and difficult to include others. The example cited in Chapter 1 focuses on the traditional east-to-west framework for organizing U.S. history courses, an arrangement that makes it somewhat difficult to talk about historical changes that moved into the present area of the United States from the Latino regions south of our present borders. The power of curriculum frameworks to emphasize some kinds of knowledge and to deemphasize others sometimes sparks attacks from groups who believe that information they are especially interested in is systematically barred from school programs.

The role schools play in *passing on the common culture* often is a target for critics' negative comments. At what point does the school's obligation to teach some shared values begin to run counter to the values that some parents and some groups want young people to acquire? Seeking an appropriate balance point constantly challenges curriculum workers. Parents and other groups are particularly apt to object to school programs that seem to encourage certain kinds of personal behavior. For example, school programs dealing with birth control are among those likely to be criticized. On the other hand, instruction designed to promote such behaviors as regular voting and responsible work habits are less frequent targets of critics' concern.

Promoting social mobility is a school role that supporters see as especially consistent with the American view that individuals' achievements in life should be based on their own competence, not on the economic or social standing of their families. Seen in this light, the school functions as a meritocracy that allows academic talent to rise to the top. Even young people from the humblest backgrounds have the potential to acquire the knowledge, skills, and predispositions needed to become leaders in their chosen fields.

The promoting-social-mobility issue occasionally prompts critics to ask whether promoting social mobility is truly an operating reality of the curriculum or whether it is just a politically correct phrase with no basis in observed fact. For example, instructional programs that appear to track some students into less challenging courses (especially when students who are advised to take them come from disadvantaged groups) may be challenged as contradictions to the social mobility obligations of the school.

Since the standard of living of every society depends on a supply of qualified workers, *preparing students for the world of work* has long been regarded as an important role for the schools. High schools, in particular, have had a kind of sorting function for future employers. Various elective course patterns prepare students with different kinds and levels of expertise. Graduates logically flow toward either further education or employment opportunities that are consistent with their levels of preparation.

School leaders encounter frequent criticisms as they attempt to prepare students for the world of work. First of all, there sometimes are allegations that students from less empowered groups are deliberately steered toward academic programs designed to produce workers for less-skilled, lower-status occupations. Second, there are concerns that the demands of the workplace change faster than school curricula. Hence, school programs that are designed to produce students for particular vocational roles may be providing them with outdated information. Finally, some critics argue that an emphasis on preparing students for the world of work diverts their attention from mastering significant academic content and learning problem-solving skills that will be of lasting benefit throughout their lives, regardless of the changing nature of the workplace.

Throughout their adult lives, today's students will find themselves working with others at work, in various organizations, and at home. Hence, one of the obligations of the school involves *teaching students appropriate social and group skills.* This role is discharged within both the formal curriculum and the informal curriculum. In school classes, lessons designed to teach students discussion and listening skills, respectful consideration for the opinions of others, and procedures for working on problems in groups help develop these skills. Informally, the many school organizations and clubs help students gain expertise and confidence in their abilities to work with others. The challenge for educators is not so much one of providing opportunities for students to develop appropriate social and group skills as it is of making certain that *all* students have opportunities to profit from these experiences.

The importance ascribed to the role of schools in *encouraging social change* varies, depending on how widespread public concern is about social problems (Goslin, 1990). For better or worse, expectations that schools have astonishing social "curing powers" are widespread. Over the past 10 years, for example, there have been proposals for schools to do something about such intractable problems as drug trafficking, illegitimate births, and alcoholism. Since the school is part of the society where these problems flourish, it is doubtful that education programs alone can solve them. However, there are demonstrated benefits for students in being exposed to important social issues. There is evidence that school programs that focus on problems that tie legitimately to life as it is lived outside the school increase students' self-confidence (Boston, 1998/1999). These programs may also help learners see a more legitimate connection between their work at school and the real world (Armstrong, Henson, & Savage, 2001).

For curriculum specialists, there is a particular challenge associated with many proposals for programs designed to respond to serious social problems. Frequently, supporters, recognizing the difficulty of establishing entirely new courses, suggest that new content be embedded within existing courses. Rarely is there an appreciation that a fixed amount of instructional time is available to teach any subject at any grade level. This means that infusing new content must be accompanied by reducing the time spent on existing topics. What is this content that is to be displaced? Who decides? The proponents of infusion rarely address these questions. Instead, problems associated with infusion land in the laps of curriculum specialists and teachers, prompt sometimes acrimonious debate, and cause great anguish to administrators who are caught between public pressure to do something about the problem and faculty and staff members who do not want to debase the existing curriculum.

Traditional Functionalist View

The term **functionalism** is applied to a traditional perspective within the discipline of sociology. Functionalists point out that, although there are many groups in society, a shared set of values exists. These shared values have led to the development of lasting institutions, such as public schools, which maintain society in its present form. These institutions play important roles as they work to maintain a harmonious and just social order, which deserves to be passed on, intact, to subsequent generations.

Talcott Parsons (1959), a strong supporter of this view, saw the school as the institution with the important responsibility of providing our society with skilled workers. He saw the school providing equal opportunities for all learners. The most talented and hardest working would learn the most. Accordingly, they would get the best jobs. The operating assumptions are that (1) individual academic merit is the criterion used to distribute economic awards and (2) schools give all students equal opportunities to earn economic awards (Dougherty & Hammack, 1990).

Because schools are seen as providing the brain power needed to fuel economic growth, functionalism provides a popular rationale for spending public money to support education. Good schools produce good workers. Good workers, in turn, increase national productivity. As a result, the average standard of living rises, and everyone benefits.

Traditional functionalists argue that school programs have the potential to serve all learners well. Critics argue that the proponents of this view fail to recognize important differences in the backgrounds of students. They suggest that a careful examination of the realities of public schooling does not support the idea that all students are benefiting from existing programs. Whereas functionalists emphasize the values they see as shared by everyone in our society, critics tend to emphasize the differences in the values among various groups. They suggest that conflict, rather than consensus, more adequately describes how Americans see public education.

Conflict Views of Schooling

Supporters of **conflict views of schooling** see "society as a battleground where competing groups strive for supremacy. In their view, schools are places where competing interest groups compete for educational advantages" (Armstrong, Henson, & Savage, 2001, p. 284). Issues that result in conflicts vary. Sometimes they are related to economics. (Are school programs diverting funds to support programs that will help a small number of children from upper-class families get into expensive colleges and universities?) Sometimes they relate to race. (Why is a much higher percentage of African-American students enrolled in special education classes than White students?) Sometimes they are related to social class. (Are students from lower-class families being advised to pursue high-school courses that fail to prepare them for college and university entrance?) Sometimes they relate to still other issues.

Conflict theorists argue that claims that schools are democratic, fair, and sensitive to individual differences are, at best, cosmetic public relations gestures. They mask practices that are too often undemocratic, unfair, and indifferent to the characteristics of individual students. Critics such as Henry Giroux (1984), Peter McLaren (1997), and Michael Apple (1998) suggest that various power groups impose their will on schools to the disadvantage of students and families who are (1) economically impoverished, (2) members of cultural, ethnic, or linguistic minorities, or (3) members of other less-empowered groups. Proposals related to issues such as school choice, more rigorous graduation standards, and increased achievement testing promote the interests of powerful groups and, more specifically, the young people in schools who come from these groups. Individuals who worry about this situation want proposals for school change and improvement to be scrutinized carefully to assure that efforts to make things better are not making things worse for some groups of students.

LEARNING EXTENSION 5–7

Functionalism, Conflict Theory, and A Nation at Risk

The 1983 report titled *A Nation at Risk: The Imperative for Educational Reform* is widely credited with stimulating unprecedented levels of public interest in improving schools. This interest has continued unabated for two decades. Locate a copy of this report or read summaries of its recommendations. Information is readily available on the web.

Your instructor may be able to suggest other places you can go to find this material. Review the report's recommendations with a view to finding answers to the following questions:

- What recommendations are most consistent with a functionalist view of society?
- What recommendations are most consistent with a conflict view of society?
- If you find recommendations leaning much more strongly in one of these directions, how do you account for this situation?

Sociological Perspectives and the Curriculum

Are there common values that all of us should prize that should take precedence over less widely held values? If so, which are they, and how should school programs respond to them? These thorny questions will challenge you as you engage in curriculum work. Proposals for curriculum revision often mask these issues. For example, arguments in support of a curriculum change often are couched in arguments that make it appear to be eminently fair, democratic, and responsive to individual student needs. As always, the devil is in the details. What will be the actual impact of the change? Who will be the beneficiaries? Will there be categories of students who cannot benefit? Will funds to support the new program be diverted from existing ones? Which students are being served by the programs to be displaced? Only by seeking answers to these and similar questions can you know whether any reality underlies the promotional rhetoric used in arguments to support a curriculum change.

Perspectives from educational sociology help you look beyond the general impact of proposed changes to consider how students from different groups will be affected. This kind of fine-grained analysis can help you make decisions that support the development and implementation of instructional programs that meet the ideal of serving *all* students.

CURRICULUM REALITIES 5–1

Consensus Is an Aspiration, Not an Expectation

Few dispute the laudable intent to serve each student's needs or to provide outstanding programs for every learner. The difficulty comes not in the thought but in the execution. Attempts to put programs in place to meet these high expectations require selecting, prioritizing, organizing, and delivering content. They demand the implementation of assessment procedures of various kinds. In a diverse society, what constitutes good or worthy approaches to accomplishing each of these needed actions generates at least as much debate as consensus. To see how quickly these differences in perspectives appear, ask a random group of 6 to 10 adults the following questions:

- Should schools require all students to take the same subjects, or should there be lots of student choices?
- What is the best way to teach children to read?
- Is it more important to teach students about problems and flaws facing our society, or is it more important to teach them citizenship skills that will allow future generations to enjoy the same benefits we have today?
- Should students be prepared for specific kinds of jobs during their years in school?
- Will attempts to teach students to think critically at school prepare them for life, or will they simply encourage students to challenge everything their parents or guardians say?
- If you went into a "good" school, what would you expect to see?

You may wish to add other questions of your own to this list.

Unless the group of individuals you select is comprised of people with unusually similar backgrounds and perspectives, you are likely to get highly varied responses to these questions. What all this means for you as a curriculum worker is that your objective should be to get strong *working majorities* in support of your decisions. There is little probability of your getting an absolute consensus in support of almost any decision.

Review and Reflection

1. What are the characteristics of idealism, realism, and pragmatism?
2. What is postmodernism, and to what extent do you think this perspective is reflected in practices in today's schools?
3. How would you compare and contrast the positions of individuals subscribing to essentialism, progressivism, perennialism, and reconstructionism? Which of these four educational applications of philosophy are most alike? most different? Which is most compatible with your own position, and why?
4. What are some legacies of both mental discipline and apperception?
5. How do you distinguish among behaviorist learning theories, cognitive learning theories, and multiple-dimension learning theories?
6. Why is it not practical for curriculum workers to simply use the findings of learning theorists as they make recommendations for selecting, organizing, sequencing, and delivering content to students?
7. How do functionalists see society, and what implications do their views have for planning school curricula?
8. How do conflict theorists see society, and how might their views of "good" school programming differ from those of functionalists?

References

Adler, M. (1982). *The paideia proposal.* New York: Macmillan.

Apple, M. W. (1998). Education and new hegemonic blocs: Doing policy the "right" way. *International Studies in Sociology of Education, 8*(2), 181–202.

Armstrong, D. G., Henson, K. T., & Savage, T. V. (2001). *Teaching today: An introduction to education* (6th ed.). Upper Saddle River, NJ: Merrill/Prentice Hall.

Ausubel, D. (1963). *The psychology of meaningful verbal learning.* New York: Grune and Stratton.

Bagley, W. (1941). The case for essentialism in education. *National Education Association Journal, 30*(7), 202–220.

Beck, C. (1993). *Postmodernism, pedagogy, and philosophy of education.* Champaign, IL: University of Chicago at Urbana-Champaign, Philosophy of Education Society.

Bestor, A. (1955). *The restoration of learning.* New York: Knopf.

Bigge, M. (1963). *Learning theory for teachers.* New York: Harper & Row.

Boston, B. O. (1998/1999). If the water is nasty, fix it. *Educational Technology, 56*(4), 66–69.

Coleman, M. (1993). *American Indian children at school, 1850–1890.* Jackson: University of Mississippi Press.

Counts, G. (1932). *Dare the schools build a new social order?* New York: John Day.

Crozier, G. (1999). Parent involvement: Who wants it? *International Studies in Sociology of Education, 9*(3), 219–238.

Dewey, J. (1902). *The child and the curriculum.* Chicago: University of Chicago Press.

Dewey, J. (1910). *How we think.* Boston: D. C. Heath.

Dewey, J. (1916). *Democracy and education.* New York: Macmillan.

Dewey, J. (1938). *Experience and education.* New York: Macmillan.

Dougherty, K. J., & Hammack, F. M. (1990). *Education and society: A reader.* San Diego: Harcourt Brace Jovanovich.

Gardner, H. (1999). *Intelligence reframed: Multiple intelligences for the 21st century.* New York: Basic Books.

Giroux, H. (1984). *Ideology, culture, and the process of schooling.* Philadelphia: Temple University Press.

Goslin, D. A. (1990). The functions of the school in modern society. In K. J. Dougherty & F. M. Hammack (Eds.), *Education and society: A reader* (pp. 29–38). San Diego: Harcourt Brace Jovanovich.

Guilford, J. P. (1967). *The nature of human intelligence.* New York: McGraw-Hill.

Hutchins, R. (1936). *The higher learning in America.* New Haven, CT: Yale University Press.

Jacobsen, D. A. (1999). *Philosophy in classroom teaching: Bridging the gap.* Upper Saddle River, NJ: Merrill/Prentice Hall.

McLaren, P. (1997). *Life in schools: An introduction to critical pedagogy in the foundation of education.* New York: Longman.

Meyer, A. E. (1975). *Grandmasters of educational thought.* New York: McGraw-Hill.

Morris, V. (1996). *Existentialism in education.* New York: Harper & Row.

National Commission on Excellence in Education. (1983). *A nation at risk: The imperative for educational reform.* Washington, DC: U.S. Department of Education.

Parsons, T. (1959). School class as a social system: Some of its functions in American society. *Harvard Educational Review, 49,* 297–318.

Sternberg, R. J. (1977). *Intelligence, information processing, and analogical reasoning.* Hillsdale, NJ: Lawrence Erlbaum Associates.

Sternberg, R. J. (1990). *Metaphors of mind: Conceptions of the nature of intelligence.* New York: Cambridge University Press.

Wertheimer, M. (1959). *Productive thinking.* New York: HarperCollins.

6

People and Roles in Curriculum Work

Graphic Organizer

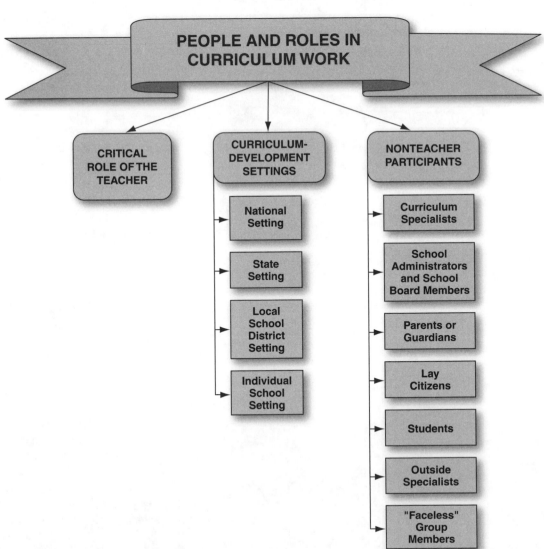

PEOPLE AND ROLES IN CURRICULUM WORK

CRITICAL ROLE OF THE TEACHER

CURRICULUM-DEVELOPMENT SETTINGS

- National Setting
- State Setting
- Local School District Setting
- Individual School Setting

NONTEACHER PARTICIPANTS

- Curriculum Specialists
- School Administrators and School Board Members
- Parents or Guardians
- Lay Citizens
- Students
- Outside Specialists
- "Faceless" Group Members

INTRODUCTION

A curriculum war raged recently in North Carolina. Though it took place in an East Coast state, it could have occurred anywhere. At issue was a proposal to change a long-standing pattern of requiring students to study state history in both the fourth and eighth grades. A committee of educators and citizens, led by a consultant from the State Department of Public Instruction, recommended cutting back state history study to a one-year course in the fourth grade and creating a new world cultures course for grade 8. This idea prompted immediate, and often strongly worded, reactions.

Proponents made several key arguments. First, they pointed out that the committee making the recommendation had acted in a consultative manner. For example, the committee surveyed a broad cross section of school administrators, teachers, parents, students, and representatives of professional organizations. Most of the individuals surveyed questioned the wisdom of having students spend two years studying North Carolina history when there is so much else to learn (Hui, 2001). They also cited the changing nature of the state's economy. Many corporations with headquarters in foreign countries now operate in North Carolina. The international outreach of economic activity suggests that the state has gone global. Many of the state's business leaders want students to learn about the larger world. Many of these young people, as adults, will work for firms with an international reach, and many of them will spend at least a part of their working lives outside of the United States.

Champions of change often have difficulty overcoming the strong hand of tradition. The opponents of the North Carolina proposal proved to be numerous, and they moved quickly, loudly, and stridently to make their views known. Many of them called attention to maturity differences between fourth- and eighth-grade students, noting that state history taught in the fourth grade, alone, could never involve students in the kind of thinking about significant issues facing the state as was possible in the existing grade 8 version of the course. Others pointed out that the eighth-grade course provided an entrée for teaching students about broader cultures. For example, the study of the "Lost Colony" on Roanoke Island might lead logically to a study of Elizabethan times and sixteenth-century European colonialism (Martin, 2001).

Other critics of the proposal pointed to the disastrous consequences of decisions in the 1970s and 1980s that briefly eliminated the required grade 8 state history course. Surveys of students taken during this period revealed astonishing ignorance about subjects that educated citizens of the state should clearly understand. For example, some students described Sir Walter Raleigh as a "prominent North Carolina tobacco farmer" and identified the "Apaches" and the "Navajos" as important North Carolina Native American tribes (Holland, 2001). Additional opposition came from many middle-school teachers and parents who, among other things, argued that state history was the first history course students take that has the potential to get them truly interested in this kind of academic content. There is an immediacy to the subject area that functions as an excellent motivator.

The State Board of Education, in the end, had to decide whether to adopt the committee's recommendation. As the date approached for the State Board to take up this issue, more and more people weighed in with their opinions. Even legislators got into the act. Two of them, one senator and one representative, filed a bill that would require North Carolina schools to continue teaching state history in both the fourth and eighth grades.

This contentious drama highlights some realities that characterize the curriculum-change process. It also tells us something about the categories of people who often become involved when curriculum change is contemplated. Some points worth taking away from a review of the North Carolina debate include the following:

- Forces aligned in support of the status quo put tremendous pressures on curriculum developers to avoid radical changes; modifications to existing patterns are an easier "sell" than are recommendations that alter the basic character of present offerings.
- Curriculum change occurs at many levels.
- Teachers are key players in curriculum-change efforts.
- The teachers whose professional lives will be most directly affected by a proposed change may have different feelings about it than teachers whose daily work it will touch less directly.

CRITICAL ROLE OF THE TEACHER

As indicated in the brief discussion of the debate in North Carolina, many people play a role in curriculum-change decisions. That of the teacher is the most important. Think back on the categories of people noted in the state history discussion. They include (1) state department of education professionals, (2) State Board of Education members, (3) state legislators, (4) professional organization representatives, (5) parents, (6) school administrators, (7) teachers, (8) students, and (9) lay citizens. Which of these groups will find the kind of work they do each day most affected by any curriculum change? In a general sense, the answer is teachers—more specifically, those who teach in the modified course or at the grade level at which the changed program will be installed.

If you are a teacher, your importance to the curriculum-development process relates to more than an obligation to implement adopted decisions. Your role is even more critical because of what you do to interpret the adopted curriculum, to modify it so it makes sense given the needs of your students, and in other ways to fit the program to the particular demands of your own setting. Researchers have found that many teachers fail to appreciate their role as an interpreter of the adopted curriculum. Though you and your colleagues may feel you are simply implementing a curriculum that may have largely been developed by others, in fact, you make many adaptations as you work with it each day (Ben-Peretz, 1990). This is true even if you teach where state or local curriculum guidelines appear to be quite prescriptive. These kinds of guidelines, though placing some limits on your options, still allow for lots of teacher interpretation. In summary, what the curriculum provides is a referent you use as you consider potential modifications to serve the needs of your own learners (Shulman, 1990).

This view of the curriculum and of teachers' roles rejects the idea that teaching is primarily a technical act. It sees what you do in the classroom as a kind of interactive dialogue, which leads to actions based on your perceptions of curricular intent, your expectations of parents and guardians and the local community, and your views of your students' needs (Henderson, 1992). If you see teaching in this way, then you have a vested professional interest in curricula that have sufficient substance, character, and relevance to function as beginning points for your own thinking. Curricula that are developed without the participation of thoughtful teachers often lack essential *gravitas*. They fail to serve as idea-rich prompts, which you and your colleagues can use to fit the curriculum to the needs of your settings and students.

LEARNING EXTENSION 6–1

Teachers' Actions to Modify the Curriculum

Teachers play active roles in modifying and interpreting adopted curricula. Their mediating function helps fit their instructional program to students' needs and to the special environmental conditions of their schools and local communities. What are some examples of specific modifications teachers make?

To respond to this question, identify a course or subject area that interests you. Identify two or more teachers who teach the same adopted program in several schools. Ask each to describe some specific modifications, adaptations, or alterations he or she has made to the official program. Seek answers to the following:

- Are most changes the results of a need to respond to the special characteristics of this teacher's students?

- To what extent have the wishes of administrators or other teachers in the building influenced the teacher's decision to make program modifications?

- Have the concerns of parents or others in the local community played a role in the teacher's decision to alter the official program?

- Does the teacher have any personal training or background that influenced his or her decision to make changes?

As important as your participation in curriculum development is, you cannot do this work alone. You need to act in concert with others who bring special perspectives to bear. Some of these individuals will bring with them an expertise in academic subject areas. Others will be able to offer helpful comments about implementation issues that go beyond the individual classroom. Some may have special insights into the availability of needed instructional support materials. Additional individuals may have skills in selling adopted decisions to the community at large. Still others may have backgrounds in other areas that can move curriculum work ahead in productive ways.

One of your key tasks in a curriculum-development group will be to remind those involved that this kind of work does not aim to develop one-size-fits-all prescriptions. The variety of teaching sites, students, community expectations, parent and guardian priorities, and available support resources militate against that proposition. Curriculum work is directed at developing plans that define an arena of concern that can prompt teachers to make stimulating, interesting, and appropriate adaptations to their own settings. Said in another way, high-quality curriculum thought by the development group should prompt further high-quality curriculum thought on the part of the people who will implement the described programs.

 ## CURRICULUM-DEVELOPMENT SETTINGS

In considering the roles various people play in curriculum development, you need to recognize that this work goes forward in at least four distinct settings:

- national
- state
- local school district
- individual school

Decisions made in one setting often impose certain obligations on educational professionals working in others and limit some of their options. For example, if you are a classroom teacher who teaches in a state that has mandatory state-level curriculum standards, you are not free to ignore these guidelines (Oliva, 1997). On the other hand, you and your colleagues enjoy considerable discretionary power in determining how programs might be organized and delivered in local school districts, particular schools, and individual classrooms.

National Setting

If you attend only to speeches made by candidates for federal office, you may be forgiven for concluding that the federal government plays a major role in paying for and operating the nation's public schools. In fact, in recent years federal dollars dedicated to supporting education have accounted for only around 7 percent of the total (Snyder, 2000). This percentage has generally decreased over the past 30 years. The lion's share of the cost is born by state and local governments.

What this pattern means is that federal, as compared with state and local, authorities can exert only modest amounts of economic power on school districts and schools. However, what federal authorities lack in terms of monetary clout they make up for in terms of their power to mobilize national opinion. Comments about education by presidents and presidential candidates have the capacity to draw enormous attention to problems associated with the schools. For example, federal officials acted quickly to publicize the findings of the 1983 report of the National Commission on Excellence in Education titled *A Nation at Risk*. This publicity stimulated many other national groups to study the schools, and there has been an almost unending stream of proposals to "make schools better," emanating from national groups—within and without the government—since its publication. For example, a 1995 book by former U.S. Assistant Secretary of Education Diane Ravitch, titled *National Standards in American Education: A Citizen's Guide* established a rationale that many states used to defend the establishment of state-level curriculum standards (Armstrong & Savage, 2001).

Curriculum work at the national level, in most cases, seeks to influence policies and practices that are largely under the control of state and local authorities. Federal legislation designed to mandate particular curricular practices is rare. Direct federal involvement runs contrary to a long-standing tradition supporting state and local control of schools. One of the few successful efforts to overcome traditional resistance to federal mandates was mounted in the 1970s by parents and interest groups who were concerned about the treatment of learners with disabilities. In 1975, their efforts resulted in passage of Public Law 94-142, the legislation that first required all of the nation's schools to provide certain kinds of instructional services to students with disabilities, including individualized instructional plans. Much more common than direct federal mandates are exhortations to states to raise standards, stiffen graduation requirements, and provide more depth in certain content areas.

National-level curriculum work tends to feature the identification of a fairly narrow agenda, which is publicized throughout the nation in the hope it will attract the interest of state and local authorities. For example, national professional organizations, such as the National Council of Teachers of Mathematics, the National Council for the Social Studies, the National Council of Teachers of English, and the National Science Teachers Association, from time to time have prepared sets of curriculum guidelines for their respective subject areas. These are presented as models to the national community to consider for state and local adoption. You might be interested in looking at some key publications of national professional groups that include suggested content guidelines; these have had a great influence on state-level curriculum standards throughout the nation:

- Aldridge, B. G. (Ed.). (1995). *Scope, sequence, and coordination of secondary school science: Vol 3. A high school framework for national science education standards.* Arlington, VA: National Science Association.

- International Society for Technology in Education. (2000). *National educational technology standards for students: Connecting curriculum and technology.* Eugene, OR: Author.

- Joint Committee on National Health Education Standards. (1995). *National health education standards: Achieving health literacy.* Reston, VA: Association for the Advancement of Health Education.

- National Association for Sport and Physical Education. (1995). *Moving into the future, national standards for physical education: A guide to content and assessment.* Reston, VA: Author.

- National Council for the Social Studies. (1994). *Expectations of excellence: Curriculum standards for social studies.* Washington, DC: Author.

- National Council of Teachers of English. (1995). *Standards for the English language arts.* Urbana, IL: Author.

- National Council of Teachers of Mathematics. (1989). *Curriculum and evaluation standards for school mathematics.* Reston, VA: Author.
- National Council of Teachers of Mathematics. (2000). *Principles and standards for school mathematics.* Reston, VA: Author.
- National Research Council. (1996). *National science education standards.* Washington, DC: National Academy Press.
- National Standards in Foreign Language Project. (1999). *Standards in foreign language learning in the 21st century.* Lawrence, KS: Author.

LEARNING EXTENSION 6–2

Curriculum Recommendations of National Professional Groups

Use a standard search engine, such as Google (http://www.google.com), to locate the home page of a national professional group that interests you. For example, you might consider going to the website of one of these: the National Council of Teachers of Mathematics, the National Council of Teachers of English, the National Science Teachers Association, or the National Council for the Social Studies.

See if the group has developed any curriculum guidelines or suggestions. If you find them, take some notes related to the following questions:

- How does the recommended program compare with what you presently have in your school or school system (or with what you experienced as a student)?
- What changes would be required in the program in your school or school system (or in a school or school system you once attended) if the recommended program of study were adopted?
- In general, what obstacles would many schools and school systems face if they decided to adopt all of the recommendations?
- Do the recommendations imply that students should spend a higher proportion of their school time studying subjects that are important to this group than is presently the case?

Business and labor groups also sometimes develop curriculum guides that showcase particular issues and perspectives they would like to see better represented in school programs. These simply become part of the total pool of programmatic options that state and local decision makers can consider as they engage in curriculum-planning work.

State Setting

Today, state legislatures exert considerable influence over curricula in individual schools and school districts. The legislatures, for the most part, lay out broad policy guidelines. In some cases, well-organized interest groups successfully lobby legislatures for the purpose of requiring schools to teach certain kinds of content to all students in the state. For example, there have been cases where schools have been required to teach such diverse topics as "the benefits of the free enterprise system" and "drug-abuse awareness." In other situations, legislators have been prompted to enact more rigorous high-school graduation standards—for example, increasing the number of years (and kinds) of mathematics or English courses students must take. In recent years, out of a desire to make schools throughout their state more accountable, many state legislatures have adopted state-level curriculum standards. For more information about state efforts to establish standards, go to the web site Mid-continent Research for Education and Learning (http://www.mcrel.org/standards). State-level standards vary considerably in terms of their specificity.

State boards of education typically are charged with implementing broad policies that are outlined in state-level education legislation. They generally have the authority to make policy in areas that have not been addressed by the state legislature. State board actions are implemented through the work of the personnel in state departments of education. (The names of these units vary from state to state.) Often, state departments of education do much of the initial organizational work associated with state-level curriculum change. State-level actions typically occur only after a process that invites involvement from many constituencies. These include state board of education members, state department of education officials, educational professional groups, teacher and administrator representatives, parents, and general citizens' representatives.

LEARNING EXTENSION 6–3

Comparing State Curriculum Standards

Use a standard search engine, such as Google (http://www.google.com), to locate the home pages of three or four state departments, including the one in your state. Try to locate information about state-level curriculum standards. As you read, seek answers to questions such as the following:

- How do the standards compare in terms of their specificity?
- Do you find information regarding which aspects teachers are obliged to follow and which are provided only as "suggestions"?
- Is there a consistent design followed from subject to subject or from grade level to grade level? (For example, do the numbers of standards, requirements, and so forth vary hugely for one year of grade 5 science, as compared with one year of grade 5 language arts?)
- Do any of the standards seem to reflect successful lobbying by particular pressure groups?
- If you had to develop an instructional program that tied to just one of the state standards you looked at, which would you choose, and why?

In years gone by, state departments of education operated with much less oversight from state legislatures and state boards of education than is the case today. Publicity accorded to public education at the national level has spawned great citizen interest in schools. As a result, legislators often feel pressured to act. These conditions by no means suggest that professional educators no longer have a voice. However, if you are a teacher, your opinions and those of other school professionals will comprise only a fraction of those that legislators will hear. As a result, the influence you and other educators have on state-level decisions often is less significant than what you can bring to bear locally.

Local School District Setting

Though state curriculum standards have been more important in recent years, much curriculum development continues to occur locally. If you are teaching, at this level you may have opportunities to participate in laying out master plans that will guide instruction throughout your school district. For the most part, teachers' perspectives receive a respectful hearing at this level, and many teachers participate actively when school districts undertake curriculum-development, revision, and improvement plans.

Individual school districts typically place specific individuals in charge of dealing with curriculum issues. In a small school district, a single person might discharge this responsibility, along with a number of other tasks. Larger school districts often have numerous curriculum specialists, some of whom have narrowly defined responsibilities for particular grade levels and/or subject areas. The relative influence of curriculum specialists within a school district varies. In part, individual personalities play an important role; their influence varies, depending on the nature of the district's administrative organization. To better understand the influence of alternative organizational patterns, you need to know something about **line relationships** and **staff relationships.** An administrator with a line relationship connection to subordinates has clear authority to impose his or her decisions on them. A school board, for example, has a line relationship with the superintendent. Similarly, the superintendent exercises line authority over his or her assistant superintendents. A staff relationship is quite different. It implies an advisory relationship. Someone who has a staff relationship with someone else in an organization may recommend, suggest, and lobby this person, but he or she lacks the authority to require the person to act in a certain way.

School districts vary in terms of whether individuals responsible for curriculum issues have line or staff authority over the principals of individual schools. Clearly, the curriculum function gets more attention from principals in administrative organizational schemes where someone responsible for curriculum issues exercises line rather than staff authority over them. See Figures 6.1 and 6.2 for a graphic representation of staff and line relationships. More school districts have arrangements featuring staff relationships between curriculum specialists and principals. What this means when you engage in curriculum work is that you and others involved cannot count on principals automatically supporting the deci-

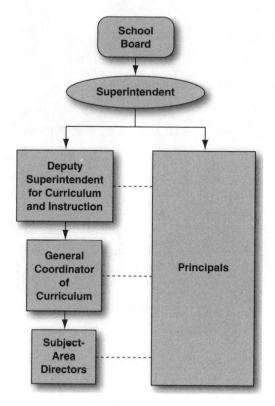

FIGURE 6.1 Organizational Pattern Featuring a Staff Relationship Between Principals and the Deputy Superintendent for Curriculum and Instruction
Note: Dotted lines represent staff relationships; solid lines represent line relationships.

sions of curriculum groups. They face pressures from many groups in the community, and they often receive contradictory advice. The case for curriculum change needs to be made to this group logically, personably, and carefully.

Individual school districts have adopted a variety of approaches for managing curriculum work. Very small districts may have no individual with exclusive responsibilities for this function. It may be something that the superintendent or a deputy handles as a routine part of his or her role. Districts enrolling more students typically have curriculum specialists and, sometimes, large staffs of curriculum professionals. The titles and responsibilities of these people vary greatly from place to place. There are also great differences in how curriculum work is approached.

For example, if you are working in a large school district, there may be a **central curriculum council,** which assists central-office curriculum specialists. A central curriculum council often includes representatives from various schools in the district, as well as representatives from constituencies including parents, students, university-based personnel, local business and community leaders, and

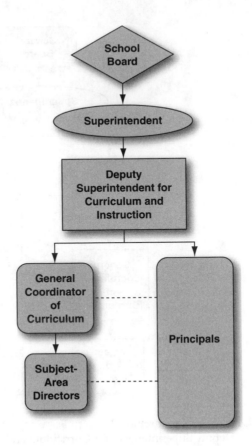

FIGURE 6.2 Organizational Pattern Featuring a Line Relationship Between the Deputy Superintendent for Curriculum and Instruction and Principals
Note: Dotted lines represent staff relationships, and solid lines represent line relationships.

lay citizens. Such councils often engage in general curriculum planning. With the assistance of central-office curriculum specialists, they may decide to lay out a curriculum-development and curriculum-management scheme that organizes the work in ways that allow for the systematic review of all curricular areas over a multi-year cycle. See Figure 6.3 for an example of such a plan.

Sometimes, particularly in larger school districts, central curriculum councils have representatives from, and oversee the work of, a number of subject-specific **program councils.** For example, there may be separate program councils for such areas as English–language arts, the social studies, mathematics, and the sciences. In some places, there are separate groups focusing on elementary-school, middle-school, and high-school programming in these areas. These groups, sometimes in consultation with the central curriculum council, often make decisions about the selection and membership of teams that will do the actual hands-on work associated with developing new programs and the review and revision of existing ones.

	Review and Recommend Changes	Begin Curriculum Revision	Ongoing Curriculum Revision	Pilot Revised Program	Modify and Install Revised Program	Assess Ongoing Program	Assess Ongoing Program
Art	2008–2009	2009–2010	2003–2004	2004–2005	2005–2006	2006–2007	2007–2008
Business	2005–2006	2006–2007	2007–2008	2008–2009	2009–2010	2003–2004	2004–2005
English–language arts	2007–2008	2008–2009	2009–2010	2003–2004	2004–2005	2005–2006	2006–2007
Mathematics	2004–2005	2005–2006	2006–2007	2007–2008	2008–2009	2009–2010	2003–2004
Music	2009–2010	2003–2004	2004–2005	2005–2006	2006–2007	2007–2008	2008–2009
Reading	2003–2004	2004–2005	2005–2006	2006–2007	2007–2008	2008–2009	2009–2010
Science	2005–2006	2006–2007	2007–2008	2008–2009	2009–2010	2003–2004	2004–2005
Social studies	2006–2007	2007–2008	2008–2009	2009–2010	2003–2004	2004–2005	2005–2006
Speech and theater	2007–2008	2008–2009	2009–2010	2003–2004	2004–2005	2005–2006	2006–2007
Technology education	2003–2004	2004–2005	2005–2006	2006–2007	2007–2008	2008–2009	2009–2010
Vocational education	2004–2005	2005–2006	2006–2007	2007–2008	2008–2009	2009–2010	2003–2004

FIGURE 6.3 An Example of a School District's Curriculum Review, Development, Implementation, and Monitoring Cycle with Examples of Major Subject Areas
Note: This example features a seven-year cycle. Note how this arrangement assures that only a few subjects each year will require the heavy personnel involvement needed during those periods when major revisions are underway.

Typically, teachers from individual buildings who teach subjects that are the focus of a particular program council are included on these teams. Especially in buildings that enroll large numbers of students, several teachers may be involved. These teachers constitute building-level curriculum groups, which gather reactions from other staff members, generate proposals for consideration of the program councils, and react to ideas from both the program councils and the central curriculum council.

Individual School Setting

Your involvement with curriculum work at the individual school level most probably will feature lots of interactions with teachers and administrators from your own building. The nature of this kind of curriculum activity varies. As noted in the previous section, some teachers and administrators are members of district-level program committees, and they serve as important liaisons to those groups. Other school-level work often features program planning that seeks to accommodate district-level and state-level guidelines in ways that make sense, given the school's unique population of students. This work cannot succeed without the thoughtful participation of teachers.

No matter how carefully programs are planned and designed by people who do not work at your school, their preparation always goes forward in an absence of the kind of specific information about your students and their needs that you and your colleagues in the building share. Your thoughtful reactions to proposals generated elsewhere and your willingness to engage curriculum modification and change suggestions are critical. Programs flowing from new or revised curricula cannot be judged in the absence of their impact on students. How they are received by students has everything to do with the care you and other teachers give to assessing change proposals in terms of the potential they provide you to deliver instructional experiences that will connect with your students and that are appropriate for their needs.

Curriculum work in individual schools often places a heavy emphasis on the development of classroom-ready instructional units. There is a strong emphasis on nuts-and-bolts planning that provides answers to such questions as the following:

- What is to be taught?
- What are some practical ideas for introducing content to *our* students?
- How will learning be assessed?
- What are some good ways to get students engaged with this content?
- Are the needed learning resources available now? If not, will they become available soon?
- If we implement these suggestions, what will we have to stop doing that we are doing now?

In one sense, state- and local-school-district-level curriculum work produces outcomes that might be thought of as sets of aspirations. The thinking you and your colleagues do as you reflect on and transform these ideas into meaningful learning experiences for your students can convert hope to reality. For this reason, curriculum work that occurs at individual schools is incredibly important.

 ## NONTEACHER PARTICIPANTS

In addition to teachers, prior sections of this chapter mentioned other categories of people who often are asked to participate as members of curriculum groups. They include school administrators, curriculum specialists, subject-matter specialists, parents, government representatives, lay citizens, and students. The particular cast of players invited to participate varies with the tasks assigned to the group and the special talents, abilities, and perspectives of potential participants (Doll, 1995; Hunkins, 1980).

The relative influence of people from various constituencies differs, depending on the level at which the work is taking place and the nature of the assigned responsibility. For example, when curriculum work takes place at a school, if the work is directed at seeking smooth grade-to-grade articulation of content in the reading program, both the principal and the classroom teachers probably will be important voices at the table. On the other hand, if the work involves the development of instructional units for the fifth-grade mathematics program, the principal is likely to have much less direct involvement in the process than are the fifth-grade teachers. As noted previously, state-level curriculum reform work often attracts the attention of large numbers of diverse groups. As a result, the perspectives of professional educators sometimes are not particularly influential at this level. See Figure 6.4 for an illustration of how the intensity of people from different groups varies with the nature of the work a particular curriculum group has been assigned to do.

Curriculum Specialists

Curriculum specialists typically are people with advanced degrees who have had specialized training in the processes associated with curriculum development,

Task	Heavy Level of Involvement	Moderate Level of Involvement	Little or No Involvement
Development of a district philosophy statement	• School administrators • Curriculum specialists • Lay citizens	• Teachers • Outside specialists	• Students
Revision of a master scope and sequence document for a school district's K–12 programs	• Curriculum specialists • School administrators	• Teachers • Outside specialists	• Students • Lay citizens
Development of a new science program for elementary-level gifted and talented students	• Curriculum specialists • Outside specialists • Teachers	• School administrators • Students	
Preparation of grade 4 instructional units to be piloted as part of a new reading program	• Curriculum specialists • Teachers • Outside specialists	• Students	• School administrators
Revision of the K–12 mathematics program	• Curriculum specialists • Outside specialists • Teachers	• School administrators	• Students

FIGURE 6.4 Ways in Which Involvement Levels of Various Categories of People Differ with the Nature of the Curriculum Work to Be Done

revision, implementation, and assessment. One of their roles is to assist others involved in curriculum work to understand the essentials of curriculum building. For example, if a group is being charged with developing a new course, the curriculum specialist might take time to explain the processes used to diagnose the learning needs of the students who will take the course, to select and organize the content, to divide material into instructional units, to develop sets of learning intentions for each unit, to provide examples of possible instructional strategies, to suggest approaches to both student and program assessment, and to provide information about learning resources for students and background materials for teachers.

Curriculum specialists often decide on the composition of the groups that will pursue a particular activity. In a large district, a curriculum specialist, working with the central curriculum committee or with one of the program committees, may put together a group with more than 30 members. On the other hand, if there is a need to develop and pilot a single unit at a given grade level, the group may have only three or four teachers, perhaps even teachers from the same building.

Often, curriculum specialists play leadership roles in curriculum-development projects. For political reasons, sometimes someone else is assigned to chair the group. However, this person frequently depends on curriculum specialists for guidance. For example, when leaders outside of education are chosen, often they need help from curriculum specialists as they seek to learn about the state-level program standards that might constrain what the group wishes to do.

Finally, curriculum specialists can help members of curriculum groups take their work seriously. If you are a teacher and are invited to participate in curriculum work, you should expect the professional curriculum specialists to buttress your confidence by providing you with assurances that you have the necessary background to do the job well. Providing good support for people involved in curriculum work helps these individuals take their responsibilities seriously. It is good insurance against the kind of "scissors-and-paste" (cut a little from program A, add a snippet or two from program B, and, presto, we have a "new" program C) approach that can result when leadership from curriculum specialists is weak.

School Administrators and School Board Members

Upper-echelon school administrators, the superintendent, and top subordinates only infrequently serve as regular members of district-level groups involved in most kinds of curriculum work. An exception to this pattern occurs when there is an effort to produce general descriptions of programs that are designed for the community at large. The superintendent and chief lieutenants work to nurture support for the schools from the entire community. As a result, they often seek involvement in planning groups when documents such as district philosophy statements and general program descriptions are being prepared. These are materials they will use in their day-to-day public relations work with various community groups.

CURRICULUM REALITIES 6–1

Establishing Priorities for Curriculum Work: The "Caste System"

Curriculum specialists Daniel Tanner and Laurel Tanner point out that actions at the federal level often convince people throughout the country that some areas of the curriculum deserve more attention than others. As noted earlier in this chapter, direct federal involvement in public schooling is modest, relative to the power exerted by state and local authorities. However, the public relations powers of federal officials and other high-profile individuals who speak out nationally about critical issues often do affect the priorities established by state and local school authorities. Actions taken nationally sometimes impose a sort of "caste system" on alternative possibilities for curriculum reform and renewal (Tanner & Tanner, 1995). State and local officials find it easier to generate enthusiasm for committing people and financial resources to work on high-caste areas of the curriculum.

Historically, during war time, concerns about the physical condition of incoming military recruits have led to calls for improved physical education programs in the schools. In the late 1950s, when the former Soviet Union succeeded in putting up the first successful orbiting earth satellite, it suddenly became fashionable for schools to take a hard look at the quality of their mathematics and sciences programs. For a time during the 1980s, many national leaders felt that Japan's schools were producing students who were so well prepared for economic life that Japan soon would leave the American economy in the dust. There were numerous calls for American educators to commit time and resources to reshape programs in American schools more along the lines of those found in Japan. (One heard much less about the excellence of Japanese education in later years when the Japanese economy was struggling.)

Are superintendents and other local-level school leaders today reacting to educational reform agendas that are being promoted at the national level? Is there a caste system in operation that makes it easier for these officials to win support for certain kinds of curriculum reform efforts than for others? As you consider a response, think about the following issues:

- Is there a highly limited number of reform issues that are being promoted nationally, or are agendas numerous and focused on widely different kinds of issues?
- What groups are behind some of the high-profile issues, and what kinds of action are they taking to win wider acceptance for their views?
- What consequences, if any, do you see for local superintendents who establish priorities that are congruent with what individuals and groups at the national level are advocating?
- Is there less or more pressure on superintendents today to provide support for a limited number of high-caste curriculum reforms than there was in earlier years? Why or why not?

Sometimes representatives from local school boards are invited to serve as members of curriculum groups. Whether or not they are invited (or choose) to participate largely depends on the scope of the group's work. School board members more frequently are involved when the product of the group's work will have broad, districtwide application—for example, board members may well be involved in an effort to develop a new framework for an entire kindergarten through grade 12 science program.

At the state level, superintendents and school board members, often operating through statewide networks or organizations, present their views when state boards of education and state education departments consider changes to state curriculum standards. They are in a position to comment on the operational implications of suggested modifications. Though their voices are important at this level, they are just one of many constituencies whose opinions receive consideration when state-level authorities ponder the wisdom of making changes.

School principals' attitudes toward a new program greatly influence its prospects for success. Hence, it is very common for the representatives of a district's principals to be invited to serve on groups considering curriculum changes. Though principals discharge many functions, increasingly they are being viewed as instructional leaders and are being held accountable for the success of the academic programs in their schools. Pressures associated with the need to promote student learning lead many of today's principals to develop a keen interest in curriculum issues. They have special insights into the ways in which proposed changes in one program area might affect the teachers and students in other grades and subjects. They also tend to be very knowledgeable about the potential budgetary implications of proposed changes. Finally, principals, with their background in management, have useful insights into the staff development implications of curriculum revision and reform proposals.

At the state level, principals' views on potential changes to state curriculum standards often are expressed through their professional associations. As administrators who are at ground zero in individual schools, they are held responsible for assuring that the instructional programs in their buildings comply with any new state mandates. They are in a position to provide information about practical implementation problems that might result if a particular change were adopted. As is true with the views of superintendents, at the state level, principals' concerns, though they receive serious consideration, are simply one of many perspectives that state-level officials weigh as they consider their options.

Parents or Guardians

Some parents or guardians of students often are invited to serve as members of school-district-level curriculum groups. Their presence serves two functions. On the one hand, they have some knowledge about what kinds of programs their own children (and presumably other students in the same age group) respond to positively. Further, they tend to bring a perspective to proposed changes that has been shaped by influences that may differ from those of the professional educator members of the group. When parents or guardians serve in groups that make recommendations for changes, these changes may prove to be an easier sell to parents or guardians in the larger community.

Some difficulties accompany decisions to involve parents in curriculum-development groups. Think about all the parents and guardians of school-age children. How many have time to accept appointment to a curriculum group? How many would feel comfortable working with such a group? How representative of all parents are those who would be willing to serve? Curriculum leaders need to ponder these questions, select parents and guardians carefully, and orient them well to the limitations imposed by operative state and local guidelines and to the particular task(s) the group will be charged with accomplishing.

At the state level, representatives of parent-teacher organizations often express views of parents and guardians. Frequently, these groups raise concerns about increased testing requirements, about changes in graduation requirements, about the fit between high-school curricula and university/college entrance requirements, about the adequacy of technology in the schools, and about other issues that parents and guardians worry about as they nurture the development of their children. At the state level, the impact of parent and guardian perspectives varies. When a particular issue prompts a large number of parents throughout the state to take a position on a proposed change in a state curriculum standard, state leaders listen. There are thousands of parents in each state, and all of them are potential voters. On the other hand, if there is little evidence that views espoused by parents' and guardians' professional organizations are deeply held by parents throughout the state, these opinions carry less weight.

Lay Citizens

In the hope that their presence will help win broad public support for any recommended changes, a few representatives from the local community may be invited to participate as members of curriculum groups. In some cases, these people are selected to represent particular constituencies. For example, in some communities, there are numerous nonschool-based groups interested in promoting literacy. If a district contemplates some changes in the structure of its K–12 language arts program, some representatives from these groups can make important contributions to the group's work and can help sell any recommendations for change to the community at large.

Lay citizens do not always come from sectors of the community with special interests in the curricular area that is the focus of a curriculum group's work. Sometimes they are selected with a view to representing the community at large. The idea is to use them as surrogates for the general public, whose reactions during deliberations may hint at concerns the community at large might have in response to a particular change recommendation. If lay citizens are to be effective participants in change-related discussions, they must receive a good orientation from curriculum leaders. For example, lay citizens are unlikely to come to their work with a solid understanding of the state and local regulations that constrain the range of decisions the group can make.

At the state level, lay citizens' views tend to be represented through the lobbying efforts of organized groups. For example, groups organized around such issues as keeping property taxes low, producing graduates with more highly developed computer skills, reducing the incidence of drug use, diminishing the incidence of school violence, and so forth make their views known to legislators, state board of education members, and state education department employees. The positions represented tend to get attention according to state officials' perception of how widespread these positions are among the entire adult citizenry of the state.

A fundamental challenge in inviting lay citizen participation in curriculum work has to do with the question "How representative are their views?" Individual citizens have hugely varied interests and affiliations. The personal agendas of citizens often incline them to join with others who share similar perspectives. By associating with like-minded individuals, people sometimes become convinced that the views they and their friends share represent general public opinion.

Curriculum experts Daniel Tanner and Laurel Tanner point out the widespread representation of narrow views by citizens who present their own positions as congruent with those of the public at large (Tanner & Tanner, 1995). Curriculum leaders must be alert to this problem when considering the positions expressed by lay citizen members of curriculum groups.

Students

Students infrequently are invited to present their views when changes to state-level curriculum standards are contemplated. A few may provide testimony before committees organized by the state legislature, the state board of education, and the state department of education. However, for the most part, there are no organized groups of students lobbying in behalf of particular positions.

Students much more frequently are asked to join curriculum groups at the local school district level. Several arguments support their involvement. For example, as receivers of school programs, they are in a position to provide comment about how students may react to changes (Marsh & Willis, 1995). Further, there is some evidence that students tend to be more receptive to curricula when they have participated in the development process (Vallance, 1981).

On the other hand, there are concerns about including students as members of district-level curriculum groups. When students are selected from individual schools and sent off to attend a districtwide meeting, leaders at their schools want a student representative who will be positively received by the entire committee membership. Typically, this reality inclines principals to select bright, well-scrubbed, articulate young people. Often, these students have outstanding academic records. Though they may portray a positive image of their school to the group, they are hardly typical students. Their views regarding what students want and need may have little foundation in reality.

Curriculum leaders face a dilemma in selecting student members of curriculum groups. As noted, if school principals do the choosing, the selected individuals may not represent the students who are not being adequately served by the present program. If curriculum leaders somehow manage to get student members who have characteristics similar to the students who will be served by the new program, these young members may not be able to articulate their needs in ways that will be helpful to the group's work. In summary, whether student representatives should be included remains an issue that curriculum professionals continue to debate.

Outside Specialists

Outside specialists have expertise that curriculum-development groups need. This category represents a huge range of people. Some examples include subject-area specialists, assessment specialists, and teaching methodology specialists. Many of these individuals are employed at colleges and universities.

At the state level, one of the most active groups of outside specialists consists of subject-area experts. Members of this group often try to influence the content of state-curriculum standards. They do this in several ways. Sometimes, individuals testify before committees of the legislature, the state board of education, or the state department of education. Academic subject specialists also are great letter writers, and they often communicate with state-level officials to express their views, and those views often are conveyed to state officials through the lobbying efforts of their professional organizations. These opinions do receive consideration, but the views of subject-area specialists are simply positions that state officials think about as they review the stands adopted by many other individuals and groups.

Sometimes, outside specialists are invited to serve as regular members of district-level curriculum groups, and sometimes they are not included. In part, the decision to request their participation has to do with the nature of a given curriculum group's task. For example, a committee charged with rearranging the sequence of required high-school English courses (but not changing any of the courses themselves) would have little need of the expertise of a university-based English specialist. On the other hand, if the group were charged with reviewing the entire scope, sequence, and content of the high-school English program, a specialist from a university English faculty might be a useful addition to the group.

When the expertise of outside specialists is needed, curriculum leaders involve them in various ways. Some advocate the appointment of outside specialists as regular members of the curriculum group. Others point out that their presence sometimes is intimidating to other members and that their views carry more weight than they sometimes should (Ben-Peretz, 1990). One solution to this is to not include outside specialists as regular committee members but to designate them as external consultants who, from time to time, will be called in to share their views with the group.

"Faceless" Group Members

When you engage in curriculum work, many people will be physically present as members engage in your assigned tasks. Precisely how many people will be involved and who these people are will vary, depending on what the group has been charged to do. In addition to these people, every curriculum group will also be visited periodically by what you might think of as the *faceless members*. These are not real people; rather, they represent perspectives that are almost certain to be voiced by one of the regular members of the group. Though the faceless members are not there in a physical sense, they exert influence on your curriculum decisions. Who are the faceless members? The following are just a few examples:

- State curriculum standards
- Textbook publishers
- Test makers
- Subject-matter-specific professional organizations
- Teacher certification requirements
- External lobbies
- The power of tradition

Let's look briefly at how the perspectives of these faceless members can influence curriculum decisions. State-level curriculum standards often constrain the range of options available to school-level committees working on curriculum revision and reform projects. They function as silent surrogates for the interests of state government. For example, these regulations prevent a curriculum group from giving serious consideration to a new grade 11 world cultures course if the adopted state curriculum mandates that American history be taught at this grade level.

Textbook publishers also exert great influence on the kinds of decisions curriculum groups make. Some years ago, a group in Texas sought to revise the state's required high-school social studies program. Some high-school American history teachers made the point that their work was made more difficult because students came to them not even knowing the locations of many places in the United States. They recommended that students be required to take a course in United States geography as a prerequisite to the American history course. For a time, the committee gave serious consideration to this proposal. However, finally someone decided to inventory the available high-school textbooks in United States geography. They found that there were none. The existing texts focused on world geography. In the absence of an existing text for the proposed new course, the committee decided to recommend against its establishment.

Despite some vocal opposition, the trend toward giving students more and more standardized tests continues unabated (Stake, 1999). Tests are being used not just to measure the progress of individual students but also to make school to school comparisons. Because of the enormous public interest in test scores, curriculum-development groups face great pressure to align the content of their programs with the tests. As you get involved in curriculum work, you are certain to encounter discussions centering on how proposed changes relate to the standardized tests students must take and whether there is any danger that the changes, when implemented, will result in lowered scores.

Today, almost every national subject-matter-related professional organization has developed a set of recommended curriculum standards. (For some examples, review the material under the earlier heading "National Setting.") If you are part of a district-level group seeking to make curricular changes related to an area of interest of one of these organizations, you can count on someone putting the national group's standards on the table for consideration. Although these standards often are well done, you and others need to remember that they are the work of people deeply committed to the subject areas they represent. Some standards propose programs that would represent a vast expansion of content in areas related to their discipline. Full implementation of these standards, in some cases, would require diminished attention to other subject areas. Such a development may or may not be a bad idea, but you and others need to know that the curriculum standards of the various subject-area groups sometimes represent a "the more of my subject, the better" perspective.

Sometimes, another presence at the table when curriculum changes are discussed is existing teacher certification requirements. Issues related to teacher-certification requirements may come up when a curriculum group considers major changes in the existing program of study. For example, someone may well ask questions about certification when a proposed curriculum change would require teachers to teach a topic that was not treated in the required academic courses they took to qualify for certification. The lack of teacher preparation may or may not be a barrier to adopting a change. The logic in support of the change may be compelling and ways may be found to provide inservice training for teachers who will deliver the revised program. (If recommended changes become widespread, over time, state officials might be convinced to make appropriate changes in certification requirements.)

Various external lobbies of all kinds have designs on school programs. Their agendas vary tremendously. Groups affiliated with organized labor often produce prototype units and study guidelines for schools to consider that cast the union movement in a positive light. Business groups of various kinds also have agendas they would like to have vigorously promoted in school curricula. Organized groups of citizens interested in issues such as tax reform, gun control, drug-awareness education, the promotion of abstinence from premarital sexual activity, better race relations, crime prevention, and phonics-based approaches to reading seek to have their views reflected in school programs. People involved in curriculum work often pick up and share ideas associated with some of these external lobbies.

Finally, the sometimes overwhelming presence of tradition looms over most groups involved in curriculum work. It is a force supporting curricular inertia that asks the "Why change?" question, and that raises doubts in the minds of curriculum workers about the wisdom of pursuing any kind of a change agenda. Tradition is a voice that will remind you that existing patterns may have their critics, but they also have their friends. During almost any curriculum-change discussion, you can count on someone to make the argument that "the status quo has served us well." Arguments in support of traditional patterns deserve a thoughtful, respectful hearing. However, history should be a force that informs enlightened decision making, not an imprisoning constraint that stands in the way of reasoned accommodations to changed conditions.

EXERCISE 6–1

The Channel One Controversy

As educators work to help young people grow toward responsible adult citizenship, they seek to expand students' interests to include a concern for important national and international issues. To facilitate this agenda, many school districts in the country have signed up for a service provided by a commercial marketing company called Channel One. Channel One, at no cost to participating schools, provides television sets, VCRs, and a satellite dish that is engineered to pick up only Channel One's transmissions. In return, schools have students watch Channel One's program for 12 minutes a day. Ten minutes of programming consists of news; the remaining 2 are filled with commercials.

In addition to the daily news service, Channel One also invites students to participate in a web-based message board and to participate in various online contests and activities. Channel One has both supporters and critics. The critics' concerns center around the question "Should students be required to watch commercials as part of their regular routine in school?"

Action

Seek out information about Channel One that reflects the perspectives of both its supporters and its critics. You might wish to begin by entering the words "Channel One" into a standard web search engine, such as Google (http://www.google.com). There are many articles on the web dealing with the Channel One controversy. You might also wish to check the *Education Index* for some recent periodical articles that have dealt with this subject. Your instructor may also have some suggestions regarding other places you might seek out information that relates to this topic.

Analysis

As directed by your instructor, prepare either a short talk for presentation to your class or a short paper in which you deal with the following:

- What are the best arguments made by Channel One and its supporters?
- What are the best arguments made by Channel One's critics?
- What position do you take on the Channel One controversy, and why?

Key Points

As you work in the field of curriculum, you will encounter many situations in which outside groups wish to have access to public school students. Some of these groups have particular agendas they wish to push. These agendas may or may not be consistent with mainstream views regarding what should and should not be provided to students as a regular part of the school day.

Review and Reflection

1. Suppose you were asked to consider whether the teacher is the most important player when curriculum changes are being discussed. If you were to prepare an editorial in support of this position, what would you say? If, on the other hand, you were charged with marshalling arguments in opposition to this idea, what key points would you make?

2. How do you assess the probability of success of some people who claim they can design a teacher-proof curriculum—that is, a curriculum that is so carefully planned and accompanied by detailed instructions that it would be virtually impossible for any teacher using it to undermine its intent? On what do you base your conclusions?

3. Why is it that politicians who seek election to federal office spend so much time promoting their views on educational reform when the federal government is only a minor player when it comes to financing education?

4. Describe some examples of educational reform activity undertaken at the national level that, over time, have affected state- and local-level educational policy decisions.

5. How would you distinguish between educational policy roles of (a) state legislatures and (b) state boards of education?

6. Some people argue that the growth in state-level curriculum standards has all but removed any influence local school district personnel have in shaping the curriculum. Do you agree? Why or why not?

7. In addition to teachers, what are some categories of people that may be involved in groups charged with accomplishing curriculum development, improvement, or revision? What factors might determine the intensity of the involvement of people from the several categories?

8. Who are some of the faceless members of curriculum groups, and what is the nature of their influence on curriculum decision making?

References

Aldridge, B. G. (Ed.). (1995). *Scope, sequence, and coordination of secondary school science: Vol 3. A high school framework for national science education standards.* Arlington, VA: National Science Teachers Association.

Armstrong, D. G., & Savage, T. V. (2001). *Teaching in the secondary school: An introduction* (5th ed.). Upper Saddle River, NJ: Merrill/Prentice Hall.

Ben-Peretz, M. (1990). *The teacher-curriculum encounter.* Albany: State University of New York Press.

Doll, R. C. (1995). *Curriculum improvement: Decision making and process* (9th ed.). Boston: Allyn and Bacon.

Henderson, J. G. (1992). *Becoming an inquiring educator.* New York: Macmillan.

Holland, R. (2001, March 2). Don't let state history become history in schools. *Greensboro News and Record,* p. A10.

Hui, T. K. (2001, February 23). Curriculum changes set on fast track. *Raleigh News & Observer,* p. B1.

Hunkins, F. P. (1980). *Curriculum development: Program improvement.* Columbus, OH: Charles E. Merrill.

International Society for Technology in Education. (2000). *National educational technology standards for students: Connecting curriculum and technology.* Eugene, OR: Author.

Joint Committee on National Health Education Standards. (1995). *National health education standards: Achieving health literacy.* Reston, VA: Association for the Advancement of Health Education.

Marsh, C., & Willis, G. (1995). *Curriculum: Alternative approaches, ongoing issues.* Upper Saddle River, NJ: Merrill/Prentice Hall.

Martin, D. G. (2001, February 21). You're a North Carolinian if you went to the eighth grade here. *Raleigh News & Observer,* p. A5.

Mid-continent Research for Education and Learning. (2001). *Standards.* [http://www.mcrel.org/standards/]

National Association for Sport and Physical Education. (1995). *Moving into the future, national standards for physical education: A guide to content and assessment.* Reston, VA: Author.

National Commission on Excellence in Education. (1983). *A nation at risk: The imperative for educational reform.* Washington, DC: U.S. Department of Education.

National Council for the Social Studies. (1994). *Expectations of excellence: Curriculum standards for social studies.* Washington, DC: Author.

National Council of Teachers of English. (1995). *Standards for the English language arts.* Urbana, IL: Author.

National Council of Teachers of Mathematics. (1989). *Curriculum and evaluation standards for school mathematics.* Reston, VA: Author.

National Council of Teachers of Mathematics. (2000). *Principles and standards for school mathematics.* Reston, VA: Author.

National Research Council. (1996). *National science education standards.* Washington, DC: National Academy Press.

National Standards in Foreign Language Project. (1999). *Standards in foreign language learning in the 21st century.* Lawrence, KS: Author.

Oliva, P. F. (1997). *Developing the curriculum.* (4th ed.). New York: Longman.

Ravitch, D. (1995). *National standards in American education: A citizen's guide.* New York: Basic Books.

Shulman, S. L. (1990). Preface. M. Ben-Peretz. *The teacher-curriculum encounter.* Albany: State University of New York Press.

Snyder, T. D. (Ed.). (2000). *Digest of education statistics, 1999.* Washington, DC: National Center for Education Statistics.

Stake, R. (1999). The goods on American education. *Phi Delta Kappan, 80*(9), 668–672.

Tanner, D., & Tanner, L. (1995). *Curriculum development: Theory into practice* (3rd ed.). Upper Saddle River, NJ: Merrill/Prentice Hall.

Vallance, E. (1981). *Focus on students in curriculum knowledge: A critique of curriculum criticism.* Paper presented at the annual meeting of the American Educational Research Association, Los Angeles.

Design Alternatives
and Needs Assessment

Graphic Organizer

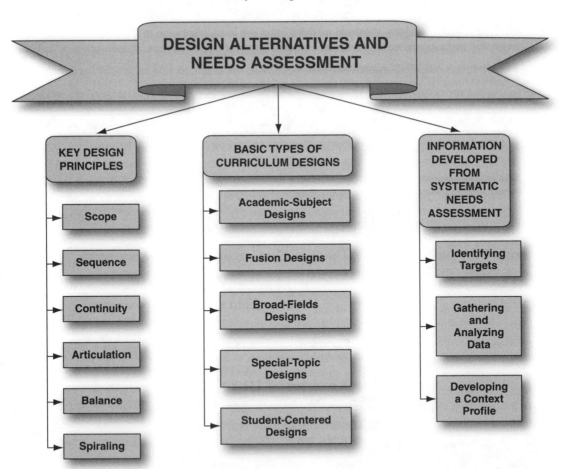

DESIGN ALTERNATIVES AND NEEDS ASSESSMENT

KEY DESIGN PRINCIPLES

- Scope
- Sequence
- Continuity
- Articulation
- Balance
- Spiraling

BASIC TYPES OF CURRICULUM DESIGNS

- Academic-Subject Designs
- Fusion Designs
- Broad-Fields Designs
- Special-Topic Designs
- Student-Centered Designs

INFORMATION DEVELOPED FROM SYSTEMATIC NEEDS ASSESSMENT

- Identifying Targets
- Gathering and Analyzing Data
- Developing a Context Profile

INTRODUCTION

As you engage in curriculum work, one of your key tasks is to impose logic and order on information to be presented to students. Decisions you make require a delicate balance between (1) the need to provide a program frame that will minimize students' difficulties in acquiring new knowledge and (2) the obligation to assure that the included information is appropriate and accurate. Nothing is gained by designing instructional experiences that students cope with easily but that leave them with only trivial understandings. Similarly, it makes no sense to prepare programs that feature excellent information but that are introduced to students in ways they cannot understand. As you work to achieve a blend of program features that makes new and important information truly accessible to students, you need to consider the following:

- Key design principles
- Basic types of curriculum designs
- Information developed from systematic needs assessments

 ## KEY DESIGN PRINCIPLES

Over the years, curriculum specialists have identified design principles that guide decisions related to selecting and organizing the content to be included in instructional programs (Armstrong, 1989; Doll, 1995; Miller & Seller, 1985; Sowell, 1996). Among these principles are those associated with

- Scope
- Sequence
- Continuity
- Articulation
- Balance
- Spiraling

Scope

Think about a subject or topic you might want to teach. If your target audience is very young children, there are obvious limits to what you can expect them to learn. Even if your intended students are advanced graduate students at a university, you face a critical limitation: It is never possible to teach it all. When you do curriculum work, this reality requires you to make decisions about what should and what should not be included in an instructional program. Decisions related to this issue define the **scope** of a program. They make explicit the extent and depth of coverage to be provided.

Scope decisions operate at several levels. Some of them describe the limits of content coverage across an entire pre-K to grade 12 instructional program.

Others focus specifically on the content to be featured at a particular elementary-school grade level or within an individual middle-school or high-school course.

Scope decisions affect instructional time. For example, suppose you and some colleagues were developing a curriculum for a survey of American literature course for 11th graders and had decided to preface your work with the following scope statement: "This course will introduce students to the works of American authors from the time of the American Revolution to the present, with particular emphases on works published since 1900." This statement suggests that no time will be devoted to writers who published before 1776 and that more time will be devoted to twentieth- and twenty-first-century authors. Though the title of the course suggests a survey of the entire period to be covered, the scope statement indicates that it will be an unbalanced survey in terms of the time allocated to various time periods within the total span of years from 1776 to the present.

LEARNING EXTENSION 7–1

Scope as Reflected in Texts Treating the Same Subject

Look at two textbooks that are designed for use either in (1) the same elementary-school subject and the same grade level or in (2) the same middle-school or high-school course. What similarities and differences are there in the scope of coverage of common topics? One measure you can use to determine this is the percentage of total book pages each text devotes to this topic. Conclude your work by responding to the following questions:

- Which topics received about the same degree of attention in each text?
- Which topics received considerably more attention in one of the texts than in the other?
- How might you explain these differences?
- If you had written one of these books, about what percentages of total book pages would you devote to major topics covered?
- How does your scheme compare with that in either of the texts you examined, and how do you account for any similarities or differences?

Decisions related to scope give voice to priorities. They not only identify specific elements of content but also have the potential to give more weight to some of them than to others. As a result, debates over the appropriate scope of an instructional program often are heated. Individual values and priorities come into play as people with contending perspectives seek to allocate instructional time to areas of content they deem important.

Sequence

The principle of **sequence** suggests that many kinds of information are learned better when they are presented to students in a particular order, rather than randomly. The degree to which sequencing situations become controversial varies with the nature of the content. For example, the tradition and logic related to sequencing are so strong within certain subjects that few disputes arise related to sequencing. For this reason, it would be hard to find a foreign language teacher who would make a case for teaching students the subjunctive tense of verbs before students first mastered the use of the present tense. Similarly, no algebra teacher would begin instruction related to the binomial theorem on the first day of class. When subsequent content requires an understanding of certain kinds of prerequisite information, sequencing decisions must assure that the more basic information is taught first.

On the other hand, as you engage in curriculum work, you will find that some subjects, topics, and kinds of content have elements that are generally freestanding. That is, students would experience no real difficulty if *A* were taught first and then *B* or if *B* were taught first and then *A*. For example, consider a typical grade 9 English course that, among other topics, includes lessons related to novels, poetry, short stories, and poetry. Though individual instructors may have their own preferences about the order in which to present the content related to each genre, there is little to suggest that one order of treatment necessarily is to be preferred over another. In other words, students' potential to learn the course material probably will not be seriously affected by their teacher's sequencing-of-content decisions.

Continuity

The principle of **continuity** is related to the principle of sequencing. Sequencing is the general ordering of fairly large blocs of content. Continuity operates at a more micro scale. It focuses on the connection between the end of "learning experience *A*" and the beginning of "learning experience *B*," which immediately follows. When the principle is observed in the program designed, there is a smooth mesh between what students have just finished mastering and the next learning experience they will encounter.

Continuity operates at many levels. In the classroom, each day teachers and their students deal with the ending points and beginning points of individual lessons. When these transitions are smooth, learning is facilitated. When they are not, students may experience problems. At another level, thought about the principle of continuity focuses on the need to ensure that that there is a relationship between what students have studied at the end of one grade level or course and what they will encounter when they enter the next one. At still another level, the principle receives attention in curriculum developers' discussions about the nature of experiences students have had in their last year at one level of schooling (for example, in elementary schools) and what they will be presumed to know when they begin work at the next level of schooling (for example, in middle schools).

The continuity principle, when it is observed in curriculum planning, prevents students' progress from being blocked because they lack the needed prerequisite knowledge to succeed as they begin their study of more advanced and complex topics. If, for example, by the end of their present lesson, young students will not yet have learned how to work with negative numbers, a subsequent lesson that presumes they know these operations will frustrate them. They will not succeed because the continuity principle has been violated and the expectations are inappropriate, given the students' present levels of understanding.

Articulation

If you do much reading in the area of curriculum, you will discover that not all authorities define terms in the same way. **Articulation** is one that sometimes is used in different ways by different people. As used in this text, the term is consistent with Albert Oliver's view that articulation properly is seen as describing a relationship between or among elements of curriculum that is simultaneous, not sequential (Oliver, 1977). For example, suppose you are developing a curriculum for all subject areas for fifth graders. In observing the principle of articulation, you may decide that students should be reading about Benjamin Franklin's experiments with electricity in their history lessons at the same time they are learning the basic principles of electricity in their science lessons.

The basic idea behind articulation is that school programs should strive to overcome the artificial divisions of content that sometimes occur when reality is divided into separate subjects. Students encounter the world as a whole. Hence, it makes sense for them to be exposed to learning experiences in schools that tie together information they receive in individual subject areas. This kind of programmatic organization makes instruction more relevant to students and helps them appreciate that what they have learned has value beyond the limits of the classroom.

CURRICULUM REALITIES 7–1

Articulation–More Easily Achieved Among Some Subjects Than Among Others

Curriculum articulation is easier to accomplish using some pairs, or clusters, of subjects than others. For example, often it is not especially difficult to plan an articulated program involving survey courses in history and English. Chronological time often is used as an organizer of such courses, and program planners face no great challenge in preparing learning experiences for students that involve them in simultaneously studying the historical developments that characterized a particular period and the works of literature produced about the same time that may help students to better understand those events. In addition, both history and English courses share an emphasis on developing students' cognitive abilities.

Curriculum developers face more significant problems when they attempt to achieve articulation across subjects that feature varying organizational patterns and that focus on different categories of student learning. Consider, for example, differences between high-school art survey courses and foreign language courses. Topics in many art survey courses tend to be free-standing. That is, it often makes little difference whether the unit on basic painting techniques precedes or follows the unit on the basic techniques of clay sculpture. The circumstances surrounding foreign language instruction are different. These courses tend to be organized according to a simple-to-complex scheme. Basic information about the language must be mastered before students can master more advanced content. Foreign language instruction is directed almost exclusively at developing students' cognitive abilities.

This discussion is not meant to suggest that there can be no articulated curricula that involve such subjects as art survey and foreign languages. Articulated curricula involving such subjects *can* be planned successfully. However, they present curriculum developers with a much more challenging set of circumstances than they face when attempting to establish articulated programs that focus on subjects that share more features.

Suppose you decided to develop an articulated program involving mathematics and physical education. Traditionally, these two subjects have not been viewed as closely related. In planning your curriculum, you would need to respond to questions such as the following. How would you answer them?

* What specific topics within existing mathematics and physical education programs might best serve as foci for articulated lessons?
* What changes would mathematics teachers have to make in delivering a program that would seek to articulate instruction in the two subjects?
* What changes would physical education teachers have to make in delivering a program that would seek to articulate instruction in the two subjects?
* What general problems do you think you would face in preparing such a program, and what steps might you take to resolve them?

Because it focuses attention on relationships among elements of content from different areas, some curriculum specialists prefer to use the term **correlation,** rather than the term "articulation" to describe these connections (Armstrong, 1989). By whatever name, the essence of the principle is that it makes sense for curriculum developers to cross subject-area boundaries and to develop lessons that enable students to see important relationships among various kinds of content. See Figure 7.1 for an illustration of the relationships among scope, sequence, continuity, and articulation.

Balance

The principle of **balance** seeks to assure that each important element in an instructional program receives its fair share of instructional time and emphasis. When the principle is violated, a small number of program components are highlighted at the expense of others. This principle has relevance at many levels of curriculum planning.

At the classroom level, individual teachers work to assure that all important content gets adequate attention. This principle often receives careful attention

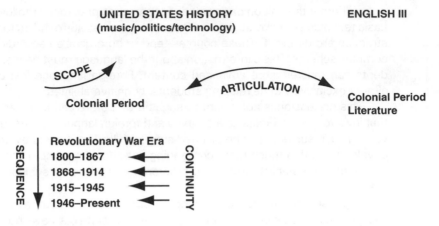

FIGURE 7.1 Basic Design Principles

when district-level curriculum-planning teams consider either new programs or revisions of old ones. Many state rules and regulations reflect decisions that relate to the issue of balance. For example, state-level curriculum standards represent policy documents that often require teachers to pay careful attention to the named content elements. High-school graduation guidelines that require students to take certain numbers of courses in a variety of areas are reflections of a concern for balance.

Concerns about the "What constitutes appropriate balance?" question often result in heated debates. Groups of various kinds and individuals have widely diverging views on this issue. In part, these discussions come about because the funds available to support school programs are limited. When a decision is made to allocate funds to support one program, it may mean that they are taken away from another. For example, organized groups of parents may push hard for more funding to support special programming for gifted and talented students. Other parents may oppose this proposal on the grounds that it will reduce the financial base for other programs and, potentially, give all students a less balanced school experience.

Spiraling

The principle of **spiraling** derives from the work of Jerome Bruner (1960) and Hilda Taba (1967). Its premise is that students of all ages are capable of learning similar basic concepts or ideas. However, there are vast differences in the levels of sophistication of their understandings. The implication for curriculum developers is that a number of key concepts need to be identified as foci for school programs. Then, curricula need to be devised that recycle students through these concepts at ever more sophisticated levels as they go through the pre-K to 12 educational system. For example, very young children might learn about "interdependence" by studying the responsibilities of individual family members. High-school students might study it in terms of the political, economic, and social relationships among nations.

The idea that students need to encounter more sophisticated treatments of ideas as they progress through the school program has wide support. Where curriculum developers sometimes have had difficulty in putting the spiraling principle into practice, the problems have tended to center on the specific concepts or ideas that should be successively revisited at more advanced levels. This issue continues to spark spirited discussions among members of curriculum-development teams. For an illustration of the spiraling principle, see Figure 7.2.

BASIC TYPES OF CURRICULUM DESIGNS

Specific responses to basic curriculum principles are reflected within **curriculum designs** (Tanner & Tanner, 1995). Curriculum designs function as basic program organizers. As you engage in curriculum work, you will find the choice of a particular design to be influenced by (1) the expectations of parents, guardians, and other influential community members, (2) the philosophical perspectives regarding the purposes of education, (3) the nature of the subject matter to be taught, and (4) the kinds of learning materials available to support instruction. Because local conditions vary, curriculum designs are not uniform across the country (Armstrong, 1989). Designs are chosen because they have features consistent with local conditions. However, in spite of place to place differences, curriculum designs tend to fall within a small number of basic patterns:

- Academic-subject designs
- Fusion designs
- Broad-fields designs
- Special-topic designs
- Student-centered designs

Academic-Subject Designs

Academic-subject designs are familiar to everyone who has attended American schools. Such staples of the school programs as courses in history, English, and mathematics are examples of applications of academic-subject designs. In these designs, the titles of traditional subject-matter disciplines give their names to elementary-school classes and middle- and secondary-school courses. Some examples include elementary-school programs in music and mathematics and secondary-school courses in chemistry, English, and economics.

A number of conditions assure the general popularity of academic-subject designs. Parents, guardians, and other adults in the community who are interested in

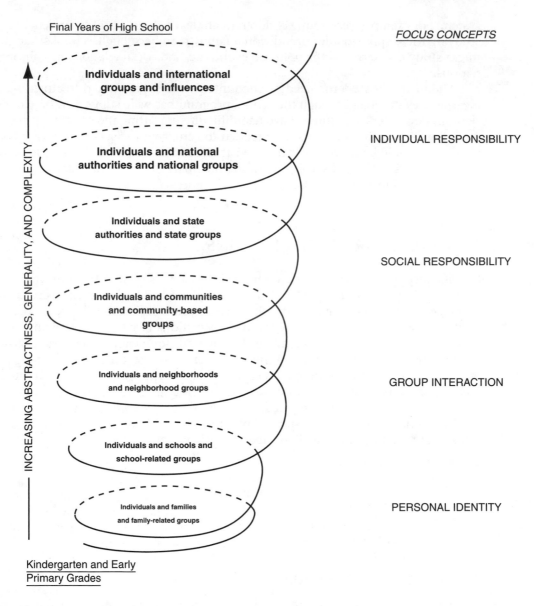

FIGURE 7.2 The Spiral Curriculum

education probably experienced school programs organized by such designs when they were in school. Hence, developers who organize new and revised curricula according to this model are unlikely to draw fire from disgruntled community members who allege that alternative models represent a deviation from a time-tested approach to program organization.

Much new academic knowledge comes from university-based researchers. Though there are some exceptions, most of these professionals operate within communities of scholars who work in traditional academic departments (mathematics, history, English, biology, and so forth). The quality of work tends to be high because, over the years, various academic disciplines have developed rigorous peer-review processes, which exercise an important quality-control function. The findings of these discipline-based professionals tend to be held in high regard. What this means is that pre-K to 12 teachers who teach in programs organized according to an academic-subjects design have a place to go for validated new information related to what they are teaching.

Patterns of teacher preparation also encourage the popularity of academic-subjects designs. Many teachers have gone through baccalaureate programs that required them to take courses from departments organized by academic discipline. As a result, they find organizing school subjects in this way to be a natural and comfortable approach.

Teachers, too, sometimes fear that an organizational pattern that deviates from one associated with traditional academic subjects may require them to spend much more time planning instructional experiences for their students. Suppose you were a new teacher and that your school district gave you the choice of teaching one of the following two courses: "American History" or "Americans' Search for Identity." If you were to make your choice simply on the ease of gathering background information, you probably would choose to teach "American History." You would have little difficulty in finding books and other materials, prepared by historians, that you could use to prepare lessons for "American History." The other course might prove tremendously interesting, but preparing lessons probably would require you to spend a great deal of time digging through widely scattered materials prepared by professionals from a variety of academic disciplines.

Finally, present public interest in testing and accountability supports the popularity of academic subject designs as organizational frameworks for school programs. The long history in the schools of these kinds of courses and classes has resulted in some fairly widespread understanding about what reasonable academic expectations of students should be. In addition, many courses with similar titles are taught in large numbers of schools. For example, virtually all fifth graders study arithmetic, and virtually all high schools have an introductory algebra course. The long-standing history of these classes and courses and the existence of common ones from school to school make it easier for assessment experts to prepare tests and for judgments to be made (based on scores) about the relative quality of the programs in one school compared with another. Where alternative organizational patterns are used, sometimes it is hard for assessment specialists to determine the reasonable levels of student performance. For example, consider the relative difficulty of establishing an appropriate performance standard for students in the previously mentioned course titled "American History" as compared with "Americans' Search for Identity."

Generally, school programs featuring academic-subject designs organize *findings* from a *single* subject area in ways that are appropriate for elementary-school, middle-school, and high-school students. There are also some variations on this basic pattern that take a somewhat different approach. Two examples are structure-of-the-discipline designs and correlation designs.

Structure-of-the-discipline designs.   In 1957, the former Soviet Union's successful launch of the first earth-orbiting satellite, *Sputnik,* stunned American political and educational leaders. Fears that American engineering talent had somehow fallen behind that of the Soviets prompted a national reexamination of the schools and school programming. One group of school reformers suggested that graduates of the pre-K to 12 program would be better served if courses and classes got away from the tendency to teach students the findings of professional scholars. Instead, **structure of the disciplines designs** should provide the framework for school programs (Schwab, 1962). That is, schools should acquaint students with (1) what questions the scholars within individual disciplines ask, (2) how these scholars go about the business of doing their work, and (3) what kinds of evidence these scholars consult as they seek to learn the "truth."

From the late 1950s until the early 1970s, national curriculum-revision groups developed a number of school programs reflecting the structure-of-the-disciplines approach. These included the Biological Science Curriculum Study (BSCS), the Earth Science Curriculum Project (ESCP), the Intermediate Science Curriculum Study (ISCS), and Man: A Course of Study (MACOS). One rationale for these programs was that they would produce high-school graduates who were so well grounded in the academic subjects that they could go through college and university undergraduate programs at an accelerated rate and quickly get involved in graduate study. The hope was to turn out more high-quality academic specialists, and to turn them out quickly.

Critics of these programs pointed out that they tended to be too oriented to the interests of students bound for colleges and universities (Armstrong, 1989). Others pointed out that it was hard to find agreement among professionals in some disciplines regarding what the "structure" of their discipline was. Still others argued that, by narrowing the focus to the methodologies used by highly trained specialists, schools were ignoring other important topics students should learn about. This final category of criticism became particularly heated in the early 1970s, as the nation struggled with such issues as race relations and the appropriateness of involvement in the war in Vietnam.

Correlation designs.   **Correlation designs** seek to provide a framework that attends carefully to the principle of articulation. They aim to identify and emphasize relationships among topics taught in different subject areas. There is no effort to eliminate the different subjects. Rather, the attempt is simply to find and take advantage of related content.

Suppose you decided to work with some high-school English and social studies teachers to prepare a program organized according to a correlation design. For a unit on World War I, you might pair content related to political, economic, social, and military developments (drawn from history) with novels and poetry produced during the war (drawn from English). The intent would be to provide students with a much broader understanding of the period than they would get from studying either only the history of the time or only the literature produced during and about the war years.

Fusion Designs

There is a similarity of intent between correlation designs and **fusion designs.** However, there is an important difference. In correlation designs, the identities of the individual subjects that are correlated remain intact. In fusion designs, the relationships have become so strong and unique that the source disciplines disappear, to be replaced by a brand-new subject label. The purpose is to generate a new content area, which describes reality more adequately than any one of its parent disciplines was able to do alone. The new subject blend draws heavily on a combination of information from its source disciplines but, over time, it begins to take on unique, defining characteristics of its own.

Fusion sometimes results in new courses within an existing, broad academic discipline. For example, high-school "World History" represents a fusion of content from independent history courses (Asian history, European history, African history, South American history, and so forth). Fusion also can involve topics from courses on different academic subjects. One example is college biophysics. Biophysics represents content fused from biology and physics. (See Figure 7.3 for a graphic illustration of fusion designs.)

Fusion designs in pre-K to 12 school programs are not common. They require a careful identification of theoretical rationales and a willingness to hold up interrelatedness as a priority high enough to warrant the replacement of the identities of the source disciplines. However, at the university level, the increasing tendency for teams of professionals from many disciplines to work on common problems may lead to more fused courses. Curriculum specialists Daniel and Laurel Tanner (Tanner & Tanner, 1995) point out, for example, that there is evidence for this trend within the biological sciences.

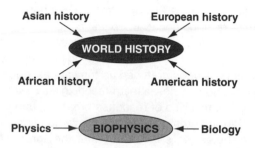

FIGURE 7.3 World History and Biophysics—Examples of Courses Featuring Fusion Designs

Broad-Fields Designs

You might think of **broad-fields designs** as grand extensions of fusion designs. Fusion designs lead to new subjects that have roots in two or more disciplines. Broad-fields designs seek a new whole, or unity, that cuts across an entire branch of knowledge. Individual parts of this branch of knowledge disappear to be replaced by a newly named "broad field."

Examples of broad-fields designs found in many schools are programs with labels such as "Vocational Arts" and "Humanities" and courses titled "Social Studies" (as opposed to economics, history, sociology, and so forth.) The term "broad fields" applies to social studies only when the actual course has this name. There is no broad-fields approach in place when social studies is simply the name of a department that continues to offer courses with titles such as "American History," "World History," "Economics," and so forth (Tanner & Tanner, 1995).

Broad-fields approaches help schools avoid expensive fragmentation. For example, a course called "Humanities" draws together content that, otherwise, might have to be taught separately in courses focusing on art, music, philosophy, history, and literature. Because broad-fields content may come from many disciplines, often instruction is organized around focus themes. For example, a humanities program might select a theme such as "Human Responses to Life Dilemmas Through Time."

CURRICULUM REALITIES 7–2

Finding Instructors for Broad-Fields Programs

One purpose of broad-fields programs is to help students see reality as a whole, rather than as something sliced into artificial compartments, called subjects. To accomplish this end, developers of broad-fields courses tend to focus instruction on large themes and to draw in content from many subject areas. For example, a broad-fields course in humanities may tap into content from history, world literature, philosophy, psychology, music, and the arts.

One of the difficulties school administrators face in sustaining broad-fields programs has to do with course staffing. Most university degree and certification programs fail to provide individuals with the range of content covered in a broad-fields program, such as "Humanities." The shortage of teachers with the breadth of academic training needed to do justice to content from the many disciplines from which they must draw content raises concerns about the quality of instruction students will receive. Those few teachers who do have the necessary breadth of expertise may find themselves very stretched as they are asked to take on a heavier than normal teaching load. Sometimes, a team-teaching approach is adopted in response to this problem. However, this kind of response presents its own set of managerial headaches.

Staffing problems certainly have not diminished interest in broad-fields programs. Nevertheless, it is fair to say that they present school leaders with challenges that are more complex than those they confront in preparing staffing plans for traditional single-subject classes and courses.

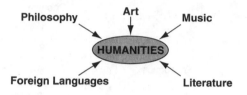

FIGURE 7.4   Humanities and Social Studies—Examples of Broad-Fields Courses

A major difficulty curriculum developers face in preparing broad-fields design is deciding which content elements to include and specific disciplines they should come from. Responses to these difficulties take many forms. For example, if you examine several broad-fields programs labeled "Humanities," it is highly probable that you will find vast differences in the content each includes and emphasizes. This lack of program to program consistency is a barrier to the expansion of broad-fields approaches at a time when accountability is a high-profile concern. When there is no consensus as to what the elements of a high-quality broad-fields program are and when there are great place to place differences in what is taught, it is all but impossible to make meaningful judgments about the quality of the programs from one school to another. (For a graphic representation of a broad-fields approach, see Figure 7.4.)

Special-Topic Designs

Special-topic designs are flexible. They can draw content from many sources. Sometimes, information comes from traditional academic subjects. Sometimes, it comes from other, less formal sources. Often, the selected topics relate to an important issue, question, problem, or area of interest. Many short courses offered by community colleges feature special-topic designs. Some examples are "Investing for Beginners," "Learn to Dance," "Building a Better Marriage," "Obedience Training for Dogs," Beginning Aerobics," and "Using Spreadsheets."

The major strength of special-topic designs is their ability to organize instruction quickly around topics that are needed because of changing conditions or changing student interests. A potential weakness of the design is that the resulting instructional programs often have little history behind them. As a result, there are no widely acknowledged quality standards. People who want schools to

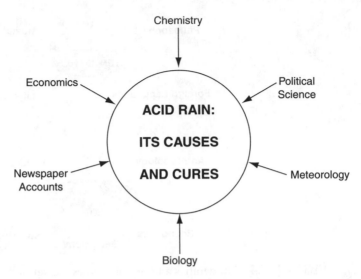

FIGURE 7.5   A Special-Topic Design Focusing on "Acid Rain: Its Causes and Cures"

be accountable often worry about programs in which there is little consensus regarding expected levels of student performance. Hence, curriculum developers sometimes find school programs developed according to special-topic designs to be a hard sell. If you find yourself involved in an effort to create such a program, you will want to pay particular attention to including explicit information about student learning expectations and how they will be assessed. (For a graphic illustration of a special-topic design, see Figure 7.5.)

LEARNING EXTENSION 7–2

Learning Expectations in a Special-Topic Course

Identify a special topic that represents something you would like to teach. Describe the kinds of students who will be in your course (approximate age level, grade level, maturational level—any information you deem relevant). You want the course you develop to be seen as a high-quality offering. To highlight your concern for quality, you decide to develop an explicit set of student learning outcomes and a system to assess students' performance levels. Develop a brief plan for your special-topic course that includes the following:

• Name of the course
• Duration of the course
• Description of the students who will take the course
• List of intended student learning outcomes
• Explanation of specifically what will be done to assess students' performance levels

Student-Centered Designs

In one sense, all curriculum designs are student-centered. Each seeks to provide a framework for the organization of instruction that will encourage students to learn. The special feature of **student-centered designs** is their attempt to be especially responsive to the interests and desires of students. Indeed, these two variables are the major focus of curriculum developers' work.

In an environment that increasingly asks teachers and school leaders to provide evidence that they are delivering high-quality instruction in areas the public at large believes to be important, student-centered designs are scarce in today's schools. Occasionally, teachers will survey students to determine some special interests and will develop some mini-courses in response. These courses are found much more frequently in middle schools and high schools than in elementary schools. Student-centered designs are much more common features of community education than public school education programs. Community education courses come and go, depending on the evolving interests of the people living within the program's service area.

One example of a student-centered design, which has been adopted, at times, by some schools, is the **core-curriculum design.** The term "core curriculum" in recent years often has been used to describe the courses required of all students. In years gone by, the term was used to suggest that all young people had certain needs in common and that school programs had an obligation to address them. It is this view of core curriculum that is reflected in the term core-curriculum design.

Programs organized around a core-curriculum design place heavy emphasis on the study of students' social and personal problems. In a variant called the **preplanned core,** teachers and other professionals identify in advance what these problems are. Then, they use this information to provide relevant learning experiences for students at each grade level. Another variation, the **open core,** features no preplanning. Instead, teachers and their students collectively determine what is to be studied as they discuss this issue together. The highest priority is given to what students want and what they see to be most relevant. This position is consistent with the existentialist philosophy, which was introduced in Chapter 5, "Influences of Philosophy, Learning Theory, and Sociology." As noted there, today this represents a view that is at odds with present public interest in accountability and testing. Few schools today have open-core programs.

 ## INFORMATION DEVELOPED FROM SYSTEMATIC NEEDS ASSESSMENT

What happens after you decide on a general curriculum design? The design decision gives you a basic framework, but it provides only a large and loose set of program-development guidelines. For example, if you commit to an academic-subject design, you still face many questions regarding exactly what will be taught. Similarly, if you and your group decide that a special-topic design makes sense, you still must confront the daunting task of selecting from at least dozens of content alternatives. To help bring more focus to your work, you need to generate additional information through the use of **needs assessment.**

Needs assessment serves two key purposes. First, it provides you with a perception check. That is, information you gather can help you better understand students' interests and backgrounds, the levels of administrator and teacher enthusiasm for a proposed new or revised program, and how the program's intentions square with community priorities. A second function of needs assessment is to produce guidelines that will enable you to make program recommendations that will result in defensible expenditures of scarce educational dollars.

The term "needs assessment" sometimes has been defined in ways that provide an illusion of specificity but that, on closer analysis, raise important additional questions—for example, "Needs assessment seeks to determine the differences between the conditions that exist now and those that should exist." This **discrepancy-analysis view** of needs assessment fails to recognize that individuals' different values often given them varied perspectives on curricular issues (Sowell, 1996). This conception of needs analysis, for example, tends to leave unanswered important questions, such as the following:

- How appropriate is it to assume that there has to be a discrepancy between the present conditions and those that should exist?
- Who are the people who have decided what conditions should exist?
- Are views about what school programs should be doing universally held, or do different people have different perspectives on this issue?

The discrepancy-analysis view of needs assessment derives from the thinking of individuals who see schools basically operating as factories. Students are the raw material. Professional educators act on the raw material in predictable ways. If their approaches are "as they should be," the student raw materials emerge at the end of the total school experience as educated adult citizens. The difficulty with this position is that, unlike the raw material going into a factory, which can be presorted to assure its consistency, there are huge student to student differences. In addition, there are enormous variations in how individuals in the society view the purposes of public education. For many reasons, the factory view of education does not fit well with the realities educators face in working with young people. Hence, an approach to needs assessment that looks only for data related to someone's potentially limited view of discrepancies between what is and what should be has little to commend it.

"Needs assessment" is better described as *a systematic effort to analyze students, the school, and the total milieu within which education occurs to generate information that can be used to allocate scarce instructional resources in ways that best serve student and community interests.* This definition builds solidly on important work by James Beane, Conrad Toepfer, and Samuel Alessi (1986). The quality of the information obtained in needs assessment is enhanced when the potential end-users of new curriculum programs, the teachers, are involved (Tanner & Tanner, 1995) and when the gathered information is carefully analyzed and actually used as a basis for making decisions (Doll, 1995).

There are many formal needs-assessment models. If you wish to see some examples, go to a standard Internet search engine, such as Google (http://www.google.com), and type in the phrase "needs assessment." Many needs-assessment approaches follow a sequence of steps, such as the following:

1. Identifying targets
2. Gathering and analyzing data
3. Developing a context profile

Identifying Targets

One purpose of identifying targets in needs assessment is to gather important information about the general environment of the school or schools where new or revised programs will be taught. Successful programs demand an appropriate physical environment. They also often require that special kinds of learning resources be available.

A second purpose of identifying targets is to focus attention on the perceptions of various groups who may be affected by or have a serious interest in a contemplated curriculum change. You will find reactions of individuals in these groups useful as you engage in curriculum development, revision, and change.

A third purpose of this phase is to establish reasonable limits for the data-gathering activity. These limits are established in two ways: (1) Identifying categories of individuals whose reactions and perceptions will be studied restricts the scope of the needs-assessment process; and (2) developing lists of questions that relate to each group prompts prior thought about what kinds of information will be useful and keeps the volume of acquired information from getting out of hand.

Suppose you and other members of a curriculum group were called together to consider the possibility of revising a middle-school language arts program. You might begin by thinking about (1) the kinds of environmental supports that might be needed; and (2) the categories of people with possible interest in changes to this part of the school curriculum. You and your group might decide to seek data related to the following topics:

- The adequacy of library holdings to support middle-school language arts programs in all schools where a proposed revision might be implemented
- The adequacy of other instructional support materials in all schools where a proposed revision might be implemented
- The reactions and perceptions of middle-school students (who are (1) students enrolled in regular classrooms, (2) gifted and talented students, (3) students with learning disabilities, or (4) students in other categories) regarding the issues related to the language arts program
- The reactions and perceptions of middle-school language arts teachers regarding the issues related to the language arts program
- The reactions and perceptions of administrators (school-level and district-level) regarding the issues related to the language arts program

- The reactions and perceptions of parents and guardians regarding the issues related to the language arts program
- The reactions of general community members to the issues related to the language arts program
- Existing local and state guidelines and any limits they impose on what might be included in the middle-grades language arts program
- The perspectives of professional organizations related to what the components of a sound middle-grades language arts program should be

These focus areas are only examples of what you and your group might find to be relevant. The number of focus areas and the number of groups to be involved vary with the scale and complexity of the contemplated curriculum change. For instance, a program focusing on a third-grade physical education program will require a needs assessment with fewer focus areas than will a program involving a massive revision of the pre-K to 12 science program.

EXERCISE 7–1

Off-the-Shelf Needs-Assessment Procedures

Type the phrase "needs assessment" into a standard Internet search engine, such as Google (http://www.google.com). Read the material provided at 10 to 12 of the listed websites.

Action

Identify those sites that include suggestions for conducting needs assessments related to programs that might be taught in elementary, middle, or secondary schools.

Analysis

Respond to the following questions:

- Are these needs-assessment procedures typically designed to generate information related to broad or narrow slices of the total school curriculum? That is, do you find more needs-assessment models designed to provide information about the total pre-K to 12 mathematics curriculum or more that focus on single grade levels or on single courses?
- In general, does there tend to be more needs-assessment models available on the web for assessments related to some subjects than for assessments related to others?

Key Points

It is difficult to find shelf-ready needs-assessment models that are designed to cover broad areas of the school curriculum. Curriculum developers charged with developing and revising such programs create many components of needs assessments themselves. More shelf-ready needs assessments are available that have a limited content or grade-level focus.

Once focus areas have been developed, general guide questions need to be created for each area and potential data sources identified. In some cases, the data sources will be obvious. For example, if you have an interest in the reactions of school administrators, information must come from members of that group. Sometimes, individuals who themselves are not members of the targeted group also provide useful information. For example, though middle-school students' perspectives deserve to be heard, it also makes sense to hear what middle-school teachers have to say about these young people, particularly regarding middle-school students' reactions to present and proposed programs.

Gathering and Analyzing Data

Many approaches are used to gather information related to needs assessment. The Joint Committee on Standards for Educational Evaluation, housed at Western Michigan University, has developed criteria for sound evaluation procedures, such as those used in needs assessments. If you are interested in this issue, on a standard Internet search engine, such as Google (http://www.google.com), type in "Joint Committee on Standards for Educational Evaluation."

Some examples of approaches used to gather needs-assessment data include

- Questionnaires
- Surveys
- Telephone interviews
- Personal interviews
- Focus groups
- Reviews of standardized test information

If you are interested in exploring a wider range of data-gathering options, you may wish to go to the website maintained by the Online Evaluation Resource Library (http://www.oerl.sri.com). Once there, follow the link to "Evaluation Instruments."

For people who are new to needs assessment, often there is a problem when all the data have been gathered. The volume of information can be huge. If there is not a system to organize this material, it may be difficult to see important patterns. To avoid this possibility, some curriculum groups find it useful to record gathered information on a **needs-assessment data summary chart.** An example that might have been developed for a proposed revision appears in Figure 7.6.

This chart in Figure 7.6 focuses on information gathered about students. Others would be developed that relate to the remaining focus areas. In practice, the chart in Figure 7.6 would take the form of a large wall chart, with sufficient space for relevant information to be added to each cell. Note on the Figure 7.6 chart that data have been gathered for different categories of students. This design appropriately recognizes that great diversity exists among students and that the "needs," more often than not, are not the same for all enrolled students (Chaplin, 1999).

	Traditional Students Enrolled in Regular Classrooms	Gifted and Talented Students	Students with Learning Disabilities	Students in Other Categories
Information about the entry-level expertise of students				
Information about performance levels of students in the existing program				
Parts of the existing program students like				
Parts of the existing program students do not like				
Kinds of content teachers say students need but are not getting now				
Kinds of instructional techniques teachers say work well with these students				

FIGURE 7.6 Format for a Needs-Assessment Data Summary Chart that Focuses on Different Categories of Students

Developing a Context Profile

Needs-assessment data cannot make curriculum decisions for you. Rather, this information provides important contextual information, which you can use to weigh the appropriateness of alternative ideas as they come up when you and others engage in curriculum-development, curriculum-design, and curriculum-revision work. This information provides an important reality check and helps you define what is possible, feasible, or desirable. To be useful, needs-assessment information must be summarized. Organizing information on needs-assessment summary charts is an important, but not sufficient, step. Data from the charts must be refined in ways that will bring to light high-priority needs and concerns.

One approach to providing a concise summary of needs-assessment data involves preparing a context profile. A **context profile** highlights important information that must be considered as alternative curriculum decisions are discussed and debated. The key points in the context profile are derived from more detailed information on the needs-assessment summary charts. Sometimes, the context profile takes the form of a brief written report. On other occasions, a list of bulleted statements will suffice. The following are a few examples of bulleted points that might be included in a context profile designed to assist curriculum workers who are looking at a middle-school language arts program:

Teachers' Concerns/Observations/Priorities

- Present program has no alternative track for gifted and talented students.
- Any new program needs to be supported by instructional materials specifically designed for students with learning disabilities.
- There must be care to tie the beginning point of any new program to what students are learning in the elementary schools.
- Developing writing skills is incredibly time-consuming; beware of adopting guidelines that greatly increase time spent on teaching writing unless teachers get more help in correcting papers.
- There is interest in assuring that any new or revised program be consistent with the guidelines of such organizations as the International Reading Association and the National Council of Teachers of English.

Administrators' Concerns/Observations/Priorities

- Any changes must prepare students to do well on state-mandated tests.
- There is little possibility of increasing the budgets for books and instructional materials to support language arts programs.
- To maintain good relationships with high schools, make certain any adopted program changes mesh well with entry-level expectations of grade 9 English teachers.

Parents'/Guardians' Concerns/Observations/Priorities

- More attention needs to be given to developing students' writing skills.
- Language arts is considered by many parents to be a very important subject; as a group, they will be especially attentive to proposed changes in this area.

Students' Concerns/Observations/Priorities

- Students in traditional classrooms rate their interest in language arts as "low."
- Students find material they are expected to read as dull.
- Students want more opportunities to work in groups and to talk during their language arts lessons.
- Gifted and talented students want to study material that is different from that offered to students in "regular" classes; some of them feel they aren't getting anything different but that they are just asked to read more pages each day and to prepare longer essays.

General Community Members' Concerns/Observations/Priorities

- There is a need to assure that community members will see the benefits of any proposed changes as cost-effective.
- Community members want assurances that there will be a heavy emphasis on developing students' writing skills.
- Faculty members from the local university's English department want to be sure that reading selections are drawn from the works of outstanding writers.

A complete version of these lists would feature many more bulleted points and might break down the major categories into a number of smaller ones. For example, there could be separate lists for (1) students in traditional regular classrooms, (2) gifted and talented students, and (3) students with disabilities.

Whether in the form of a long bulleted list or a written report, the context profile gives you highly useful information. For example, when you and your group make decisions consistent with the priorities reflected in the context profile, you will not anticipate great difficulty in gaining support for your recommendations. There may be other times when members of your group conclude that a decision is warranted that runs counter to the attitudes reflected in the context profile. When you have this information in advance (e.g., from your review of the context profile), you and others in your curriculum group gain time to develop strategies for winning support for your ideas among groups that may have little initial enthusiasm for them.

Review and Reflection

1. Why do discussions about policies that can affect the scope of school programs sometimes become quite heated?
2. How do you distinguish between the principle of sequence and the principle of continuity? What consequences might there be for students if the continuity principle is ignored when a new instructional program is planned?
3. Think about any one of the following: (a) an elementary-grade level, (b) an entire elementary-school program, (c) an entire middle-school program, or (d) an entire high-school program. What would be taught in the area you chose

if you were in a position to make a decision to create what, in your view, is a perfectly balanced program of study? Explain your choices.

4. Today, more school programs are organized around an academic-subject design than around any other alternative. Do you think this condition will persist in the future? Why or why not?

5. To what extent does the interest in holding schools accountable drive curriculum specialists to favor some curriculum designs over others? If all standardized testing were to cease, what impact do you think there would be on the kinds of curriculum designs found in most schools?

6. How would you describe the major functions of needs assessment?

7. What are some general steps you might follow in conducting a thorough needs assessment?

8. On the one hand, educators are admonished to fit programs to the needs of individual students. On the other hand, they are told to prepare students to get high scores on standardized tests. Is there a conflict between these two agendas? Why or why not?

References

Armstrong, D. G. (1989). *Developing and documenting the curriculum*. Needham Heights, MA: Allyn and Bacon.

Beane, J. A.; Toepfer, C. F., Jr.; & Alessi, S. J., Jr. (1986). *Curriculum planning and development*. Boston: Allyn and Bacon.

Bruner, J. (1960). *The process of education*. Cambridge, MA: Harvard University Press.

Chaplin, D. (1999). *Summary of capacity and needs assessments: Youth activities in the District of Columbia*. Washington, DC: The Urban Institute.

Doll, R. C. (1995). *Curriculum improvement: Decision making and process* (9th ed.). Boston: Allyn and Bacon.

Miller, J. P., & Seller, W. (1985). *Curriculum: Perspectives and practice*. New York: Longman.

Oliver, A. I. (1977). *Curriculum improvement: A guide to problems, principles, and process* (2nd ed.). New York: Harper & Row.

Schwab, J. J. (1962). The concept of the structure of a discipline. *The Educational Record, 43*, 197–205.

Sowell, E. J. (1996). *Curriculum: An integrative introduction*. Upper Saddle River, NJ: Merrill/Prentice Hall.

Taba, H. (1967). *Teacher's handbook for elementary social studies*. Reading, MA: Addison-Wesley.

Tanner, D., & Tanner, L. (1995). *Curriculum development: Theory into practice* (3rd ed.). Upper Saddle River, NJ: Merrill/Prentice Hall.

8

Selecting, Sequencing, Organizing, and Prioritizing Content

Graphic Organizer

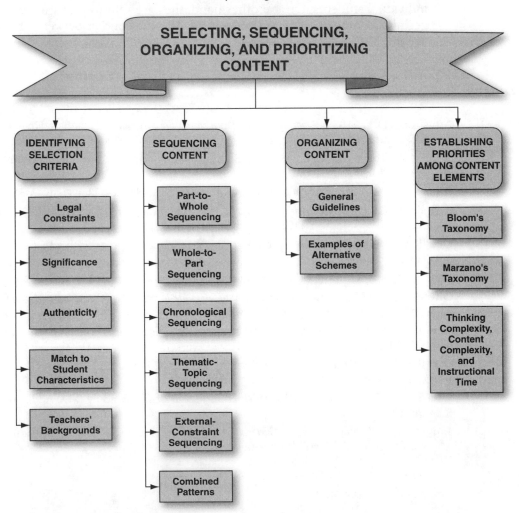

SELECTING, SEQUENCING, ORGANIZING, AND PRIORITIZING CONTENT

IDENTIFYING SELECTION CRITERIA
- Legal Constraints
- Significance
- Authenticity
- Match to Student Characteristics
- Teachers' Backgrounds

SEQUENCING CONTENT
- Part-to-Whole Sequencing
- Whole-to-Part Sequencing
- Chronological Sequencing
- Thematic-Topic Sequencing
- External-Constraint Sequencing
- Combined Patterns

ORGANIZING CONTENT
- General Guidelines
- Examples of Alternative Schemes

ESTABLISHING PRIORITIES AMONG CONTENT ELEMENTS
- Bloom's Taxonomy
- Marzano's Taxonomy
- Thinking Complexity, Content Complexity, and Instructional Time

INTRODUCTION

Curriculum work requires difficult choices. Even after a careful study of needs-assessment information and protracted discussion about desirable new or modified programs, you will still find yourself confronted with more content options than can possibly be accommodated within any instructional program. You will have to sort through various views regarding (1) the relative importance of differing content alternatives and (2) the relative amount of attention that should be devoted to each. You will face these issues even when the focus of your work is as narrow as a single instructional unit for a particular course or grade level. The range of content possibilities becomes even more daunting when a curriculum project seeks to improve instruction in a broader area that ranges across the entire grades pre-K to 12.

Conflicts among the supply of potential content options, various views of the relative importance of alternative content possibilities, and the limited amount of instructional time available force curriculum developers to make decisions related to

- Identifying selection criteria
- Sequencing content
- Organizing content
- Establishing priorities among content elements

Ideally, you will want to make decisions related to these categories that (1) ensure that students are being taught the appropriate kinds of information, (2) sequence information according to patterns that will make it easy for students to acquire the new knowledge, and (3) allocate more instructional time to higher- than to lower-priority content.

 ## IDENTIFYING SELECTION CRITERIA

The volume of information available about almost any topic is vast. For example, you could construct a series of courses that would require several years to complete on such narrow topics as agriculture in Tasmania, Bulgarian writers of the nineteenth century, and insects of Wibaux County, Montana. Because of time constraints and because there is an expectation that school curricula will introduce content that large numbers of people consider to be important, it is unlikely that these extremely narrow topics would rank high on the priority lists of most people concerned about the quality of school programs.

To help you as you think about decisions related to content selection, you will want to consider content-selection criteria such as the following:

- Legal constraints
- Significance
- Authenticity
- Match to student characteristics
- Teachers' backgrounds

Legal Constraints

Members of curriculum-development and curriculum-revision groups find that some content decisions have been made for them. For example, if your state is typical, there are legal mandates that require all high-school students to complete a certain number of courses in such areas as history, the basic sciences, English, and mathematics. Some states go beyond naming categories of content that schools must teach and indicate how much instructional time must be devoted to each required subject. For example, all students may have to enroll in one full year of American history during one of the high-school years, a year of state history during one of the middle-school grades, and reading instruction in every one of the elementary-school grades. Some state policies even specify the number of minutes per week, semester, or year that must be devoted to instruction in a given subject area.

In some places, local school districts impose content requirements. Where such policies exist, they and those of the state constitute a set of "givens" that place limits on curriculum developers' content-selection options. Often, curriculum groups begin their content-selection work by sharing information about these legal constraints, so that all group members gain a clear understanding of the range of their discretionary authority to make additional decisions about what programs should and should not include.

Significance

In general, content is determined to have **significance** when there are yes answers to two key questions:

1. Is the mastery of this content essential if students are to do more advanced work in this area?
2. Does the mastery of this content give students control over information that will transfer in useful and productive ways to other settings and situations?

The first question encourages curriculum developers to gather information about areas of content that form important building blocks for later, more sophisticated kinds of learning. For example, students must master information about basic arithmetic facts and operations before they can deal with concepts associated with more advanced mathematics. Developing students' proficiency in reading makes it possible for them to productively engage more sophisticated content in many subject areas. Helping students master basic keyboarding skills enables them to have the proficiencies needed to profit from more advanced, computer-based instruction. The basic idea is to be sure that sufficient basic content is embedded within instructional programs, so that there will be no learning blockage because students lack the basic skills and knowledge needed to master more advanced content.

The second question seeks to pinpoint the kinds of content that will prove useful to students in settings beyond the one where they learned the information. In general, identifying content of this kind is more difficult than identifying basic skills and basic information content. Often, curriculum developers seek guidance from subject-matter specialists, learning theory experts, educational psychologists, and other professionals. Frequently, even experts have differing views regarding what kinds of content are truly important and which best help students transfer what they have learned to new settings. You will also find that many curriculum specialists, administrators, teachers, students, parents, and other community members have diverse views on this issue. Because the priorities of individuals vary, you can expect to encounter a great deal of debate and discussion whenever questions come up about which content best promotes the transfer of learning.

Authenticity

The principle of **authenticity** speaks to the need to include information that is intellectually sound. You will not find it particularly difficult to determine accuracy when all that is involved is a question of fact. Controversies related to authenticity boil up much more frequently when issues of judgment are involved. To make responsible judgments about accuracy, you cannot simply take a vote and make a decision to support the views of the majority. The hard reality is that not everyone has the expertise necessary to make a reasoned judgment about all content-related issues. Although you cannot ignore the views of the wider community, you also must give serious consideration to the views of specialists who may be able to share arguments and evidence with you that support conclusions that differ from those of people who lack their training. Sometimes, you can use information from experts to build a case that, in time, will change the opinions of people with less formal training in areas relevant to the controversy.

Selecting content that stands up well to the test of authenticity gives programs credibility, both with the community at large and with students. When programs fail the authenticity test, people may lose faith in the educational process. This negative turn of events can have disastrous public relations consequences for educators. In recent years, for example, there have been recurring concerns about the inaccuracies found in many school textbooks. There is even an organization called The Textbook League, which publishes a journal called *The Textbook Letter.* Issues of this publication include numerous articles focusing on content errors in school texts. Newspapers also have featured articles about this situation. As a result, some parents, guardians, and members of the general public raise questions about the intellectual integrity of teachers and administrators. These concerns can undermine the political and financial base of schools, and educational leaders are working hard to correct the situation and to reassure the public that educational professionals are committed to providing students with instruction that features authentic content.

EXERCISE 8–1

Accuracy of Information in Textbooks

Go the website of The Textbook League (http://www.textbookleague.org). If you have trouble getting to the site using this electronic address, enter the words "The Textbook League" into a standard search engine, such as Google (http://www.google.com).

At this site, you will find a long list of web-accessible articles from various issues of *The Textbook Letter,* The Textbook League publication that features critiques of the contents of school textbooks.

Action

From this list, find and read critiques of two texts. If possible, choose two from the same general content area.

Analysis

Respond to the following questions:

- What specific deficiencies did the critique writers cite?
- Were the cited errors more frequently errors of fact or errors of interpretation?
- What recommendations for improvement were suggested?
- What was the general tone of the critiques? For example, did you get the impression that the writer presumed that errors were made because of (1) poorly informed authors, (2) insufficient final reading of materials by experts before publication, (3) a desire to push a particular political agenda, or (4) other reasons?
- What general impression do you have about how widespread the concerns about textbook accuracy are?

Key Point

Errors in instructional materials have the potential to undercut public faith in the quality of the schools. This diminished confidence can result in eroded support for budgets and can provide ammunition for individuals and groups interested in diverting to other purposes some money that now goes to maintain public schools.

Match to Student Characteristics

There are two basic concerns related to selecting content that is well fitted to the characteristics of students. The first of these has to do with the issue of content complexity. The second has to do with the issue of motivation. Let's look first at the complexity issue.

The focus question is a simple one: "Is the proposed content appropriate, given the ages, mental-development levels, and previous instructional experiences of the students to be taught?" In some cases, this question is easy to answer. For example, you would be highly unlikely to recommend a lesson titled "Red Means Stop—Green Means Go: Learning About Stoplights" for inclusion in a health course designed for high-school students. Similarly, you naturally would shy away from introducing a lesson titled "Fun with the Pythagorean Theorem" in a program designed for kindergarten youngsters.

Sometimes, answers to this question are not so easy. You have to consider variables beyond students' ages and grade levels. For example, even quite young gifted and talented students can handle content that would be far too difficult for their more typical age mates. Similarly, students with certain kinds of disabilities cannot profit from instruction that would provide few serious difficulties for many other students in their age group.

To get a better feel for whether a certain kind of content is at an appropriate level of complexity for the target group of learners, you need to look carefully at the available instructional materials. Textbooks, in particular, need to be scrutinized carefully. Are readability levels appropriate? What kinds of instructional aids are provided throughout? In addition, it makes sense to look at other kinds of learning supports, including instructional software, websites with related information, videotapes, and periodicals.

The potential of proposed content to motivate students to learn also bears consideration when you make selection decisions. As you think about the relative motivational appeal of several content alternatives you are considering, you may wish to consult professional articles that focus on the general issue of motivation. In addition, you might want to pilot test several alternatives to see which one students like best. You might also consider interviewing a small sample of students to find out their reactions to the alternatives you are considering.

Finally, does the content have the potential to develop students' higher-level thinking skills? Will it encourage them to make comparisons and contrasts and to engage in other activities that will have explanatory utility beyond the context in which the material was learned? Yes answers to these questions will support the appropriateness of including the information.

LEARNING EXTENSION 8–1

Adequacy of Recommendations for Matching Content and Instructional Materials to the Needs of Individual Students

Today, commercial publishers of instructional materials understand that selection committees want to know how well items they might purchase will serve the needs of various kinds of students. For example, instructor's guides often provide some guidelines for adapting materials and instructional approaches to subgroups of students within the general school population.

Review several instructor's guides that have been prepared as part of a total instructional program or to accompany a textbook. Then, respond to the following questions:

1. Do the recommendations recognize that there are many categories of students who may have special needs and that accommodating these needs may require quite varied approaches?

2. If the answer to question 1 is yes, is the information about what might be done to help the students in each group about the same in term of its extent, depth, and appropriateness?

3. In general, does the information provided seem to have been developed by people who truly understand the practical realities of dealing with diverse groups of

students, or do you get the impression that the information is just a cosmetic response provided because of a political need to say something about meeting the needs of individual students?

4. If you were to make changes to the provided recommendations, what would they be, and why would you wish to include this information?

Teachers' Backgrounds

When curricula are being developed or revised at the local school district level or the state level, most teachers who will implement the changes are not personally part of the process. Often, those teachers who are involved develop a strong sense of ownership in the work and are eager to teach the new program. Their participation in the development process leaves them well acquainted with the rationale for the program, the embedded elements of content, the suggested teaching approaches, and the available instructional support material.

Teachers who have not been actively involved in the curriculum development effort lack these insights. When you are engaged in curriculum work, you and others in your group need to respond to this reality during the developmental phase, as well as when you prepare to implement the changes. One approach you might take is to invite selected representatives of the teachers who will be potential users to meetings of the curriculum committee, where members of your group can provide them with updates and can solicit their reactions. You might also provide summaries of your group's evolving thinking to an even larger number of potential program users. Efforts to stay connected with potential users help ensure that the completed program will not deviate too far from their interests, priorities, and backgrounds. If it does, problems may surface when it is implemented.

Once your new or revised program is completed, it must be introduced to all potential users in a systematic way. Good staff-development work will help assure a smooth transition from the old to the new program. For more information on the staff-development issue, see Chapter 10, "Implementing Curriculum Changes."

 SEQUENCING CONTENT

In what order should the individual components of an instructional program be presented to students? Sometimes, the nature of the content to be taught suggests the importance of teaching certain content elements before others. In other situations, the order of presentation can be varied without jeopardizing students' abilities to master the material. There are five basic content-sequencing arrangements. A sixth approach features a combination of two or more of the five basic arrangements:

- Part-to-whole sequencing
- Whole-to-part sequencing

- Chronological sequencing
- Thematic-topic sequencing
- External-constraint sequencing
- Combined patterns

Part-to-Whole Sequencing

Part-to-whole sequencing is also sometimes known as the *simple-to-complex* model. If you organize instruction according to this approach, you will arrange individual content parts in such a way that simple elements are taught before more complex ones. The idea is that more sophisticated "wholes" cannot be understood before students have a thorough understanding of their constituent parts. Mathematics and foreign language courses often have this kind of sequencing pattern. The internal logic of both the mathematics and the foreign languages disciplines supports the logic of this scheme. Students simply cannot grasp the more complex aspects of these subjects without having first mastered the less complex ones.

Whole-to-Part Sequencing

Whole-to-part sequencing is the reverse of part-to-whole sequencing. Students are first presented with the big picture; then they are introduced to the parts that collectively make up the whole. Some subject areas lend themselves more naturally than others to this arrangement. A subject that often is organized this way is geography. For example, world geography courses often begin with an overview of the entire globe. Frequently, the continents are introduced, as are global wind systems, weather systems, and ocean current systems. Following this overview, lessons often narrow their focus to deal in-depth with large global regions. These, in turn, may be followed by lessons focusing on countries within regions and perhaps of regions within individual countries.

Chronological Sequencing

In **chronological sequencing**, you order the content elements based on the variable of time. This scheme makes sense for some content areas, but not for others. History courses often are organized this way. When this is done, lessons focusing on earlier periods of time usually precede those focusing on later periods. (The chronological approach does not mandate an earliest-to-latest sequence, but it is more common than a latest-to-earliest sequence.)

Subjects other than history sometimes also are organized chronologically. For example, some English and language arts courses arrange materials to be studied chronologically. A survey of American literature course may begin with a study of colonial era literature, proceed to a consideration of the literature of the early republic, and use similar units of time to move students forward toward a concluding unit featuring present-day literature.

Thematic-Topic Sequencing

Thematic-topic sequencing occurs in content areas where individual topics do not build on others. For example, in a high-school art survey course, basic information presented in a unit on metal sculpture is not a prerequisite for units on working with pastels or the coil method of making clay pots. An elementary-school language arts program may have separate units focusing on short stories, creative writing, plays, and poetry. Since none of these topics builds on the others, the order in which they are taught makes little difference.

In courses of this kind, individual units logically can be sequenced in many different ways. If you are involved in developing curricula with this kind of focus, sequencing suggestions (if you make them at all) will be based on some general feelings you and others involved in creating or revising the program have about an order of presentation that seems well suited to accommodate student needs and interests.

External-Constraint Sequencing

External-constraint sequencing demands sometimes force you to make sequencing decisions that are based on neither the nature of the content to be taught nor student needs. External constraints may require you to recommend certain topics to be covered at certain times. For example, if a high-school biology course regularly features a field ecology unit that is taught in an outdoor laboratory facility serving many schools, the date this facility will be available fixes the time in the instructional program when the unit will be taught.

Sometimes, the availability of important support media also influences sequencing decisions. Years ago, the author worked in a school in a thinly populated state that had only one centralized educational film library to serve all of its schools. Teachers who wanted to use films had to schedule them months in advance, and often the dates of their availability exercised considerable influence over content-sequencing decisions.

Combined Patterns

Sometimes, the basic sequencing patterns are combined. For example, many English and language arts programs include topics that reflect a thematic-topic sequence. However, a chronological sequencing scheme is used under each theme. Such arrangements facilitate the development of lessons designed to enhance students' higher-level thinking skills. For an example of such a combined arrangement, see Figure 8.1.

LEARNING EXTENSION 8–2

Alternative Sequencing Arrangements

Identify a course or topic you might like to organize for instructional purposes. (If you choose a topic, be certain it is large enough to be broken into a number of divisions.)

Survey of Twentieth-Century American Writing

- **The Evolution of Plays as a Genre**
  - o 1900–1918
  - o 1919–1945
  - o 1946–1975
  - o 1976–Present

- **Emerging Patterns in Short-Story Development**
  - o 1900–1918
  - o 1919–1945
  - o 1946–1975
  - o 1976–Present

- **Variations Related to Theme, Setting, and Characterization in the Novel**
  - o 1900–1918
  - o 1919–1945
  - o 1946–1975
  - o 1976–Present

- **Changes in the Character of American Poetry**
  - o 1900–1918
  - o 1919–1945
  - o 1946–1975
  - o 1976–Present

FIGURE 8.1 A Combined Thematic-Topic/Chronological Sequencing Arrangement

Note: A thematic sequence has been used for the major divisions. Subordinate divisions use a chronological approach. The common time periods under each major heading allow teachers to engage students in activities requiring them to compare and contrast the characteristics of plays, short stories, novels, and poetry written both within common time periods and across time periods.

Prepare three sequencing schemes you might use. Select a different one of the following approaches for each of your first two schemes: (a) part-to-whole sequencing, (b) whole-to-part sequencing, (c) chronological sequencing, or (d) thematic-topic sequencing. For your third scheme, use a combined pattern.

When you have finished, answer the following questions:

- Which of these schemes was easiest for you to develop?
- Which was the most difficult?
- How do you account for these differences in difficulty?

 ## ORGANIZING CONTENT

If you look at a number of school textbooks for almost any subject and grade level, you probably will discover variations in the number of chapters, the titles of chapters, and the topics that are covered. Even when you find chapters with generally similar names, frequently you will note great differences in the nature of the specific information that is provided. Why do these differences exist?

Differences result because the personal values of the developers of individual curricular materials vary. Further, developers differ in their reactions to alternative philosophical positions, their perspectives on learning theory, their interpretations of legal mandates, their concerns about community expectations, and their levels of attention to other external influences.

When you are charged with identifying content headings for a new instructional program, your task is to seek a balance between breadth and number. On the one hand, you have to recognize the importance of selecting headings that have the capacity to carry within them significant quantities of important information. On the other hand, you need to recognize that students sometimes feel intimidated when material they are asked to learn lacks fairly numerous internal divisions. Generally, older, more mature students can handle materials with fewer internal divisions than can younger, less mature students.

General Guidelines

In thinking about developing a scheme for dividing a large body of content into smaller sections, you might consider these guidelines:

- Major headings need to be broad enough to encompass large numbers of important ideas, but not so broad as to organize a volume of content that students will find intimidating.
- Student characteristics must be considered. In general, instructional programs designed for younger students need more internal divisions than those designed for older students.
- The sequencing of internal divisions needs to make sense, given the nature of the content to be taught.
- The relative emphases given individual program components should vary, depending on such variables as identified student needs; the availability of instructional support materials; legal mandates; and teacher, administrator, parent, and community preferences.
- If the instructional program is part of a larger sequence that ties to a preceding instructional experience, to a subsequent instructional experience, or to both, it makes sense to consider the fit of the proposed set of divisions with kinds of content divisions that students have experienced or will experience.

Examples of Alternative Schemes

Even when there is careful attention to the selection criteria, the content-organization patterns of courses and units with similar names can be quite different. To illustrate this point, look carefully at Figure 8.2. It illustrates three

Arrangement One

Our Country's Beginnings
- Our People
- Our Land
- The First Americans

Developing the English
Colonies
- Southern Colonies
- New England Colonies
- Middle Colonies

The New Nation Is Born
- The Road to Revolution
- Governing the New
  Nation
- Early Growth

Expanding the Frontiers
- Americans Move West
- On to the Pacific
- A Changing Nation

The North and South
at War
- A House Divided
- The Civil War
- Reconstruction

The New Industrial Age
- Twilight of the Old West
- Growth of Industry
- Immigrants and Cities

A New World Power
- Becoming a World Power
- Challenges in the New
  World and Old
- Prosperity and
  Depression
- World War II and the
  Atomic Age
- Today and Tomorrow

Arrangement Two

Settlement in the Colonial
Period
- From the Atlantic Coast
  to the Fall Line
- West of the Mountains

Settling the United States
- 1800–1850
- 1850–1910
- 1910–Present

Arrangement Three

Earning a Living
- Age of Discovery to 1776
- 1776–1820
- 1820–1870
- 1870–Present

Inventions and Innovations
- Age of Discovery to 1776
- 1776–1820
- 1820–1870
- 1870–Present

Social Life and Recreation
- Age of Discovery to 1776
- 1776–1820
- 1820–1870
- 1870–Present

How Political Decisions
Were Made
- Age of Discovery to 1776
- 1776–1820
- 1820–1870
- 1870–Present

Involvement in World
Affairs
- Age of Discovery of 1776
- 1776–1820
- 1820–1870
- 1870–Present

FIGURE 8.2 Alternative Organizational Patterns for Contents in a United States History Course

distinctive schemes for organizing topics for three versions of a survey course called "United States History."

In Figure 8.2, consider "Arrangement One." You will notice several key features. First of all, the content is broken down into a large number of separate parts. In general, a chronological sequencing arrangement has been adopted. That is, the early units focus on earlier time periods than the later ones. Except for the last unit, the number of major topics in each unit is very consistent. Finally, you may have observed that there is a very unequal weighting of attention to different time periods. This course purports to cover the entire span of United States history. Although the course arrangement does direct some attention to the entire period from the days of early exploration to the present, much more attention is devoted to events that occurred prior to 1870. Note that five of the seven units deal with this period of United States history. All the topics related to the events and situations occurring between 1870 and the present are covered within the space of just two units.

You will also note in Figure 8.2 that "Arrangement One" features a large number of content divisions. This feature suggests that this course was designed to meet the needs of younger students, who sometimes find it difficult to cope with extremely long units of study. The organizational scheme in "Arrangement One" is typical of those often found in United States history courses designed for fifth graders. Why did the course developers of Arrangement One decide to frame the course in this way? The decision probably was based in part on a recognition that, in addition to studying United States history in grade 5, most students also study United States history for at least one additional year in high school. Many school districts also require students to take a United States history course in either grade 7 or grade 8. Knowing that students will have other opportunities to study this material, the developers of this fifth-grade program assumed that its heavy emphasis on earlier periods in United States history would be counterbalanced in subsequent courses by emphases on more recent periods of history.

In addition, the developers probably recognized a long-standing tradition in grade 5 elementary programs to highlight content dealing with explorers, the lives of early settlers, and the interactions of pioneers with Native American groups. Vast quantities of instructional materials designed for use by elementary-school teachers and students are available that focus on the earlier periods of United States history. Supplies of instructional materials to support teaching fifth graders about more recent historical episodes, such as the Great Depression of the 1930s, are much less abundant.

The people who developed the course in Figure 8.2, if asked to provide a rationale for their decisions, might have included comments such as the following:

> Students in this course should receive more intensive instruction in topics related to precolonial days, colonial days, the early republic, early settlement of the frontier, the Civil War, and Reconstruction than in topics related to developments from 1870 to the present. Even though coverage of developments since 1870 is sparse, there is sufficient coverage of this material to justify the standing of this course as a general survey of United States history. In addition, excellent instructional support materials exist to support instruction related to the earlier years of United States history. The many con-

tent divisions this design features are appropriate, given the developmental levels of the students who will enroll in this course.

In Figure 8.2, "Arrangement Two" organizes the course content in a very different way. Notice that it features a much smaller number of internal divisions. The course organization also has been designed to focus students' attention on a single, overriding theme—the settlement of the land area of today's United States. A rationale developed by the curriculum developers who proposed this arrangement might have included comments such as the following:

> There is a single essential understanding that students who take a United States history course must acquire. It is that issues associated with "settling the country" are critical to developing an appropriate appreciation of our history. The tradition of presenting history according to a chronological sequencing arrangement is strong; hence, though issues associated with settlement will remain the "meat" of the course, it makes sense for students to examine these patterns as they evolved from the earliest periods of our history to the present.

"Arrangement Three" divides the course into more component parts than does "Arrangement Two." It features a number of major themes as the major course organizers. A common set of time periods is used to provide content divisions under each theme. A rationale prepared by the developers of this arrangement might have included comments such as the following:

> There are important themes that have recurred throughout United States history that students should come to understand. The tradition of presenting history according to a chronological sequencing arrangement supports studying each theme in a chronological sequence, using a set of common time periods as subordinate topics under each major thematic heading. Students' thinking abilities are enhanced when the content is organized in ways that allow them to compare and contrast developments related to individual themes that were occurring (1) during common time periods and (2) at different time periods.

LEARNING EXTENSION 8–3

Imposing Order on Unorganized Content

There is a virtually limitless supply of information available about any subject. One of the challenges you face as you do curriculum work is finding an organizational structure that will help students derive meaning from what they are taught. A good organizational scheme facilitates student learning. It also imposes order in a way that tends to highlight certain aspects of content while giving less attention to others.

Developing a good organizational structure is not easy. You need to think carefully about the issues described in the content-organization guidelines described at the beginning of this section. Review the guidelines, and then do the following:

1. *Step One:* (a) Develop an extensive list of specific information related to a large subject you might wish to organize for instruction, *or* (b) use topics from the

list below. These topics were included in a textbook unit titled "Days on the Last Frontier: 1865–1900," a component of a middle-school-level American history course:

> Rainfall beyond the 100th meridian
> Failure of reservations for Native Americans
> Bows and arrows
> Invention of the revolver
> New transportation systems
> Buffalo slaughter
> Custer's last stand
> The Dawes Act (about reservations for Native Americans)
> The Cattle Kingdom
> Latinos and Native Americans in the Old West
> The long rifle
> The open range
> Making fortunes in cattle
> New kinds of fences
> The Homestead Act
> Railroads and settlers
> Materials for houses
> Water problems
> Windmills
> Barbed wire
> Steel plowshares
> Double-disk harrows
> Adjustable smoothing harrows
> The Forty-Niners
> Pikes Peak
> The Comstock Load
> Innovations in mining technology
> Wars with Native Americans

2. *Step Two:* Create an organizational scheme with headings and subordinate headings that will accommodate the specific items you either identified yourself or chose from the list from the middle-school American history course.

3. *Step Three:* (a) Develop a short list of generalizations that would guide the overall instruction of this material and that you hope students would master, (2) develop an accompanying list of major concepts (key ideas) you wish students to grasp as a result of their exposure to this material, and (3) summarize one or two hoped-for student attitudes or dispositions toward this material that you would like students to have after they have been exposed to it.

4. *Step Four:* Prepare a short paragraph in which you explain your rationale for preparing a scheme that tends to highlight some content elements while downplaying others.

5. *Step Five:* Share your responses to the following questions in a manner suggested by your instructor:

- What problems or frustrations did you encounter in developing your organizational scheme?

- Were there some content elements that did not seem to fit well under any of your headings?

- Were there other potential arrangements you considered before deciding on the final organizational scheme you adopted? If so, what led you to reject them?

 ## ESTABLISHING PRIORITIES AMONG CONTENT ELEMENTS

Sometimes, you will be asked to make recommendations regarding the relative importance of the individual components of a curriculum you are developing, refining, or revising. This information will be helpful in several ways. First of all, it gives school leaders a rationale for committing more money to purchase instructional resources to support the program's higher-priority components. Second, this information helps potential users understand which aspects of the content the developers believe to be most significant. Armed with this knowledge, they may decide to allocate the time they spend preparing to teach the new program in ways that respond to the relative importance of its various parts.

The priorities accorded individual program components take on a particular significance once instruction begins. This is true because there is an expectation that, at the end of their instruction, students will leave with a more sophisticated grasp of the content associated with high-priority than low-priority program elements. It takes considerable time for students to develop in-depth understandings of complex content. The operational reality is that more instructional time needs to be devoted to high-priority than to low-priority content.

In deciding how to prioritize program elements, you may want to consider the opinions of subject-matter specialists and other authorities. Sometimes, this kind of information can be found through reviewing articles in professional journals. (Many relevant articles can be found in the *Education Index,* a guide to professional literature in education that is available in many libraries.) Finally, many subject-area specialist groups (National Council of Teachers of English, International Reading Association, National Council of Teachers of Mathematics, National Science Teachers Association, National Council for the Social Studies, and so forth) publish curriculum guidelines that call for heavy emphases on certain kinds of content.

Though guidelines from external sources are helpful, you and others involved in curriculum work probably will need to make your own decisions about prioritizing content divisions. In general, it makes sense to assign high priorities to the segments of a program that

- Have broad explanatory power
- Focus on critical issues
- Promote the transfer of knowledge to many new settings and situations (Armstrong, 1989)

As noted previously, since you will expect program users to considerable instructional time to high-priority content elements, you will expect students to emerge with quite sophisticated levels of understanding of the new material they encounter. One way to present a visual representation of the priorities accorded to different content elements is to make explicit what kinds of thinking might be expected of students at the conclusion of their exposure to the instruction related to each element. Several schemes seek to scale various kinds of thinking in terms of their complexity. Often called **taxonomies,** these arrangements attempt to arrange categories of thinking in a simple-to-complex order. These taxonomies can be sorted into three basic types, each of which focuses, respectively, on the *cognitive domain,* the *psychomotor domain,* or the *affective domain.*

The **cognitive domain** comprises rational or intellectual thinking. Much of the mental activity associated with learning the academic content of basic school subjects such as history, chemistry, English, and mathematics requires students to engage in cognitive processes.

The **psychomotor domain** embraces the kinds of learning that require students to develop control over the body's muscular system. The kinds of psychomotor controls that students must develop vary, ranging from those requiring the use of the large muscles to those demanding the highly coordinated use of fine muscle systems. Raising pots using a potter's wheel, developing good keyboarding skills, and producing legible handwriting are all examples of school activities that engage students in psychomotor learning.

The **affective domain** focuses on the issue of attitudes and predispositions. David Krathwohl and his colleagues (Krathwohl, Bloom, & Masia, 1964) developed a taxonomy that organizes levels of affective learning into a hierarchical structure. See Figure 8.3 for a graphic representation of their **affective taxonomy** and a brief explanation of each of its levels. In affective learning, the focus is not on students' abilities to succeed at individual school tasks but, rather, on their reactions to these tasks. This issue is of concern because, when students are negatively disposed to certain kinds of school experiences, they do not do well (Good & Brophy, 2000). It is somewhat unusual for curricula to feature topics that have the sole purpose of teaching students specific attitudes and values. More frequently, learning in the affective domain is seen as a kind of overlay on topics that primarily focus on developing students' cognitive or psychomotor proficiencies.

The division of thinking into separate cognitive, psychomotor, and affective categories may be a useful way for looking at each of the categories in isolation. However, in reality, all operate at the same time. For example, consider a student whose grades are poor on handwritten essays assigned by an English teacher. The student's less than adequate performance may be explained by a combination of cognitive, affective, and psychomotor factors. In the cognitive area, this person may lack an essential understanding of the information that is tested. Part of his or her failure to master this information may result because the student has an extreme dislike for English and, therefore, refuses to do the assigned background reading. Finally, the person's handwriting may be extremely difficult to read. The

Level	Brief Description
Characterized by a value or value complex	Certain values become a permanently embedded part of a person's existence and direct his or her actions and statements.
Organization	At this level, individuals think about their values, work to clarify them, and set about arranging them in a systematic way.
Valuing	At this level, individuals accept and prefer certain things and become committed to them.
Responding	At this level, individuals willingly react or respond to new circumstances.
Receiving	At this level, individuals demonstrate an awareness of something new or unfamiliar and are willing to acknowledge its existence, receive it, or attend to it.

FIGURE 8.3 Categories of the Affective Domain

Source: Based on *Taxonomy of educational objectives handbook II: Affective domain,* by Krathwohl, D.R., Bloom, B.S., & Masia, B.B., 1964, New York: McKay.

student's poor handwriting, a product of inadequate development of a psychomotor skill, may make it difficult for the teacher to understand and properly credit the student for what he or she has written.

Bloom's Taxonomy

As you engage in curriculum work, you will probably spend a great deal of time focusing on cognitive learning. Of the several cognitive taxonomies that have been developed over the years, the best known is the framework that Benjamin Bloom and others (Bloom, Engelhart, Furst, Hill, & Krathwohl, 1956) developed half a century ago. Widely known as **Bloom's Taxonomy,** this scheme features the following six simple-to-complex levels:

Level	Abbreviated Description
Knowledge	Ability to recall specific elements of previously learned information
Comprehension	Ability to engage in simultaneous recall of several bits of information, to organize information, to transform the form of information, and to extrapolate from the information
Application	Ability to use new information in contexts different from the one in which it was initially learned
Analysis	Ability to describe the characteristics of something by identifying the relationships between and among its parts

| Synthesis | Ability to put together elements of something in a creative or new way (or at least in a way that is creative or new to the person engaged in the task) |
| Evaluation | Ability to make judgments about something in terms of specific and credible criteria |

Some critics have pointed out that Bloom's Taxonomy focuses on thinking processes in isolation and fails to consider how they might operate differentially on various categories of information (Marzano, 2001). For example, because the objects toward which thinking can be directed vary enormously in their complexity, it cannot always be assumed that knowledge-level thinking is less demanding than application-level thinking—developing a good knowledge-level grasp of the principles associated with a nuclear reaction is more intellectually challenging than developing an application-level ability to locate points on a globe using measures of latitude and longitude.

LEARNING EXTENSION 8–4

Critiquing Bloom's Taxonomy

Many educators acknowledge Bloom's contributions to professional thought about how cognitive processes might be ordered from simplest to most complex. At the same time, critics have raised questions about the adequacy of the hierarchical structure in Bloom's Taxonomy. To extend your understanding of some issues the critics have raised, you might wish to read several of the monographs in the following volume, and your instructor may suggest some other materials you might consult that relate to this topic: Anderson, L. W., & Sosniak, L. A. (Eds.). (1994). *Bloom's Taxonomy: A forty-year retrospective: Ninety-third yearbook of the National Society for the Study of Education.* Chicago: University of Chicago Press.

Marzano's Taxonomy

Robert Marzano (2001) developed a taxonomy that looks simultaneously at levels of thinking and at the kinds of knowledge toward which these levels are directed. It also includes information related to learning in the psychomotor domain. Figure 8.4 shows Marzano's model of thinking. **Marzano's Taxonomy** features three types of knowledge and six levels of processing.

Types of knowledge.   The three types or domains of knowledge in Marzano's Taxonomy are

- Declarative knowledge, or information
- Procedural knowledge, or mental procedures
- Psychomotor procedures

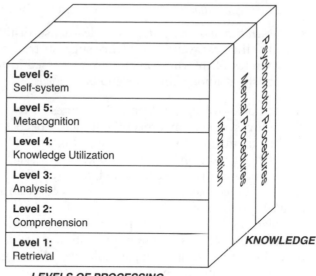

FIGURE 8.4 Marzano's Taxonomy

Source: From Robert J. Marzano. *Designing a New Taxonomy of Educational Objectives.* Thousand Oaks, CA: Corwin Press, Inc. , 2001, p. 60. Copyright © 2001, Corwin Press, Inc. All rights reserved.

Declarative Knowledge, or Information **Declarative knowledge**, or information, includes content information that students are expected to learn as a consequence of their exposure to instruction. Marzano divides this category into two major divisions, which are used to separate less complex, easier to learn content from more complex, more difficult to learn content. He uses the term **details** to describe the kinds of declarative knowledge associated with the easier-to-learn category and the term **organizing ideas** to describe the kinds of declarative knowledge associated with the more-difficult-to-learn category.

The details category includes the following:

- *Concepts, or vocabulary terms:* the basic words and ideas that form the intellectual foundation for understanding instruction related to a specific topic or subject
- *Facts:* specific items of information, which are often bound by time or place
- *Time sequences:* chronological orderings of events that occurred between two precise times or time periods
- *Cause and effect sequences:* series of events that chain together in ways that result in a specific effect or outcome
- *Episodes:* descriptions of particular events that occur at a particular time and place, involve specific individuals or groups, have a specific duration, follow a particular sequence, and reflect the operation of certain causes and effects (Martin Luther King's "I Have a Dream" speech is an example)

The *organization of ideas* category includes the following:

- *Generalizations and principles:* idea-dense distillations of "truth," or at least what the best available evidence suggests truth to be; they draw together huge volumes of information and are expressed in terms that often identify relationships among concepts and basic ideas

Procedural Knowledge, or Mental Procedures **Procedural knowledge**, or **mental procedures**, focus on processes students need to know. It is knowledge that teaches them how to do something. Marzano (2001) suggests that procedural knowledge can be divided into two key types: *skills* and *processes*. In general, **skills** are procedures that, once mastered, require little additional conscious thought by students. Once mastered, the processes become an almost automatic part of a student's repertoire of abilities.

Marzano uses the term **processes** to describe more sophisticated and demanding procedures. These require students to use collections of less complex procedures to accomplish a particular task. For example, many sophisticated procedures are involved when students are engaged in writing a research-based term paper. Among other things, they must know how to locate background information, take notes, organize their thinking, prepare rough drafts, proofread their material, provide appropriate internal citations, and follow appropriate procedures for listing references. More instructional time is required for students to master procedural knowledge processes than procedural knowledge skills.

Psychomotor Procedures **Psychomotor procedures** focus on student learning that requires them to develop highly coordinated activities involving their large and fine muscle structures. Marzano (2001) divides psychomotor procedures into two basic categories, skills and procedures. Psychomotor *skills* involve limited numbers of procedures that students can learn relatively easily and that, once mastered, students can repeat almost automatically. For example, once students learn how to stay upright on a moving bicycle, they can continue to do so with little or no reflection on the subtle things they are doing to retain their balance.

Psychomotor procedure *processes* include complex series of movements that need to be applied differently in response to the specific context in which they occur. For example, a student may have mastered some general procedures associated with woodcarving. However, when he or she engages in carving a particular object, conscious thought is required related to such issues as the angles of the cuts to be made, the general hardness of the wood being used, and the way the grain is oriented. The mastery of procedures requires the ability to apply basic skills in ways that make sense, given the constraints of the situation in which they are applied. More instructional time is required for students to master psychomotor procedure processes than psychomotor procedure skills.

Levels of processing.   Marzano's taxonomy includes six levels of information processing. The top two of these—level 5, metacognitive system, and level 6, self-system—involve general student dispositions and actions that stand outside of their actual intellectual engagement with new content. The *metacognitive system* has to do with students' perceptions of the goals of learning, their thoughts about organizing their thinking processes to achieve these goals, and the self-monitoring and adjustments they may make as they work on an academic task. The *self-system* focuses on students' attitudes toward academic work and includes information related to students' thoughts about the importance of what they are asked to do, the degree to which they have negative or positive feelings about the proposed work, and their thoughts about their probable success in accomplishing an assigned task.

The remaining four levels of Marzano's taxonomy comprise the "cognitive system." They describe various levels of thinking that can be applied to (1) details and organizing ideas in the area of declarative knowledge, (2) skills and processes in the area of procedural knowledge, and (3) skills and processes in the area of psychomotor procedures. These four levels are

Level 4: *Knowledge utilization.* At this level, students (1) make decisions when faced with situations in which no clearly superior answers are initially evident; (2) successfully meet, confront, and develop solutions to difficult problems; (3) generate and test the validity of hypotheses they develop to explain unfamiliar phenomena; and (4) engage in comprehensive judging of evidence, which leads to conclusions about highly complex situations and events.

Level 3: *Analysis.* At this level, students (1) identify similarities and differences among individual content elements, (2) group information into appropriate superordinate and subordinate categories, (3) process new information in terms of the "reasonableness of fit" with existing knowledge, (4) make inferences that extend applications of what they have learned to novel situations and settings, and (5) make information-based predictions.

Level 2: *Comprehension.* At this level, students are able to (1) impose patterns on elements of content they have learned, which includes placing them in appropriate categories and sequencing them properly and if requested, (2) generate representations of the new learning in symbolic form.

Level 1: *Retrieval.* At this level, students take in new information, process it, and store it as part of their supply of acquired information. This process features the basic recall of knowledge.

Each of these levels of processing has the potential to be applied to components of each knowledge type. This means, for example, that, given the appropriate conditions, students may be involved at various times in retrieval tasks, comprehension tasks, analysis tasks, and knowledge-utilization tasks that focus on both the details category and the organization of ideas category of declarative knowledge. Similarly, at appropriate times, students may be involved in these tasks as they deal with content associated with the skills and processes categories associated with procedural knowledge and psychomotor procedures.

Thinking Complexity, Content Complexity, and Instructional Time

The nature of the intended interaction between the sophistication of required thinking and the complexity of the content has implications for curriculum development. Consider these examples:

- If both complexity of thinking and complexity of content are at low levels, less instructional time is required than when they are both at higher levels. For example, this will occur when retrieval-level thinking is directed at declarative knowledge content at the level of details.

- More instructional time will be required when there are expectations that students will perform at higher levels of thinking complexity, even when complexity of content remains the same. For example, this will occur when there is an expectation that students' thinking will increase in complexity from retrieval to analysis while the sophistication of knowledge is kept constant at the declarative knowledge level of details.

- More instructional time will be required when there is an increase in the complexity of the content, even though there is no increase in the complexity of the expected level of student thinking. For example, this will occur when the level of expected thinking remains at retrieval and there is an increase in sophistication of content to the declarative knowledge level of organizing ideas.

- Large blocks of instructional time are essential when there is an expectation that students will engage in high-level thinking tasks that are directed at the acquisition of complex, sophisticated kinds of information. For example, this situation will occur when the level of expected thinking is at the level of knowledge utilization and when they will apply these thinking skills to the declarative knowledge level of organizing ideas.

CURRICULUM REALITIES 8–1

Some Issues Associated with Allocation of Instructional Time

Curriculum developers confront conflicting realities as they struggle to make recommendations on how the limited supply of instructional time ought to be allocated. These difficulties become especially pronounced when they attempt to make recommendations about varying instructional time to accommodate both the content to be taught and the nature of the individual students to be served.

Let's consider a situation in which low-ability students are expected to master fairly sophisticated content. On the one hand, we know that such students profit from exposure to multiple examples of new information. On the other hand, we also know that many of these students are poor readers and have limited attention spans. To provide them with access to the additional examples they need, our proposed remedy may be to require these students to engage in a highly intensive use of their poorly developed reading and attending skills. Unless we provide students with much additional time to master the material, this approach has dim prospects for success. Regrettably, an attempt to give these students more time to learn the material introduces another set of difficulties.

As more instructional time is devoted to providing skill-deficient students with additional examples related to one topic, there is a reduction in the time that can be allocated to instruction in other topics. In making this decision, we have two alternatives. One is for us to acknowledge that some future topics will be less complex and that even students with poorly developed learning skills will master them quickly. The other is to reduce the total number of topics that will be taught to this group of students. Neither option is attractive.

The expectation that later topics will be learned more quickly, even by students with underdeveloped skills represents a triumph of faint hope over reality. Although occasionally this will happen, more typically, students who need a considerable amount of time to master topics A, B, and C will also require a considerable amount of time to master topics D, E, and F. There are also problems that accompany a decision to reduce the number of topics treated. With today's emphasis on standardized tests, there is an expectation that certain topics will be covered at specific grade levels and within individual courses. If we eliminate instruction related to some tested topics for students with poorly developed learning skills, their test scores have a high probability of going down. Although such highly respected curriculum thinkers as Theodore Sizer (1984) make a strong case that less is more and that our school programs should be emphasizing depth rather than breadth of understanding, the high-stakes testing environments within which schools operate today make it difficult to put this idea into practice.

When you assign priorities to the components of instructional programs based on (1) the breadth of their explanatory power, (2) their focus on critical issues, and (3) their potential for promoting transfer, generally you have an associated expectation that students will leave with two kinds of learning benefits. First, you will expect them to be capable of engaging in sophisticated thinking regarding this high-priority information. Second, you will expect them to have dealt with quite sophisticated kinds of knowledge. Accomplishing both purposes requires time. One of your objectives should be to make recommendations that result in the allocation of more instructional time to high-priority than low-priority content elements.

One approach you can use to highlight differences in time demands associated with topics that vary in terms of the levels of expected thinking and the complexity of their featured content is to develop a *thinking/content-complexity matrix*. A **thinking/content-complexity matrix** is a chart. Across one axis are the names of topics or other major content divisions. The other axis features information that relates both to the levels of expected thinking and to the relative complexity of the content the students are expected to learn. Figure 8.5 features an example of a completed thinking/content-complexity matrix that focuses on declarative knowledge content. Note that information listed in the vertical axis on the left

	Topic A	Topic B	Topic C	Topic D	Topic E
Retrieval					
Information: details	3	3	3	3	3
Information: organizing ideas	1	1		1	
Comprehension					
Information: details	3	3		3	3
Information: organizing ideas		1		1	
Analysis					
Information: details		3		3	3
Information: organizing ideas		1		1	
Knowledge Utilization					
Information: details		3			
Information: organizing ideas		1			
Totals:	7	16	3	12	9

FIGURE 8.5 An Example of a Thinking/Content-Complexity Matrix Focusing on Declarative Knowledge Content

side includes information about both thinking processes and content complexity. Earlier the curriculum group that prepared this chart identified Topics B and D as the two having the highest priority.

In preparing the Figure 8.5 matrix, the developers decided that considerable time will be required for students to think about and master the content at the details level (facts, definitions of terms and concepts, cause and effect sequences, time sequences, episodes). Once students have mastered this information, additional time will be required for them to think about and master content at the organizing ideas level. In this case, the developers decided that about three times as much time will be needed for instruction directed at thinking about details as will be needed later to expand thinking directed at organizing ideas.

In Figure 8.5, you will see that the number 3 has been assigned in each cell where there is an expectation that instruction will demand thinking about declarative knowledge at the level of details. The number 1 has been assigned in each cell where there is an expectation that instruction will go on to demand additional thinking directed at declarative knowledge at the level of organizing ideas. Empty cells mean that there is no expectation that instruction will occur at these levels of thinking for content either at the details level or at the organizing ideas level.

This weighting scheme represents a decision curriculum developers have made in light of information they have received from teachers with credible insights into the relative amounts of time students need to engage in various levels of thinking that are directed at kinds of knowledge that differ in complexity.

You can use a completed chart such as the one in Figure 8.5 to make some general decisions about how much instructional time logically should be devoted to each topic. To do this, you need to add the total points associated with each topic. If you do this using the Figure 8.5 data, you will get the following results:

Topic A: 7
Topic B: 16
Topic C: 3
Topic D: 12
Topic E: 9

This pattern, in general, suggests that Topics B and D deserve more instructional time than the other topics. Topics E and A merit a smaller allocation, and instruction related to Topic C should require fewer instructional hours than instruction devoted to any of the others. For example, for a six-week block of instruction featuring these topics, time might be allocated in the following way:

Topic A: 1 week
Topic B: 2 weeks
Topic C: ½ week
Topic D: 1½ weeks
Topic E: 1 week

The strength of this approach is that time allocations are made based on a consideration of two key variables: (1) expected complexity of thinking and (2) complexity of content. It recognizes that instructional time implications flow from both the kinds of thinking we expect of students and from the difficulty of the content we ask them to learn.

Review and Reflection

1. What criteria can you use to identify the content to be included in a proposed instructional program?
2. What differentiates more significant from less significant content?
3. How would you go about establishing the authenticity of content you might consider for inclusion in a new program?
4. What are the characteristics of each of the five basic content-sequencing arrangements?
5. Suppose you were asked to organize a large body of content into major and subordinate topics. How would you approach this task, and what guidelines would you follow in making your decisions?
6. What influences can content organization have on what students take away from their exposure to instruction related to a given topic?

7. How would you compare and contrast the features of (1) Bloom's Taxonomy and (2) Marzano's Taxonomy?

8. How can a *thinking/content-complexity matrix* be used to suggest how instructional time might be allocated to different components of an instructional program?

References

Armstrong, D. G. (1989). *Developing and documenting the curriculum.* Needham Heights, MA: Allyn and Bacon.

Bloom, B. S., Engelhart, M. D., Furst, E. J., Hill, W. H., & Krathwohl, D. R. (Eds.). (1956). *Taxonomy of educational objectives: The classification of educational goals. Handbook I: Cognitive domain.* New York: David McKay.

Good, T. L., & Brophy, J. E. (2000). *Looking in classrooms* (8th ed.). New York: Longman.

Krathwohl, D. R., Bloom, B. S., & Masia, B. B. (Eds.). (1964). *Taxonomy of educational objectives: Handbook II: Affective domain.* New York: David McKay.

Marzano, R. J. (2001). *Designing a new taxonomy of educational objectives.* Thousand Oaks, CA: Corwin Press.

Sizer, T. (1984). *Horace's compromise: The dilemma of the American high school.* Boston: Houghton Mifflin.

9

Documenting Curriculum Decisions

Graphic Organizer

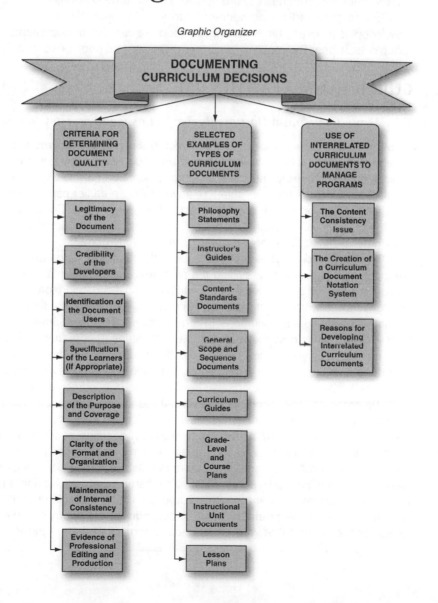

DOCUMENTING CURRICULUM DECISIONS

CRITERIA FOR DETERMINING DOCUMENT QUALITY
- Legitimacy of the Document
- Credibility of the Developers
- Identification of the Document Users
- Specification of the Learners (If Appropriate)
- Description of the Purpose and Coverage
- Clarity of the Format and Organization
- Maintenance of Internal Consistency
- Evidence of Professional Editing and Production

SELECTED EXAMPLES OF TYPES OF CURRICULUM DOCUMENTS
- Philosophy Statements
- Instructor's Guides
- Content-Standards Documents
- General Scope and Sequence Documents
- Curriculum Guides
- Grade-Level and Course Plans
- Instructional Unit Documents
- Lesson Plans

USE OF INTERRELATED CURRICULUM DOCUMENTS TO MANAGE PROGRAMS
- The Content Consistency Issue
- The Creation of a Curriculum Document Notation System
- Reasons for Developing Interrelated Curriculum Documents

INTRODUCTION

Suppose that you and others have been at work for 18 months on a new grade 8 mathematics program. You have spent hundreds of hours on the project. Some meetings have been contentious. Others have featured pleasant interchanges among people with differing views. Notes reflecting the group's collective decisions fill an enormous notebook. At this point, everyone involved feels a sense of accomplishment and, at the same time, a great deal of relief that the difficult, tedious process is coming to an end. What happens next?

There are many possibilities. However, all too often, the actual drafting of new and revised materials continues to the very end of the time scheduled for the project. Not long before the deadline, someone has to say, "Enough! No more changes." What may follow is an overly hasty attempt to generate curriculum documents based on the group's decisions. The resulting documents may not be good ones, and that is too bad.

CURRICULUM REALITIES 9–1

Why Many Curriculum Documents Are Not as Good as They Should Be

If you have occasion to look over a selection of **curriculum documents** produced by different people in different places for different purposes, you may be struck by their uneven quality. You may find many of them to be incompletely worked out (often, material in the latter sections is "thin," relative to that in earlier parts), deficient in terms of organization, and poorly organized, edited, and produced. Certainly, many fine examples of curriculum documents exist, but startlingly high numbers of them feature glaring deficiencies. Why are so many of them poorly done?

The answer does not lie in indifference to their importance on the part of most people involved in creating and revising the programs the documents describe. When you and others commit one to two years of hard work on a curriculum project, it is natural for you to want the written documentation of your work to reflect the same effort and quality that went into your deliberations. In large measure, others will draw conclusions about your work based on how they react to the written documents that describe and build a case in support of your decisions. The last thing you want are documents that suggest to other educators and the community at large that what you have done is unimportant and, hence, not worthy of being described in high-quality curriculum documents.

The pressures that often occur toward the end of a curriculum project can lead to conditions that make creating high-quality curriculum documents a challenge. Frequently, as time winds down toward a final project deadline, much work remains to be done. In an effort to complete the project on time, additional funds may have to be spent for additional personnel time and materials. As a result, some of the funds initially budgeted to purchase personnel time for careful drafting and editing and for printing documents may be spent for other purposes. Under such circumstances, final documents may be hastily prepared, inadequately edited, and poorly representative of the quality of the thought that went into the development of the programs.

Curriculum documents, which stand as formal expressions of curriculum decisions, are incredibly important kinds of materials. They communicate your group's decisions to wider audiences. Good ones effectively describe what has been decided in ways that can generate widespread support for your group's views. For this reason, curriculum documents deserve to be prepared carefully. Even curricula developed through eminently professional design processes will fail to garner needed support if only sparse attention is devoted to preparing high-quality documents to carry descriptive information to wider audiences.

As you begin thinking about curriculum documents, you need to recognize that these materials serve both an internal purpose and external purpose. The **internal purpose of a curriculum document** has to do with its function to serve the needs of the individuals who will directly use this information as part of their daily work. For example, an instructional unit has the internal purpose of providing guidance to teachers as they think about organizing instruction related to a particular topic. A textbook has an internal purpose of serving the learning needs of the students who use it. An instructor's guide has the internal purpose of providing specific guidance for the teacher who uses the text or the instructional program to which it relates.

The **external purpose of a curriculum document** relates to its capacity to provide information to parents, guardians, legislators, taxpayers, and others who may not be the beneficiaries of the included information as they discharge their normal life roles. These individuals often have views about what schools do, and the information in curriculum documents provides them with insights into the learning outcomes and instructional experiences being recommended for students. When documents are prepared with a careful eye to their external purpose, they build interest in and support for proposed programs. Let's consider the case of **philosophy statements,** which describe the basic beliefs and assumptions that are embedded in school districts' programs of study.

Philosophy statements provide a rationale that school leaders use to build general support for their districts' instructional programs. Because philosophical positions, personal values, ideas about effective teaching, and general thoughts about what constitutes a good education vary widely among communities of people as large as many school districts, philosophy statements have to be prepared with great care. Many of them include components that are specifically designed to respond to the concerns of important subsets of the total community. The idea is that, collectively, information in the adopted philosophy statement will generate attitudes toward the school district that, in the main, are favorable.

LEARNING EXTENSION 9–1

The Multiple Varieties of Curriculum Documents

Curriculum documents embrace an enormous variety of materials. Specific titles of these items and specific formats differ greatly from place to place. To gain insight into the scope of these differences, go to a standard web search engine, such as Google (http://www.google.com) and type in "curriculum document." Look at about 10 of these documents. Answer the following questions:

- Do these documents have specific names? If so, what are they?
- What are the intended functions of the various documents you found?
- Are you able to identify both *internal* and *external* purposes of some of these documents? If so, what are they?
- What are some features of the documents you liked, and what bothered you most about some of those you did not like?

Another example of how curriculum documents serve external audiences is found in the preface sections of college and university textbooks. The main body of these texts seeks to serve the needs of the students who will use the information these books contain. The preface, on the other hand, is directed at people who will make textbook-selection decisions; the information focuses on how the content fits in with typical course organizations, what kinds of supplementary materials are available for instructors to use, and how the textbook's scholarship reflects up-to-date thinking in the field.

CRITERIA FOR DETERMINING DOCUMENT QUALITY

Curriculum documents that fail to provide relevant information do not get used (Doll, 1995). How can this problem be avoided? More specifically, when you and others with whom you work are ready to begin preparing written materials that will describe your curriculum decisions, what characteristics should these documents have?

Over the years, curriculum specialists have identified a number of characteristics of high-quality curriculum documents (Armstrong, 1997; Armstrong & Shutes, 1981). You may find it useful to consider a list of quality criteria as you prepare your own curriculum documents. You might also find it worthwhile to examine existing documents in light of these criteria to identify their strengths and weaknesses. A review of several documents can help you identify ideas worth considering for inclusion in your own documents, as well as pitfalls you will wish to avoid. As you develop curriculum documents, think about how you are addressing each of these quality criteria:

- Legitimacy of the document
- Credibility of the developers
- Identification of the document users
- Specification of the learners (if appropriate)
- Description of the purpose and coverage
- Clarity of the format and organization
- Maintenance of internal consistency
- Evidence of professional editing and production

Criteria	Questions
Legitimacy of the document	Does the name of the issuing school district or educational agency appear along with a printed list of responsible administrative officials and a facsimile signature of the chief administrative officer?
Credibility of the developers	Do the names of the developers appear along with specific references to their training or expertise in areas related to the subject of the document?
Identification of the document users	Is there information provided regarding the categories of people for whom the document is intended along with the reasons these people will find the information in the document useful?
Specification of the learners (if appropriate)	If the described program is designed to serve students, does the document provide specific information about their grade levels and/or age levels, as well as about the presumed learning characteristics of this group (gifted and talented, limited English proficient, and so forth)?
Description of the purpose and coverage	Is the document specifically labeled as to its purpose, does the body of the material include elaborated information about its purpose and breadth of coverage, and is there information about other available kinds of curriculum documents that might interest some users?
Clarity of the format and organization	In the beginning pages of the document, Is there a clear description of how the material is formatted, and is this plan implemented consistently throughout the document?
Maintenance of Internal consistency	Are all similar sections or components of the document worked out in ways that reflect a similar volume of information and level of detail?
Evidence of professional editing and production	Has the document been printed using commercial printing technology, and is it free from spelling and mechanical usage errors?

FIGURE 9.1   Some Questions to Answer in Meeting the Criteria for Well-Prepared Curriculum Documents

Some questions you may wish to ask yourself as you and others prepare curriculum documents are included in Figure 9.1.

Legitimacy of the Document

The **legitimacy** criterion speaks to the legal standing of the document. Is there evidence that the included information has been approved for dissemination by a recognized authority? A potential user will want some assurance, for example, that a curriculum document that purports to describe a grade 5 science program represents the official, adopted program. As part of the document-preparation process, you will want to build in a step that requires some kind of formal approval of your documents, and they should not be disseminated without it. In the document itself, legitimacy often is reflected in a sentence or two containing phrases such as "Approved by the Jones Township School Board on January 25, 2003" or "Issued Under the Authority of the Superintendent, Jones Township Schools, January 2003."

Credibility of the Developers

Many, probably most, users of the curriculum documents you prepare will not have been personally involved in the development process. Large numbers of them may have no acquaintance at all with you or with any other people who took part. These potential users need assurances about the expertise and backgrounds of the people who made the decisions. You add significantly to the comfort level of likely program adopters when you include specific information on the developers' expertise in the areas referenced in the document. This information can include details about such areas as their educational backgrounds, their subject-matter expertise, their grasp of the learning-style characteristics of different kinds of students, and their actual experience in teaching students similar to those for whom the program is designed.

You often will find great attention to the credibility-of-the-developers criterion in textbooks designed for elementary- and high-school students. For example, one middle-school geography text, *Geography: The World and Its People* (Boehm, Armstrong, & Hunkins, 2002), in its introductory pages states (1) the academic, professional, and teaching backgrounds of the three authors; (2) the names and positions of 10 national and international consultants; and (3) the names and locations of 31 teacher reviewers.

Identification of the Document Users

People who use curriculum documents are busy. The kind of information wanted by individuals who play different roles within and without education varies enormously. Although kindergarten teachers have a certain level of professional interest in how the entire pre-K to 12 mathematics program is organized, they probably will not see a document devoted to a general description of this multigrade sequence to be of compelling relevance to their daily work. On the other hand, they might be highly interested in the contents of a document that focuses specifically on proposed mathematics-related units for kindergarten youngsters. To encourage document use, you want to provide clear information about who the intended document users are. Some simple phrases at the beginning of the document will make it easy for users to make reasoned judgments about the pertinence of the material for their own work. The following are some examples:

- This document includes specific suggestions for teaching a unit focusing on basic number facts to first-grade students.

- This document describes grade-level topic emphases and individual middle-school and secondary-school course titles for the entire pre-K to 12 English/language arts program.

- This document describes the general philosophy that supports all instructional activities in the Jones Township schools.

- This manual provides general suggestions for teachers who will use the text *Our America: From Sea to Shining Sea.*

Specification of the Learners (If Appropriate)

If you have occasion to look at large numbers of curriculum documents that describe programs directed at students, you may be surprised to discover that many of them provide only limited information about the kinds of students for whom the program was designed. Occasionally, the developers of documents (inadvertently, one hopes) fail to mention this issue at all. An inadequate description of the kinds of students a proposed program is supposed to serve is frustrating to potential document users. Sometimes, this situation can result in serious consequences.

One case several decades ago involved an outstanding social studies program that initially was developed for the "most talented one-fourth" of the high-school population. As the curriculum documents describing the program were prepared, someone failed to include information to alert potential users that it was designed for the most talented one-fourth of high-school students. The initial users, not having this information, attempted to use it with the general population of high-school students. Predictably, the results were a disaster. Many teachers who taught the material found that their students had great difficulty with the content, and they concluded that the program was poorly designed. Had the documents describing the program carefully identified the nature of the targeted group of students, the teachers probably would have used it only with classes of high-ability students. Under these circumstances, the teachers' reactions might have been much more positive.

The specification-of-the-learners criterion is not applicable to every curriculum document. Some kinds of curriculum documents do not describe programs for students. For example, when you are involved in preparing a school district philosophy statement, you are organizing information that ultimately will be directed at members of the general community, not at students.

Description of the Purpose and Coverage

You and others involved in preparing a curriculum document need to ensure that it includes adequate information about its purpose and breadth of coverage. Is the document designed to assist fourth-grade teachers by providing (1) a unit title,

(2) guiding generalizations, (3) key ideas, (4) alternative instructional approaches, (5) suggestions for evaluating students, and (6) the titles of useful instructional support materials that these teachers might use in preparing and teaching a single unit in the grade 4 science program? Is the document intended to serve as a management tool for all subject areas of the entire grades pre-K to 12 school instructional program? Well-designed curriculum documents provide clear answers to questions such as these. Potential users of documents have many calls on their time. When they encounter a new curriculum document, they should not have to read it in its entirety to infer its purpose. Explanations related to a document's function and scope, in addition to enabling potential users to understand the nature of the material, provide an opportunity for developers to mention the possible existence of other, related documents that might better serve users' needs.

For example, suppose an elementary-school principal picked up a copy of a document with detailed information about presenting content related to a single unit in the grade 4 science program. Material in this document tends to focus on micro issues associated with the delivery of a small part of the grade 4 science program, information that a fourth-grade teacher might find highly relevant but that might be too detailed to be of much practical use to a principal. In preparing information regarding the purpose and scope of the unit document, the developers might also have mentioned the existence of another curriculum document that describes in more general terms the nature of the entire grade 4 science program. This information would inform a user, such as a principal, that a different but related curriculum document exists that includes details better matched to his or her informational needs.

Clarity of the Format and Organization

Good curriculum documents are easy to use. Ease of use improves when documents feature formats and organizational schemes that allow the quick location of individual document parts. At a minimum, when you prepare documents, you need to provide numbered pages, a good table of contents, and a common set of heading and subheading formats that are used consistently throughout the materials. You might also think about adding features such as an index and a glossary of terms related to the document content.

Maintenance of Internal Consistency

One challenge you will face in preparing curriculum documents relates to the number and diversity of people involved in developing the included information. Individuals have varied writing styles, ideas about the volume of descriptive information individual topics deserve, and thoughts about what headings and subheadings should be used to organize materials. Because of these differences, a curriculum document that represents a simple assemblage of parts developed by various people may lack good internal consistency and, therefore, be difficult to use. Good documents result from careful editing. A well-edited document that features information developed by large numbers of people will read as though the material has been produced by a single, highly organized person who writes clear, consistent, coherent prose.

Documents that are internally consistent work out all sections to approximately the same level of specificity. Sometimes, you will encounter curriculum documents that feature content in the latter sections that appears "thin," relative to what you will see in earlier parts of the material. Often, this situation results when members of a curriculum team have faced a tight time deadline to complete their tasks and have devoted only sparse attention to the aspects of the program described in the final sections of the curriculum document.

Evidence of Professional Editing and Production

To the extent you can do so, make your influence felt in support of committing adequate money to produce professionally edited and printed documents. If you examine curriculum documents, you will note that many have spelling and typographical errors and were produced using the cheapest available production technologies. (Some that you will find in libraries and other repositories were even produced using old purple spirit masters.) Poorly edited and poorly printed documents might as well have this message on the cover sheet: "Ignore—this material is not important!"

Documents that are professionally produced stand a much better chance of being taken as serious pieces of professional work. Given the expense associated with completing a long-term curriculum project, it is a false economy to embed decisions in documents that fail to honor the professionalism that has gone into the development of their content. Documents that are well edited and professionally produced can greatly assist you and others who have been involved in program development and revisions as you seek to build widespread support for the recommended changes.

LEARNING EXTENSION 9–2

Critiquing the Quality of Curriculum Documents

Identify a curriculum document that focuses on a program that interests you. The document type (lesson plan or instructional unit document, for example) is strictly a matter of your own preference. Assess the quality of the document using the criteria introduced in this section. Then respond to the following questions:

- What are the areas of strength in this document?
- What are the areas of weakness?
- If you were to make several specific changes to this document, what would they be? How would these changes make the document better?

SELECTED EXAMPLES OF TYPES OF CURRICULUM DOCUMENTS

In their capacity as physical carriers of curriculum decisions, curriculum documents include a huge range of formats and serve many purposes. They range in length from less than a single page to hundreds of pages. Some common document types include philosophy statements, instructor's guides, content-standards documents, general scope and sequence documents, curriculum guides, grade-level plans and course plans, instructional unit documents, and lesson plans.

Individual document types have specific purposes and are designed for use by particular audiences. The following subsections introduce the features of several examples of widely used types of curriculum documents.

Philosophy Statements

Today, many school districts develop philosophy statements, which attempt to summarize the values and priorities that underpin the programs offered to students. Philosophy statements tend to be rather brief documents, rarely exceeding more than two pages. Though there are important place to place differences, philosophy statements tend to share some characteristics.

Key features.   Writers of philosophy statements seek to fulfill two goals. On the one hand, they attempt to identify a general sense of direction for a school district's programs. On the other hand, they try to anticipate and respond to different (and sometimes contending) views in the local community regarding what constitutes a good education. The latter purpose recognizes that philosophy statements, in part, function as political communications that seek to build as broad an audience as possible in support of the school district's programs. These documents attempt to weave together positions that speak both to the general orientation of a school district and to the concerns of the individuals in the community who have varying conceptions of educational excellence. For an example of language from a typical school district philosophy statement, see Figure 9.2.

Note that the document in Figure 9.2 includes mention of commitments to positions that may conflict with one another. The overriding theme reflected in this document is a concern for identifying and responding to students' needs. In addition, the statement references many additional program goals. There is something in this material to satisfy community members who believe the purpose of education should be (1) to develop intellectual competencies, (2) to produce students who are ready for the world of work, (3) to develop students' sense of self-understanding, (4) to enhance students' abilities to solve problems, and (5) to produce students who will be committed to social reform.

Philosophy statements seek to bring together many different perspectives on the purposes of instructional programs. If you find yourself involved in developing a document of this kind, others will probably join you who represent a broad cross section of school administrators, teachers, parents, students, and other in-

The Jones Township Public Schools commit to developing each student's potential to its maximum. This purpose will be achieved as learning experiences are developed and delivered that respond to legitimate student interests, promote clarity of understanding of the larger world, support the development of the characteristics of effective citizenship, foster the development of economic survival skills, and develop students' feelings of self-worth and personal understanding.

Achieving educational balance is a high priority for the Jones Township Public Schools. Sound academic skills needed for survival in a competitive world must be part of the repertoire of every school district graduate. Young people, too, must leave school having solid control over basic workplace skills. To prepare effective future citizens, programs seek to help students commit to participation in democratic efforts to improve the quality of local, state, national, and international life. These skills take shape as students take advantage of both academic offerings and extracurricular experiences.

Tomorrow's world promises to confront today's students with challenges barely dreamed of today. For this reason, programs in the Jones Township Schools work to develop students' problem-solving and thinking skills. Intellectual soundness and adaptability are essential in a world where change, increasingly, is one of life's few constants.

Programs to achieve all of these purposes have been and must continue to be developed by individuals representing the entire community. Parents, leading citizens, and students themselves accept an obligation to join with professional educators to plan and keep up-to-date the best possible learning experiences for Jones Township's future—its children.

FIGURE 9.2   Philosophy statement—Jones Township Public Schools

terested citizens. Because philosophy documents help build an important base of understanding and support for a school district's entire pre-K to 12 program, the leadership of groups charged with developing philosophy statements often is assigned to top-level school administrators or curriculum staff professionals.

LEARNING EXTENSION 9–3

Working with Philosophy Statements

Read carefully the philosophy statement in Figure 9.2. Next, review the material in Chapter 5 regarding the philosophies of education, learning theory, and sociology of education. When you have finished doing so, respond to the following questions:

- Identify the portions of this philosophy statement that seem to have been written to satisfy people with specific philosophical positions. Who are these people, and what philosophical positions do they seem to represent?

- How would you assess the relative importance accorded statements consistent with individual philosophical positions? In other words, did the people who prepared this document tend to devote more prose to statements consistent with some philosophical positions than others? How satisfied are you with these differences?

- Do you get any feel for the kinds of learning theory that appear to be favored in the school district's programs? Are you satisfied with the degree of attention to this issue? Why or why not?
- What positions from the sociology of education do you see reflected in this document? Are you satisfied with this selection? Why or why not?

To conclude, prepare a version of a philosophy statement for the Jones Township Schools. Assume that 75 percent of the people in the district are committed reconstructionists who hold conflict views of schooling. Assume the remainder are people who are about equally divided between (1) essentialists who hold traditionalist functionalist views of schooling and (2) perennialists who hold traditional functionalist views of schooling.

Primary users.   The general community is the intended audience of philosophy statement documents, particularly the segments of the general community with interest in schools and school programs. The information in these documents is highly general. Their comments tend to be couched in terms of general intentions, rather than in terms of specific guidelines for program implementation. Hence, these documents tend to be of relatively marginal interest to teachers, principals, and others who need much more detailed information about content coverage, instructional delivery, and student evaluation information.

Because philosophy statements provide an indication of a school district's general orientation toward instruction, they often provide a useful context for curriculum-development activities that result in the preparation of documents tied more closely to day-to-day instruction, such as course and grade-level plans, instructional unit documents, and lesson plans. The intent is to assure that there is consistency between the perspectives reflected in the philosophy document and those embedded in documents that focus more narrowly on the content to be delivered, instructional methodology, and student assessment.

Instructor's Guides

Instructor's guides exist in many forms. They typically accompany programs or materials that are designed for use by students. For example, there are instructor's guides for learning materials such as textbooks, educational software, educational videos, and various multicomponent instructional packages.

Key features.   The major purpose of an instructor's guide is to provide assistance to teachers who will be using the instructional program to which it relates. Because programs vary greatly in their length and complexity, there is also much variation in the amount of material individual guides contain. Some of them provide all the information anyone could possibly want in 1 or 2 pages; others go on for 30 pages or more.

Many instructor's guides include components such as the following:

- Overview of the material
- List of student learning objectives
- Identification of and elaboration of key points
- Discussion questions
- Glossary of important terms
- Assessment device or general suggestions for assessing student learning
- Recommended follow-up activities

If you are called on to prepare an instructor's guide, how you treat each of these components will vary according to the nature of the program to which the guide relates. If you undertake to develop an instructor's guide for a textbook or a complex series of educational films, you will need to include a substantial volume of material. Indeed, in the case of extremely complex and lengthy programs—for example, a television series involving a dozen or more individual programs that tie to a common organizing topic—you may need to prepare multiple guides, one for each program and one master "guide to the guides."

You may find it interesting to review several instructor's guides to determine how many of the components are included and to make judgments about the quality of each. Many guides tend to be especially weak in terms of the information they provide about assessing student learning. You may discover others that provide inadequate student learning objectives. With regard to the quality of the information about the provided components, pay special attention to the tone of the prose. Good guides tend to couch ideas in terms of "suggestions" or "recommendations," rather than in terms of "must do's." Many potential users are turned off by language that presumes they need heavy-handed direction. In addition, the circumstances within which individual teachers operate vary so much that recommendations made by a developer of an instructor's guide may not make sense for every teacher who is a possible user of the program.

EXERCISE 9–1

Preparing an Instructor's Guide

A good instructor's guide fits information closely to the needs of the intended users. This reality sometimes poses a dilemma. Consider the case of this textbook, which seeks to familiarize users with the general dimensions of the curriculum field. Potential users of this book include a highly diverse group. For example, there may be (1) people who are newcomers to education or educators of many years standing, (2) kindergarten teachers or university instructors, and (3) classroom practitioners or central office administrators.

Action

Prepare two versions of a short instructor's guide for this chapter. Include the components listed under the "Key Features" heading in the discussion of instructor's guides.

Identify the specific audience for which each version is intended. Identify your audience for each version from the following options:

- Inexperienced elementary-school teachers
- Experienced high-school teachers
- Newcomers to central office curriculum leadership

Analysis

When you have completed your work, be prepared to explain the characteristics of your two guides. You will want to answer questions such as the following:

- In what ways are the two versions the same?
- In what ways are the two versions different?
- Did you have more difficulty preparing one version than the other? If so, why?
- Do the two versions vary in length? If so, what contributed to the difference?

Key Points

The utility of individual instructor's guides depends, in large measure, on how well their content responds to the specific needs of the audiences who will use them. When instructional programs are designed for use by wide and diverse groups, developers find it difficult to prepare instructor's guides that adequately serve the needs of all.

Primary users.   Individuals who will teach programs to which the document relates constitute about the only audience for an instructor's guide. Since there is virtually no market for guides beyond this group, commercial publishers of textbooks, educational videos, and other instructional materials often do not charge for instructor's guides. They are automatically provided *gratis* to teachers in schools that have purchased the instructional programs to which they relate.

Content-Standards Documents

Content-standards documents contain information on the kinds of information that should be treated within particular courses at individual grade levels. In some cases, there are legal mandates requiring coverage of the identified content. In others, the standards serve as recommendations that educators are urged to consider in planning and delivering instruction related to the subject area that the standards reference.

Key features.   Individual standards typically include two distinct but related categories of information. On the one hand, they focus on content associated with a particular school subject. On the other, they specify the particular aspects of that content that are to be introduced to students at different points in their school experience. In some instances, there are separate standards for individual grades (pre-K standards, K standards, grade 1 standards, and so forth). In other cases, the standards cover ranges of grades (primary-grades standards, middle-grades standards, middle-school standards, and so forth) (Marzano & Kendall, 1997; *McREL's contributions to K–12 standards,* 2001).

Content-specialty organizations, such as the National Council of Teachers of English (NCTE), the National Science Teachers Association (NTSA), the National Council of Teachers of Mathematics (NCTM), and the National Council for the Social Studies (NCSS), are among the many content-specialty organizations that have developed curriculum standards. In recent years, departments of education in the individual states have developed standards to guide instruction in the schools (American Federation of Teachers, 1999). Some local school districts have adopted content standards of their own. See Chapter 4, "Working with Curriculum Standards," for more information about curriculum standards.

Primary users.   Content standards receive a great deal of attention. Some of them are backed by legal authority that requires teachers to cover certain kinds of content when teaching a particular subject at a given grade level. Even voluntary content standards, such as those developed by many national specialty organizations, exert important moral authority on people who develop and revise instructional programs. This moral authority comes about because of the high regard and respect many educators have for the perspectives of the leaders and members of national content-specialty groups.

Top-level school officials, at some point, may face an audit by state education officials that includes requests for information about how mandated content standards are reflected in the district's programs. From time to time, they also may find it useful to provide information to the general public regarding how instructional programs match with the voluntary standards that national content-specialty groups have proposed. The concerns of upper-echelon school leaders about content standards tend to be shared by others with interests and responsibilities associated with curriculum development. It is highly probable that you and others involved in developing and revising instructional programs will pay close attention to the content standards of the subjects that are the focus of your work.

General Scope and Sequence Documents

Typically, **general scope and sequence documents** are part of an interrelated set of documents that, collectively, provide a structure for a school district's entire instructional program. Some school districts split these documents into separate sections for (1) elementary-school-level programs, (2) middle-school-level programs, and (3) high-school-level programs. Because of their extraordinarily wide scope of coverage, these documents provide only limited information about individual courses and grade-level programs.

These documents highlight the key features of the entire instructional program. Hence, central office leaders who are responsible for the overall management of the school district and its instructional function play important roles in their design. Often, top-level curriculum specialists take the lead in developing these materials. Some decisions regarding the contents to be included may be mandated by state law. Others may be determined locally.

Key features.   Because they function as overall program-management documents, general scope and sequence documents reference other kinds of curriculum documents that provide more specific information about what is taught at individual grade levels and in individual courses. Well-constructed general scope and sequence documents also embed features consistent with the quality criteria that you learned about earlier in this chapter. Specific components vary from place to place, but many general scope and sequence documents include elements such as the following:

1. Front matter, including
   1.1. A title (e.g. "All Programs, Grades Pre-K to 12")
   1.2. The name of the school district
   1.3. A foreword, which concludes with a statement of approval and a signature from an authority empowered to sign off on behalf of the school district
   1.4. A short list of the names of the responsible developers and their qualifications
   1.5. A table of contents
2. A brief description of all the document types that are included in the district's interrelated set—for example, curriculum guides, course plans, grade-level plans, and instructional unit documents
3. An explanation of a notation system or another mechanism used to tie together in a logical way all the documents in a district's interrelated set (more information about working with an interrelated set of documents appears in a later section of this chapter)
4. A list of subjects taught in the district and subordinate information about each related to
   4.1. The grade levels and course titles (e.g., grade 1 arithmetic, algebra 1)
      4.1.1. The units and topic titles associated with each grade level and course
         4.1.1.1. Sometimes, generalizations, principles, or key ideas associated with each unit and topic title

Primary users.   The primary users of general scope and sequence documents are central office personnel who have the responsibility for overseeing (1) the entire pre-K to 12 program, (2) the district's entire elementary-school program, (3) the district's entire middle-school program, or (4) the district's entire high-school program. Individuals such as the superintendent, his or her associates who are responsible for overseeing instructional programs, and district-level curriculum directors are among the individuals who often work with general scope and sequence documents.

Curriculum Guides

As you engage in curriculum work, you may encounter a problem that vexes even people who have worked in the field for years—the lack of a common professional vocabulary. You often will find similar terms being used by different people to refer to quite different things. The term **curriculum guide** tends to be used to refer to many different kinds of documents. Sometimes, it refers to a document that lists all the courses available at a given school. Sometimes, it is used as a synonym for "curriculum document," in which case it is a broad, generic term that includes virtually all written expressions of curricular decisions. In still other cases, the term is used to provide a general overview of the entire instructional program of a school district.

The term "curriculum guide" is used in this chapter in a restrictive sense. It refers to a subset of a general scope and sequence document that does one of two things. It can either bring together in one document all information about pre-K to 12 instruction in a given subject area (e.g., what is done in the area of social studies from pre-K to grade 12), or it can bring together in one document all the information about instruction provided to students at one grade level (e.g., what students in grade 6 are taught about each included subject). Often, school districts find it useful to produce a number of these curriculum guides. General scope and sequence documents tend to be huge, multivolume affairs. Often, it proves more manageable to shred out information from these enormous documents and repackage it as individual subject-area or grade-level curriculum guides.

Key features.   As is the case with other document types, the formatting characteristics of curriculum guides vary from place to place, even in situations where the term "curriculum guide" is used as it is in this chapter. Formatting follows closely that used in general scope and sequence documents. Some typical components include

1. Front matter, including
   1.1. A title ("Mathematics, Grades pre-K to 12")
   1.2. The name of the school district
   1.3. A foreword, which concludes with a statement of approval and a signature from an authority empowered to sign off on behalf of the school district
   1.4. A short list of the names of the responsible developers and their qualifications. In the case of curriculum guides that reference a single subject area, the names include individuals with expertise in that subject area (reading, mathematics, and so forth). In the case of curriculum guides that reference a particular grade level, the names indicate their familiarity with students in the general grade covered by the document (primary-grades specialists, intermediate-grades specialists, and so forth).
   1.5. A table of contents

2. A brief description of all the document types that are included in the district's interrelated set—for example, curriculum guides, course plans, grade-level plans, and instructional unit documents

3. An explanation of a notation system or another mechanism used to tie together in a logical way all the documents in a district's interrelated set (more information about working with an interrelated set of documents appears in a later section of this chapter)

4A. If the document references a particular *subject area,* there is information related to

    4A.1. The names of all grade-level programs and courses associated with this subject (grade 2 science, grade 3 science, biology 1, biology 1 gifted and talented, and so forth)

        4A.1.1. The units and topic titles associated with each grade level and course (if the subject focus area is science, these topics and titles all tie to the science program in each grade and to the individual secondary-school science courses)

            4A.1.1.1. Sometimes, generalizations, principles, or key ideas associated with each of the topics

4B. If the document references a particular *grade level,* there is

    4B.1. A list of all the subjects taught at that grade level (for example, if grade 5 is the focus, then there is information about all grade 5 content related to English/language arts, music, science, social studies, mathematics, art, physical education, and other subjects taught at that grade level)

        4B.1.1. The units and topic titles associated with each of these subject areas (e.g., grade 5 units for English/language arts, music, science, and so forth)

            4B.1.1.1. Sometimes, generalizations, principles, or key ideas associated with each of the topics

Primary users. Curriculum guides tend to be used by somewhat wider audiences than general scope and sequence documents. In addition to central office personnel, including senior administrators responsible for the overall school program, subject-area curriculum guides are used by subject-area specialists who are in charge of specific areas of the curriculum (director of science, director of social studies, and so forth) or of specific grade levels (associate superintendent for elementary instruction, director of middle-school instruction, supervisor of high-school instruction, and so forth). These guides often are also of interest to building principals who, from time to time, have to answer questions about how instruction related to a single subject ties together over multiple years. Any group involved in a curriculum revision related to a given subject area or grade level also may be interested in seeing how elements in the present program tie together.

Grade-Level and Course Plans

A **grade-level plan** is a curriculum document that summarizes the content to be taught in one subject area at one grade level. Some examples include grade-level plans focusing on grade 2 reading, grade 3 science, and grade 4 mathematics. A similar document that describes some middle-school programs and many high-school programs is called a **course plan.** Course plans focus on the content treated within individually named courses. Some examples include course plans for algebra 1, United States history, basic bookkeeping, and physics.

Key features.   As is true with many other document types, the specific formats for grade-level and course plans vary greatly from place to place. The following components are among those many of them feature:

1. Front matter, including
   1.1. A title (e.g., "Grade 2—Mathematics")
   1.2. The name of the school district
   1.3. A foreword, which concludes with a statement of approval and a signature from an authority empowered to sign off on behalf of the school district
   1.4. A short list of the names of the responsible developers and their qualifications. In the case of grade-level plans, the names include individuals with expertise in providing instruction in a specific school subject to students at a given grade level or a given range of grade levels. Similarly, course plans reference the names of the people known to have expertise in teaching content related to the focus subject.
   1.5. A table of contents
2. A brief description of all the document types that are included in the district's interrelated set—for example, curriculum guides, grade-level plans, course plans, and instructional unit documents
3. An explanation of a notation system or another mechanism used to tie together in a logical way all the documents in a district's interrelated set (more information about working with an interrelated set of documents appears in a later section of this chapter)
4. Descriptions of the units to be covered within the grade-level program or unit
   4.1. Sometimes, generalizations, principles, or key ideas associated with each of the units

Primary users.   Grade-level and course plans are used by district-level grade-level program directors (e.g., director of primary education, director of middle-grades education) and by subject-area directors (e.g., director of music, director of mathematics). (The actual titles of these individuals vary widely from district to district.) Principals in individual buildings often use these documents as a primary source of information about what is being taught at each grade level and in each course. Teachers who serve as grade-level team leaders and as department heads in middle schools and high schools also frequently work with these documents. The contents provide some guidance to individual teachers as they engage in activities designed to build an instructional support program related to each described unit.

Instructional Unit Documents

Instructional unit documents provide teachers with specific information about approaches they might wish to take in delivering instruction to students and assessing their progress. Huge numbers of these documents have been developed, and many now can be accessed on the World Wide Web. For example, large numbers of content-specialty organizations make sample units available on their websites. Many formats have been developed for instructional units. The following are some components that many well-designed instructional unit documents have:

1. Front matter, including
   1.1. A title (e.g., "The American Novel from 1900 to 1920," "The Arthropods," "Life in Pioneer Days")
   1.2. The name of the school district
   1.3. A foreword, which concludes with a statement of approval and a signature from an authority empowered to sign off on behalf of the school district
   1.4. A short list of the names of the responsible developers and their qualifications. The individuals named have expertise related to the subject of the unit and to teaching this kind of content to students at the grade level for which the unit is intended.
2. A table of contents
3. A brief description of all the document types that are included in the district's interrelated set—for example, curriculum guides, grade-level plans, course plans, and instructional unit documents
4. An explanation of a notation system or another mechanism used to tie together in a logical way all the documents in a district's interrelated set (more information about working with an interrelated set of documents appears in a later section of this chapter)
5. Descriptions of approaches to teaching and evaluating the unit
   5.1. An introduction, including comments about the subject matter, the nature of the students to be served, and approaches to diagnosing their readiness for the new material
   5.2. A list of generalizations, principles, or key ideas associated with the unit
      5.2.1. A list of learning objectives or learning intentions related to the generalizations, principles, or key ideas
      5.2.2. A list of suggested instructional approaches that might be used to teach the generalizations, principles, or key ideas
      5.2.3. Suggested ways to evaluate student learning related to the generalizations, principles, and key ideas associated with the unit
   5.3. A list of resource materials needed to teach the unit

Primary users. Classroom teachers are the primary users of instructional unit documents. The level of detail these materials provide guide teachers as they think about developing lessons related to the unit titles. This information provides them with a useful beginning point as they work to adapt instruction to meet the needs of their students. Grade-level program leaders and secondary-school department heads also occasionally work with instructional unit documents. Because these documents contain so much detailed information on recommended teacher actions, they tend to be used less frequently by principals and central office personnel who, in many cases, can get the kinds of information they need from documents such as grade-level and course plans, which provide more general program descriptions.

LEARNING EXTENSION 9–4

Formatting Instructional Units

Approaches to formatting instructional units vary. Some components included in many instructional units are described in this section of the text. You may find it useful to look at some other guidelines for formatting units. To locate this information on the World Wide Web, go to Merrill Education's General Methods resource site (http://www. prenhall.com/methods-cluster/). At the bottom of the web page, you will be invited to click on a topic. Choose Topic 17, "Planning Instructional Objectives and Goals," and click on "Begin." This will take you to a page providing an overview of this topic. On the left side of this page, you will see several options listed. Click on "Web Links." This will take you to a page with two clickable topics, "Instructional Planning guides" and "Planning Instruction." Click on each for an extensive list of additional links. Many of these include material related to formatting instructional units. Follow two to four links with this focus, and read the material related to unit formatting information. Then, respond to the following questions:

- What differences did you find between the unit components discussed in the chapter and those listed on the website?
- What similarities did you note?
- Given these alternatives and your own experiences, what might you include in a list of instructional unit components that you develop?

Lesson Plans

A **lesson plan** is a highly teacher-specific document type. Lesson plans describe in considerable detail a teacher's instructional intentions for a brief period of time, sometimes covering a single day, sometimes covering a longer period of time. A lesson plan represents a written summary of what a teacher plans to do. These intentions flow from a consideration of the content to be covered, the characteristics of the students to be served, the available instructional support materials, and other information that is unique to the teacher's instructional setting.

Key features. Many examples of lesson plans are available on the web from content-specialty organizations and other sources. Formats for lesson plans vary widely, according to individual teacher needs and preferences. The one depicted in Figure 9.3 includes elements that many of them have.

Number of This Lesson Plan _____

Title _____

Unit to Which This Lesson Relates _____

Lesson Objectives or General Learning Purposes _____

_____

_____

Knowledge and Skills Related to the Lessons That Students Should Already Have _____

_____

Most Important General Ideas and Key Terms _____

_____

Plans for Accommodating Special Needs Students _____

_____

Time	Lesson Sequence	Materials
	1. Securing attention/informing students of objectives or purposes	
	2. Introducing new material	
	3. Checking for understanding and monitoring students	
	4. Guided student practice with new learning and teacher feedback	
	5. Independent student practice/ application/extension	
	6. Lesson closure/evaluation of learning	

Teacher Evaluation of Lesson Effectiveness

_____

_____

FIGURE 9.3 A Typical Lesson Plan Format

Large numbers of present-day lesson plans continue to include components that track the elements of lessons associated with the now outdated theory of apperception (*preparation, presentation, comparison, generalization, and application*). (You may wish to review the information on apperception in Chapter 5.) It is interesting that, although the theory of apperception now is largely discounted, its prescription for organizing content into lessons has been found to be compatible with many modern theories of learning.

Primary users.   Lesson plans are used most frequently by individual classroom teachers. They include highly detailed information about what instructionally related activities will go on in the classroom over a relatively short period of time. The specificity of this information and the decisions that the preparers of the lesson plan make to accommodate the instructional setting make lesson plans only marginally useful to audiences other than classroom teachers. In some places, principals regularly review lesson plans. These actions ordinarily are taken to ensure that content related to prescribed standards and other legal mandates is adequately addressed in the school's instructional program.

LEARNING EXTENSION 9–5

Features of Lesson Plans

Probably more lesson plans are available on the World Wide Web than any other kind of curriculum document. If you type "lesson plan" into a standard search engine, such as Google (http://www.google.com), you will find links to many sites where lesson plans are available. Professional groups, such as the National Council of Teachers of English, the National Council for the Social Studies, the National Science Teachers Association, the National Council of Teachers of Mathematics, and the International Reading Association, often put up good examples of lesson plans. Organizations such as the Discovery Channel, PBS, and the Library of Congress also have them available on their websites. Hundreds of school districts around the country also make lesson materials available through their Internet sites.

Locate lesson plans from two or three different sources. Then review the format used to display the lesson plan depicted in Figure 9.3. To conclude, respond to the following questions:

- What are some components you found in some of the lesson plans you viewed that differ from those included in the example in Figure 9.3?

- Are there any features of the Figure 9.3 example that were lacking in some or all of the other lesson plans you reviewed?

- If you were to develop a format for a lesson plan that included components you think to be really important, what would those components be? What rationale might you use to encourage others to adopt your general design?

USE OF INTERRELATED CURRICULUM DOCUMENTS TO MANAGE PROGRAMS

Forces are in play that encourage school districts to emphasize some common content to students enrolled in the same grade or course in all schools. The need to comply with state content standards pressures school leaders to make certain that each school provides instruction consistent with state requirements. In addition, public interest in the issue of accountability and, more specifically, public wishes to have data available that allow for convenient school to school comparisons, influence similar kinds of schools to embed common content within programs targeted for given categories of students. Obviously, if students in School 1 study contents A and B, whereas students in School 2 study contents Y and Z, any comparison of the relative performance of the students in the two schools is meaningless.

The Content Consistency Issue

As you study school districts' responses to the content consistency problem, you will find that many of them have developed an overall program-management scheme that features an interrelated set of curriculum documents. The content elements that are to be common features of all instructional programs for similar categories of students often appear first in a district-level general scope and sequence document. These required content elements must be included in subordinate documents, such as grade-level plans, course plans, and instructional unit documents. When an **interrelated curriculum document system** is well designed, you can readily identify the common content elements in all of the district's basic program-management documents.

Recall that different categories of curriculum documents include information that varies greatly in scope and detail. The highly detailed information for teachers found in instructional unit documents provides extensive guidance in the issues of day-to-day instruction that goes far beyond that found in a general scope and sequence document. On the other hand, a general scope and sequence document lacks an instructional unit document's tight focus on a single topic related to a single subject. The function of a general scope and sequence document is to provide much broader information about the entire pre-K to 12 program. If a general scope and sequence document carried as much detailed information as an instructional unit document, hundreds of enormous volumes would be necessary to package the information. Such an elephantine document would have little practical value.

To avoid this problem, many school districts use a **curriculum document notation system,** which allows for the information in subordinate documents to tie back to general scope and sequence documents and curriculum guides in ways that do not require each item of information to be written out in its entirety. Instead, numbers tied to specific content elements are used to reference some of a document's content information. This approach provides a space-efficient way to acknowledge common content across a set of interrelated documents without requiring all the common content to be reprinted in each document.

The Creation of a Curriculum Document Notation System

If you wish to use a curriculum document notation system, you begin by identifying the categories of information that might be denoted using a **notation system** in some documents. Suppose you decided to build a set of interrelated documents comprising three kinds of documents: (1) a general scope and sequence document, (2) grade-level plans and course plans, and (3) instructional unit documents. The first step is to identify some categories of information that, in some of the documents, you might choose to reference by notation alone, rather than by actually printing out all of the details. You might build a notation system that focuses on three areas, organized in the following order of subordination:

Subject area

      Grade-level course title

         State curriculum standard

You need to think about the likely maximum number of entries you might have under each heading. Assume that you'll not need more than 99 entries for any one heading. If this is the case, then a numeric scheme can be adopted that allocates numbers ranging from 01 to 99 for each category. The next step is to prepare a numbered list of elements for each category. The completion of a master list is a huge task. In practice, the master list may be developed for the district's entire set of programs over time. As a beginning point, programs associated with such key subject areas as English/language arts, mathematics, social studies, and science often make sense. This information can be easily stored in a computer and relevant sections printed out as needed.

See Figure 9.4 for an explanation of how a section of a master notation system that focuses on a grade 4 English/language arts program might look. To refer to the documents in this system that are subordinate to the general scope and sequence document (grade-level plans, course plans, instructional unit documents, for example), you may decide to save space by referencing information on the master list using only the notation. You can briefly summarize a great deal of information by using a *line of notation*. For an explanation of the elements in a line of notation based on categories from the master content list illustrated in Figure 9.4, see Figure 9.5. Note the explanations of the meanings of the individual sections of the notation line. Note, too, how various components of the line are separated from one another using periods.

See Figure 9.6 for an example of saving space on an instructional unit document by referencing the subject area, the grade level, and the related state curriculum standard using only the notation. This leaves more space for critical information related to (1) focus generalizations, principles, and key ideas associated with the unit, (2) suggested procedures for teaching unit content, (3) ideas for evaluating student learning related to the unit, and (4) instructional resources that might be used to support instruction on unit-related content.

Subject Area
01 Social studies
02 Mathematics
03 Science
04 English/language arts
05 Health
06 Vocational education
(Same pattern continues for other subjects.)

Grade level or Course Title
   01 Social studies
   02 Mathematics
   03 Science
   04 English/language arts
      01 English/language arts—pre-K
      02 English/language arts—K
      03 English/language arts—1
      04 English/language arts—2
      05 English/language arts—3
      06 English/language arts—4
   (Same pattern continues.)

State Curriculum Standards
   01 Social studies
   02 Mathematics
   03 Science
   04 English/language arts
      05 English/language arts—pre-K
      06 English/language arts—K
      07 English/language arts—1
      08 English/language arts—2
      09 English/language arts—3
      10 English/language arts—4
         01 Grasp main ideas and identify pertinent supporting details provided in prose selections.
         02 Make predictions and describe, with reference to specifics, how new information ties to previous learning.
         03 Provide well-argued oral, written, or artistic responses to what has been read and compare feelings with those of others.
         04 Identify basic genres of literature and describe their defining characteristics.
         05 Compare and contrast new information from prose sources with present knowledge and develop data-based conclusions.
         06 Explain main ideas contained in written works with reference to supporting facts and details.
         07 Accurately summarize reading in both written and oral form.
      (Same pattern is followed for other grade levels and courses associated with English/language arts.)

FIGURE 9.4 Components Related to Grade 4 English/Language Arts from a Master List That References Subject Areas, Grade Levels or Course Titles, and State Curriculum Standards

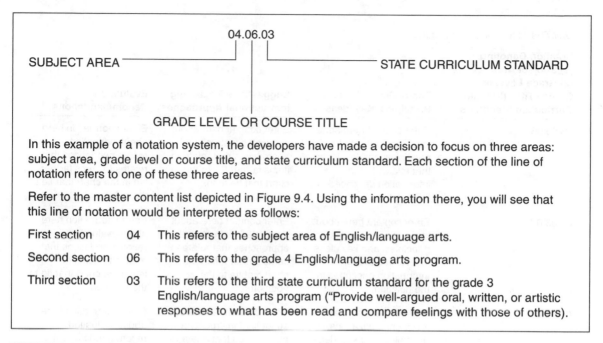

FIGURE 9.5 Explanation of the Meaning of a Line of Notation

Reasons for Developing Interrelated Curriculum Documents

Are the efforts to prepare a set of interrelated curriculum-management documents and an accompanying notation system worth the trouble? Your answer to this question may depend on the role or roles you play within the educational system. If you are a classroom teacher, you might argue that you find instructional unit documents particularly helpful and that it makes little difference to you whether the information they contain ties directly to that in grade-level plans, course plans, or your district's general scope and sequence document. This position has merit to a point. However, it is increasingly likely that you must include certain information in your instructional program that is required because of mandates embedded in state or local content standards. By using a notation system to tie information in your instructional unit documents to related course plans, grade-level plans, and the general scope and sequence document, you are in position to verify that your program complies with state and local content mandates.

If you are a school principal, a central office curriculum specialist, or a senior-level school district administrator, the likelihood is high that you will be subjected to occasional audits focusing on how the content standards are addressed in your instructional programs. Your reporting task is much easier when you have interrelated documents that allow for the quick identification of places in the overall school program where the information delineated in the content standards is

Unit Title: "Thinking as a Scientist"

Notation Denoting (1) Subject Area, (2) Grade Level or Course Title, (3) State Curriculum Standards	Focus Generalizations, Principles, Key Ideas	Suggestions Regarding Instructional Approaches	Evaluation Recommendations
03.05.06	Enter content here about focus generalizations, principles, and key ideas that relates to the information described in the notation.	Enter content here about suggested instructional approaches that relate to items farther left in the chart that tie to the notation.	Enter information here about evaluation recommendations that relates to items farther left in the chart that tie to the notation.
03.05.07	Enter content here about focus generalizations, principles, and key ideas that relates to the information described in the notation.	Enter content here about suggested instructional approaches that relate to items farther left in the chart that tie to the notation.	Enter information here about evaluation recommendations that relates to items farther left in the chart that tie to the notation.
03.05.08	Enter content here about focus generalizations, principles, and key ideas that relates to the information described in the notation.	Enter content here about suggested instructional approaches that relate to items farther left in the chart that tie to the notation.	Enter information here about evaluation recommendations that relates to items farther left in the chart that tie to the notation.
(Same pattern continues.)	(Same pattern continues.)	(Same pattern continues.)	(Same pattern continues.)

List of Resources to Support Instruction in This Unit

_____

_____

_____

Explanation: Refer to Figure 9.4 for information about the master content list and to Figure 9.5 for information about how to decipher a line of notation. In this instance, the line of notation reading 03.05.06 references the subject area of science (03), the third-grade program in the area of science (05), and the sixth state curriculum content standard that relates to the third-grade science program (06). The next notation (03.05.07) provides information related to the seventh state curriculum standard for third-grade science, and the next one (03.05.08) provides information related to the eighth state curriculum standard for third-grade science.

FIGURE 9.6   Example of an Instructional Unit Document Format that Uses a Notation Scheme to Identify Some Information Categories

addressed. Formal content audits by state and local officials represent just one category of inquiry you might face as a school leader with regard to how your programs accommodate the required content standards. Quite often, parents and other community members want to have this information simply as a matter of interest. When interrelated documents are available, questions related to this issue are easy to answer.

Sophisticated computer-management systems make it relatively easy to store vast quantities of information about the contents of interrelated curriculum documents. Such systems allow for the speedy production of information responsive to many questions associated with a school district's entire program. For example, well-designed systems can provide quick responses to dozens of questions, such as the following:

- What are the names of the available instructional units for the grade 8 science program?
- In what units in the grade 4 English/language arts program is there content related to grade 4 content standard number six?
- Is there evidence that all of the state content standards related to United States history are included in the district's instructional program?

One of the easiest ways to survive an audit against state and local curriculum standards is to design programs from the beginning so that they accommodate the required content. This approach does not mean that mandated content should displace other information that you and others believe should be included to serve students' needs. It simply recognizes that some information must be included in adopted programs because of state or local policy actions. If you have a plan from the very beginning for interrelating documents, such as a general scope and sequence document, course plans and grade-level plans, and instructional unit documents, you can stop periodically to ensure that all mandated content is being included. These checks can identify gaps and can encourage the solution of problems before your curriculum group completes its work.

Review and Reflection

1. How would you describe the general functions of curriculum documents?
2. How do you distinguish between the internal purposes and the external purposes of curriculum documents?
3. What are some quality criteria you might use as guidelines in preparing new curriculum documents and in critiquing existing ones?
4. What conditions associated with curriculum-development work sometimes get in the way of preparing high-quality documents at the conclusion of projects?
5. Why is it that many philosophy statements lack a consistent, narrowly focused point of view?
6. What are some examples of common curriculum documents, and what are some typical internal characteristics of each type?
7. If someone asked you to justify a school district's decision to develop of a set of interrelated curriculum documents, what would you say?
8. How can a notation system be used to tie together the information contained in different documents that are part of an interrelated document system?

References

American Federation of Teachers. (1999). *Making standards matter 1999: An update on state activity. Educational Issues Policy Brief, 11*. Washington, DC: Author.

Armstrong, D. G. (1997). Rating curriculum documents. *The High School Journal, 81*, 1–7.

Armstrong, D. G., & Shutes, R. E. (1981). Quality in curriculum documents: Some basic criteria. *Educational Leadership, 39*(3), 200–202.

Boehm, R. G., Hunkins, F. P., & Armstrong, D. G. (2002). *Geography: The world and its people.* New York: Glencoe/McGraw Hill.

Doll, R. C. (1995). *Curriculum improvement: Decision making and process* (9th ed.). Boston: Allyn and Bacon.

Marzano, R. J., & Kendall, J. S. (1997, September). *The fall and rise of standards-based education.* Alexandria, VA: National Association of State Boards of Education.

McREL's contributions to K–12 standards. (2001). Aurora, CO: Mid-continent Research for Education and Learning. [http://www.mcrel.org/standards/factsheet.asp]

10

Implementing Curriculum Changes

Graphic Organizer

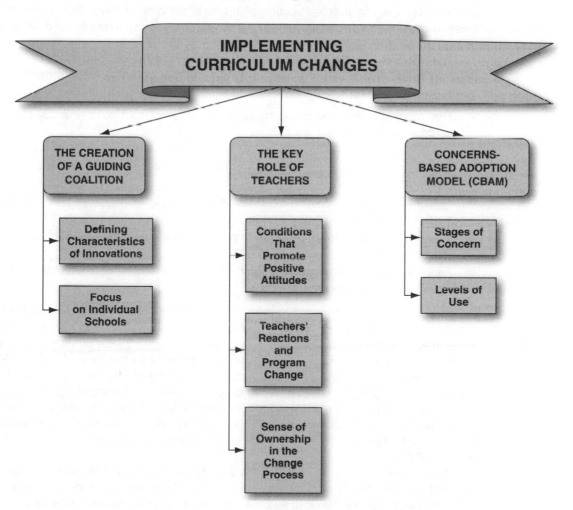

IMPLEMENTING CURRICULUM CHANGES

THE CREATION OF A GUIDING COALITION
- Defining Characteristics of Innovations
- Focus on Individual Schools

THE KEY ROLE OF TEACHERS
- Conditions That Promote Positive Attitudes
- Teachers' Reactions and Program Change
- Sense of Ownership in the Change Process

CONCERNS-BASED ADOPTION MODEL (CBAM)
- Stages of Concern
- Levels of Use

INTRODUCTION

Let's lay out an ideal set of conditions. Suppose you and a group of others have been engaged in a project to develop an exemplary new grade 7 mathematics program. You have had two years to work on the project. During this time, the school district has provided you with abundant time to meet, discuss, and plan. You have also received an extra stipend to work on the project during the summer months. Funds have been sufficient to bring in needed external consultants. The sophisticated project leadership team has made sure that group members include influential representatives of parents' organizations, the business community, and the local community college and university, as well as teachers, administrators, and students from the school district. At various stages in the development of the program, the individual components have received a trial in local classrooms, and reactions from teachers and students have been given considerable weight as the group has continued to refine the program. Schools representing a cross section of those in the district have pilot tested the close-to-final version. Information from the pilot test has led to a few minor additional refinements.

The leadership of the curriculum-development effort has decided to present the program to the local board of education with a strong "do adopt" recommendation based on the following information:

- The program has received a strong endorsement from all members of the curriculum-development group.
- Student scores on standardized mathematics exams were higher for students who were exposed to the pilot program than for students who were taught the program it will replace.
- Teachers in the schools who have reviewed the program have made generally supportive comments about its contents.
- The proposed program is consistent with state curriculum guidelines for grade 7 mathematics.
- Funds are available to support the purchase of the instructional materials needed to implement the program.

Suppose the local school board, given this evidence, extended congratulations and thanks to the curriculum-development group and voted to adopt the new program. What then? With an innovation that seems to be this good, individual schools and teachers will eagerly abandon the old program and endorse the new one, right? Although this outcome may seem logical, the long history of attempts to implement new curricula suggests that, even when cases for change are compelling, it is by no means certain that a new or revised program will easily displace an older one. "One of the most common and serious mistakes . . . is to presume that once an innovation has been introduced . . . the intended users will put the innovation into practice" (Knoll, 1987, p. v).

This reality may surprise you. There is a widespread myth that something "good" or "better" immediately attracts supporters. Few people who saw the film *Field of Dreams* questioned the "build it, and they will come" mantra that led to the construction of a major league baseball diamond in a cornfield in Iowa. However, a leading researcher in the area of innovation, Everett M. Rogers (1995), points out that little evidence supports the proposition that people will always stand in line to buy a better mousetrap. To illustrate this point, he cites the QWERTY keyboard found on most typewriters and computer keyboards. The name comes from the letters on the top left row of keys. This arrangement was initially developed in the nineteenth century to slow the rate at which typists could hit the keys, which tended to jam if struck too rapidly. The letters were arranged in a way that would require moving the fingers off the "home keys" to strike such frequently used letters as e, i, and o.

In time, typewriter technology advanced to the point that there was no need to slow down the rate at which typists struck the keys. In the 1930s, August Dvorak developed a keyboard that placed the most frequently used keys on the row of home keys. Typists trained on the new keyboard were able to type faster. Further, they experienced less fatigue than those using the traditional QWERTY arrangement (Rogers, 1995). Despite these advantages, the Dvorak keyboard never caught on. Today, more than 70 years after the invention of a more efficient keyboard arrangement, the older, slower, and more cumbersome QWERTY arrangement continues to be found on the overwhelming majority of keyboards.

The QWERTY vs. Dvorak example underscores several points. Vested interests, which sometimes you are not able to discern immediately, may have a stake in maintaining a present practice. One of the most frequently overlooked realities is the comfort-of-the-familiar phenomenon, which makes it much easier for people to think positively about change when it exists as an abstract idea or a hypothetical condition. When a change promises to impinge on people's regular routines, new procedures and processes that may have attracted considerable verbal support may encounter unexpected resistance. In addition to individuals who may find cherished routines threatened by a change, often, existing practices are sustained by a complex support infrastructure. In the case of school programs, the publishers of instructional materials have hundreds of thousands, even millions, of dollars invested in the development of books, software, and other materials designed to serve existing programs. They may be reluctant to commit the resources needed to supply new materials for an innovative program, particularly if it is one that will be used by only a small number of schools and school districts.

LEARNING EXTENSION 10–1

Pressures to Maintain the Status Quo

Few people question that the successful introduction of complex innovations poses significant challenges for groups and individuals interested in improving school practices. The fact that suggestions for even modest change often prompt strong resistance is a less widely appreciated reality. In part, this resistance is explained by the advantages that present practices confer on certain individuals and groups. In part, it is a reflection of a level of comfort that often comes to people who have learned to cope successfully with existing practices and patterns. To better appreciate some of the difficulties you might encounter as a member of a group promoting the adoption of new or modified practices, consider the kinds of resistance you might encounter, even in a situation in which you are seeking to implement only one change, as opposed to a more typical curriculum revision, which requires adopters to make multiple changes. As a focus for this activity, choose a change from the following short list. Alternatively, identify one of your own.

- To give elementary teachers a longer lunch period, the school day will be extended by 30 minutes.

- To give students and teachers an extra day each semester to prepare for standardized tests, the school year will be extended by two days.

- To improve secondary students' writing proficiency, all secondary-level English teachers will require all students to produce at least one essay per instructional week.

- To save on air-conditioning bills, during September, October, May, and June, all schools will start one hour earlier and dismiss one hour earlier.

- To assure that students receive a truly well-rounded education, each student will be taught to play one musical instrument by the time he or she completes grade 8.

Think about the change you have selected as a focus. Then, respond to the following questions:

- Are there particular individuals and groups who are advantaged by the present arrangements and practices? If so, how do they benefit?

- What implications will the proposed change have for individuals and groups outside of the school, and how will they react to the change?

- As you begin thinking about the kinds of resistance to the change you might encounter, what ideas do you have that you could use in building a case designed to win over those who, initially, oppose it?

You may recognize a number of professional realities that today's teachers face that can act as barriers to enthusiasm for curricular innovations. For example, they are faced with the challenge of working in schools where the results of standardized tests assume increasing importance and where the diversity of students becomes more pronounced each year. On the one hand, they are pressured to produce students who do well on standardized tests. On the other hand, they are encouraged to vary their instruction to accommodate the needs of young people with widely divergent backgrounds. To succeed at bringing all the members of today's highly varied student body to levels of learning that will allow them to achieve good scores on standardized tests, many teachers feel they must be as flexible as possible about what and how to teach the young people under their charge (Hargreaves, Earl, Moore, & Manning, 2001). Researchers have found that teachers pull back their commitment to change and even reduce their basic interest in their professional work when they feel that a proposed change will restrict the range of their professional judgment (Woods, Jeffrey, Troman, & Boyle, 1997).

Both the compelling allure of tradition and the professional conditions in schools underscore the folly of assuming that even the most eminently worthy curriculum innovation will immediately attract enthusiastic adopters. Successful changes require both time to take root and careful planning. Often, the time condition is one of the most difficult to achieve. School boards and, sometimes, the central office administrators responsible for approving curriculum changes have unrealistic expectations about how long the innovations should be in place before they are evaluated for the purpose of retaining or rejecting them. Gene Hall and Shirley Hord (2001), who have studied curriculum-adoption processes for decades, conclude that "a pattern has developed: introduce a new program, give it a year to take hold, immediately assess its effectiveness, and reject it when no increased program outcomes are found" (p. 31). More time is required for teachers to become familiar with a curriculum change, to commit to its use, to master its nuances, and to develop patterns of use that include all the critical components. Hall and Hord (2001) contend that "most changes in education take three to five years to be implemented at a high level" (p. 5).

The challenges associated with moving an innovation from the planning and development stage to the point that most intended users implement it enthusiastically and appropriately make a strong case for careful planning for implementation. Increasingly, there is support for the idea that (1) planning for curriculum development and revision and (2) planning for curriculum implementation, though related, need to be considered as two independent activities (Hall & Hord, 2001). This pattern is rarely followed today. Typically, planning for implementation is an add-on task for the curriculum-development team. Its complexity often goes unrecognized. In addition, there are concerns about the appropriateness of involving the same people who developed a curriculum change in the quite different task of building commitment for the change among potential users. Curriculum development and revision are taxing. At the end of a project, the people involved often are tired. It makes more sense to charge a new and enthusiastic group with the task of planning and putting into play a sound implementation plan. In addition, even when pilot testing has been extensive, when large numbers of teachers begin implementing a curriculum change, they may discover that the innovation would profit from adjustments to its design. It makes sense for there to be a mechanism that allows information to flow back from the change-implementation group to the curriculum-design group.

 ## THE CREATION OF A GUIDING COALITION

School reform leader Phillip Schlechty (2001) stated that "compared to sustaining change, starting change is relatively easy" (p. 39). He notes that few schools and school systems are **change-adept organizations**—institutions in which leadership expertise and support conditions routinely are deployed to encourage and support altered ways of doing business. One approach to moving educational institutions from change-inept to change-adept institutions is to assign **guiding coalitions.** These consist of individuals who are "empowered to lead and manage the change process" (Schlechty, 2001, p. 47). Their work supports the dissemination and installation of curriculum innovations to enable them to become sustainable features of the school program.

Defining Characteristics of Innovations

The number of individuals involved in a guiding coalition varies with the general character and complexity of the curricular innovation the members will work with. In general, individual curricular innovations differ in terms of three characteristics (Hall & Hord, 2001):

- Their emphasis on a new or revised product
- Their emphasis on a new or revised process
- Their size

Curriculum projects that produce novel or revised *products* seek to introduce schools and students to tangible innovations such as new textbooks (for example, a "fused" science text including content from multiple science disciplines, as opposed to traditional separate texts for chemistry, biology, and physics), new technological hardware (computers, scanners, personal digital assistants, and so forth), and new assessment devices (formal examinations, authentic assessment approaches, rubrics, and so forth). Curriculum projects that seek to introduce new or revised *processes* aim to encourage the use of specific instructional methodologies and procedures (inquiry strategies, clearly defined questioning strategies, simulations, cooperative learning approaches, and so forth). The issue of curricular innovation *size* has to do with two variables: complexity and scope. Complexity relates to the defining characteristics of the innovation. Does the change involve the modification or introduction of something that suggests that potential users alter only one or two things they are doing? For example, will they be asked to use a particular questioning technique once or twice a week? Or does the change involve a complex cluster of innovations that, when implemented, will require the potential users to do many things that differ from present practices? For example, will they be encouraged to embrace a new program that, for the first time, requires them simultaneously to engage in team teaching, base their reading program on a whole language approach, and deliver 40 percent of new content to students via computer software or the Internet? Clearly, the work of guiding coalitions becomes more challenging when they deal with innovations that ask potential users to make many changes in what they do.

LEARNING EXTENSION 10–2

Organizing a Guiding Coalition for a School

Suppose you were charged with organizing a guiding coalition to promote the adoption of an innovation in a given school. If you are presently working in a school, assume your own school is the setting. If this is not your situation, choose a school you know about. Then, prepare responses to the following questions:

- Who will the members of the group be?
- What is your rationale for selecting these people?
- How will the members relate to one another? (Who will be in charge? Who will report to whom?)
- How will information be provided to teachers and others who will implement program changes?
- What actions will be taken to assure that information from new users will be carefully gathered and shared with others? You will need a mechanism to get information into the hands of (1) other teachers in the building, (2) other building-level guiding coalitions in different schools, (3) the members of a district-level guiding coalition coordinating group, and (4) the members of the group responsible for developing and modifying the innovation.

The scope of an innovation has to do with the issue of scale. Is the proposed curricular change something designed for use within a single school or by a small subset of the total group of students in a district? Or is it to be implemented districtwide or statewide? More people need to be involved in guiding coalitions charged with promoting the adoption and encouraging the sustained use of large-scale innovations. Where the proposed scope is huge (districtwide in large school districts, statewide, and so forth), there may be a central guiding coalition management team, which coordinates the work of many smaller groups assigned to individual school districts and schools.

Focus on Individual Schools

Researchers who have studied the change process emphasize the importance of using the individual school as the unit of analysis when establishing guiding coalitions (Hall & Hord, 2001). Even if the innovation is a large one to be applied across all like schools in a school district (for example, in all grade 8 social studies classrooms), separate guiding coalitions should be established in each building. Some members of this group will also serve as members of a district-level coordination group. These individuals fulfill an important liaison function between district-level leadership and professional personnel in buildings where curriculum changes are to be implemented. For example, they can take back suggestions related to possible design modifications that the district-level guiding coalition coordination group might wish to share with all members of the group.

Although some kind of central guiding coalition coordinating group may make sense, the day-to-day work of selling the change and supporting the work of potential adopters goes on in individual buildings. Advocates for change who, in most cases, are part of the professional community of the individual school have the credibility needed to advocate successfully on behalf of the proposed change or changes.

The composition of building-level guiding coalitions may vary, depending on the nature of the innovation, the priorities of the school personnel, and other contextual variables associated with the setting. Gene Hall and Shirley Hord (2001) recommend school-based coalitions that include three or more individuals from the school, as well as one person who has no institutional tie to the school. A school-based guiding coalition organized according to this pattern might include the following members:

- A coalition leader
- An assistant coalition leader
- Interested teacher advocates
- An outside consultant

Change cannot be sustained in the absence of strong support from school administrators (Hall & Hord, 2001). Hence, it makes sense for someone from the school's central administration (often, the principal) to serve as building leader of the guiding coalition. The principal's leadership signals strong support for the change to the entire school community. It also suggests that there will be administrative advocacy for the resources that might be needed as teachers adopt and implement the new program.

Hall and Hord (2001) propose that an assistant coalition leader might be a member of the school's instructional staff who has been assigned to assist school leadership in exchange for a reduced teaching load. When a curricular change is contemplated, this person can be directed to promote schoolwide interest in the change and to take other actions to encourage its adoption and sustained use.

Because many innovations require important alterations in what teachers do, it is especially helpful for someone with heavy teaching responsibilities to advocate for the change. This might be an early adopter of the innovation who is willing to model its use for other members of the staff. It might be someone who has been in the building for a long time, has seen various enthusiasms come and go, and who has become personally convinced that the one being proposed is "a keeper" and should be supported. The opinions of highly respected teachers carry great weight with their colleagues, and it is important for one or more of them to be involved as members of school-based guiding coalitions. The next section of this chapter contains more information about the important role that teachers play in the process of implementing and supporting curricular changes.

In addition to guiding coalition members from within the school, it also often makes sense to include an external consultant as a member. This person may have a background in general curriculum development and may have knowledge concerning design features embedded within the change. He or she might serve as a member of guiding coalitions in several schools. If this proves to be the case, this individual can share ideas about approaches to implementation that have worked well in other settings and those that have not gone as well as innovation supporters hoped they would (Hall & Hord, 2001). Finally, this person may serve as a member of a central district guiding coalition coordinating group. In this capacity, the external consultant helps link adoption efforts in individual schools with efforts going on throughout the entire school district.

THE KEY ROLE OF TEACHERS

You may recall from the Chapter 6 discussion of teachers' roles in curriculum development that new and revised curricula can prompt them to think about ways to modify suggested changes to better meet the needs of the students in their classrooms. Abundant research supports the view that teachers make many adaptations to the information contained in curriculum guidelines as they seek to modify the programs to accommodate the unique characteristics of their students (Ben-Peretz, 1990; Hall & Hord, 2001). Curriculum developers have not always recognized this reality.

For example, in the 1960s many major curriculum projects went forward on the assumption that new programs would be delivered exactly as designed if (1) the explanations of the content to be covered were clear, (2) needed instructional materials were provided for students to use, and (3) teachers were given explicit directions about the instructional techniques they were to use. In the main, these so-called *teacher-proof curricula* failed to take root (Hargreaves et al., 2001). Follow-up research revealed that many programs were quickly abandoned or modified and implemented in ways that differed greatly from the developers' intents (Tanner & Tanner, 1995). As Daniel Tanner and Laurel Tanner (1995) point out, this turn of events should have been expected, given the abundant evidence supporting the idea that "effective teaching is not mechanical. It is dependent on individual variation and the professional teacher's latitude in interpreting the subject matter and in effecting one's own teaching style . . ." (p. 441).

If you have been an active professional educator in recent years, you will recognize some present realities that prompt teachers to be especially wary of program-improvement proposals. Increasingly, teachers are being held accountable for students' levels of performance on standardized tests. The pressures associated with testing lead many teachers to approach new or revised curricula with a skeptical eye. Teachers are skittish about committing to programs that, in their view, may lead to poorer student performance on test scores. If scores fall, they, not the members of the curriculum development group, will take the heat. This set of conditions underscores the point that, "if reform of any kind is to succeed, teachers must believe that they will have a meaningful voice in decisions and will not become the lone scapegoats of a failure to reach goals" (Marsh, 1999, p. 192).

Conditions That Promote Positive Attitudes

You will find it easier to win commitment to a new or revised program when you point out to teachers that change is a *process,* not an *event* (Hall & Hord, 2001). Processes imply ideas such as "long-term," "modifying," and "adapting." When change is seen as a process, potential adopters are better able to understand that new and revised practices will take time to root and that there is no expectation that, on a fixed date, all the elements of the old program will be displaced by the new. On the other hand, when curriculum change is seen as an event, there is an implication that decisions have been made, packaged, and prepared under the assumption that all the elements will be implemented, with no modification, by a certain time. This conception presumes teachers to be technicians whose only role is to serve as passive conduits who will deliver changed programs to students precisely as they have been designed. This patronizing view does not go down well, and it can lead to passive and even active resistance on the part of potential program adopters.

Teachers more readily commit to a new program when they perceive it to have an important *relative advantage* over the one it is to replace (Rogers, 1995). This means that members of the guiding coalition who are championing a new or revised program need to be as conversant with the one it is replacing as with the new one. They need to be prepared to answer questions such as

- What aspects of the old and new programs are similar?
- What aspects of the old and new programs are different?
- What is the rationale for assuming that the changes in the new program are superior to what presently is included in the old program?
- What differences in preparation time will there be when the new program is introduced?
- What differences are there in terms of how the existing and proposed programs accommodate state curriculum guidelines and the content expectations of standardized tests?

Individuals who have participated in the development of new and revised curricula become highly conversant with their features and with any specialized vocabulary included in documents that have been prepared to record and disseminate recommendations. Potential teacher users of these programs sometimes are put off by what they perceive to be their excessive *complexity* (Rogers, 1995). In response to this possibility, guiding coalition members must be prepared to describe the new or revised program in clear and detailed language. They need to provide potential users answers to questions such as the following:

- Exactly what new content will I be expected to teach?
- If I lack background in this content, what plans are there to provide me an opportunity to acquire it before I am expected to teach the new material?
- What are the readability levels of student materials that will be provided? If these are too high, given the reading proficiency of some students I teach, will supplementary materials at a lower readability level be available?
- How many class periods are recommended for each unit in the program?
- How much freedom do I have to deviate from the content that is provided and the suggested instructional approaches?

You may find teachers who are potential adopters to be greatly concerned about the issue of transition from the existing program to the changed program. Researchers have found that commitment to a change is facilitated when an innovation has a high level of *trialability*, a set of conditions that allows potential adopters to try small parts of a larger change to get used to how it differs from what they have been doing. These small-scale trials tend to increase the comfort levels of potential users and to be associated with a higher incidence of strong commitment to the change (Rogers, 1995). Members of guiding coalitions need to be prepared for questions such as

- May I begin using part of the program on an experimental basis?
- What components of the total program would you recommend for a trial run?
- What if I disagree with the instructional technique suggestions and decide to teach the new content in a different way? Will this be a problem if I try parts of the new program with my students?
- Who will listen to me if I have questions or concerns as a result of my trial use of part of the changed program?

Teachers' Reactions and Program Change

Teachers who use a new or modified program will make some alterations as they attempt to fit it to their own students and instructional setting (Hall & Hord, 2001). This kind of teacher involvement is to be expected from thoughtful professionals. However, there are some limits to the modifications a teacher can make without changing the basic character of the new program. Indeed, a new or revised program may include some features that teachers are barred from modifying or deleting. For example, the proposed change may embed content newly mandated in a changed state curriculum standard—for example, specific subject-area content that is part of an official state curriculum standard—which teachers must not delete. (A later section of this chapter, dealing with the concerns-based adoption model, introduces more discussion of the issues raised by program-design changes that occur during implementation. See the heading "Levels of Use.")

Though there are some limitations on the kinds of changes teachers can make, most new and revised curricula give teachers considerable flexibility in making modifications that will make learning easier for the students they teach. In approaching teachers about this issue, you need to emphasize not only that there is room for them to adapt the new or revised program but also that some modifications are highly desirable. Many alterations made by individual teachers may make sense for other users, and it is helpful to provide a mechanism that will allow teacher reactions, suggestions, and proposed modifications to be fed back to the people responsible for developing and revising the proposed program. The members of the guiding coalition who oversee the process of installing the curriculum change can arrange to get teachers' views to the appropriate people.

You will find that attempts to sell new programs to teachers by trashing existing ones lead to more anger than commitment. Because of the political difficulties attendant to getting a hearing for change proposals in large and complex school bureaucracies, sometimes promotional rhetoric soars beyond the boundaries of reality. Existing practices may be described as "hopelessly antiquated," "academically soft," or "ill suited to today's workplace." Proposed new ones may be touted as being "cutting-edge," "fostering high-level thinking," or being "technologically advanced." Describing existing programs in highly negative terms and counterbalancing these comments with glowing characterizations of proposed replacements may win initial political support for a change among community leaders and school-district-level administrators. However, such talk suggests that teachers have failed to perform in a professional manner and have not been doing all in their power to serve their students well. Quite naturally, teachers bristle at attempts to characterize their work in such a negative way. They are reluctant to get behind change recommendations that seem to imply that their previous levels of performance were inferior. As you think about enlisting teachers' support, it makes far more sense to assume high levels of teacher competence and to suggest that this kind of expertise provides exactly the kind of foundation needed to make the present programs better.

LEARNING EXTENSION 10–3

Accentuate the Positive

Identify a potential program revision in an area of your interest. Next, think about the teachers who, you hope, will embrace the program and commit to it with genuine enthusiasm. These teachers are professional people whose work you respect. You wish to avoid leaving any impression that their present work has been deficient. Identify four to six bulleted points you might use in working with these people to win their support. Think about the following concerns as you prepare your list:

- The need to provide assurances that the change will build and extend many features of the existing program
- The fact that suggestions regarding instructional approaches are just that—*suggestions*, not *mandates*
- Openness to teacher recommendations regarding modifications to the innovation (based on their experiences in using it in their classrooms)
- The desirability of providing praise for past performance

Sense of Ownership in the Change Process

Winning teachers' commitment to a new or revised program requires actions, not just supportive words. If you have been a professional educator for many years, you will appreciate that there is much public talk about the importance of thinking teachers who function as leaders and act as independent, professional decision makers. Such phrases have become staples of politicians' comments about education and, frequently, of keynote addresses at educators' professional meetings. What, too often, have been lacking are substantive changes in teachers' work conditions that allow them to behave in ways consistent with how speakers often define their roles. The point is simple. If you want teachers (1) to think about a proposed curriculum revision; (2) to modify it, so that it functions well in their own classrooms; and (3) to give their honest reactions to the people charged with developing and refining the innovation, then you need to assure that their perspectives will be heard and seriously considered as bases for action. If teachers feel that nothing ever happens as a result of their recommendations, many (perhaps most) of them will see comments about "the need for teacher involvement" as cosmetic verbiage having no grounding in reality.

One approach to providing a structure that will promote active involvement comprises four key phases, which are largely built around three assumptions. The first assumption is that teachers are competent professionals who know their content, a variety of instructional and assessment techniques, and the nature of the students they teach. The second assumption is that many elements of what they are doing prior to the installation of an innovation can be used as they begin working with the change. The third assumption is that there will be a mechanism in place for their ideas to be heard by the individuals responsible for developing and revising the proposed change and that the teachers will receive feedback from these people regarding the disposition of any ideas they send forward.

Phase one: analyzing the new and the old.   Phase One involves the teacher in comparing and contrasting existing practices with the new or revised program. The idea is to identify specific aspects of the present program that can be continued with little or no modification as the new one is introduced. Some focus questions teachers should be encouraged to answer during this phase are

- What elements of the present program can be continued with no change when the new program is implemented?
- What elements in the present program can be continued with some modification when the new program is implemented?
- What elements of the present program will have to be abandoned when the new program is implemented?

Phase two: working to promote the effectiveness of the new program.   Phase Two focuses on developing responses to the most important concerns of teachers. School reform expert Phillip Schlechty (2001) suggests that changed curricula must respond appropriately to three key teacher concerns:

1. Providing learning experiences that engage students
2. Designing instruction that encourages students to persist when they have difficulty
3. Leading students to develop a sense of satisfaction and responsibility as they successfully complete assigned tasks

During this phase, teachers are asked to examine the new program carefully, to look at issues such as content difficulty and recommended instructional strategies, and to consider suggestions embedded in the innovation in light of the three concerns. Teachers are encouraged to make modifications to the new program to assure a good fit with their own instructional needs. You will find that teachers who do this often develop strong commitments to the change. Their work gives them a personal investment in the change process, and their modifications give them more confidence that the new program will have characteristics that are appropriate for the kinds of students they teach. Some questions that teachers may ask during this phase include

- What elements of the proposed program will attract the initial attention of my students? If some sections seem to lack good potential to do this, what specific alternatives might work better?
- What aspects of the proposed program promise to be sufficiently interesting and motivating for my students that they will willingly stay the course until all needed work is completed? If the proposed configuration of the changed program includes parts that students might quickly lose interest in, what might be modified to better sustain their interest?
- Are the difficulty levels of the proposed program set in ways that will give my students a legitimate opportunity to succeed? If not, what changes might be made that will enable them to experience success and gain a sense of self-worth and self-confidence?

Phase three: making, trying, and reporting modifications.   In Phase Three, teachers make program adjustments in light of the analyses completed in Phase Two. Then, they implement these changes on a trial basis. In light of their experiences during these trials, they decide to adopt the modification or to make additional revisions. Finally, they prepare reports of their proposed modifications and transmit them to the people responsible for developing and revising the innovation. Often, a member of the guiding coalition will work with teachers to transmit their reports to the curriculum-development and -revision group.

Some questions that teachers might ask during this phase include

- Given my analysis of the new program, what changes need to be made to better serve my own students? How can I put these changes into practice?
- How can I test my ideas about modifications of the new or revised program that seem to make sense, given my own students and school setting?
- After trying some of my proposed changes on a trial basis, what do I conclude? What specific information and recommendations should I provide to the curriculum-development and -revision group?

Phase four: providing feedback to teachers.   Phase Four is important. It assures that information from teachers to the curriculum-development and -revision group gets serious consideration. To give the entire process of teacher participation credibility, it is important that teachers receive feedback once they have taken the time to study the elements of a change proposal, to think about and try out modifications, and to share their thoughts (in writing) with members of the curriculum-development and -revision group. Feedback promotes teachers' sense of professionalism and underscores their importance as members of a wider professional community with sincere interests in providing high-quality programming to students. You will find teachers to be much more receptive to implementing a change when they have tangible evidence that their ideas receive a serious hearing. Feedback on their recommendations and suggestions assures them that their views carry weight.

Some questions that the members of the curriculum-development and -revision group might think about in preparing feedback responses to teachers include

- Do the suggestions and recommendations make sense only in the particular setting of this teacher, or do they deserve to be shared with a wider audience, in the hope that other teachers might also wish to implement them?
- Are the suggested changes acceptable modifications that continue to support the defining characteristics of the innovation?
- What costs might be associated with implementing the proposed suggestions and changes, and can the budget sustain any needed increases?

 ## CONCERNS-BASED ADOPTION MODEL (CBAM)

In the 1960s, researcher Frances Fuller (1969) determined that people who want to become teachers have different feelings about their information and training needs, depending on where they are in their preparation programs. She further discovered that these feelings and concerns fall into a predictable sequence. For example, during the early phases of the programs, future teachers typically feel "nonconcern" about student teaching. As student teaching begins, this attitude shifts to "concerns about self"—worries about specific actions to be taken, tasks to be completed, and other work associated with getting through the school day. Fuller discovered that typical student teachers begin to think seriously about how their instruction affects their students only toward the end of their student teaching experience. By this time, they have developed confidence in their abilities to handle the routines of classroom teaching and are able to think seriously about the impact of their instruction.

In the early 1970s, a group of scholars associated with the Research and Development Center for Teacher Education, then located at the University of Texas at Austin, began considering how the stages of concerns Fuller identified might be applied to educational innovations. Their work resulted in the development of the **Concerns-Based Adoption Model (CBAM).** Research based on the framework has continued for more than 30 years (Hall & Hord, 2001).

One part of CBAM focuses on **Stages of Concern.** The seven stages describe how teachers' concerns change as they continue to work with and become familiar with an innovation (Hall, G. E., & Loucks, S. F., 1977). Another part of CBAM looks at **Levels of Use.** Researchers have identified seven basic patterns that change over time as teachers implement, think about, and revise innovations (Hall, G. E.; Loucks, S. F.; Rutherford, W. L.; & Newlove, B. W., 1975). You may

0 *Awareness:* Little concern about or involvement with the innovation is indicated.

1 *Informational:* A general awareness of the innovation and interest in learning more detail about it is indicated. The person seems to be unworried about himself/herself in relation to the innovation. She/he is interested in substantive aspects of the innovation in a selfless manner such as general characteristics, effects, and requirements for use.

2 *Personal:* Individual is uncertain about the demands of the innovation, his/her inadequacy to meet those demands, and his/her role with the innovation. This includes analysis of his/her role in relation to the reward structure of the organization, decision making, and consideration of potential conflicts with existing structures or personal commitment. Financial or status implications of the program for self and colleagues may also be reflected.

3 *Management:* Attention is focused on the processes and tasks of using the innovation and the best use of information and resources. Issues related to efficiency, organizing, managing, scheduling, and time demands are utmost.

4 *Consequence:* Attention focuses on impact of the innovation on students in his/her immediate sphere of influence. The focus is on relevance of the innovation for students, evaluation of student outcomes, including performance and competencies, and changes needed to increase student outcomes.

5 *Collaboration:* The focus is on coordination and cooperation with others regarding use of the innovation.

6 *Refocusing:* The focus is on the exploration of more universal benefits from the innovation, including the possibility of major changes or replacement with a more powerful alternative. Individual has definite ideas about alternatives to the proposed or existing form of the innovation.

FIGURE 10.1 Stages of Concern

Source: From G. E. Hall & S. F. Loucks, "Teacher Concerns as a Basis for Facilitating and Personalizing Staff Development," *Teachers College Record, 80* (1), 1978, (36–53), p. 41. Reprinted with permission of Blackwell Publishers. Copyright © 1978 by Teachers College Press.

find the Stages of Concern and Levels of Use helpful as you think about the issues associated with implementing changes and revised curricula. Let us look first at the seven Stages of Concern. For an illustration of these stages and a brief description of each, refer to Figure 10.1.

EXERCISE 10–1

Using Findings from CBAM Research in Preparing Plans for Promoting the Adoption of Curriculum Innovations

Space limitations in this text prevent more than a cursory discussion of the findings associated with the more than three decades of work associated with the Concerns-Based Adoption Model. The findings of researchers who have associated themselves with this model represent a rich resource you can use in planning for and supporting the adoption of new and revised school programs.

Action

Seek additional details about the Concerns-Based Adoption Model. You will find abundant information available on the web. Use a search engine, such as Google (http://www.google.com), and type in "Concerns-Based Adoption Model." Over the years, numerous journal articles have reported CBAM-related research. You should be able to find some by referring to the *Education Index* in your library. Several books have been published, summarizing work related to CBAM. The following is an especially good one, which you may wish to consult:

Hall, G.E., & Hord, S.M. (2001). *Implementing change: Patterns, principles and pitfalls.* Boston: Allyn and Bacon.

Analysis

As you read the materials you locate, write down ideas you might use in putting together a plan to win initial support for a program change and to sustain and support users for the first three to five years of their involvement with the change. Include these ideas in a brief outline of your overall plan.

Key Points

Many research studies focus on various aspects of implementing change. There are two especially noteworthy strengths of research that have been conducted around the Concerns-Based Adoption Model. First of all, there has been a sustained record of accumulating studies that now has extended more than 30 years. This kind of long-term focus on a relatively narrow topic focus is unusual. Second, the model focuses not only on issues associated with the initial adoption of an innovation but also on issues related to its sustainability.

In summary, the CBAM work represents an impressive, sophisticated body of knowledge that stands as a key resource for professionals interested in implementing new and revised programs.

Stages of Concern

Suppose you knew nothing about the stages depicted in Figure 10.1 and were charged with preparing a plan to sell an innovation to a group of teachers. Since a major responsibility of teachers is to help students acquire knowledge, you might decide to build your case around the positive impact the changed program promises to have on students. Given today's concerns about standardized test scores, you may even choose to frame many of your comments around the idea that the new program will result in students' mastering new content so well that their test scores will go up. Stages of Concern research findings suggest the folly of trying to generate initial teacher enthusiasm for an innovation by describing how it will benefit students. It is true that the developers of a new or revised curriculum and the school board and other authorities that endorsed it probably based their decisions on the assumption that the changes would enhance student learning.

However, teachers and others who will work with the changes on a day-to-day basis first want to know how these changes will affect what they do as they discharge their responsibilities.

Stages of Concern research suggests that the kinds of staff-development work required will vary over time, depending on where people are in terms of their familiarity with the change and with the problems and potentials associated with its use (Hall & Hord, 2001). Individuals who are at the first two stages, "awareness" and "informational," have yet to confront the possibility that they personally will participate in implementing a proposed change. Their interest tends to be at a somewhat removed, intellectual level. It is much the same as what you might experience as you read about new equipment used to make ascents of Mt. Everest easier. You might have a keen interest in reading about these developments, but chances are small that you will personally take advantage of these innovations and actually climb the mountain. If you have a realistic possibility of doing so, then you want much more information. You might ask questions such as "What would the new equipment cost?" "How much would it weigh?" and "How comfortable would I find it?"

A similar change in intensity of interest in and demand for additional information occurs when teachers recognize that they will have some involvement in implementing a curriculum change. They begin to have "impact on self" questions that are reflected in concerns at the levels of "personal" and "management" (Hall, George, & Rutherford, 1977). Only after teachers who are new adopters of an innovation have had experience with and have become comfortable with the changed procedures and processes are they ready to start thinking seriously about the impact of the new program on students, how they might collaborate with others to make the change more effective, and how the program might be modified to become more effective. These concerns are reflected at the levels of "consequence," "collaboration," and "refocusing." Researchers have found that it may be two or three years before impact on learners becomes a high-priority concern of the users of a curriculum innovation (Hall & Rutherford, 1975).

What this information suggests is that the details provided to new and inexperienced users of a curriculum innovation should focus heavily on the issues related to how the change will affect them and to how it might be managed. In planning staff-development sessions designed to generate a commitment to a curriculum change, you might consider using a checklist such as the one provided in Figure 10.2. As you design your staff-development approaches, you can use the checklist to assure that the information and experiences you provide will respond to all of the listed questions.

Although it is true, in general, that the potential adopters of a curriculum innovation have more initial worries about the changes it will require in their behavior and work than about how they will affect learners, when you find yourself charged with planning staff-development activities for groups of new users, you may want information about the specific feelings of the members of your group. This kind of information can help you better tailor staff-development experiences related to the innovation to the specific concerns of the members of the group or

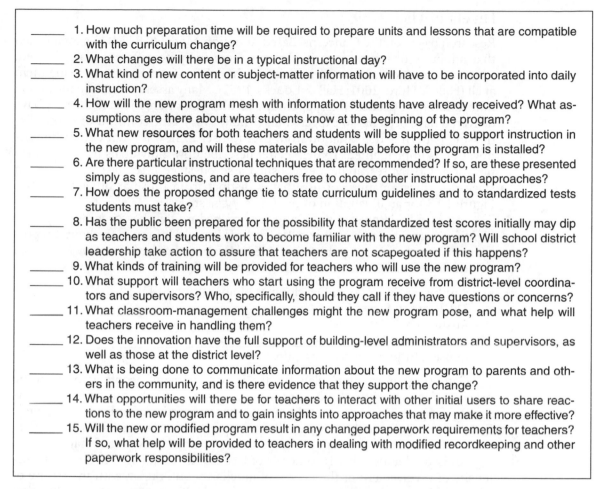

_____ 1. How much preparation time will be required to prepare units and lessons that are compatible with the curriculum change?

_____ 2. What changes will there be in a typical instructional day?

_____ 3. What kind of new content or subject-matter information will have to be incorporated into daily instruction?

_____ 4. How will the new program mesh with information students have already received? What assumptions are there about what students know at the beginning of the program?

_____ 5. What new resources for both teachers and students will be supplied to support instruction in the new program, and will these materials be available before the program is installed?

_____ 6. Are there particular instructional techniques that are recommended? If so, are these presented simply as suggestions, and are teachers free to choose other instructional approaches?

_____ 7. How does the proposed change tie to state curriculum guidelines and to standardized tests students must take?

_____ 8. Has the public been prepared for the possibility that standardized test scores initially may dip as teachers and students work to become familiar with the new program? Will school district leadership take action to assure that teachers are not scapegoated if this happens?

_____ 9. What kinds of training will be provided for teachers who will use the new program?

_____ 10. What support will teachers who start using the program receive from district-level coordinators and supervisors? Who, specifically, should they call if they have questions or concerns?

_____ 11. What classroom-management challenges might the new program pose, and what help will teachers receive in handling them?

_____ 12. Does the innovation have the full support of building-level administrators and supervisors, as well as those at the district level?

_____ 13. What is being done to communicate information about the new program to parents and others in the community, and is there evidence that they support the change?

_____ 14. What opportunities will there be for teachers to interact with other initial users to share reactions to the new program and to gain insights into approaches that may make it more effective?

_____ 15. Will the new or modified program result in any changed paperwork requirements for teachers? If so, what help will be provided to teachers in dealing with modified recordkeeping and other paperwork responsibilities?

FIGURE 10.2   Checklist to Assure That Staff-Development Information Responds to the Personal and Management Concerns of the Potential Users of a Curriculum Innovation

groups you will be working with. You may be interested in administering and studying responses to the _SoC questionnaire,_ a questionnaire designed to provide information about where individuals are located in terms of the seven stage of concern levels. The following are two sources of copies of the _SoC questionnaire:_

- Southwest Educational Development Laboratory (SEDL)
  211 East 7th Street
  Austin, TX 78701-3281
  phone: 800-476-6861
  website: http://www.sedl.org/pubs/

- Hall, G. E., & Hord, S. M. (2001). _Implementing Change: Patterns, Principles, and Potholes._ Boston: Allyn and Bacon.

Levels of Use

Research based on the Concerns-Based Adoption Model (CBAM) has established that adopters of innovations implement them in quite different ways. Indeed, some people who claim to use innovations have been found not to be using them at all (Hall & Hord, 2001; Hall & Loucks, 1977). Many assessments of educational innovation have produced disappointing results. Too often, the benefits they have delivered have been below expectations (Knoll, 1987). One contributor to this distressing pattern is the variation from user to user in how a given curriculum innovation is implemented. To help better describe how individuals use a given innovation, CBAM researchers established a seven-stage *Levels of Use* scale. Each stage describes a pattern of use that is distinct from those at other levels. See Figure 10.3 for an illustration of the *Levels of Use* stages.

You may be interested in an interview procedure that has been developed to identify where a given person is on the *Levels of Use* scale. Information about this procedure is contained in a publication titled *Measuring Levels of Use of the Innovation: A Manual for Trainers, Interviewers and Raters*. It is available from the following source:

- Southwest Educational Development Laboratory (SEDL)
  211 East 7th Street
  Austin, TX 78701-3281
  phone: 800-476-6861
  website: http://www.sedl.org/pubs/

Gathering information related to the Levels of Use of people who are in the process of implementing a new or revised program can help you better tailor inservice support efforts to meet the unique characteristics of individual adopters. For example, individuals who are still at the "preparation" stage have vastly different needs than those who are at the "refinement" and "integration" stages.

An issue that ties closely to Levels of Use has to do not so much with the intensity of involvement or the degree of familiarity but, rather, with the nature of what is being done in the name of the innovation. If you have been in education for very long, you recognize that certain enthusiasms sweep through the profession from time to time. A few people adopt the labels used to identify these phenomena (e.g., inquiry-based teaching, concept learning, computer-based instruction, co-operative learning, and so forth) without actually embracing all (or, in some instances, any) of the practices they describe. Even individuals who are very committed to a changed or modified program and who believe they are implementing it as designed inevitably make some modifications as they work with it in their own classrooms (Ben-Peretz, 1990; Hall & Hord, 2001). Indeed, this probably is a desirable state of affairs. Teachers and students vary, and it makes sense for programs to be modified to take advantage of both teachers' individual backgrounds and the characteristics of the students they teach.

On the other hand, as Gene Hall and Shirley Hord (2001) point out, some innovations have tremendous potential to improve student learning. In such cases, it makes sense to assure that modifications of the original design do not undermine the ability of the proposed change to help students. For this reason, there

Level 0—Nonuse	State in which the user has little or no knowledge of the innovation, has no involvement with the innovation, and is doing nothing toward becoming involved
Level 1—Orientation	State in which the user has acquired or is acquiring information about the information and/or has explored or is exploring its value orientation and its demands on the user and user system
Level 2—Preparation	State in which the user is preparing for the first use of the innovation
Level 3—Mechanical use	State in which the user focuses most effort on the short-term, day-to-day use of the innovation with little time for reflection. Changes in use are made more to meet user needs than client needs. User is primarily engaged in a stepwise attempt to master the task required to use the innovation, often resulting in disjointed and superficial use.
Level 4a—Routine	Use of the innovation is stabilized. Few, if any, changes are being made in ongoing use. Little preparation or thought is being given to improving innovation use or its consequences.
Level 4b—Refinement	State in which the user varies the use of the innovation to increase the impact on clients within the immediate sphere of influence. Variations are tested for knowledge of both short- and long-term consequences for clients.
Level 5—Integration	State in which the user is combining own efforts to use the innovation with related activities of colleagues to achieve a collective impact on clients within their common sphere of influence
Level 6—Renewal	State in which the user reevaluates the quality of use of the innovation, seeks major modifications of or alternatives to present innovation to achieve increased impact on clients, examines new developments in the field, and explores new goals for self and the system

FIGURE 10.3   Levels of Use of an Innovation

Source: Adapted from G. E. Hall, S. F. Loucks, W. L. Rutherford, & B. W. Newlove. "Levels of Use of the Innovation: A Framework for Analyzing Innovation Adoption." *The Journal of Teacher Education*, 1975, *26*(1), pp. 52–56. Reprinted with permission. Copyright © 1975 by The American Association of Colleges for Teacher Education.

may be times you will want to know how much a given user of an innovation has changed the original design. To obtain this information, consider developing a chart along the lines of the one depicted in Figure 10.4. You can include categories that make sense in light of your specific areas of concern.

CURRICULUM REALITIES 10–1

Issues Associated with Innovation Complexity

Is it more desirable for a curriculum innovation to feature only a small number of embedded changes, or is it more desirable for it to include many concurrent changes? There are arguments on both sides of this issue. From the standpoint of teachers and

Categories	Original Design	What This Teacher Is Doing	Thoughts/Comments/Reactions
Topics covered			
Student learning resources used			
Recommended instructional techniques			
Patterns of teacher-student interaction			
Procedures for assessing students			
Modifications for students with special needs			

FIGURE 10.4   Chart for Gathering Information about Alterations to the Original Design of a New or Revised Program

other potential adopters, an innovation that asks them to make only a few changes from present practices may be more welcome than one that suggests they do many new things at once. On the other hand, some present-day school improvement and reform specialists suggest that there will be little meaningful improvement unless a broad range of concurrent changes is implemented.

The concerns of both individual teachers and advocates of large-scale school reform point out a need for school-district-based change proponents to seek a middle ground between too little and too much. This prescription is easier to describe than to implement. If the change is a modest one that teachers will find easy to install, critics may suggest that the school district has committed to cosmetic rather than substantive reform. On the other hand, if teachers see the change as imposing large numbers of new and unfamiliar expectations, they may develop negative attitudes. If such attitudes persist, it is doubtful that the proposed change will produce the benefits envisioned by its promoters.

The work of individuals in school districts and schools who are charged with winning enthusiastic support for large and complex innovations is especially challenging. Individuals who do this successfully need a keen political nose. They must respond in meaningful ways both to the concerns of outsiders who may be frustrated at what they see as the slow pace of school reform and to the concerns of school professionals who must implement the proposed changes.

Review and Reflection

1. How do you explain the difficulties that often are associated with implementing even well-designed program changes? More particularly, what conditions in schools today often contribute to some teachers' reluctance to embrace change?

2. What does research say about the appropriateness of making evaluations related to the impact and worth of an innovation that are made after it has been in place for one year? What political realities lead to evaluations of new programs being made relatively soon after they have been installed?

3. What is the function of a *guiding coalition,* and what categories of people might be included in one established in a single school?

4. What are some general characteristics of innovations designed for implementation in schools?

5. What steps might you take to increase teachers' interest in and commitment to an innovation?

6. How might you use information related to the *Stages of Concern* identified by CBAM researchers in planning staff-development opportunities for potential and new users of a program innovation?

7. What is the importance of information related to teachers' *Levels of Use* of an innovation?

8. How might you go about determining the extent of modifications to an innovation that individual users have made?

References

Ben-Peretz, M. (1990). *The teacher-curriculum encounter.* Albany: State University of New York Press.

Fuller, F. F. (1969). Concerns of teachers: A developmental conceptualization. *American Educational Research Journal, 6,* 207–226.

Hall, G. E., George, A. A., & Rutherford, W. L. (1977). *Measuring stages of concern about the innovation: A manual for use of the SoC questionnaire.* Austin: The Research and Development Center for Teacher Education, The University of Texas at Austin.

Hall, G. E., & Hord, S. M. (2001). *Implementing change: Patterns, principles, and potholes.* Boston: Allyn and Bacon.

Hall, G. E., & Loucks, S. (1977). A developmental model for determining whether the treatment is actually implemented. *American Educational Research Journal, 14*(3), 263–276.

Hall, G. E., Loucks, S. F., Rutherford, W. L., & Newlove, B. W. (1975). Levels of use of the innovation: A framework for analyzing innovation adoption. *Journal of Teacher Education, 26*(1), 52–56.

Hall, G. E., & Rutherford, W. L. (1975). *Concerns of teachers about implementing the innovation of team teaching.* Austin: The Research and Development Center for Teacher Education, The University of Texas at Austin.

Hargreaves, A., Earl, L., Moore, S., & Manning, S. (2001). *Learning to change.* San Francisco: Jossey-Bass.

Knoll, M. K. (1987). Foreword. In S. M. Hord, W. L. Rutherford, L. Huling-Austin, & G. E. Hall (Eds.), *Taking charge* (pp. v–vi). Alexandria, VA: Association for Supervision and Curriculum Development.

Marsh, M. S. (1999). Life inside a school: Implications for reform in the 21st century. In D. D. Marsh (Ed.), *Preparing our schools for the 21st century: The 1999 ASCD yearbook* (pp. 185–202). Alexandria, VA: Association for Supervision and Curriculum Development.

Rogers, E. M. (1995). *Diffusion of innovations* (4th ed.). New York: The Free Press.

Schlechty, P. C. (2001). *Shaking up the school house: How to support and sustain educational innovation.* San Francisco: Jossey-Bass.

Tanner, D., & Tanner, L. (1995). *Curriculum development: Theory into practice.* Upper Saddle River, NJ: Merrill/Prentice Hall.

Woods, P., Jeffrey, B., Troman, G., & Boyle, M. (1997). *Restructuring schools, reconstructing teachers.* Bristol, PA: Open University Press.

Evaluating the Curriculum

Graphic Organizer

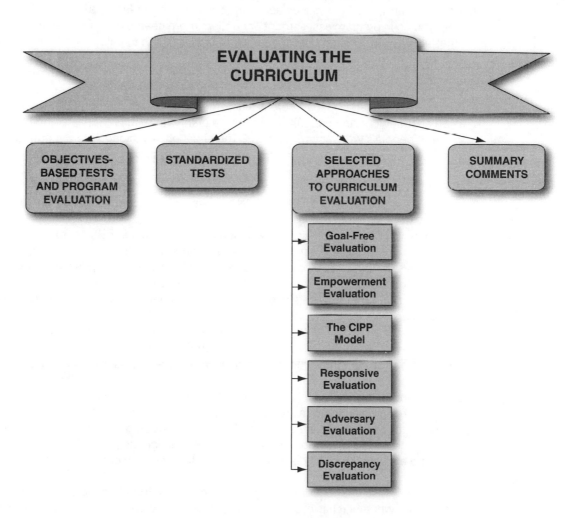

EVALUATING THE CURRICULUM

- **OBJECTIVES-BASED TESTS AND PROGRAM EVALUATION**
- **STANDARDIZED TESTS**
- **SELECTED APPROACHES TO CURRICULUM EVALUATION**
  - Goal-Free Evaluation
  - Empowerment Evaluation
  - The CIPP Model
  - Responsive Evaluation
  - Adversary Evaluation
  - Discrepancy Evaluation
- **SUMMARY COMMENTS**

INTRODUCTION

As measurement specialist Michael Scriven (1967) pointed out many years ago, evaluations of educational programs demand more than simply assembling information. They also require people to make *judgments* about gathered data. The hope is that the results of these judgments will suggest approaches that lead to improved teaching and better educational programs (Tanner, 2001). If you immerse yourself in the educational evaluation literature, you will find examples of numerous research-based approaches that you might use to make judgments about new or revised instructional programs. You will find few challenges to the idea that program evaluation is a legitimate and valued activity.

The consensus in support of the idea that new and revised curricula *should* be evaluated by no means suggests that assessments of particular programs typically are smooth, warm, and harmonious activities. They are not. In fact, you may find that the work you do in program assessment engenders more heated disputes than almost any other activity you engage in as a curriculum specialist. This reality sometimes comes as a surprise to newcomers to the field.

How can there be conflict when there is such wide support for the idea that schools should use evaluation to weed out mediocre programs and support stronger ones? The explanation is that there is a difference between commitment to evaluation as an abstract idea and commitment to evaluation with results that have the potential to affect people's work and reputations. The situation is analogous to the attitude of a small, owner-operated hardware store toward the idea of business competition. If you ask the store owner whether he or she believes in the value of competition, you are likely to get an enthusiastic yes answer. If you ask the same individual how he or she would welcome the opening of a national hardware chain superstore on the next block, you may get a different response.

A key to working in program evaluation is developing a sensitivity to how various kinds of judgments will affect people. These judgments often impact individuals in different ways. A few people may not care whether the evaluation is positive or negative. Others, probably including many who opposed the new or revised program from the beginning, may hope for a negative evaluation. Still others may be desperately anxious for some positive evaluation results.

To illustrate this reality, think about members of a school board who have authorized the development of a new program. When they were considering supporting the development of the innovation, they may have learned that some community members (perhaps even a large number) opposed the change. It is possible that board members expended considerable political capital when they decided to support the development of the new program. Authorizing the change and providing scarce financial resources to pay for it may have placed them at considerable risk. Under these circumstances, the people who are charged with evaluating the program may sense that the board expects them to "discover" evidence that the new or revised program is doing well.

You may also find that different groups focus on different aspects of a program in considering whether it has merit. For example, school board members may attend very carefully to the issue of program cost. The superintendent and other central office administrators may focus heavily on how student scores on standardized tests have been affected by a new or revised curriculum. The parents and guardians of students may have concerns about how well a changed program prepares their sons and daughters for college and university work. Teachers, among other concerns, often want evaluation information that focuses on the adequacy of the provided instructional support materials. Representatives of minority groups may seek information from the evaluation that specifies how well the new or modified program serves students from ethnic and language minorities.

Well-designed evaluation processes are complex. They must be implemented in pressure-filled political environments that pose frequent challenges to the professional integrity of evaluators. These circumstances have led to much discussion among the members of the American Evaluation Association (AEA), the leading national professional group for experts in the evaluation of educational programs. In recent years, there has been some consideration of proposals to establish a certification system for evaluators (Worthen, 1999). The idea is that certified evaluators should be individuals who have been screened both for their knowledge of evaluation approaches and for their understanding of the pressures evaluators feel when doing their work. To date, no formal action has been taken to implement such a certification plan. Part of the difficulty has been in establishing a set of criteria to be used in the certification process. The discussion of this issue continues.

OBJECTIVES-BASED TESTS AND PROGRAM EVALUATION

Serious systematic efforts to evaluate school programs, as opposed to school students, began about 70 years ago (Stufflebeam & Shinkfield, 1985). Interest in program evaluation accelerated in the middle of the 20th century when Ralph Tyler (1949), an important pioneer in the educational evaluation field, proposed that specific learning objectives be developed for individual courses. He recommended that tests be developed that tie closely to these objectives. Then student performance on these **objectives-based tests** could be used to judge the adequacy of the instructional program.

Over time, objections to this approach began to appear in the professional literature. For one thing, critics pointed out that many objectives could be developed for a given instructional program. It proved easier to develop tests for some of these objectives than for others. There were concerns that this approach encouraged the selection of objectives that could be tested easily, rather than those that had greater educational significance (Armstrong, 1989). If this tendency became widespread, the effort to establish evaluation programs could result in weaker instructional programs.

Tyler's approach tended to assume that all students in a given classroom should be pursuing the same objectives. Over the years, the populations of American classrooms have become more, not less, diverse. This has been particularly true since the passage of federal legislation that promoted the inclusion of students with various disabilities as members of regular classrooms. The increasing diversity in classrooms has been a force militating against the idea that all students should pursue the same learning objectives.

Tyler (1949) emphasized the importance of teachers' writing their own objectives in light of the needs of the students they were teaching. In the second half of the twentieth century, as standardized testing became more common, some teachers began to develop objectives based on the items on standardized tests. Critics pointed out that such a practice provided a basis for developing school programs that failed to respond to the unique characteristics of the students. Concerns about the inappropriateness of using common standardized tests to assess the quality of educational programs for all students continue today. Harold Howe II (2001), a former U.S. commissioner of education, voiced a concern about a proposal for some schools to require all students to take the same standardized tests and to achieve the same proficiency levels. He noted that "such an arrangement would be a well-organized disaster for a country moving rapidly toward cultural, economic, and social diversity."

The idea of assessing the curriculum by creating tests based on instructional objectives also is problematic when totally new programs are developed. If you were assigned to identify the objectives of a course, such as high-school introductory algebra, you probably would not have too much difficulty. The course has been taught for years. Though there are some differences in individual texts and approaches taken by specific teachers, there also is much consensus about this course's content. On the other hand, if you were asked to develop an evaluation plan for a new course for a community-college evening program on film appreciation for adults who have educational backgrounds ranging from eighth-grade graduates to master's degree holders, you would face considerable difficulties. What kinds of objectives would be reasonable for such a course? What would your expected levels of proficiency be? There are no obvious answers to these questions.

Finally, objectives-based assessment approaches have been criticized because assessment information is not gathered until after instruction related to the objectives has been completed. The evaluation results come too late to be of any immediate use to the teachers of specific groups of students (Cohen & Leonard, 2001). Although the gathered information may prompt them to modify their practices with a subsequent group of students, it will not help the group that initially was tested.

Evaluation specialist Michael Scriven (1967) proposed that evaluators make a distinction between **summative evaluation** (evaluation at the end of the instructional experience) and **formative evaluation** (evaluation that gives results to program users while instruction is still ongoing, so that they can make needed changes). Over the years, interest has increased in the ways to provide evaluative feedback to teachers while their programs are being taught. Formative evaluation information of this kind gives them opportunities to rethink procedures and make midcourse adjustments. Many contemporary evaluation procedures build in a strong formative evaluation component.

LEARNING EXTENSION 11–1

Timely Receipt of Evaluation Information

There is much sentiment among evaluation and measurement specialists for conducting assessments frequently as programs are being delivered. The idea is to gather data, to provide this information to teachers, and to allow them (perhaps in consultation with specialists of various kinds) to modify their instructional approaches to better serve students' needs. How often is the approach followed?

Take time to survey some teachers regarding this issue. You might consider some focus questions, such as these:

- Are the results of mandated tests provided to you early enough in the school year for you to use this information to consider changes in how you teach the students who took them?

- Is there any formal mechanism in your school or in your school district that brings people together to consider how test data might be used to improve instruction?

- If you were able to change the ways in which test data are now used in your school or school district, what would you do?

In summary, what are your conclusions about the degree to which patterns of student scores on required tests are being used to improve instruction in the schools (and possibly school districts) where the teachers you surveyed are employed?

STANDARDIZED TESTS

Standardized tests, as you may know, are tests constructed from the test scores of scientifically selected samples of groups (for example, all fifth graders) to establish **norms** (expected scores). For many years, members of the general public paid sparse attention to standardized test scores. For the most part, teachers and administrators used them as they considered modifications to instructional programs. Some standardized test scores also were among the data used by college and university admissions offices when considering prospective students' applications. These somewhat benign applications of standardized test information have given way in recent years to the increasing use of them in making judgments about the relative excellence of school districts, specific schools, central office and school-based administrators, and individual classroom teachers. If you have been in education long, you recognize that many national and state political leaders, leading representatives of the media, and members of the general public today use standardized test scores to draw conclusions about the relative excellence of our schools. This interest has supported a huge increase in standardized testing. It is now estimated that all American students take more than 100 million standardized tests each year (Weaver, 1995). Standardized tests are used nowhere else in the world as frequently as they are in the United States (Kohn, 2000b).

Widespread belief in the proposition that standardized test scores provide good information about the quality of school programs has consequences for administrators and teachers. In some places, financial and other rewards go to administrators and teachers in buildings where scores are high, and negative sanctions (sometimes even the loss of jobs) result when standardized test scores are low.

The importance standardized tests now have for audiences outside the school places tremendous pressure on school personnel to shape instructional programs in ways that will lead to high student scores. This circumstance suggests that, when you work to design an evaluation scheme for a new program, you may feel considerable pressure to embed a standardized test component as part of your plan. Whether this is desirable or not, an important part of the judgment of the "worth" of any new or revised program will be based on any observed changes in students' scores on related standardized tests.

The supporters of standardized testing see these exams as providing a mechanism that will allow honest comparisons among school districts, schools and school leaders, and individual teachers. If students in different places and in different schools take different tests, there is no legitimate way to make these kind of quality distinctions. Some people who favor standardized testing hint that the opposition of some educators is based not so much on honest concerns about the legitimacy of the approach as on a reluctance to have their performance held up to close public scrutiny.

Although a few educators who are concerned about standardized tests may harbor I-don't-want-my-work-carefully-scrutinized motives, there *are* legitimate, professional concerns about these kinds of assessments. Let's consider a few points that critics often make. As noted in Chapter 4 in the discussion of state standards, the movement to develop standards generally came after the movement to develop and administer standardized tests. If you have prepared a new or revised program and have worked to tie it to state curriculum standards, it may be that no standardized test exists that will adequately sample the content of your program. The development of standardized tests is a time-consuming and expensive process (Stake, 1998). It may be years before new standardized tests are developed that adequately sample the content of any new or revised programs you develop.

What this means is that students who are taught the program may have to take an off-the-shelf standardized test that relates only tangentially to the content of the program you have developed and wish to assess. (It is highly doubtful that you will be able to make a case in support of the idea that students should be excused from standardized testing, pending the development of a new one that better fits the content of the new or revised program.) Under these circumstances, the school district may base a decision to keep or abandon the program on student scores on a standardized test that samples content not included in your new or revised program.

For decades, critics of overreliance on standardized test data have struggled to make their views understood by individuals outside the professional community of educators. In the early 1980s, Ernest Boyer (1983) reported that, increasingly, teachers were preparing their students to answer the kinds of multiple-choice questions featured on standardized tests. To accomplish this purpose, their instruction was becoming more and more focused on teaching students to memorize isolated bits of information, rather than to develop their abilities to engage in more sophisticated kinds of analyses. Over the years, many other observers have confirmed Boyer's observations (Goodlad, 1984; Kohn, 2000a; Weaver, 1995).

Why don't standardized tests probe students' higher-level thinking abilities? Two conditions militate against this. First of all, there is the issue of numbers. Standardized tests are given to enormous numbers of students. It is not practical for answers to be reported in a way that does not lend itself to speedy electronic correction. This circumstance forces test makers to opt for forced-choice test items that can be scored quickly. Test items of this kind (multiple-choice, true-false, and matching, for example) are not capable of assessing sophisticated levels of student thinking. Essay examinations and other kinds of exercises that allow students to bring a variety of information to bear on an issue are better suited to this purpose. However, such items cannot be scored electronically. Given the volume of tests to be graded, it has not proved feasible to embed many items of this type on standardized tests. There have been attempts to assess students' writing abilities by having them prepare samples of their work. When this is done, graders apply an assessment **rubric,** a set of guidelines that tells the grader what to look for in assessing the quality of the student's performance. The correction of these items takes a great deal of time, and in some places there have been issues related to the reliability of assessments made by different graders.

In addition to concerns about the kind of instruction the overuse of standardized testing may promote, critics have pointed out some other important problems. Though people today often use these test scores to make judgments about the quality of instructional programs, there is evidence that students' scores are affected most strongly by variables having little to do with the nature of the teaching they encounter at school. For example, *The Nation's Report Card: Mathematics 2000* (U.S. Department of Education, 2001) reported that students' scores were strongly associated with such variables as poverty, their parents' levels of education, and their school's community setting.

Standardized tests sample student performance at a single point in time. It is questionable whether this kind of brief performance snapshot provides enough evidence for people to draw conclusions about what students have been taught and what they have learned. Further, scores from standardized tests often are reported back to schools and teachers weeks, even months, after students took the tests. Many of the tests are given late in the school year. These conditions do not allow teachers to use the information to modify their instructional programs in time to serve the interests of the students who have been tested (Cohen & Leonard, 2001).

Critics of standardized tests have been especially vocal in their concerns about fairness. Many minority students have not done as well on standardized tests as their majority-group peers. Large numbers of such students have economically impoverished backgrounds. In addition, there is evidence that some minority children have been unfairly perceived as slow learners, placed into low-ability tracks, and provided with instructional experiences that are inferior to those provided to other students. Too many minority students receive poor instruction; hence, it is no surprise that their standardized test scores tend to fall below those of majority-group learners (Ferguson, 1998). Critics of standardized tests suggest that poor scores often are interpreted as evidence of minority students' inability to learn, rather than as evidence they have received poor instruction.

CURRICULUM REALITIES 11–1

Gaining Widespread Commitment to Closing the Majority-Minority Achievement Gap

The fact that minority students' scores on achievement tests continue to lag behind those of majority White students has been widely documented. Many efforts are underway to close this gap (Jencks & Phillips, 1998), yet the political environment within which curriculum change takes place has not always supported aggressive efforts to respond to this problem. Part of the difficulty is that many people in the majority White community fail to see the importance of the problem. A survey commissioned by *The Washington Post,* the Henry J. Kaiser Family Foundation, and Harvard University found that over half of all the White respondents felt that issues related to race were receiving too much attention. Only 17 percent of the African-Americans, 31 percent of the Latinos, and 28 percent of the Asian-Americans shared this view (Morin, 2001).

Evaluation expert Robert Stake (2000) is among those who have worked to draw attention to the differences between what standardized test scores are *supposed* to measure and what they *do* measure. By design, high test scores are intended to indicate students who have mastered the material well. The intent is for the scores to be indicators of achievement. Stake argues that standardized tests, instead, measure students' scholastic *aptitude.* This quality is greatly influenced by life circumstances, beyond their personal control, that have to do with such things as opportunities to manipulate verbal and numerical symbols during the early years of their childhood. Individual students, too, have little personal control over the quality of the instruction they receive in their classes.

As noted earlier in this chapter, some educational leaders see an inherent incompatibility between (1) the idea that all students in a given grade level or a given course should take the same kind of standardized test and (2) the reality that we live in a nation that honors diversity and where differences among students are increasing. The one-size-should-fit-all assumption of standardized testing runs contrary to what some educational leaders see as the essential nature of good education. Speaking to this issue, Robert Stake (2000) points out that "professionalism in teaching means such things as treating individual children differently, seeking out the teachable moment, and looking at education more as problem-solving experience than as amassing basic skills" (p. 3).

Despite efforts to draw public attention to the limitations of standardized tests, they continue to draw strong support from many people who are concerned about the quality of American schools. For example, the Republican presidential administration that assumed office in 2001 made an early commitment to "improve education" by establishing a mandatory annual testing program. At present, political support for standardized testing remains strong. As you engage in curriculum work and consider the evaluation issue, you can expect at least some of the judgments that will be made about the quality of new and revised programs will be based on standardized test scores. What you will want to avoid are situations in which *only* standardized test information is used to assess program quality. It is unlikely that such tests will be appropriately fitted to all of the special features of new and changed programs. Although the results of such tests may provide a small part of the information you need, you will want to argue for more comprehensive assessments that tie clearly to the unique characteristics of the program to be judged.

SELECTED APPROACHES TO CURRICULUM EVALUATION

Over the years, many curriculum-evaluation approaches have been developed. These vary tremendously in complexity and in basic design features. The examples in this section will introduce you to the range of available options.

Goal-Free Evaluation

When you and others develop a revised curriculum, your work typically is guided by assumptions about what benefits the students will derive from their exposure to that program. Many evaluation approaches base assessments on student goals and objectives that the program developers have identified. Such approaches tend to indicate progress (or lack of progress) in terms of how well student achievement conforms to the identified goals and objectives. However, there is always some tension between externally developed program goals and objectives and the characteristics of the students taught by particular instructors in specific classes and schools. Is it more appropriate for a new or modified program to be assessed based on the expectations of its developers, or is it more appropriate for it to be judged in terms of how well it responds to the unique needs of the students who are being taught? The proponents of **goal-free evaluation** commit strongly to the second position. Their primary interest is seeking information about how well the program serves students' needs.

Goal-free evaluation is an approach first promoted by evaluation specialist Michael Scriven (1972). Scriven argued that evaluators should not have their perspectives biased by information on what a program was supposed to accomplish. Rather, evaluators should simply be told to go into a school where the new program has been implemented, to gather information about what students are doing and learning, and to judge how well students' needs are being met. This approach honors and legitimizes the actions teachers take to modify programs to fit the characteristics of their students and other special features of their instructional circumstances.

The supporters of goal-free evaluation argue that assessment information that focuses on what students are actually doing and learning may reveal patterns consistent with what the program developers had in mind. If that proves to be the case, the individuals who prepared the new or revised program will be interested in the information. However, goal-free supporters suggest that, if evaluation data confirm that students' needs are being met, even if what learners are doing and learning varies considerably from the program developers' intentions, that, too, is cause for celebration. Such a finding indicates that teachers are responsibly modifying the program to fit the special needs of their own students.

For the supporters of goal-free evaluation, negative assessments are merited when instructional programs fail to respond adequately to the special characteristics of the students who are being taught. Even if students are achieving the goals and learning objectives established by the program developers, a negative evaluation judgment will be rendered if the program fails to respond well to the students' individual needs.

Today's schools exist in a political and social environment that does not comport well with goal-free evaluation. Widespread public interest in standardized testing is indicative of support for assessment approaches that hold students to common patterns of teacher and learner performance. Goal-free evaluation places a higher priority on varying patterns of teacher and student performance. Few school boards today will enthusiastically commit funds to a goal-free evaluation plan that directs evaluators to "see what is happening and let us know whether students' needs are being met." They face great pressure to generate information that can be used to inform the general public about how well teachers are transmitting common content and how well students are mastering it.

Empowerment Evaluation

David M. Fetterman (1996) points out that **empowerment evaluation** "is designed to help people help themselves and improve their programs using a form of self-evaluation and reflection" (p. 5). It is based on the idea that people respond best when they play an active and substantive role in making decisions about issues that affect their lives. The key words are "active" and "substantive." It is not sufficient for decision makers simply to appoint advisory groups consisting of people who will be affected by their decisions. The representatives of these groups need to play an active role as initial decisions are made.

Empowerment evaluation attempts to provide all individuals with a stake in decisions with opportunities to affect decisions. These stakeholders are invited to establish goals that are as compatible as possible with their own interests. The idea is to build collective ownership and interest. Self-determination is a strong, underpinning value of empowerment evaluation (Fetterman, 2001). People who sense they are exercising control over their lives grow as human beings and tend to commit strongly to decisions in which they participate.

Because so many stakeholders have interests in decisions that are made, empowerment evaluation always involves groups of people. Every effort is extended to achieve some representation from all groups who may be affected by decisions. Supporters of empowerment evaluation are especially concerned about getting representation from traditionally marginalized groups (the economically impoverished, those with poor English language skills, and so forth). Empowerment evaluation has been used successfully in many settings. For example, Henry Levin's (1996) Accelerated School Project (ASP) includes parents, teachers, and administrators, who work together to improve all aspects of the school setting.

Further, empowerment evaluation tends to have a strongly formative character. With a view to promoting continuous improvement, individuals engage in continuous patterns of assessment and modification of the programs as they are delivered. The idea is to engage in continuous program improvement at the same time that the individuals participating in the process extend their personal horizons. To avoid any appearance of heavy-handed, top-down, prescriptive leadership, evaluation specialists act more as facilitators than directive experts. Their role is to "teach people to conduct their own evaluations and thus become more self-sufficient" (Fetterman, 1996, p. 9). The evaluation specialist works with an evaluation team, which includes representatives of all the relevant stakeholders.

The following phases are recommended when an empowerment-evaluation approach is used (Fetterman, 1996, 2001):

1. Developing a mission
2. Taking stock
3. Setting goals/developing strategies
4. Documenting progress/planning for the future

Developing a mission. If you are involved in empowerment evaluation, in developing a mission, you and other group members will work together to develop a common understanding of how the new or revised program should function. You may call in people who participated in its development to explain the developers' initial intentions and to respond to questions and concerns. Follow-up discussions will give you and other members of your group a clear picture of how an idealized version of the program might operate. You will use this version as a common reference point as your group continues to study the program and learn how its operation in practice deviates from your understanding of how it originally was intended to operate.

Taking stock. In *taking stock*, members begin the process of rendering judgments about the program. If you were a member of such a group, you and others would begin by identifying a list of the important components of the innovation. Depending on the complexity of the program, you would then designate some of these as critical or high-priority features. Next, the members of your group would gather information about how each component is being implemented. Each person in your group would evaluate how well individual program features are functioning by assigning a rating from 1 (the lowest rating) to 10 (the highest rating) to each program component. Next, each group member would share his or her feelings and provide the evidence used to arrive at his or her conclusions. This sharing of information and the associated careful listening and discussion build a consensus on which aspects of a program are working well, satisfactorily, or in undesirable ways. As David Fetterman (1996) points out, work accomplished during the taking stock phase provides "a baseline from which future progress can be measured" (p. 19).

Setting goals/developing strategies.   During the setting goals/developing strategies phase, you and other participants think about program features that are not operating as well as you would like. Your task is to identify any changes that might result in program improvement. These take the form of goals. Once goals are identified, you go on to identify strategies that might be used to accomplish them. In addition, you identify the kinds of evidence to be used in determining whether these goals have been met.

The kinds of goals set during the setting goals/developing strategies phase may differ from those that were provided by the original developers of the new or revised program. Often, at least some individuals involved in initial curriculum-development work will themselves be little affected by the actual operation of the new or changed programs they recommend. Because empowerment-evaluation teams are comprised of program stakeholders, the goals they establish tend to speak clearly to the interests of the people whose lives will be influenced by the program. Typically, these goals are shorter or more intermediate than goals developed by the original curriculum-development group. Often, however, the achievement of the goals established by empowerment-evaluation teams over time will result in the accomplishment of many of the larger goals originally formulated by the program-development group.

Documenting progress/planning for the future.   During the documenting progress/planning for the future phase, you and others support the implementation of strategies designed to accomplish the goals established during the previous phase. In addition, you develop and implement the procedures for systematically gathering information related to the effectiveness of these recommended changes. Great care is taken at the beginning of this phase to identify the kinds of documentation needed and the ways in which each recommended type provides relevant information. The intent is to make documentation a highly focused activity that seeks to gather only the information that is really needed to make judgments about how well a particular aspect of the program is functioning. An examination of this evidence is used as a basis for ongoing review of the program and to recommend additional changes to make it better in the future.

The nature of the documenting progress/planning for the future phase underscores a key characteristic of empowerment evaluation: It views evaluation as a continuous process, not as a series of events with definite beginning and end points. In empowerment evaluation, stakeholders with clear interests in how well programs function engage in activities that simultaneously expand their capacities as human beings and reshape programs in ways that make them more effective.

The CIPP Model

Daniel L. Stufflebeam, a leading authority on program evaluation, has long promoted the view that useful evaluation is formative. As he notes, the best approaches "lead to evaluations that would aid in managing and improving programs" (Stufflebeam & Shinkfield, 1985, p. 155). Stufflebeam developed a scheme that provides useful information for making basic program planning decisions, organization decisions, implementation decisions, and review and revision decisions. His evaluation model, one of the most widely used in education, requires evaluations of four focus areas:

- Context
- Input
- Process
- Product

Stufflebeam's (2000) model takes its popular name from the first letters of the names of these four focus areas. It is almost always referred to as the **CIPP** (pronounced "sip") **model.** For an illustration of the model, see Figure 11.1. Let's look at each of its four components.

Context. Certain assumptions underpin decisions that curriculum-development groups make in planning new and revised programs. Are these assumptions appropriate? *Context evaluation* seeks to provide answers. The issue is an important one. For example, if planning for a given program presumes that students already have a solid background in certain kinds of information but, in fact, they do not, they will not fare well when the program is implemented. Their failure is unlikely to have anything to do with the expertise of the teachers, the quality of the instructional support material, or the way new content is sequenced. It has everything to do with an unacceptable gap between what students presently know and what the program developers expected them to know.

Context-evaluation information does not only reveal that students know too little to profit from a proposed program. It can also point out that students have already mastered content that developers erroneously may presume to be new to them. For example, consider a situation in which a large number of seventh graders attended a summer scholarship camp and that part of their summer involved an introduction to algebra. If program developers lack this kind of information, they may presume that no students entering the eighth-grade algebra program have had previous exposure to the subject. As a result, new programs they plan may assume that all students need the basics. Students who already know this material may become bored, even resentful.

	Context Evaluation	Input Evaluation	Process Evaluation	Product Evaluation
Objective	• To define the institutional/service context • To identify the target population and assess its *needs* • To identify pertinent area *assets* and *resource opportunities* for addressing the needs • To diagnose *problems* underlying the needs • To judge whether *goals* are sufficiently responsive to the assessed needs	• To identify and assess *system capabilities* and alternative service *strategies* • To closely examine planned *procedures, budgets,* and *schedules* for implementing the chosen strategy	• To identify or predict *defects* in the procedural design or its implementation • To provide information for the programmed decisions • To record procedural events and activities for later analysis and judgment	• To collect descriptions and judgments of *outcomes* • To relate outcomes to *goals* and to *context, input,* and *process* information • To interpret the effort's *merit* and *worth*
Method	• By using such methods as survey, document review, secondary data analysis, hearings, interviews, diagnostic tests, system analysis, and the Delphi technique	• By *inventorying and analyzing* available human and material resources • By using such methods as *literature search,* visits to *exemplary programs, advocate teams,* and *pilot trials* to identify and examine promising solution strategies • By *critiquing* procedural designs for relevance, feasibility, cost, and economy	• By *monitoring* the activity's potential procedural barriers and remaining alert to unanticipated ones • By obtaining specified *information for programmed decisions* • By *interviewing* beneficiaries, *describing* the actual process, maintaining a *photographic record,* and continually *interacting* with and observing the activities of staff and beneficiaries	• By operationally defining and *measuring* outcomes • By *collecting judgments* of outcomes from stakeholders • By performing both *qualitative* and *quantitative analyses* • By *comparing outcomes* to assessed needs, goals, and other pertinent standards
Relation to decision making in the change process	• For deciding on the *setting* to be served • For defining *goals* and setting *priorities* • For surfacing and addressing potential *barriers* to success • For providing *assessed* needs as a basis for judging outcomes	• For selecting *sources of support* and solution *strategies* • For explicating a sound procedural *design,* including a budget, schedule, and staffing plan • For providing a *basis for monitoring and judging implementation*	• For *implementing and refining the program design and procedures*—that is, for effecting *process control* • For logging the actual process to provide a *basis for judging implementation* and *interpreting outcomes*	• For deciding to *continue, terminate, modify,* or *refocus* a change activity • For presenting a clear *record of effects* (intended and unintended, positive and negative) • For *judging* the effort's merit and worth

FIGURE 11.1 Four Categories Associated with the CIPP Model

Source: From Daniel L. Stufflebeam. "The CIPP Model for Evaluation." In Daniel L. Stufflebeam, George F. Madaus, and Thomas Kellaghan (Eds.). *Evaluation Models: Viewpoints on Educational and Human Services Evaluation.* 2nd edition (pp. 279–317). Boston: Kluwer Academic Publishers, 2000, p. 302. Copyright © 2000 by Kluwer Academic Publishers. Reprinted with permission.

Context evaluation seeks to uncover information about issues such as students' backgrounds to make sure that proposed and modified programs are appropriate for the settings in which they will be delivered. It acts as a kind of reality check, which provides program developers with assurances that their assumptions about students, teachers, facilities, and other features of the instructional setting are accurate.

Input.   *Input evaluation* seeks to provide information about the appropriateness of the recommended means of meeting program goals and objectives. As Armstrong (1989) notes, evaluators during this phase ask the key question "Given the options available for meeting established goals, is this the best choice?" (p. 241).

Suppose that context evaluation has reaffirmed that a goal related to familiarizing gifted and talented high-school freshmen with *The Merchant of Venice* as an introduction to Shakespeare's works is appropriate. Input evaluation might look for answers to questions such as the following:

- What, if anything, do these students know about Shakespeare and his literary works?
- More specifically, do students know anything about *The Merchant of Venice?* If so, what proportion of students know something and, in general, what do they know?
- What aspects of *The Merchant of Venice* will be selected to illustrate patterns that recur in other works by Shakespeare?
- Is there a specific edition of *The Merchant of Venice* that is better suited to these students' needs? If so, what makes this edition better than other choices?
- Are there particular reasons that *The Merchant of Venice* will be a better introduction to Shakespeare for these students than some of his other works?

Input evaluation also considers alternative approaches to instructional design and delivery. Information can be gathered that relates to questions such as the following:

- What instructional techniques should be recommended? Why are those to be preferred over others?
- How should information be sequenced? What are the sequencing decisions based on?
- How is student progress to be measured? Are the selected approaches to evaluation the best ones for this purpose?

In summary, you will find that input evaluation provides data that are useful in planning a new or revised instructional program. Its purpose is to help you and others make the best possible decisions before implementation begins.

Process.   You will use *process evaluation* to monitor carefully a new or revised program as it is being implemented. Details gathered during this phase of evaluation provide information that will help you learn whether the program is being implemented properly. Often, there is room in a program design for teachers to make some adaptations to fit their own instructional circumstances. However, there may be some features that cannot be changed without compromising the program's integrity. Process-evaluation data can help you determine whether this is happening and whether some actions need to be taken to remedy the situation.

To accomplish the purposes of process evaluation, the formative information that is obtained needs to be shared frequently with the participating teachers.

Process-evaluation information may suggest the need for various kinds of intervention. For example, one reason some teachers fail to adopt certain critical features of a new or revised program may be that they have received inadequate training. If you determined this to be the situation after process evaluation, you and others involved in the assessment activity probably would suggest strategies for providing program users with program-related inservice training. Process-evaluation data can also identify basic flaws in the program design. For example, you may uncover information that suggests that the program requires teachers to do things that simply are not reasonable, given their personal backgrounds and the nature of the students they teach, such as expectations that too much complex content be covered in a short period of time, recommended reading materials beyond the capacity of some students, and requirements that computer software be used but there are not enough computers available.

Product.   *Product evaluation* provides information related to how well the goals of the instructional program were achieved. It tends to be summative information. For this reason, you will typically engage in activities associated with product evaluation at the end of the period when a new or revised instructional program has been delivered. Information you gather during this evaluation phase will be used as modifications in the program are considered before it is taught again. The idea is to engage in an ongoing cycle of product evaluation, so that programs can be made better over time.

Responsive Evaluation

Evaluation specialist Robert Stake (1975) developed an assessment approach called responsive evaluation. **Responsive evaluation** assumes that the worth of an evaluation process is measured by the usefulness of its findings to people who are affected by the program being assessed. For this reason, responsive evaluation requires active participation by program stakeholders, including teachers, administrators, parents, community representatives, program developers, and specially trained evaluators.

LEARNING EXTENSION 11–2

Identifying the Stakeholders

Suppose you were asked to name the members of an evaluation group that would use a responsive-evaluation approach to assess a new instructional program. Who would you identify as the stakeholders? What would be your rationale for selecting these individuals? How many from each category would you include? What differences in values, perspectives, and expectations of the program would you anticipate as the stake-

holders began their work? How would you balance (1) a need to honor diverse perspectives and (2) a need to move the assessment process forward?

The supporters of responsive evaluation believe that all stakeholders apply
certain subjective criteria to what they observe, based on differing personal values.
Part of the responsive-evaluation process requires stakeholders to make explicit
their value orientations and their unique expectations of the program being evaluated. The evaluator's role is "to find out what is of value to his audiences" (Stake,
1975, p. 5). The concerns of individual stakeholders tend to be framed in terms of
issues, such as "Are teachers being required to do too much when implementing
the program?" "Will students in the program be more interested in it than they
were in the one it replaces?" and "Will discipline problems in any way be different, now that the new program is underway?" These issues become the focus of
the data-gathering activities. Data are gathered using a variety of informal and formal means.

If you are involved in responsive evaluation, you will find that you and the
other stakeholders engage in a pattern of continuous observation and reporting
as the evaluation process goes forward. In Michael Scriven's (1967) terms, responsive evaluation is formative, not summative. Its emphasis is always on responding to the issues, contexts, and concerns of stakeholders. The assumption,
too, is that there will be ongoing modifications of the new or revised program as
evaluation information is gathered, shared, and reflected on by those involved in
the process.

Stake proposes a framework for processing data as information is gathered
that relates to stakeholders' issues. You will note that members of the evaluation
group are to attend to three basic categories of information: antecedents, transactions, and outcomes. *Antecedents* include information that may be available before
a new or revised program is implemented. Data gathered in this category shed
light on special conditions that might affect students, teachers, and other stakeholders before instruction begins. For example, information gathered during this
period might reveal that many students in a particular school or school district are
the sons and daughters of recent immigrants to this country and are from a culture that teaches young people that it is impolite to challenge the opinions of
adults. If a new or revised instructional program features a teaching model that
calls on teachers to make frequent use of a methodology that requires students to
challenge teachers' opinions, some students from these groups may not do well.
This kind of information can prompt revisions of some program-design features
before instruction begins, in the hope that the initial implementation will represent a better fit to the settings where it will be used.

When you are involved in an assessment of *transactions,* you are looking at
individual parts of a new or modified program as it is being delivered. This activity is similar to Stufflebeam's (2000) process evaluation. Among the program
elements that you and other stakeholders might consider are patterns of interactions between teachers and students, student responsiveness to the provided

instructional materials, and student reactions to recommended assessment techniques.

The *outcomes* category features judgments about observations that relate to issues that stakeholders have identified. It is similar to what Stufflebeam (2000) calls "product evaluation." Sometimes, traditional evaluations have focused only on how new and revised programs have affected students. In responsive evaluation, outcome data are gathered that is of interest to all stakeholders. Hence, there may be information that seeks to respond to the interests, values, and concerns of administrators, teachers, community members, and other identified stakeholder groups.

The categories of antecedents, transactions, and outcomes describe when evaluation information is gathered (before program implementation, during program implementation, and after program implementation). Stake (1967, 1975) also describes a multicomponent evaluation process to be followed when antecedent, transaction, and outcome information is gathered. First, Stake recommends that stakeholders develop a *rationale* for the program. The rationale describes its overall purpose.

The *intents* category provides an opportunity for stakeholders to identify what they would like to see happen in response to the critical issues they have identified. As a member of a responsive-evaluation group, you will generate intents information that relates to antecedents, transactions, and outcomes. Next, you and others will conduct *observations* to determine what actually is happening.

Once information is available to your group, you will decide on some *standards* that make as explicit as possible what the stakeholders view to be acceptable behaviors and circumstances. The final step is for the group to make *judgments* about the degree to which the observed program meets the identified standards. The purpose of these judgments is to provide an indication of general levels of satisfaction with the program. They are not intended as summary "continue/ discontinue" recommendations. Indeed, responsive evaluation rejects these kinds of judgments as a legitimate purpose of evaluation. Rather, the intent is to use the views of stakeholders and gathered data as prompts to modify programs in ways that, over time, will make them better. See Figure 11.2.

Adversary Evaluation

A quarter of a century ago, many educators became interested in a proposal to base educational evaluations on procedures similar to those followed in a legal trial. Such **adversary evaluation** is premised on the idea that two clear sides to assessment issues can be identified. If you find yourself involved in an adversary-evaluation activity, you will be assigned to one of two teams. One seeks to uncover as much positive and supporting information about the new or revised program that is the focus for the exercise. The other group works to discover as much negative and opposing information about the same program. When members of the contending teams have completed their work, they make presentations before an individual or a group of individuals who considers the testimony and renders a final decision.

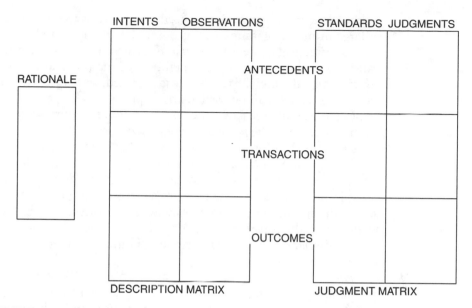

FIGURE 11.2   Robert Stake's Antecedents, Transactions, and Outcomes Model

Source: From Robert E. Stake. "The Countenance of Educational Evaluation." *Teachers College Record, 68* (April 1967), p. 529. Reprinted with permission of Blackwell Publishers. Copyright © 1967 by Teachers College Press.

One argument made in support of adversary evaluation is that it overcomes a presumed tendency of some evaluators to become too closely associated with the people who are implementing and committed to new and changed instructional programs. The fear is that some evaluators who are involved in an assessment process with a strong formative bias (e.g., a bias toward using information that is gathered to make immediate changes in the program to make it function better) develop such a vested interest in the program they are considering that they fail to adequately consider its faults. The design of adversary evaluation assures that there will be as much emphasis on negative as on positive information.

Sequence of adversary-evaluation activities.   An early supporter of adversary evaluation, Robert Wolf (1975) identified the following stages as characterizing many assessments of this kind:

1. Issue generation
2. Issue selection
3. Preparation of arguments
4. Hearing

At the *issue-generation stage,* evaluators work to identify the issues for the members of both the "pro" and "con" evaluating teams to consider as they work to identify the program's strong and weak points. This stage concludes with the generation of an extensive list of issues the evaluators believe relevant to their assessment work. At the issue-generation stage, the work tends to encourage the development of large numbers of issues. At this point, the attempt is to be as inclusive as possible. As a practical matter, time constraints place limits on the number of issues that can be actively pursued by the members of the pro and con teams. At the *issue-selection stage,* the initial list of issues is trimmed, with a view to retaining only those that are considered to be particularly important.

Once a limited set of issues is identified, the members of the pro and con teams move on to the *preparation-of-arguments stage.* The members of the pro team gather as much information as they can that reflects positively on the new or revised program. Similarly, the members of the con team gather as much information as possible about its negative features. For example, suppose one of the identified issues is how well the new program is serving minority-group students. In such a situation, the pro team evaluators seek out as much data as they can find to illustrate the positive effects on minority students. The con team evaluators make a similar effort to find information pointing to the program's negative effects on minority students.

After the members of the pro and con teams have finished their work, the evaluation process moves on to the *hearing stage,* in which the pro and con team members present their findings to one or more individuals, who listen to testimony, weigh the presented arguments, and render a final decision.

Criticisms of adversary evaluation.   Although adversary evaluation provides a mechanism that assures that both negative and positive information will be presented in a public forum, other features of the approach draw criticism. For example, it is not at all clear that the complex issues associated with educational change divide neatly into issues for which clear pro and con positions can be identified (Arnstein, 1975). Additionally, the approach presumes that the arguments made by the pro team and the con team will be made with equal skill. If they are not, then the quality of the rhetoric used, rather than the quality of the presented information, may influence the decision that is rendered. Also, unlike in a court of law, where legal counsel who feel irregular procedures and processes have been used can appeal decisions, many adversary-evaluation procedures have no built-in appeal process. This presumes that decision makers have no irresponsible biases and will not make errors in judgment. Critics suggest that this situation fails to mirror reality (Popham & Carlson, 1977). Finally, because adversary evaluation often requires the active involvement of fairly large numbers of people—multiple members of both pro and con teams and, often, people who serve as decision makers during the hearing stage—and because the data-gathering and data-presentation processes require considerable time, the approach costs more than some other approaches to program evaluation.

Discrepancy Evaluation

Over 30 years ago, Malcolm Provus (1971) developed an approach to program assessment that he called **discrepancy evaluation.** The idea is a simple one. You develop a clear idea, or standard, about how a program ought to be functioning. Then, you gather information about how it is functioning. The difference is the "discrepancy," and it provides you with information about what might need to be done to close the gap between the reality and the ideal.

Discrepancy evaluation is both formative and summative. It is used as new and revised programs are designed, as they are delivered, and after students have been exposed to them. Provus (1971) identified five stages associated with discrepancy evaluation:

1. Design stage
2. Installation stage
3. Process stage
4. Product stage
5. Cost stage

When you are working at the *design stage,* you and others will use evaluation information as part of the process of developing a new or revised program. You seek out information about how a new or modified program should function. You may provide a list of questions to teachers and other relevant parties, asking what they would like to see going on in their classrooms. For example, you may ask, "What kinds of instructional procedures would we see most frequently in your classroom were we to visit it today?" "What kinds of instructional support do you have available?" and "What kinds of student behavioral problems do you face regularly?" The responses to such questions can be considered as your group works to identify a profile of what is in present classrooms. Next, working with outside experts and other professionals, the group attempts to contrast this reality with an ideal design. This design is modified in ways that allow it to conform both to the special characteristics of the local school district and to more broadly held views regarding the characteristics of excellent schools. After much additional work, the new or revised program is ready to be installed.

During the *installation stage,* you and other evaluators work closely with school administrators and teachers to assure that the changed program is being delivered as designed. If you find that some teachers are using the program in ways that are inconsistent with its design, you have two basic decisions to make. On the one hand, you may conclude that there is a flaw in the program design and that it should be changed to fit the way teachers are using it. On the other hand, if you determine that the design is fine, you may wish to consider other options. For example, the explanation for teachers' failure to follow the recommended program design may be a lack of needed instructional support materials. If this proves to be the case, you and others in the evaluation group will want to advise the administrators of this problem in the hope it can be remedied quickly. Another possibility is that teachers have not been sufficiently trained to use the new program. If this is the situation, you will wish to recommend more inservice opportunities for teachers.

In the *process stage,* your task is to look at the individual components of the new or modified program. The purpose is to assess some short-term student learnings that provide a necessary foundation for larger, more complex program outcomes. For example, one purpose of a new algebra program may be to develop students' abilities to handle complex quadratic equations with multiple unknowns. Evaluation during the process stage may look at how well the new program enables them to solve simple, one-unknown equations. If students who have been taught how to do this in the new program are not able to perform this task at an acceptably high level of proficiency, you and others involved in the evaluation process will be prompted to look at the adequacy of both the program design and its implementation.

Evaluation at the *product stage* is more summative than is evaluation at the process stage. At this point, you look at how well the standards established for the overall program have been met. When there are differences between the actual and the hoped-for program outcomes, you and others involved in developing the innovation and the evaluation process will meet to consider what might have caused these discrepancies. You may determine that there were flaws in the initial program design, mistakes in interpreting the quality of student learning when process-stage evaluations were done, inadequate supplies of needed instructional materials in the classroom, inadequately trained teachers, or other factors that contributed to these differences.

EXERCISE 11–1

Gathering Data from Students as Part of a Curriculum-Evaluation Plan

Students are the recipients and potential beneficiaries of instruction provided to them when new and revised instructional programs are implemented. Quite naturally, then, you will want to gather data related to students as part of any comprehensive evaluation scheme you devise.

Action

Think about a new or modified instructional program that interests you. Suppose that you and others have been charged with developing an overall evaluation plan. Your assignment is to design the part of the program-evaluation scheme that will report on information related to students. Respond to this task first by going to Merrill Education's Link to General Methods website (http://www.prenhall.com/methods-cluster/).

At the site, you will be provided some topic options at the bottom of the page. Select "Curriculum Development" and click on "Begin." This will take you to a page titled "Topic 1: Curriculum—Overview." On the left side of this page, you will find several links. Select "Web links." This will take you to a page titled "Topic 1: General Links." Scroll down until you find the link to the "Online Curriculum Evaluation Resource Library." Click on this link. This will take you to the home page of the Online Curriculum Evaluation Resource Library.

On this page, you will find the heading "Project Types." Under this heading, you will find several links. Select "Curriculum Development." This will take you to a page titled "Curriculum Development Projects." On this page, you will find the heading "Evaluation Resources." Select "Curriculum Development Instruments," which takes you to a page titled "Illustrations of Sound Evaluation Instruments in Curriculum Development Projects." On this page, you will find the heading "Student Instruments," under which you will find links to *surveys about courses, surveys about materials, attitude surveys, interviews,* and *content assessment.* Each of these links takes you to examples of validated instruments that provide information on their respective topics.

Analysis

Look at a number of the instruments listed and identify several that might have relevance for you as you begin designing an evaluation plan for the student-data section of the program-evaluation approach your curriculum-assessment group is designing. Using information you find at the links under the "Student Instruments" heading, identify some data-gathering approaches that might help you find information related to *any three* of the following topics:

- Students' reactions to teaching methods
- Students' reactions to instructional materials
- Students' ratings of the importance or relevance of the program content
- Students' reactions to the expected workload
- Students' reactions to topic sequencing and other organizational features
- Students' levels of achievement

Key Points

An issue that concerns many people who are concerned about the quality of our schools is the potential impact of new and revised programs on students' academic achievement. Achievement levels are affected by many variables. For this reason, it makes sense for comprehensive program evaluations to gather student-related information that goes beyond achievement scores on tests related to program content.

The final phase of the evaluation process, the *cost stage,* requires a careful weighing of the benefits of the new or modified program, as compared with its benefits. The essential question that must be asked at this time is "How much 'good' is delivered for 'how much money'"? (Armstrong, 1989). During this stage, you and others may be asked to prepare information that demonstrates the comparative costs of the focus program and those of other, somewhat similar programs.

 ## SUMMARY COMMENTS

When you work in the area of curriculum evaluation, you operate in an environment that seems much different from the pristine world that sometimes is depicted in program-evaluation texts. As has been noted, various constituencies may want you to use quite varied criteria as you seek to determine the relative excellence of a given program. Often, you will find yourself operating in a politicized environment, where the individuals who will be affected by the evaluation results work hard to make their perspectives known, in the hope that they will influence the judgments that are made. These conditions suggest the importance of selecting an evaluation design that will allow you to maintain the integrity of the evaluation process while, to the extent possible, responding to the legitimate concerns of the individuals who have a vested interest in the outcome.

This prescription for a sound approach to program evaluation is easier to describe than to implement. In fact, difficulties associated with implementing evaluation processes often are the despair of the supporters of various program-improvement initiatives. Indeed, the desire to "do something to make schools better" often has led to strong advocacy for reform proposals that have little evaluation and research support to back up the claims of their proponents. To appreciate how widespread is the practice of promoting improvement proposals in the absence of abundant evidence about their actual impact on student learning, you may wish to visit a website maintained by the American Association of School Administrators (AASA) (http://www.aasa.org/reform/approach.htm). At this site, you will find an organized listing of more than 20 reform initiatives. They are compared in terms of a number of criteria, including the extent to which validated information exists about their effectiveness in helping students learn. A disappointingly small number are supported by evaluation evidence that attests to their effectiveness in enhancing student achievement.

This situation highlights a dilemma you will face when you are involved in discussions of curriculum evaluation. The complexities associated with high-quality evaluation practices are daunting. These approaches require time to implement, may involve a number of people, feature difficult confrontations with individuals "who just know" the innovation is wonderful (or terrible), and require commitments of large sums of money. Challenging as these conditions are, the alternative of doing no serious evaluation has even more associated negatives. Installing new programs that are grounded in little beyond their proponents' assurances that they will improve students' learning is dangerous. When such programs fail to deliver, they promote cynical and distrustful public attitudes toward schools and school leaders.

What does all this mean for you? As a curriculum professional, your long-term credibility, in large measure, will be determined by the congruence between your statements about the relative effectiveness of program alternatives and how well these alternatives serve students when they are implemented. To increase the likelihood that your views about what will work are put forward in support of approaches that, in fact, improve student learning, you would do well to be circumspect in your comments about new and modified programs until good evaluation evidence is in hand. By doing so, you build a strong case for yourself as a serious professional, rather than as an enthusiastic purveyor of cosmetic, and unsubstantiated, promises.

Review and Reflection

1. How do you explain the intense controversy and conflict that sometimes surround evaluations of educational programs?

2. Suppose someone proposed to you that an evaluation of a new instructional program should be based simply on how well students did on tests related to a list of program objectives. How would you react to this idea, and why?

3. Schools have administered standardized tests for years. Why is it they have become such a large issue today?

4. What are some characteristics of goal-free evaluation, and what arguments might confront you, were you to suggest this approach be used to assess a new or modified instructional program?

5. In what ways does empowerment evaluation differ from more traditional ways of evaluating school programs?

6. Daniel Stufflebeam's CIPP model describes an approach to program evaluation that has proved highly attractive to the assessors of school programs for many years. Why do you think the model has attracted so many supporters?

7. What are some challenges you might face if you were responsible for implementing either a responsive-evaluation approach or a discrepancy-evaluation approach?

8. Are the criticisms of adversary evaluation justified? Why or why not?

References

Armstrong, D. G. (1989). *Developing and documenting the curriculum.* Needham Heights, MA: Allyn and Bacon.

Arnstein, G. (1975). The outcome. *Phi Delta Kappan, 57*(3), 188–190.

Boyer, E. (1983). *High school: A report on secondary education in America.* New York: Harper & Row.

Cohen, M. A., & Leonard, S. (2001). Formative assessments: Test to teach. *Principal Leadership, 1*(5). [http://www.nassp.org/news/pl_test2teach_101.htm]

Ferguson, R. F. (1998). Can schools narrow the black-white test score gap? In C. Jencks & M. Phillips (Eds.), *The black-white test score gap* (pp. 318–374). Washington, DC: The Brookings Institution.

Fetterman, D. M. (1996). Empowerment evaluation: An introduction to theory and practice. In D. M. Fetterman, S. J. Kaftarian, & A. Wandersman (Eds.), *Empowerment evaluation: Knowledge and tools for self-assessment and accountability* (pp. 3–46). Thousand Oaks, CA: Sage.

Fetterman, D. M. (2001). *Foundations of empowerment evaluation.* Thousand Oaks, CA: Sage.

Goodlad, J. I. (1984). *A place called school: Prospects for the future.* New York: McGraw-Hill.

Howe, H. II (2001, July 23). Testing and diversity. *New York Times.* [http://www.nytimes.com/2001/07/23/opinion/L23SCHO.html]

Jencks, C., & Phillips, M. (Eds.). (1998). *The black-white test score gap.* Washington, DC: The Brookings Institution.

Kohn, A. (2000a). *The case against standardized testing.* Portsmouth, NH: Heinemann.

Kohn, A. (2000b, September 27). Standardized testing and its victims. *Education Week on the Web.* [http://www.edweek.org/ew/ewstory.cfm?slug=04kohn.h20]

Levin, H. M. (1996). Empowerment evaluation and accelerated schools. In D. M. Fetterman, S. J. Kaftarian, & A. Wandersman (Eds.), *Empowerment evaluation: Knowledge and tools for self-assessment and accountability* (pp. 49–64). Thousand Oaks, CA: Sage.

Morin, R. (2001, July 16–22). It's not as it seems: A national survey shows that misperceptions cloud whites' views of blacks. *The Washington Post National Weekly Edition,* p. 34.

Popham, W. J., & Carlson, D. (1977). Deep, dark deficits of the adversary evaluation model. *Educational Researcher, 6*(6), pp. 3–6.

Provus, M. (1971). *Discrepancy evaluation for educational program improvement and assessment.* Berkeley, CA: McCutchan.

Scriven, M. (1967). The methodology of evaluation. In R. W. Stake et al. (Eds.), *Perspectives on curriculum evaluation* (pp. 39–53). AERA Monograph Series on Curriculum Evaluation, No. 1. Chicago: Rand McNally.

Scriven, M. (1972). Pros and cons about goal-free evaluation. *Evaluation Comment, 3*(4), 1–7.

Stake, R. E. (1967). The countenance of educational evaluation. *Teachers College Record, 68,* 523–540.

Stake, R. E. (1975). *Program evaluation—Particularly responsive evaluation.* Paper #5, Occasional Paper Series. Urbana-Champaign: University of Illinois Center for Instructional Research and Curriculum Evaluation.

Stake, R. E. (1998). Some comments on assessment in U.S. education. *Educational Policy Analysis Archives, 6*(14). [http://epaa.asu.edu/epaa/v6n14.html]

Stake, R. E. (2000, January 6). *Evaluation and assessment: Discriminatory against minorities?* Paper delivered at the RACE 2000 conference, Tempe, AZ.

Stufflebeam, D. L. (2000). The CIPP model for evaluation. In D. L. Stufflebeam, G. F. Madaus, & T. Kellaghan (Eds.), *Evaluation models: Viewpoints on educational and human services evaluation* (2nd ed., pp. 279–317). Boston: Kluwer.

Stufflebeam, D. L., & Shinkfield, A. J. (1985). *Systematic evaluation.* Boston: Kluwer-Nijhoff.

Tanner, D. E. (2001). *Assessing academic achievement.* Boston: Allyn and Bacon.

Tyler, R. W. (1949). *Basic principles of curriculum and instruction.* Chicago: The University of Chicago Press.

U.S. Department of Education. (2001). *The nation's report card: Mathematics 2000.* Washington, DC: National Center for Education Statistics.

Weaver, C. (1995). *Facts: On standardized tests and assessment alternatives.* [http://homepage.tinet.ie/~seaghan/articles/10.htm]

Wolf, R. L. (1975). Trial by jury: A new evaluation method. *Phi Delta Kappan, 57*(3), 185–187.

Worthen, B. R. (1999). Critical challenges confronting certification of evaluators. *American Journal of Evaluation, 20*(3), 533–555.

Glossary

academic-subject designs Curriculum designs in which traditional academic disciplines give their names to school subjects and school courses. *See also* broad-fields designs; correlation designs; curriculum designs; fusion designs; special-topic designs; structure-of-the-disciplines designs; student-centered designs.

academy The dominant form of secondary school in the nineteenth century. These were private institutions that flourished in the days before a legal precedent had been set in support of the public funding of secondary schools.

advance organizers Category headings provided by teachers to help students organize information and, as a result, to make learning the information easier.

adversary evaluation An evaluation approach, based on judicial proceedings, in which a pro side gathers as much positive information as possible about the focus program, a con side gathers as much negative information as possible about the focus program, and a final decision is rendered by one or more individuals who hear the evidence and then render a judgment.

affective domain The category of thinking that focuses on attitudes and values. *See also* cognitive domain; psychomotor domain.

affective taxonomy The type of taxonomy, such as the one developed by David Krathwohl and others, that scales categories of affective thinking in order of their complexity or sophistication. *See also* affective domain; Bloom's Taxonomy; Marzano's Taxonomy; taxonomies.

apperception The now largely discarded learning theory, associated with the work of Johann Friedrich Herbart, that saw the mind as a collection of ideas that acted as a mechanism to screen out new ideas that were inconsistent with those already there and

to admit new ideas that were consistent with those already there.

articulation The curriculum-design principle that describes a relationship among content elements (often embedded within different subjects) that is simultaneous, as opposed to sequential. *See also* scope; sequence; continuity; balance; spiraling.

authenticity The content-selection criterion that seeks to ascertain the accuracy of information included in an instructional program.

axiology The area of philosophy that focuses on the nature of values and ethics.

balance The curriculum-design principle that seeks to assure that each important element in an instructional program receives a fair share of instructional time and emphasis. *See also* articulation; scope; sequence; continuity; spiraling.

behaviorism The orientation to learning theory that assumes that the world perceived through the senses is real and that complex content is best mastered by studying its constituent parts.

benchmarks As related to standards-based education and, more particularly, to state curriculum standards, indicators of clear expectations of what students are to know and do, which are tied to variables such as their age, grade level, and developmental level. *See also* standards-based education.

Bloom's Taxonomy The hierarchical arrangement of cognitive skills, developed by Benjamin Bloom and others, that purports to scale categories of cognitive thinking in a simple-to-complex order. *See also* cognitive domain; Marzano's Taxonomy; taxonomies.

Boston English Classical School The nation's first high school, this institution was established in Boston in 1821.

Boston Latin Grammar School   This early secondary school was established in 1635 to prepare boys for Harvard.

broad-fields designs   Curriculum designs that sometimes are thought of as grand extensions of fusion designs. They seek new unities that draw together the contents of a wide range of sources within an entire branch of knowledge. *See also* curriculum designs; academic-subject designs; fusion designs; special-topic designs; student-centered designs.

CBAM   *See* Concerns-Based Adoption Model (CBAM).

central curriculum council   The group in a school district that, working with central office curriculum leadership, has the authority to oversee the general management of the curriculum function.

change-adept organizations   Organizations or institutions in which leadership expertise and support conditions routinely are deployed to encourage and support altered ways of doing business.

chronological sequencing   The approach to content sequencing that orders content in terms of chronological time, either from earliest time to latest time or from latest time to earliest time. *See also* external-constraint sequencing; part-to-whole sequencing; thematic-topic sequencing; whole-to-part sequencing.

CIPP model   The comprehensive evaluation model, which Daniel Stufflebeam developed, that allows for assessment data to be gathered as programs are being planned, as they are being implemented, and after they have been installed. "CIPP" derives from the first letters of the words "context," "input," "process," and "product."

cognitive domain   The category of thinking that focuses on rational, or intellectual, thinking. *See also* affective domain; psychomotor domain.

cognitive theory   The orientation to learning theory that presumes that reality does not come to us unaltered through our senses but, rather, that reality is developed in our minds as we think about and ascribe meaning to these inputs.

common school   The type of school associated with the work of Horace Mann, it refers to a publicly-supported institution that provides an education to all members of society, irrespective of wealth, class, or other social markers.

componential intelligence   One of the categories of intelligence included in Robert Sternberg's triarchic theory of intelligence. *See also* triarchic theory of intelligence; experiential intelligence; contextual intelligence.

Concerns-Based Adoption Model (CBAM)   Initially developed at the Research and Development Center for Teacher Education in the 1970s, a model that provides a framework for the findings and ongoing research related to installing and sustaining the use of innovations. *See also* Levels of Use; Stages of Concern.

conflict views of schooling   Sociological perspectives that challenge the fairness and adequacy of present social, economic, and political arrangements. Educational decisions are seen as the product of conflicts among groups who are either advantaged by or disadvantaged by particular decisions. *See also* functionalism.

content standards   As used in the context of discussions of state standards, standards that describe what students should know or be able to do as a result of their exposure to classroom instruction. *See also* standards-based education.

content-standards documents   The category of curriculum documents that identifies content standards associated with a given subject area as identified by a state, an outside subject-area specialty group, or a school district. *See also* course plan; curriculum document; curriculum guide; general scope and sequence documents; grade-level plan; instructor's guides; instructional unit documents; lesson plan; philosophy statements.

context profile   A summary of needs-assessment data that provides a succinct distillation of high-priority findings. *See also* needs assessment.

contextual intelligence   One of the categories of intelligence included in Robert Sternberg's triarchic theory of intelligence. *See also* triarchic theory of intelligence; componential intelligence; experiential intelligence.

contextual standards   In the context of discussions of content standards, standards requiring students to become proficient in the knowledge and skills that take on a special meaning because of the special conditions within which they occur. *See also* content standards.

continuity The curriculum-design principle that focuses at a micro scale on the importance of ordering the elements of instruction in such a way that the "ending points" of the preceding content mesh well with "beginning points" of the content that follows. *See also* sequence; scope; articulation; balance; spiraling.

core-curriculum design The subcategory of student-centered designs that places a heavy emphasis on identifying and responding to the general personal and social problems of students. *See also* curriculum designs; academic-subject designs; fusion designs; special-topic designs; student-centered designs.

correlation The curriculum-design principle that describes a relationship among content elements (often embedded within different subjects) that is simultaneous, as opposed to sequential. *See also* articulation; scope; sequence; continuity; balance; spiraling.

correlation designs The subcategory of academic-subject designs that seeks to embed the principle of correlation within a formal curriculum design. *See also* curriculum designs; academic-subject designs; fusion designs; broad-fields designs; special-topic designs; student-centered designs.

course plan The curriculum document that describes the contents of a middle-school or high-school course. *See also* content-standards documents; curriculum document; curriculum guide; general scope and sequence documents; grade-level plan; instructor's guides; instructional unit documents; lesson plan; philosophy statements.

critical theorists Scholars who take the position that groups in positions of power have acted on behalf of narrow interests and have failed to actively seek an end to social injustice.

curriculum A set of decision-making processes and products that focuses on the preparation, implementation, and assessment of general plans to influence students' behaviors and insights.

curriculum designs Overall organizational frameworks for an instructional program. *See also* academic-subject designs; fusion designs; broad-fields designs; student-centered designs.

curriculum document A document that packages curriculum decisions. *See also* content-standards documents; curriculum guide; general scope and sequence documents; grade-level plan; course plan; instructor's guides; instructional unit documents; lesson plan; philosophy statements.

curriculum document notation system A system that indicates the relationships among individual documents in an interrelated system by using a notational scheme to identify common components.

curriculum guide As used in this text, a subset of a general scope and sequence plan that includes one of the following components: (1) information about all subjects taught at a specific grade level or (2) information about what is taught in a single subject area across all grade levels. *See also* content-standards documents; course plan; curriculum document; general scope and sequence documents; grade-level plan; instructor's guides; instructional unit documents; lesson plan; philosophy statements.

curriculum standards In the context of discussions of state standards, standards that refer to the kinds of activities that should take place in classrooms as teachers work to convey specific types of information to students. *See also* standards-based education.

declarative knowledge (information) Content that students are expected to learn as a consequence of their exposure to instruction. *See also* details; Marzano's Taxonomy; organizing ideas; procedural knowledge (mental procedures).

declarative standards In the context of discussions of content standards, standards that require students to identify specific information related to particular topics. *See also* content standards.

deductive logic The thought process that begins with a general conclusion and that elucidates it by presenting relevant examples. *See also* inductive logic.

details The component of the declarative knowledge (information) category of Marzano's Taxonomy that includes concepts, facts, time sequences, cause and effect sequences, and episodes. *See also* Marzano's Taxonomy; organizing ideas.

discrepancy-analysis view As applied to needs assessment, the practice of identifying discrepancies between existing and ideal school practices. *See also* needs assessment.

discrepancy evaluation   The approach to program evaluation that is based on discrepancy analysis. *See also* discrepancy-analysis view.

empowerment evaluation   Evaluation that seeks to give all people with a stake in decisions related to a given program an opportunity to be heard and to experience personal growth as part of their involvement in the process.

epistemology   The area of philosophy that seeks information about the nature of knowledge.

essentialism   The educational application of philosophy that places a high value on teaching students basic, or "essential," information required to maintain the benefits associated with the present social, political, and economic structures of American society. *See also* progressivism; perennialism; reconstructionism; existentialism.

existentialism   The educational application of philosophy that holds that each person must make his or her own sense of reality and that schools should work hard to avoid imposing the perspectives of others on students.

experiential intelligence   One of the categories of intelligence included in Robert Sternberg's triarchic theory of intelligence. *See also* triarchic theory of intelligence; componential intelligence; contextual intelligence.

external-constraint sequencing   The pattern of content sequencing that orders content in response to an external condition, such as the time when a needed instructional facility might be available for use. *See also* chronological sequencing; part-to-whole sequencing; thematic-topic sequencing; whole-to-part sequencing.

external purpose of a curriculum document   The role a given curriculum document plays in serving the needs of individuals who will not use the information it contains as part of their daily work but who may be generally interested in these details for other reasons. *See also* internal purpose of a curriculum document.

formative evaluation   The approach to evaluation in which results are fed back to teachers while the instructional process is still ongoing for the purpose of allowing them to make needed improvements.

Franklin Academy   A private secondary, free from religious ties, that Benjamin Franklin established in 1751 to teach students practical subjects including mathematics, bookkeeping, and navigation.

functionalism   The sociological view that suggests that the present social, economic, and political arrangements are fair, good, and abiding and that the role of the school as an institution is to provide future workers with the varied kinds of expertise needed to maintain present patterns. *See also* conflict views of schooling.

fusion designs   Curriculum designs that reflect a blending of two or more source disciplines or subjects into a new entity, which draws content from the sources and, over time, takes on some defining characteristics of its own. *See also* curriculum designs; academic-subject designs; broad-fields designs; special-topic designs; student-centered designs.

generalization   A statement of relationship among ideas that summarizes the best available information about a topic or an issue.

general scope and sequence documents   Master curriculum-management documents for a school district that provide very basic information about all of its programs. *See also* content-standards documents; course plan; curriculum document; curriculum guide; grade-level plan; instructor's guides; instructional unit documents; lesson plan; philosophy statements.

goal-free evaluation   The approach to program evaluation in which evaluators embark on the process to see what actually is happening as a program is implemented without any prior information regarding what it is supposed to be accomplishing.

grade-level plan   A curriculum document that summarizes content to be taught about one subject area at one grade level. *See also* content-standards documents; course plan; curriculum document; curriculum guide; general scope and sequence documents; instructor's guides; instructional unit documents; lesson plan; philosophy statements.

guiding coalitions   Groups of people charged with disseminating, installing, and sustaining an innovation.

idealism   A philosophical tradition, tracing back to the thought of Plato, that contends that reality cannot be discerned through the senses but exists only in a mental world of ideas.

inductive logic A thinking process that begins with a consideration of examples and leads to an appreciation of a larger, explanatory conclusion. *See also* deductive logic.

inner curriculum The curriculum that is perceived by individuals after information is filtered through their unique values and personal perspectives.

instruction The specific means used to achieve the purposes of the overall plan reflected in the curriculum.

instructional unit documents Curriculum documents that contain specific information about teaching content and evaluating students on the material taught in a single unit of study. *See also* content-standards documents; course plan; curriculum document; curriculum guide; general scope and sequence documents; grade-level plan; instructor's guides; lesson plan; philosophy statements.

instructor's guides The category of curriculum document that provides information for instructors regarding how to approach the tasks associated with teaching and evaluating students as they work with the program to which the guide relates. *See also* content-standards documents; course plan; curriculum document; curriculum guide; general scope and sequence documents; grade-level plan; instructional unit documents; lesson plan; philosophy statements.

internal purpose of a curriculum document The role a given curriculum document plays to serve the needs of the individuals who will directly use the information it contains as part of their work. *See also* external purpose of a curriculum document.

interrelated curriculum document system A system of documents used to manage a school district's overall instructional program in which individual documents share certain elements.

Kalamazoo case A famous court case, decided in 1874, that established the legal grounds for using public tax money to support secondary schools.

legitimacy A curriculum document quality criterion that refers to the legal standing and authority of a given curriculum document.

lesson plan A curriculum document that provides details related to instructional planning for a brief period of time, sometimes as short as a single class meeting. *See also* content-standards documents; course plan; curriculum document; curriculum guide; general scope and sequence documents; grade-level plan; instructor's guides; instructional unit documents; philosophy statements.

levels of use A series of levels, identified by researchers associated with the Concerns-Based Adoption Model, that suggests that individuals vary enormously in how they react to and implement an innovation. *See also* Concerns-Based Adoption Model (CBAM); Stages of Concern.

line relationships An administrative arrangement in which a higher-level authority has the right to impose a decision on a subordinate.

logic The area of philosophy that focuses on issues related to the nature of exact thought.

Marzano's Taxonomy Developed by Robert J. Marzano, a scaled arrangement of both cognitive and psychomotor thinking that emphasizes both levels of thinking and the complexity of content to which the thinking is directed. *See also* Bloom's Taxonomy; cognitive domain; psychomotor domain; taxonomies.

Massachusetts School Law of 1642 The first American legislation directed at making schooling compulsory.

mental discipline An outmoded learning theory, which argued that the mind is composed of discrete faculties, each of which can be "strengthened" by exposing students to difficult and appropriate learning experiences.

metaphysics (ontology) The area of philosophy that focuses on the nature of reality.

multiple-dimension theories A category of learning theories, which presume that individual intelligence is not unitary but is, instead, a composite of many abilities or variables.

needs assessment A systematic effort to analyze students, the school, and the total milieu within which education occurs for the purpose of generating information that can be used to make decisions about allocating instructional resources in ways well-fitted to student and community needs. *See also* needs-assessment data summary chart; context profile.

needs-assessment data summary chart A chart that provides categories under which needs-assessment data can be organized and displayed.

normal school　A type of institution established in the nineteenth century for the purpose of training future teachers.

norms　Expected scores that have been established by examining the results of many scores of students in similar groups. *See also* standardized tests.

notation system　The system of codes used to identify common elements that appear within two or more documents that are part of a set of interrelated curriculum documents.

obliterative subsumption　According to David Ausubel, a pattern associated with forgetting that involves a gradual movement of more detailed and specific categories into larger and more general ones. *See also* progressive differentiation.

objectives-based tests　Tests designed to assess objectives that have been developed to guide instruction.

Old Deluder Satan Act　Legislation passed in colonial Massachusetts in 1647 that required each town of 50 or more families to hire a teacher to be paid out of local funds.

ontology　The area of philosophy that focuses on the nature of reality, sometimes also referred to as "metaphysics."

open core　An approach to developing a core curriculum in which preplanning is avoided and teachers and students together discuss what is to be studied. *See also* core-curriculum design.

organizing ideas　The component of the declarative knowledge (information) category of Marzano's Taxonomy that includes generalizations and principles. *See also* details; Marzano's Taxonomy.

part-to-whole sequencing　The approach to content sequencing that orders content according to a simple-to-complex or easiest-to-most-difficult order. *See also* chronological sequencing; external-constraint sequencing; thematic-topic sequencing; whole-to-part sequencing.

perennialism　The educational application of philosophy that holds that certain knowledge has been validated over time and that schools should dedicate themselves to immersing students in the study of these enduring verities. *See also* essentialism; progressivism; reconstructionism; existentialism.

performance indicators　Clusters of specific behavior that are examined in an effort to determine whether a student has met a given curriculum standard. *See also* standards-based education; benchmarks.

philosophy statements　The category of curriculum document that seeks (1) to provide an indication of a school district's general direction and purpose and (2) to accommodate the priorities of different groups represented within a school district. *See also* content-standards documents; curriculum document; curriculum guide; general scope and sequence documents; instructor's guides; instructional unit documents; lesson plan.

postmodernism　A perspective that holds human uniqueness as an extremely high value and that asserts that many benefits of new technologies have come at the cost of damage to large numbers of individuals.

postmodern philosophy　The worldview that is characterized by suspicion of traditional positivistic scientific thinking, is dubious about the benefits of technology, and is committed to upholding the uniqueness of the individual human being as a high value.

pragmatism　The philosophical tradition that focuses on the changing nature of the universe and that rejects the idea that there is a huge body of unchanging knowledge, which all should learn.

preplanned core　A type of core-curriculum program in which teachers and professionals identify the student-oriented problems and concerns that will be the focus of instruction before the program is taught. *See also* core-curriculum design.

procedural knowledge (mental procedures)　The category of Marzano's Taxonomy that focuses on the processes that students need to know and that is divided into two basic types: skills and processes. *See also* declarative knowledge (information); Marzano's Taxonomy; processes; skills.

procedural standards　In the context of discussions of content standards, the processes that students need to master. *See also* content standards.

processes　As related to Marzano's Taxonomy, complex clusters of skills that students must draw on as they seek to accomplish procedural and psychomotor tasks. *See also* Marzano's Taxonomy; procedural knowledge (mental procedures); skills.

program councils School-district groups responsible for the curriculum decisions in a given subject area or at a given grade level or group of grade levels.

progressive differentiation According to David Ausubel, the process of adding detailed information to larger and more general categories as more and more is learned about a topic. *See also* obliterative subsumption.

progressivism The educational application of philosophy that views change as a constant of life and that stresses the importance of teaching students effective problem-solving skills. *See also* essentialism; perennialism; reconstructionism; existentialism.

psychomotor domain A category of thinking that focuses on the development of control over the body's large and small muscle systems. *See also* affective domain; cognitive domain.

psychomotor procedures The psychomotor dimension of Marzano's Taxonomy, including two basic components: skills and processes. *See also* Marzano's Taxonomy; processes; skills.

realism The philosophical tradition, historically associated with Aristotle, that truths exist as they can be found in the real world.

reconstructionism The educational application of philosophy that believes the present social, political, and economic arrangements of society to be unfair and believes that school programs should prepare students to be in the vanguard of changes that will promote a more just society. *See also* essentialism; progressivism; perennialism; existentialism.

reinforcers According to B. F. Skinner, environmental events that increase the likelihood of recurrence of the behavior they follow.

responsive evaluation The evaluation approach, developed by Robert Stake, that presumes that the worth of an assessment process should be measured by the findings' usefulness to the people who are affected by the program that is the focus of the activity; hence, it requires active participation by all stakeholders.

rubric A guideline or set of guidelines designed to tell an assessor what he or she should look at in making judgments about the quality of student performance on a given task or set of tasks.

schema As described by cognitive learning theorists, internal thought structures people use as they process new information.

scope The curriculum-design principle that describes the breadth and depth of content to be included within a given curricular program. *See also* sequence; continuity; articulation; balance; spiraling.

sequence The curriculum-design principle that references the order in which major blocks of content are introduced to students. *See also* scope; continuity; articulation; balance; spiraling.

seven liberal arts Subject areas that developed within the *Trivium* and *Quadrivium* at Middle Ages cathedral schools. *See also* Quadrivium; Trivium.

significance As applied to content selection, the need to choose content that will help students do more advanced work and that will have good potential for transfer to settings beyond the one in which information initially is learned.

skills As related to Marzano's Taxonomy, individual task competencies that students must acquire to the point they become automatic as students go about the business of accomplishing basic procedural and psychomotor tasks. *See also* Marzano's Taxonomy; procedural knowledge (mental procedures); processes.

special-topic designs Curriculum designs that focus on a single issue, question, problem, or area of interest and that draw content from many kinds of information sources. *See also* curriculum designs; academic-subject designs; fusion designs; student-centered designs.

spiraling The curriculum-design principle that suggests that all students can learn common concepts in an intellectually honest and appropriate way and that, as students progress through school programs, key principles should be revisited and studied with a view to developing progressively more sophisticated levels of understanding. *See also* articulation; scope; sequence; continuity; balance.

staff relationships Administrative relationships that do not empower one party to impose a decision on a second party. The first party must rely on logic as he or she recommends, suggests, and lobbies the second party in the hope that he or she will make a personal decision to accept the recommendation.

stages of concern A series of stages, identified by researchers associated with the Concerns-Based Adoption Model, that indicates various levels of concern about an innovation people have. These tend to be scaled from concerns focusing on personal information and mechanical-use issues to concerns about how changes will affect students and how additional modifications of the innovation might improve its quality. *See also* Concerns-Based Adoption Model (CBAM); Levels of Use.

standardized tests Tests that are constructed from the test scores of scientifically selected samples of groups (for example seventh graders) to establish expected scores, or norms. *See also* norms.

standards-based education Educational practices that include (1) clear, measurable descriptions of what students should be able to know and do as a result of their learning in school and (2) accompanying measurements used to assess student achievement levels.

structure-of-the-disciplines approach An approach to drawing on knowledge from academic disciplines that would have students in grades K–12 master the *processes* used by subject-matter specialists to acquire new knowledge, rather than the *findings* of these experts.

structure-of-the-disciplines designs A subcategory of academic-subject designs that uses the structure-of-the-disciplines approach as the basis of a formal curriculum design. *See also* curriculum designs; academic-subject designs; fusion designs; broad-fields designs; special-topic designs; student-centered designs.

structure-of-the-intellect model A multiple-dimension model of the intellect, proposed by J. P. Guilford.

student-centered designs Curriculum designs that feature programs that are especially responsive to the interests and desires of students. *See also* curriculum designs; core-curriculum design; academic-subject designs; fusion designs; special-topic designs.

summative evaluation Evaluation that takes place at the conclusion of an instructional sequence.

taxonomies As used in education, hierarchical listings of thinking skills that typically are ordered in terms of either ascending or descending complexity. *See also* affective domain; Bloom's Taxonomy; cognitive domain; Marzano's Taxonomy; psychomotor domain.

thematic-topic sequencing The approach to content sequencing that is used in programs in which no element of content need either precede or follow any other; hence, the order of presentation represents a generally arbitrary decision on the part of program planners and instructors. *See also* chronological sequencing; external-constraint sequencing; part-to-whole sequencing; whole-to-part sequencing.

thinking/content-complexity matrix A chart that highlights differences in instructional time that might be allocated to lower-priority and higher-priority program components.

triarchic theory of intelligence A multiple-dimension view of intelligence, proposed by Robert Sternberg, which proposes three categories of intelligence. *See also* componential intelligence; experiential intelligence; contextual intelligence.

whole-to-part sequencing The approach to content sequencing in which students first are exposed to the big picture and then gradually introduced to its smaller, constituent parts. *See also* chronological sequencing; external-constraint sequencing; part-to-whole sequencing; thematic-topic sequencing.

Name Index

Subject Index